LONG TERM CARE AND THE LAW

LONG TERM CARE AND THE LAW

Edited by   Thomas C. Fox

*The National Health Lawyers Association
Tenth Annual Symposium*

 **NATIONAL HEALTH PUBLISHING**

Printed in the United States of America
First Printing
ISBN: 0-932500-39-0
LC: 85-63150

CONTENTS

PART I

CASE LAW: LEGISLATION POLICY UPDATE

Speaker:

Joel M. Hamme

Speakers:

Peter Bouxsein *The Legislative Perspective*
David W. Curtiss *The Financial Community Perspective*
Thomas C. Fox *The Legal Perspective*
Thomas J. Jazwiecki *The Industry Perspective*

Speaker:

Robert A. Streimer

Speaker:

Donald C. Yesukaitis

PART V

PROVIDERS: ICFs, CORFs, AND HOME CARE

ABOUT THE SPEAKERS

EDWIN M. BLADEN

Edwin M. Bladen serves as the Assistant Attorney General in Charge, Economic Crime Division, State of Michigan. He has lectured extensively and authored publications relevant to white collar crime, antitrust, and consumer participation.

PETER BOUXSEIN

Peter Bouxsein is Counsel, Subcommittee on Health and the Environment for the U.S. House of Representatives Committee on Energy and Commerce and is responsible for health care financing, health care technology, and other related issues. He has held many posts with the Department of Health, Education, and Welfare and the Department of Health and Human Services.

ROBERT E. BURKE

Robert E. Burke is a Professional Associate with the Institute of Medicine, National Academy of Sciences in Washingtion, D.C. In this capacity, he is involved in a 22-month study of nursing home regulation which is expected to serve as the basis of significant modifications in regulatory policy on both the federal and state levels. Previously, Mr. Burke was Project Director and Senior Analyst for Abt Associates Inc. in Cambridge, Massachusetts.

DIANE E. BURKLEY

Diane E. Burkley is an Associate with the Washington, D.C. firm of Pierson, Ball and Dowd representing clients before federal executive branch agencies and the Congress on such issues as labor, pensions, equal employment, and environmental concerns. Prior to this, Ms. Burkley was an Associate with the firm of Shaw, Pittman, Potts and Trowbridge where she handled equal employment, labor, and nuclear licensing cases.

PATRICIA A. BUTLER

Patricia A. Butler served most recently as Staff Director for the Colorado Task Force on the Medically Indigent, which examined issues of financing care for the uninsured poor. She currently participates as the only attorney member of the

Institute of Medicine Committee on Nursing Home Regulation which is developing a revised federal system of enforcing quality care in nursing homes.

JAMES L. BUXBAUM

James L. Buxbaum is a certified public accountant and a partner in charge of the Buxbaum and Sacks Healthcare Group. As such, he is responsible for overseeing the accounting, budgeting, and third-party reimbursement services for over 60 skilled nursing facilities, home care agencies, and other health care providers.

MICHAEL H. COOK

Michael H. Cook is associated with the Washington, D.C. law firm of Wood, Lucksinger and Epstein. His practice primarily involves litigation on behalf of hospitals and long term care facilities relevant to Medicare and Medicaid program matters. He is a member of the Healthcare Financial Management Association Advisory Task Force on Long Term Care.

DAVID W. CURTISS

David W. Curtiss is a Vice President of Newman and Associates, Inc. of Denver, Colorado. He specializes in underwriting tax-exempt debt issues for health care facilities. Mr. Curtiss is a Certified Public Accountant and was associated with Arthur Andersen and Co. as an accounting and audit manager. His client responsibilities included audit and feasibility consulting work for a broad range of health care facilities including multihospital systems, freestanding hospitals, outpatient surgery centers, and long term care centers. Mr. Curtiss is a member of the Healthcare Financial Management Association, the American Institute of Certified Public Accountants, and the National Association of Accountants.

THOMAS C. FOX

Thomas C. Fox is a partner with the Washington, D.C. firm of Pierson, Ball and Dowd and specializes in health care law. He serves as the chairman and program monitor (1976-1985) for the National Health Lawyers Association's annual programs on "Long Term Care and the Law." Mr. Fox also serves as Advisor, Volunteer Lawyers Project, NRTA-AARP Legal Counsel for the Elderly, Washington, D.C.

ARTHUR S. FRIEDMAN

Arthur S. Friedman serves as Supervising Attorney with the Office of the Inspector General, United States Department of Health and Human Services. Among his responsibilities is the provision of Federal oversight for the

$42 million State Medicaid Fraud Control Grant Program. For the past 15 years, he has been involved in the investigation and prosecution of white collar crime, especially that relating to health care.

ALAN S. GOLDBERG

Alan S. Goldberg is a member of the Boston law firm of Goulston and Storrs, and his special area of concentration is the long term care needs of the elderly, as well as home health care and new modes of health services delivery to the elderly. He is also currently involved in counselling national and local for-profit and nonprofit health providers (hospital and nursing home). In addition, he serves as general counsel to the Massachusetts Federation of Nursing Homes and as special counsel to the American Health Care Association.

DONALD W. GRIMES

Donald W. Grimes is currently involved in the general practice of law in Cary, North Carolina. Previously, he was the Assistant Attorney General and Director, Medicaid Fraud Control Unit, with responsibility for directing all investigative and prosecutive activities.

JOEL M. HAMME

Joel M. Hamme is a partner in the Washington, D.C. law firm of Pierson, Ball and Dowd with a specialty in health care law. He is a member of the Pennsylvania and District of Columbia bars, and serves as a contributing editor for *Contemporary Administrator for Long Term Care*. Mr. Hamme is also Associate Professional Lecturer in Law, Health Care Delivery Systems at the National Law Center, George Washington University.

DAVID S. HOUGHTON

David S. Houghton is a partner in the law firm of Fitzgerald, Brown, Leahy, Strom, Schorr and Barmettler, Omaha, Nebraska. He has also been a member of the Omaha, Nebraska State House of Delegates since 1982.

THOMAS J. JAZWIECKI

Thomas J. Jazwiecki serves as Director of Reimbursement and Financing for the American Health Care Association. In this capacity, he is responsible for long term care financing issues, including nursing home reimbursement under the Medicare and Medicaid programs. In addition, Mr. Jazwiecki is currently a member of the Congressional Office of Technology Assessment Advisory Panel on Disorders Causing Dementia.

CALVIN P. JOHNSON

Calvin P. Johnson is affiliated with Barrett & Hanna, Washington, D.C. He specializes in Medicare and Medicaid reimbursement issues with an emphasis on claims processing. Previously, Mr. Johnson was Assistant Washington Counsel, Health Insurance Association of America, where he served as representative before Congress on all health issues affecting the health insurance industry.

JUDITH A. JOHNSON

Judith A. Johnson is an associate in the Health Law Department of the law firm of Ropes & Gray, Boston. She is a member of the National Health Lawyers Association and has spoken at several educational meetings of the various hospice organizations in the New England region.

K. PETER KEMEZYS

K. Peter Kemezys, a member of the Illinois Bar, serves as Assistant General Counsel and Assistant Secretary of Manor Care, Inc. and Manor Healthcare Corp., Manor Care's wholly owned health care subsidiary. Prior to this post, Mr. Kemezys was Senior Staff Attorney for the American Hospital Association in Chicago.

MARY H. MICHAL

Mary H. Michal focuses on insurance law and health care matters with the firm of Whyte and Hirschboeck in Madison, Wisconsin. She was formerly the Director of the Bureau of Complaints and Market Conduct with the Wisconsin office of the Commissioner of Insurance. She presently serves as counsel to the Association of Wisconsin HMOs and sits on the Board of Independent Living, Inc.

KATHLEEN A. MICHELS

Kathleen A. Michels is the Assistant Director, Congressional and Agency Relations for the American Nurses' Association in Washington, D.C. Prior to this, Ms. Michels served as Nurse Attorney/Legislative Liaison for the Wisconsin Nurses Association in Madison. She is a frequent lecturer on the legal and legislative aspects of being a health care provider in today's constantly changing health care environment.

GREGORY J. NACLARIO

Gregory J. Naclario is employed by the New York State Deputy Attorney (Special Prosecutor) for Medicaid Fraud Control and is presently the Regional

Director of the Long Island Regional Office. He also serves as the Chairman of the National Association of Medicaid Fraud Control Unit's Training Strategy Committee and is Co-chair of the Special Prosecutor's Training Committee.

FRANK S. OSEN

Frank S. Osen is currently the Assistant General Counsel for Beverly Enterprises, specializing in corporate real estate transactions and the acquisition and disposition of long term care facilities throughout the country. Previous to this, he was counsel to Coldwell Banker and Co., the largest real estate brokerage company in the United States.

RICHARD E. PLYMALE

Richard E. Plymale is the Assistant Deputy Attorney General of Kentucky and serves as the Director of the Medicaid Fraud Control Unit with responsibility for the statewide investigation and prosecution of fraud in the Medicaid program and abuse of nursing home patients. He has been admitted to practice by the bars of New York, Kentucky, and California.

STEPHEN E. RONAI

Stephen E. Ronai is a member of the law firm of Murtha, Cullina, Richter, and Pinney, with offices in both Hartford and New Haven. He is currently the Chairman of the firm's health care section. Mr. Ronai serves as general counsel and labor counsel to the Connecticut Association of Health Care Facilities, and he also represents numerous nonprofit health care providers, such as long term care facilities and hospitals.

JOHN H. SEYLE

John H. Seyle has been the Assistant Administrator at Summit Nursing Home, Catonsville, Maryland since 1970. He currently serves as a member of the American Health Care Association Legal Task Force and as the Chairman, Legal Services, Legislative and Government Relations Committee of the Health Facilities Association of Maryland.

ROBERT A. STREIMER

Robert A. Streimer serves as the Deputy Director of HCFA's Bureau of Eligibility, Reimbursement and Coverage. For the past eighteen years, he has held various positions with the federal government in the field of health insurance, such as Director of Coverage Policy, Director of Alternative Reimbursement Systems, and Deputy Director for Reimbursement Practices. Mr. Streimer has lectured extensively on the topic of financing of health care.

JOHN K. SUTHERLAND

John K. Sutherland is a partner in the law firm of Miller, Starr & Regalia of Oakland, California and specializes in real estate law with an emphasis on the acquisition and syndication of health care facilities. In addition to his extensive lecturing on real estate and tax law, Mr. Sutherland is a contributing author to the six-volume treatise of Miller and Starr, *Current Law of California Real Estate.*

SANFORD V. TEPLITZKY

Sanford V. Teplitzky is a partner in the law firm of Ober, Kaler, Grimes & Shriver and he has done extensive work in the area of Medicare and Medicaid reimbursement issues and policies. Mr. Teplitzky presently serves as general counsel to the Health Facilities Association of Maryland, the nursing home trade association.

SAMUEL D. TURNER

Samuel D. Turner handles litigation and special projects for a variety of health case clients in the private practice of Kaye, Scholer, Fierman, Hays & Handler. He was formerly Deputy General Counsel at the U.S. Department of Health and Human Services during the first term of the Reagan Administration.

J. MARK WAXMAN

J. Mark Waxman is a principal in the firm of Weissburg and Aronson, Inc. and is responsible for litigation of issues relating to the operation of health care facilities before administrative and judicial tribunals. He is the immediate past president of the Venice Family Clinic and serves on the Board of Directors of Alternative Living for the Aging and Bet Tzedek Legal Services. In addition, Mr. Waxman is an Adjunct Professor in the School of Public Administration, University of Southern California.

PAUL R. WILLGING

Paul R. Willging is presently the Executive Vice President of the American Health Care Association. In this capacity, he serves as director of the Government Services Division for the trade association which represents multifacility, single-owned, and nonproprietary nursing homes.

DONALD C. YESUKAITIS

Donald C. Yesukaitis is a principal in the Washington, D.C. World Headquarters Office of Arthur Andersen and Co. and serves as that firm's liaison on health care with the federal government. Among his various responsibilities are maintaining dialogue with different government agencies and with the Congress, as well as monitoring and analyzing health care legislation and regulations. He has lectured extensively across the nation on health care financial matters.

FOREWORD

This book is based on the proceedings of the Tenth Annual Program on Long Term Care and the Law held in Nashville, Tennessee during February, 1985. We want to thank the faculty for participating in the education program and for agreeing to have their presentations recorded and subsequently edited for this book. Our particular thanks go to the program chairman, Thomas C. Fox of Pierson, Ball and Dowd, Washington, D.C., for taking time from his busy schedule to organize these programs for the National Health Lawyers Association. As in previous years, Mr. Fox has agreed to chair our Eleventh Annual Program on Long Term Care and the Law to be held in San Diego, California, February 5-7, 1986. We would like to thank National Health Publishing for producing this book.

The National Health Lawyers Association is a nonprofit association of attorneys and health professionals involved with or practicing in the area of health care. The association publishes two monthly periodicals, *Health Law Digest* and *News Report* and also conducts educational programs in other areas of health law. All of the programs are open to physicians, administrators, health executives, and attorneys, and they have been granted continuing education credits for attorneys, CPAs and nursing home administrators.

To obtain more information on the National Health Lawyers Association, its publications, and educational programs, write to:

David J. Greenburg
Executive Director
522 21st Street, N.W.
Suite 120E
Washington, D.C. 20006
(202) 833-1100

PREFACE

This book contains speeches delivered at the Tenth Annual Long Term Care and the Law conference held at the Opryland Hotel in Nashville, Tennessee. The speakers included leading health care lawyers and other professionals, such as government officials and public advocates who provided information and led discussions on important and emerging legal issues confronting those involved in the field of long term care.

For the new lawyer as well as the seasoned practitioner, the Case Law Update is an excellent presentation. It encompasses a review of recent cases involving the Boren Amendment payment standard. Two special features of this session were a review of the Eighth Circuit's decision in the Minnesota rate equalization case and the Tenth Circuit's opinion in *In Re Estate of Smith v. O'Halloran*.

In a session which included representatives from the legal field, the long term care industry, the financial community, and the federal agency and legislative staffs, the controversial Section 2314 amendment of the Deficit Reduction Act of 1984, which provides federal limitation on the revaluation of capital assets of hospitals and skilled nursing homes upon a change in ownership, was discussed. The session addressed the various issues raised by the amendment, among them the effective date for state Medicaid plans, state capital payment methodologies affected, and ways in which states demonstrate compliance. The legislative perspective included a discussion of the legislative history and budgetary savings projection, as well as an analysis of the statute and possible legal challenges. The financial perspective offered views on how a financial institution that is active in financing the acquisition and construction of long term care facilities might be affected. Of particular interest to providers was the industry perspective which discussed the potential impact on various state Medicaid Plan payment methodologies. In reviewing this material, the reader should also examine the presentation by a Health Care Financing Administration official in the Bureau of Eligibility, Reimbursement and Coverage. This presentation evaluated certain unique arrangements currently in use in the delivery and financing of long term care.

For a more in-depth look to the future, the reader should examine the presentation by a representative of Arthur Andersen and Co., which used the Delphi forecasting method to study the future direction of the health care system.

This material may be of particular interest to providers in strategic planning and to public officials involved with identifying future directions in long term care.

Providers might also be interested in the session which identified the goals and possible recommendations of the Institute of Medicine committee on nursing home regulations. There was an excellent commentary on the potential impact of this project on the nursing home enforcement system.

Providers considering the possibility of bed reservation agreements as a result of the Medicare DRG prospective payment system for hospitals should be aware of the session on developing such contractual arrangements, and the presentation which focused on the current federal and state prohibitions on discrimination against admission and discharge of Medicaid patients, as well as the impact of these statutes and regulations on the development of bed reservation agreements.

The "state of the industry" presentation by Dr. Paul R. Willging, Deputy Executive Vice President of the American Health Care Association has become a regular feature of the annual program. As a former high official in the Health Care Financing Administration who now represents the long term care industry, his insights are of particular interest.

A special feature of the program this year was the specialty workshops and discussion groups where participants had an opportunity to gain useful information and share experiences. Included were presentations by attorneys representing investors and syndicators who acquire nursing homes for the purpose of leasing to qualified operators. Corporate counsel from two major nursing home organizations examined the contractual concerns in acquiring, managing, and selling long term care facilities. There was also a session on legal considerations of the mortgage lender in financing nursing home acquisitions.

Several sessions included presentations geared especially for the long term care facility administrator. These included the interdisciplinary audit with a panel composed of an attorney, a nursing home administrator, and a certified public accountant, who discussed how a preventive internal audit can be performed. There was also a presentation by an Assistant North Carolina Attorney General and Director of the North Carolina Medicaid Fraud Control Program who directed the criminal prosecution of eight nursing homes and nine employers for misappropriation of funds. For the nursing home administrator, this session included a discussion on the legal aspects of handling patient funds. Nursing home administrators were made aware of a problem in California faced by owners and attorneys in defending against punitive damage claims, a new area of concern. For the administrator, there was also a discussion of the major ethical issues which arise in the nursing home setting. A representative of the American Nurses Association, who is both a lawyer and a registered nurse, discussed the legal issues in nursing which confront the long term care provider.

For the lawyer who must deal with the problem of investigation, the panel discussion led by the Chief of the State Fraud Branch of the Office of the

Inspector General should be particulary helpful. State Medicaid Fraud Control Unit directors from three states were involved with this.

For the administrator or attorney connected with a long term care facility serving the mentally retarded, the discussion by the former Deputy General Counsel for the Department of Health and Human Services, which included current congressional and regulatory issues in this area, should be of interest. For anyone with a strong interest in developing commercial insurance for home care and nursing home care, the remarks of an attorney in the Wisconsin Office of the Commissioner of Insurance may be helpful. Finally, a session was presented on the impact of federal labor and wage laws on the long term care providers. This session focused on the position of the Department of Labor under the Service Contract Act, which applies to nursing homes which have contracts with the Veterans Administration.

In conclusion, I want to express my sincere appreciation to our faculty for their excellent presentations and for their preparation in editing the transcripts which are included. I strongly recommend this book and trust that it will be a valuable resource. For those who have not attended our programs, please consider doing so in the future.

Thomas C. Fox
Pierson, Ball and Dowd
Program Chairman

PART 1

CASE LAW:
Legislation Policy Update

Chapter 1

Case Law Update

Speaker: Joel M. Hamme

This chapter discusses the case law decisions that have been made since February 1984 regarding the Boren Amendment and its standards, which establish the federal Medicaid reimbursement criteria for long term care Medicaid facilities. This review will also summarize the issues that are frequently raised in Boren Amendment litigation and how those issues are being resolved by the courts. We will also examine the strategic considerations that determine whether or not a Boren Amendment case should be brought to court, and if so, whether it should be brought in a federal or a state court, how the case should be presented, and the types of evidence that should be adduced to ensure a successful result.

LEGISLATIVE HISTORY

When the Medicaid statute was first enacted in 1965, it did not provide any reimbursement standard whatsoever for Medicaid payments to nursing homes. This situation existed until April 1, 1968, when Congress specified that nursing home payments should not be in excess of reasonable charges consistent with efficiency, economy, and quality of care. This enactment, which was effective from April 1, 1968, created a ceiling or a maximum standard, but not a floor or a minimum standard, for a state's Medicaid payments to long term care facilities. In other words, the states remained, for the most part, free to pay something less than that ceiling and frequently did so. They were merely prohibited from paying rates that were in excess of reasonable charges consistent with the efficiency, economy, or quality of care.

In 1972, Congress amended the Social Security Act, effective July 1, 1976, to require that there be a minimum standard for Medicaid payments to long term care facilities. This provision, commonly known as section 249, required that, effective July 1, 1976, long term care services under the Medicaid act be paid by the states on what was known as a reasonable cost-related basis, to be determined

3

in accordance with methods and standards developed by the states on the basis of cost-finding methods approved and verified by the Secretary of Health, Education, and Welfare. The Secretary by regulation attempted to postpone the effective date of section 249 requirements from July 1, 1976, until January 1, 1978. That regulation was invalidated by a number of federal district courts, and about the time a number of the courts in the country started to look into the substantive requirements of section 249, Congress again changed the standard.

Effective October 1, 1980, Congress enacted a provision, commonly known as the Boren Amendment, which deleted section 249's requirement of reasonable cost-related reimbursement. In its place, the amendment substituted a provision that states that the Medicaid reimbursement standards for long term care facilities are to entail the use of rates that the state finds and makes assurances satisfactory to the Secretary of Health and Human Services (HHS) are reasonable and adequate to meet the costs that must be incurred by efficiently and economically operated facilities in order to provide care and services in conformity with applicable state and federal laws, regulations, and quality and safety standards.

That provision was applied one year later by Congress to inpatient hospital services under the Medicaid act, so that the Boren Amendment cases that arise frequently involve not only nursing home reimbursement but also often hospital reimbursement. While the statutory standards differ in some small respects for hospitals as opposed to nursing homes, the case decisions involving hospitals often have an influence on the nursing home decisions and vice versa.

The Boren Amendment was enacted by Congress because it was felt that the federal approval process that had existed under section 249 had unduly restrained the states' fiscal and administrative discretion, and many states had complained that they were required to utilize Medicare reimbursement principles that mandated payment of reasonable cost. Congress's desire, therefore, was to grant the states greater flexibility in developing Medicaid methods of payment for long term care services. Congress viewed the Medicare reasonable cost provisions as not entirely satisfactory, as they lacked cost and efficiency incentives, and were inherently inflationary because they reimbursed any costs that were in fact reasonable.

Although the states were free to establish Medicaid long term care rates on a statewide or geographic basis, on a class basis, or on an institution-by-institution basis without reference to Medicare under the Boren Amendment, Congress made clear that this flexibility was not intended to encourage arbitrary reductions by the states in the Medicaid rates that would detrimentally affect patient care. In addition, Congress specified that the rates established by the states under the Boren Amendment, despite the flexibility accorded to the states, were supposed to take account of the projected economic conditions for the periods for which the rates were set. Finally, in the House conference report prior to the enactment of the Boren Amendment, there is an indication that Congress, while giving the states greater flexibility than they had had under section 249, intended that the states were not supposed to develop Medicaid rates for long term care facilities based solely on budgetary appropriations or restraints.

Subsequent to the enactment of the Boren Amendment and to the time that that amendment was applied in large part to hospital rates under Medicaid, HHS issued interim final regulations. Those regulations came out on September 30, 1981. The federal review process under the final Boren Amendment regulations, which came out in December, 1983, is very much diminished from what it was under section 249, and in fact from the process that was used under the interim final regulations of 1981. For example, under the interim final regulations, states had to submit annual assurances that the rates met the statutory standard imposed by the Boren Amendment, and they had to submit related information and findings to support that assurance, regardless of whether they changed the methodology for setting their Medicaid rates. Under the final regulations, this requirement was dropped. Now the states have only to make annual findings that the Medicaid rates meet the Boren Amendment standard; they are not required to submit assurances or related information unless the state makes what is considered a significant change in its Medicaid reimbursement methodology.

RECENT LITIGATION

The Boren Amendment litigation that has occurred since February 1984 falls into four separate areas. First, there are cases that represent substantive challenges under federal law. These are challenges to the merits of the actual rate-setting reimbursement methodology imposed by a state under the Boren Amendment. Second, there are cases that represent federal procedural challenges under the Boren Amendment, that is, challenges to the process by which the Medicaid rate-setting methodology was promulgated or implemented. In other words, the challenge was not necessarily to the merits of that reimbursement methodology but to the process by which it was either approved, promulgated, or implemented. Third, a group of cases presented substantive challenges under state law. Finally, another group of cases represented procedural challenges under state law. The last two categories, substantive and procedural challenges under state law, technically might not be considered as Boren Amendment litigation. Frequently, however, they are combined with substantive Boren Amendment challenges, or they involve state laws and regulations that have been established because of the Boren Amendment or because of federal Medicaid regulations and requirements.

SUBSTANTIVE CHALLENGES UNDER FEDERAL LAW

Two Medicaid rate freeze decisions came out of Wisconsin and the United States Court of Appeals for the Seventh Circuit during the year: *Wisconsin*

Hospital Association v. Reivitz (733 F.2d 1226) and a companion case known as *Hillhaven Corporation v. Wisconsin Department of Health and Social Services* (733 F.2d 1224). Both of these cases arose out of the same factual circumstances affecting Medicaid hospital and long term care facility rates in Wisconsin.

a.   The *Wisconsin Hospital Association* Case

In 1982 the Wisconsin legislature enacted a provision requiring that Medicaid hospital rates in Wisconsin be frozen for a three-month period, from July 1 through September 30, 1982. In addition, the same legislation required that Medicaid nursing home rates be frozen for a three-month period, from January 1 through March 31, 1983. The Wisconsin Hospital Association filed suit contending, among other things, that the rate freeze resulted in rates that violated the Boren Amendment. The federal District Court in Wisconsin awarded summary judgment to the hospitals, finding that the rate freeze was inherently unreasonable because the state had assured HHS that its methodology took account of inflationary increases. In reaching this result, the court relied upon a number of rate freeze cases, including another rate freeze case in Wisconsin that had been litigated under section 249. Essentially, the court said that a rate freeze was per se unlawful and did not require the court to inquire into the facts and circumstances that spawned the legislation or to review any particular evidence regarding the effects of that rate freeze.

b.   The *Hillhaven Corporation* Case

At about the same time, the Hillhaven Corporation on behalf of its facilities in Wisconsin filed suit in federal court and sought a preliminary injunction against the Medicaid rate freeze for nursing homes. The district court judge, who happened to be the same judge who had ruled on the *Wisconsin Hospital Association* case, granted a preliminary injunction largely on the basis of the earlier decision in that case. The court noted that the freeze had been implemented without any objective analysis of the effects of the freeze and that the freeze therefore appeared to be based entirely on budgetary considerations, which was contrary to the Boren Amendment.

The state of Wisconsin ultimately appealed both of these cases to the United States Court of Appeals for the Seventh Circuit. In the *Wisconsin Hospital Association* case, the Seventh Circuit reversed the district court and held that a rate freeze, or at least a rate freeze for a limited period of time such as three months, is not necessarily unreasonable or unlawful under the Boren Amendment. The court found that it could not be presumed that the rates that had existed prior to the rate freeze represented the lowest level of reimbursement that the state found adequate to meet the Boren Amendment. Thus, a freeze might not have rendered the rates unreasonable; the rates might have been higher than they had to be, and so a freeze was simply bringing them down somewhat and perhaps not to a level that was unreasonable. Accordingly, the Seventh Circuit remanded the case to the district court for further evidentiary hearings to determine several other things. First, the district court had to review the effect that the rate freeze had had on the hospitals' quality of services, on their Medicaid patient utilization, and on their financial operations. When the district court had entered its summary judgment, it had never reviewed any evidence relating to those topics, because it had found that a rate freeze by its very definition was inherently unlawful. Second, the circuit court asked the district court to review whether the state of Wisconsin had violated the Boren Amendment by failing to submit assurances and related information to HHS when the state had implemented the rate freeze. In fact, the state had not submitted a plan amendment to be approved by HHS, and it had not submitted the assurances, because the state of Wisconsin contended that the rate freeze for hospitals was not a substantial change in its existing plan. Therefore, under the Boren Amendment, the state felt that it was not required to make a plan amendment or to submit assurances or related information.

In the *Hillhaven* case, the circuit court again reversed the district court, largely relying on the reasoning that it used in the *Wisconsin Hospital Association* case. Therefore, the *Hillhaven* case was similarly remanded to the district court for further proceedings. The *Wisconsin Hospital Association* case has since been tried in the district court, and the parties are awaiting a decision. In the litigation brought by the Hillhaven Corporation, the parties are involved in settlement negotiations and the case has not been tried.

c.   The *Nebraska Health Care Association* Case

The next group of cases involves Medicaid rate cut litigation, in which the rates are not merely frozen but actually reduced. The first case is *Nebraska Health Care Association v. Dunning*, decided by the federal district court in Nebraska on July 9, 1984. This case is reported at paragraph 34,100 of the CCH Medicare and Medicaid guide (1984-2 Transfer Binder). The facts in the Nebraska case were that the Nebraska legislature on July 1, 1982, had enacted several statutory provisions. Under the first provision, if at any time during the state's fiscal year it appeared that Medicaid funds were being spent at a rate at which they would exceed available appropriations, the single-state agency would be required (1) to impose a pro rata reduction of reimbursement rates for all optional services including intermediate care services offered by nursing homes, and (2) under circumstances of budgetary emergency where pro rata reductions for optional services had gone into effect and reached the level of 10%, to impose pro rata reduction on all services, both optional and required services under Medicaid in order to achieve the cost savings needed to stay within the budget.

Under the second provision of the statute, the part that relates to pro rata reductions to tailor rates to meet what the budgetary appropriation had been, nursing care facilities, Medicaid rates for the period beginning July 1, 1982, through the end of June 1983 could not exceed the rates that were in effect on April 1, 1982, by more than 3.75%. In other words, there was a ceiling of 3.75% on the increases that could be given Medicaid long term care facilities over this 15 month period. Subsequently, the Nebraska legislature extended this provision to cover the fiscal year July 1, 1983, through June 30, 1984. That extension required that the Medicaid rates for the entire 24-month period (July 1, 1982, through June 30, 1984) not exceed by more than 3.75% the rates in effect on April 1, 1982.

HHS approved a plan amendment that incorporated both of these provisions effective August 1, 1982. Ultimately, however, HHS withdrew approval of the emergency cuts provision and asked Nebraska to delete that provision from its state plan. About the same time, and immediately after Nebraska had promised to delete the provision, the state encountered a budget crisis, the pro rata reductions provision went into effect, and the state proposed that effective April 1, 1983, intermediate care facility rates in the State of Nebraska would be reduced by 14.4% and skilled nursing facility rates for Medicaid by 4.4%.

A federal district court entertained a challenge to this provision and issued a preliminary injunction against the Medicaid rate cuts effective April 1, 1983. Later in 1983, that same court upheld HHS's interim final Boren Amendment regulations and found that, although the term "efficiently and economically operated facilities" needed to be defined, that responsibility lay not with the Secretary of HHS but with the states.

In July of 1984 the district court considered the merits of both the 3.75% rate increase limitation and the pro rata rate reduction provision and invalidated both provisions. The court offered four reasons for invalidating the rate cut provision. First, it found that HHS had refused to approve the provision and therefore that the provision could not be implemented without federal approval. Otherwise, the plan would be in violation of federal law.

Second, the court found that the pro rata reduction provision had not been accompanied by any studies conducted by the state, or any analysis performed by the state, to determine the effect that the reductions would have on areas such as patient care. The court ruled that, without such studies, the assurances that were required to be given to HHS could not properly be given, and therefore the state's rate could not be deemed to meet Boren Amendment standards.

Third, the court found that the across-the-board reductions were based entirely on budget considerations--in fact the formula specified that the reductions went into effect when it was threatened that the budget would be exceeded--and it found that the reductions reduced the rates for all of the long term care facilities in Nebraska, including facilities that the state itself had already found were economically and efficiently operated. Thus, if a facility, for example, had a rate of $25 per day and the state had found that that was an efficient and economic facility, that facility also had to take a rate cut just the same as a provider that received $45 per day Medicaid rate.

Finally, the court found that the testimony offered by the plaintiffs indicated that the rate cuts would force a reduction either of services or of the number of Medicaid patients. Such a reduction could result in harm to patients and/or a violation of certification standards or, alternatively, private-pay patients would unfairly be asked to bear those losses through additional rate increases in the private-pay rate.

Not only did the court invalidate the pro rata rate reduction provision, but it also found the 3.75% rate increase limitation under the statute to be arbitrary and capricious. In that respect, the court found that the approved Nebraska state plan indicated that Nebraska would pay Medicaid rates up to a ceiling that was set at the 65th percentile of Medicaid patient days. In looking at the evidence that was presented, the court determined that the effect of the limitation, even for the first year that it was in effect (1982-83), was to deny full reimbursement of allowable costs to numerous facilities that were under the 65th percentile. In effect, then, the state was no longer paying at the 65th percentile even though it had represented to HHS that it would pay at that level, and even though its state plan required it to do so.

Additionally, the court found that the 3.75% limitation did not correlate to any relevant inflation index that covered the 1982-83 period. The state was unable to offer any evidence that inflation over that period had been projected at 3.75%. Moreover, the court said, the extension of that limitation into another year beyond 1982-83 meant that the state was estimating annual inflation at a rate of about 1.36%. The court said there certainly was no index that the state has offered to support an annual inflation rate of that amount. Accordingly, even though HHS had approved the rate limitation, the state agency had done no objective study or analysis to determine the effects of the limitation on the care that was being rendered to Medicare patients. The state agency also had no analysis or study of the extent to which the rate limitation would continue to have an effect on the willingness of facilities either to continue in the Medicaid program or to take Medicaid patients. The court said that, without such an analysis, there was no factual basis for the assurances that the state had given to HHS in order to get HHS to approve the plan. Thus, the assurances were invalid because there was no factual or objective study on which they were predicated.

The Nebraska decision thus not only invalidated a rate reduction system based on budgetary appropriations, but also invalidated a rate limitation provision that: (1) was not in accordance with any reasonable index to cover inflation over the periods involved and (2) the state had never conducted any studies to support.

d. The *Illinois Hospital Association* Case

A second case that involves what amounts to Medicaid rate reductions is the *Illinois Hospital Association* case, reported at 576 F.Supp. 360 (N.D. Ill. 1983).

In that case, decided in 1983, a federal District Court in Illinois had issued a preliminary injunction against a new prospective Medicaid rate reimbursement methodology for hospitals in Illinois. Under that methodology, the state of Illinois proposed to defer payment of about one-quarter of all the reimbursement that the hospitals were entitled to until there were sufficient appropriations to cover those costs and to cover the payments that would be made under that methodology. In issuing a preliminary injunction, the district court found that this standard probably violated the Boren Amendment.

Since February 1984, a settlement agreement was finalized in which the state of Illinois agreed to pay the difference between the interim and final rates that were proposed under its rate reimbursement methodology. The state also agreed to create an outpatient hospital fund of about $6 million, and it agreed to increase its Medicaid rate ceilings to the 65th percentile. The litigation in Illinois on behalf of the hospitals was therefore quite successful.

e. The *Cascade County Convalescent Nursing Home* Case

A third category of cases under substantive Boren Amendment challenges involved Medicaid inflation and rate adjustment factor litigation. A case in Montana similar to the *Nebraska* case discussed above, was *Cascade County Convalescent Nursing Home v. Montana Department of Social and Rehabilitation Services.* Effective July 1, 1982, the state of Montana had decided to implement a prospective reimbursement system for nursing homes in that state. The new system was designed to provide annual rate increases over a three-year period. Accordingly, the methodology utilized rate adjustment factors, and in this instance those rate adjustment factors were designed to yield annual increases in Medicaid rates of approximately 6% to facilities in Montana.

At the time this methodology was issued, those rate adjustment factors had been based on an analysis that showed, in the judgment of the state agency, that inflation would run about 6% annually over the next three years. When the prospective methodology was enacted, the state promulgated regulations not only adopting the methodology, but specifying that the rate formula itself could be altered during the three-year period, but only if certain events occurred, one of which was a material change in the assumptions on which the existing rate methodology had been based.

In the spring of 1983 the Montana legislature, which holds biennial sessions, appropriated Medicaid funds for the next two fiscal years. When it appropriated those funds, the Montana legislature utilized rate adjustment factors that were less than what the state agency had indicated that it was going to use over the remaining two-year period in which the rate formula was in effect. After the legislature adjourned, the Montana single-state agency proposed a temporary rate freeze to try to make up the funds that were necessary to account for differences between what the reimbursement methodology would have paid and what the legislature had appropriated.

There was considerable opposition to that proposal, and ultimately the state, instead of imposing a rate freeze, reduced the rate adjustment factors. Interestingly, the state agency decided not only to use the rate adjustment factors that the legislature had used, which were lower than those that were contained in the rate formula, but reduced them even further, apparently to give themselves a little bit of cushion. Thus, instead of producing 6% annual rate increases, the new rate adjustment factors that were promulgated by the Montana single-state agency would have approximated about 4% increases annually.

Four nursing facilities in Montana filed a class action suit in state court against the amended rate methodology. In August 1983 that court issued a temporary restraining order which prohibited implementation of the changes and required that the old methodology, which produced the 6% annual rate increases, be continued. The parties agreed by stipulation to continue that temporary restraining order in effect until the court issued its preliminary injunction decision after a hearing and after briefing.

On August 30, 1984, the court issued a preliminary injunction. The court found, among other things, that the plaintiffs were likely to prevail on various legal claims that they had made. It found that the plaintiffs were likely to prevail on their claim that the Boren Amendment was violated by the reduction of the rate adjustment factors, because the change in the methodology had been based entirely on state budgetary constraints and did not account for inflation that the state agency projected would occur in the next two years. The evidence showed that the state agencies had begun drafting revised rules right after the legislature went out of session. The initial drafts of the revised rules explicitly said that the revisions were necessary because of budget constraints due to the legislature failing to appropriate enough money.

In addition, the state agency, at the time it was changing the rate methodology, did an analysis of anticipated inflation over the next two-year period and found that inflation would, they believed, run about 6% annually over those two years. In other words, the agency found exactly what it had found previously. Thus, the state's decision to reduce the rate adjustment factors to a 4% level was not supported even by the state's own data. The court found also that the plaintiffs were likely to prevail on their claim that the rate revisions violated state law because, contrary to the state regulations, the state agency had *not* shown a material change of assumptions concerning the level of inflation, again because its analysis projected annual inflation to continue at about 6%, which was its original assumption.

The court further found that the proposed reductions in the rate adjustment factors would adversely affect the quality of care and the operations of nursing homes in Montana. The plaintiffs showed that numerous facilities in Montana had undertaken rather extraordinary cost containment measures when the prospective Medicaid reimbursement methodology was first enacted in July

1982. They had thus already undergone significant changes in their operations just to meet the initial reimbursement methodology. The state's reduction of those levels would, of course, have forced further staffing reductions and further cuts that would have adversely affected patient care.

Following the court's issuance of the preliminary injunction, as so often happens in these cases, the parties entered into a settlement agreement under which the plaintiffs received about three-quarters of all the sums that were in dispute, and in addition to that provision, the state promised certain other future changes in the methodology that would give the plaintiff class additional sums of money that were not in dispute in the litigation. The state also entered into an agreement indicating that they would not tailor the rates over the next several years to recoup from the facilities what the facilities had gained through the litigation. Thus, the litigation essentially enabled the providers in Montana to hold to what they originally expected in July 1982, and to get back what the state in July 1983 had attempted to take away.

f.   The *Colorado Health Care Association* Case

Colorado had a prospective Medicaid reimbursement system for long term care facilities in which costs were divided into two components: health care costs, which were not subject to any ceiling whatsoever, and administrative costs. The administrative costs were capped at the 90th percentile of the Medicaid patient days within each of the classes that Colorado established.

Those administrative costs were adjusted based on the Consumer Price Index to account for inflation during the periods that the rate would be in effect. Additionally, Colorado had what was called an incentive allowance, which permitted facilities that had administrative costs below the 90th percentile to keep one-half of the difference between the 90th percentile ceiling and their actual costs. Thus, if a facility's administrative costs were $25 per day, and the ceiling was $30 per day, the facility could keep one-half of the $5 difference, or $2.50 per day. This incentive factor was mandated by state statute, which provided that the incentive allowances were to be paid subject to the availability of appropriations.

In February 1983 the state agency, acting in response to what it perceived as a funding shortage, eliminated the incentive allowance. The Colorado Health Care Association and a number of nursing homes thereafter filed suit in state court to block that action, alleging that the elimination of the incentive factor violated a number of provisions of both federal and state law. Interestingly, the defendants removed the case to federal court and claimed that it involved primarily issues of federal law. After the removal, the parties entered into a stipulation--apparently some funds were found or there had been a mistake-- under which the state agreed to pay the incentive retroactively back to the beginning of February 1983 and to continue to pay it as long as there were funds for it. If the funds ran out and the incentive allowance could not be paid, then, under the stipulation, the parties agreed to submit the dispute to the court.

Two months after the stipulation had gone into effect, the state agency started failing to make payment under the incentive allowance, and the parties asked the court to make a ruling. The court ultimately held against the Colorado Health Care Association and found that the elimination of the incentive factor did not violate the Borne Amendment because the state was not required under any federal provision to pay such an allowance. The allowance was not an allowance for costs actually incurred but simply an incentive factor to try to keep costs down. The court's decision is reported at 598 F.Supp. 1400 (D. Colo. 1984).

The court found that the state continued to pay for actual administrative costs under the 90th percentile cap, and it found that that ceiling was certainly higher than other ceilings that have been approved under the Boren Amendment, and accordingly the elimination of the incentive allowance did not violate any aspect of federal law.

The court held additionally that budgetary considerations, while they may have entered into the state's rate-setting process, were permissible in this instance. It is noteworthy that the defendants had actually stipulated that they had eliminated the incentive allowance entirely because of lack of appropriations. The court never sought to reconcile the fact that the move was solely budgetary with the legislative history of the Boren Amendment. What might be derived from this opinion is that, although the states cannot set rates, or rates based on cost, totally on the basis of budget considerations, discretionary payments, that is, payments not required under federal law, can be eliminated even if the reasons for the elimination are solely budgetary. Such an exception, if it is one, might mean that the state can engage in totally budgetary considerations to eliminate efficiency allowances that are not based on cost.

The court emphasized that the plaintiffs had not shown or argued that the termination of the efficiency incentive adversely affected the quality of patient care. It held, moreover, that the elimination of the efficiency incentive was not arbitrary or capricious, nor did it violate any aspect of the Fourteenth Amendment in terms of due process rights or equal protection rights. In addition, the court rejected various state law claims that the Colorado administrative procedure act had been violated and that the elimination of the efficiency allowance was not based on any objective studies. The court found that the action did not have to be based on any objective studies--again, perhaps, an exception to other Boren Amendment standards--and that the provider in this case had not had its provider agreements breached by the elimination of the incentive.

One conclusion that can be drawn from this case is that, as in a ruling several years ago in a case involving a group called the Coalition of Michigan Nursing Homes, there is great difficulty of winning profit or incentive allowance cases under the Boren Amendment substantive standards. The reason is that federal law simply does not require payment of efficiency incentives or allowances. If a state reduces or eliminates those incentives, to the extent that its ensuing payment rate violates the Boren Amendment, it obviously is not in violation because of the elimination of the incentive allowance but because the rate-setting methodology is not in compliance with the amendment in some other way. Thus, if a state needs an efficiency incentive in order to comply with Boren, there is some other defect in the state plan that needs to be attacked when the efficiency incentive is disallowed.

g.   *Troutman v. Cohen*

A substantive case under the Boren Amendment that involves changes in rates based on level of care alterations is *Troutman v. Cohen,* out of the Eastern District Federal Court in Pennsylvania. In that case a group of plaintiffs who were nursing home residents challenged a revision to Pennsylvania's definition of skilled care. Pennsylvania had a patient care ratio or census of approximately 70% skilled nursing patients and 30% intermediate care patients. As a result of the change in definition, which the state said federal law required, Pennsylvania hoped to change its census from 70-30 in favor of skilled nursing patients to 30-70 in favor of intermediate care patients. Thus, the regulatory revisions changing the level of care and determinations in Pennsylvania were designed to shift a large number of skilled care patients to the status of intermediate care patients.

The patients in this case challenged that shift and the effects it would have on them, and they sought a preliminary injunction to require the state to continue certain interim measures that it had undertaken when it first engaged in the level of care changeover.

One of those interim measures was that the state recognized nursing hours in excess of the skilled, the maximum skilled, or the minimum skilled, and intermediate levels required under state licensing law. In addition, the state had given a temporary 6% increase in the intermediate care facility rate ceilings for Medicaid providers in the state.

Both of those interim measures had expired on December 31, 1983, and the plaintiffs were seeking to extend them. The court, however, denied a preliminary injunction to the plaintiffs. Many of the arguments in the case are unrelated to the Boren Amendment and do not require discussion here. However, part of the decision that is noteworthy is the fact that the plaintiffs had challenged Pennsylvania ceilings for Medicaid long term care facilities and that this was a group of patients, not facilities, that were challenging the ceilings.

Pennsylvania essentially establishes a ceiling at the median of a facility's allowable costs. In other words, the state arrayed the costs of each facility as allowable, from lowest to highest, then went to the midpoint and selected that level as being the ceiling, so that approximately 50% of the facilities were over and 50% under the ceiling. In upholding this ceiling, the court acknowledged that Pennsylvania had not established why it selected the median as a ceiling, but the court ruled that the plaintiffs had the burden of proving that the ceiling was arbitrary and capricious.

The court noted that there had been testimony by the single-state agency that the Pennsylvania median ceiling was actually higher than the 50th percentile. Pennsylvania used unaudited cost reports submitted by the providers. The audits, it was argued, would more likely find areas of disallowance rather than areas for which the facilities would get more money. The state contended that, in adjusting those unaudited cost reports to account for inflation, they felt that probably 70% of the facilities were getting their costs, and only 30% were under the ceiling. The court found that piece of evidence relevant to its determination, and it upheld, at least in a preliminary injunction proceeding, the fact that the plaintiffs were unlikely to prevail on their claim that that ceiling violated the Boren Amendment.

Procedural Challenges Under Federal Law

Boren Amendment litigation frequently involves procedural issues, such as whether or not Medicaid rate-setting methodologies were properly promulgated or approved under federal law. One issue is whether a particular revision involving a significant change requires state plan approval. The *Wisconsin Hospital Association* case and the *Hillhaven Corporation* case, both discussed above, raised that issue.

Second, the issue has come up as to whether or not prior federal approval is required before proposed changes by the states are implemented. There were two apparently differing views in 1984. In the *Wisconsin Hospital Association* case and the *Hillhaven Corporation* case, the Seventh Circuit intimated that states were free to implement the plan before HHS approved it, and that the plan when subsequently approved would relate back to the first day in the quarter in which it had been submitted. That has been HHS's position as well. The *Nebraska Health Care Association* decision, however, says that state plans cannot be enforced until HHS approves them. Both this and the Wisconsin decision really did not have to address those issues, because in Wisconsin the state had never submitted a plan amendment to begin with, and in the *Nebraska Health Care Association* case the state had submitted a plan amendment, and at least part of the amendment was approved and part disapproved.

Those two decisions have thus had some impact on the federal approval question. Frequently, too, the issue comes up as to whether or not changes are significant. If they are deemed to be significant, the state must engage in certain public notice and comment provisions and requirements under federal law. I am not aware of any significant cases under that provision in 1984.

Finally, one area that has been litigated in the past, although I have seen no cases on it in 1984, is whether the state in changing its methodology has consulted the medical care advisory committee.

Challenges Under State Law A number of other cases have raised issues, both procedural and substantive, under state law. An example is the *Cascade County* case in Montana, mentioned before. It involved a change in methodology without a material change of assumptions that was required under the state regulation. There are also cases from Washington (*United Nursing Homes, Inc. v. McNutt*, Nos. 59035, 80-2-01440-1, 81-2-0076-0 (Wash. Super. Apr. 3, 1984)), Illinois (*Senn Park Nursing Center*, 34,184 of CCH Medicare and Medicaid Guide, 1984-2 Transfer Binder), and the *South Carolina Health Care Association* decision, 740 F.2d 963 (4th Cir. 1983). Each of these cases involved procedural challenges under state law.

The Colorado case also involved procedural challenges under Colorado law, and the *Troutman* case likewise raised those issues but the court refused to decide them. A decision early in 1984 by the U.S. Supreme Court in a case called *Pennhurst State School and Hospital v. Halderman* (104 S.Ct. 900), was the basis for the court's decision in *Troutman* to refrain from deciding state law questions. In *Pennhurst*, the Supreme Court interpreted the Eleventh Amendment to the Constitution to bar federal courts from awarding relief against state officials based solely on state law. Previously, federal courts took what was called pendant jurisdiction over state law claims. This meant that, when there was a federal claim against the state, and a state claim as well, the federal court would resolve either or both the federal and the state claims. The Supreme Court's decision in *Pennhurst* said that the federal courts cannot resolve state law claims against states or their officials in this type of litigation.

TYPES OF RELIEF

A question raised by Boren Amendment cases is what type of relief should be sought. There is particular hazard in seeking preliminary injunction relief, because one of the factors that the plaintiff has to show is irreparable harm. Most courts are interested not so much in irreparable harm to the facilities, although that is something you should try to show if you can, but in irreparable harm to patients.

Every successful case under the Boren Amendment and virtually every unsuccessful case have been dissimilar in one respect: the successful cases tend to show that the patients are going to be very adversely affected, and the unsuccessful cases are unable to show that. Thus, in making their assessment on the merits, or on a preliminary injunction analysis, the courts are greatly swayed by patient care considerations. One hazard of seeking a preliminary injunction is that, if you cannot show that there is irreparable harm, the courts frequently do not stop their analysis there. They frequently go on to pontificate as to the plaintiff's likelihood of success on the merits. Generally, the court ends up convincing itself that the plaintiff does not have much of a case on the merits either. Therefore, if you cannot show irreparable harm, you automatically throw your case away, generally, if you try to seek preliminary injunction relief.

Important, too, is whether or not there is really any deference accorded to HHS or to its approval process. Without attempting to sound cynical, the fact is that the courts that uphold Boren Amendment state plans that have approved by HHS usually find that HHS is expert in this area. On the other hand, the courts that have invalidated plans approved by HHS under the Boren Amendment normally find that HHS should not be accorded very much deference because its review is rather cursory. HHS does not really take a detailed look at the state's assurances, which are rather superficial, and the state often does not produce the studies on which the assurances are supposed to be based.

Was any distinction made in the Nebraska and Wisconsin cases between interim and final rates?

The question is whether or not they make any distinction in the Nebraska and Wisconsin cases between interim and final rates, and the answer is that the decisions do not talk about those. I don't remember the decisions in either of those cases talking about interim versus final rates.

Now, my understanding in Wisconsin is that there was a rate freeze, and the facilities weren't going to get any more than that, regardless of what their final costs showed. In Nebraska, the rate--I'm assuming that the way that the statute read, the pro rata reductions were permanent, and the facility got no more money, and the state didn't intend to go back and pay it that money. I don't know whether that was a device simply to try to get supplemental appropriations or not, but I'm not aware of any distinction between interim and final rates in those instances. Those particular cases seem to suggest that the rates that were at issue were for all intents and purposes final.

Did I understand you to say that in the Nebraska case there was some mention made by the court about shipping some of the cost through Medicaid patients and private patients?

Right. In the Nebraska case, the district court suggested that the evidence showed that there had been no analysis or study of the effects of either the pro rata reductions or the limitations on increases, both of which were statutory. The court said that the evidence showed that, in order to comply with either of those provisions, the nursing homes were going to have to cut services to Medicaid patients, or, alternatively or both, would

have to shift costs to private-pay patients. The court felt that
the burden of cost shifting would be unfair.

Now, the court did not provide a lengthy legal analysis as to
whether that was unlawful or not. The whole Medicaid system
in every state other than Minnesota has been predicated on cost
shifting, but it isn't a legal ruling so much as it is a factual
observation as to the evidence.

*Is there any specific statutory prohibition or other case that
holds that it is illegal to try to shift the cost over to a private
patient population?*

In Minnesota, obviously, it's unlawful because Minnesota
requires rates to be equal for similar services. Aside from that,
I personally am not aware of anything. Certainly, there is
nothing in the federal Medicaid statute and regulations that
prohibits such cost shifting. Notably, the federal Medicare
statute does, however, contain such a prohibition.

What often happens, and what happened in both Nebraska
and Montana, is that evidence is produced about the effect of
the cuts, or the challenged provisions, on patient care. And it is
a very effective tool to come in and show, "Here's the
differences between our private-pay rates and our Medicaid
rates to begin with. If this Medicaid rate that we are
challenging goes into effect, here is what we are going to have
to do. We are either going to have to cut these X, Y, and Z
services, or cut our staffing, which is going to have these
effects on the patients, or we are going to have to change our
differential from, let's say, $10 per day to $12 per day, so that
the private-pay patients are paying that much more." That will
simply produce a private-pay patient that spends down more
quickly, that becomes Medicaid eligible more quickly, thus,
creating more problems both for the state and the facility.

So, it's not so much a legal ruling as it is, I think, a comment
on the evidence. But that is what the district court in Nebraska
said that it found to be unfair.

Chapter 2

Federal Limitations on the Revaluation of Assets: §2314 (DEFRA)

Speakers: Peter Bouxsein
David W. Curtiss
Thomas C. Fox
Thomas J. Jazwiecki

THOMAS FOX When Section 249 was enacted as part of the Social Security Amendments of 1972, the statute indicated that Section 249 had an effective date of July 1, 1976. The Department at that time said that the effective date was January 1, 1978. Thereafter ensued a controversy, a number of suits were filed, and the federal courts ultimately upheld the proposition that when a statute says July 1, 1976, in fact, that is what the Congress means.

When we talk about Section 2314 of the Deficit Reduction Act, we probably face a similar controversy. The Department maintains on one hand that the certain amendments made by this section have an effective date of July 18, 1984, while the industry takes the position that the effective date is October 1, 1984 or later.

The other irony in this is that we have been so accustomed to the Department's position on the Boren Amendment, that it provides rather broad discretion and administrative responsibility to the states, that the federal government should have absolutely no role whatsoever in defining such crucial terms as "efficient" and "economically operated," and now we have an issue before us where the federal government is attempting to impose certain restrictions upon the states, which have that same discretion.

Faced with that very controversial problem, I thought it would be appropriate to convene a body of experts on this issue where I am certain we would receive unbiased and objective opinions from all of the members involved; and so I've asked the gentlemen that we have here today to participate in a discussion on this particular section of the Deficit Reduction Act of 1984.

We will have formal remarks for approximately 10 to 15 minutes from each of the speakers and then at the conclusion of all of the speakers having the opportunity to state their position, we'll have an opportunity for questions and answers from the audience as well as other members from the panel.

The members of the panel are: Peter Bouxsein, counsel to the Health Sub-Committee on Health and the Environment, who was involved in one way or another in this legislative enactment; Dave Curtiss, a vice president of Newman and Associates, who will present the financial community perspective on this issue; Tom Jazwiecki who is the Director of the Office of Reimbursement and Finance of the American Health Care Association, and will present the industry perspective.

The Legislative Perspective

PETER BOUXSEIN I will give you an indication of what kinds of concerns led to this issue being on the agenda last year, and then give you a sense as to what the decision environment was like at that time, and still is, and then trace the emergence of the final policy and talk about the savings estimates.

The concerns that put revaluation of assets on the agenda last year were essentially these. That, first of all, it has become generally accepted that cost reimbursement rules are simply wasteful. It is not an efficient way of paying for health care services, particularly passing through the costs of depreciation and interest. Even a return on equity is not a good way of going about paying for capital. One reason is that it encourages debt financing, which may or may not be a bad thing, but it certainly does not provide incentive for the operators of the facilities to shop around for better interest rates or to delay or forego building or expansion because the interest rates are too high. It also encourages turn over of facilities for a variety of reasons, including the fact that it tends to overcompensate at the beginning of a cycle, at least compared to the debt payments, and to underpay in the later years; it ensures the buyer that he'll be able to recoup his costs. And the provision allowing for a step-up in the value of the assets after a sale or transfer tends to exacerbate these factors and leads to higher expenditures under Medicare and Medicaid that don't seem to make any discernable improvement in access or quality of care. All these factors were highlighted in a report from the General Accounting Office having to do with a purchase of Health Affiliates, Inc. by the Hospital Corporation of America, indicating that the result of that was a substantial increase in Medicare expenditures for capital. So, those were the concerns, the premises on which we were operating at the time.

The decision environment was one in which concerns about the budget and about the deficit had primacy over any health policy considerations. In fact since 1981, health policy had to struggle to be heard when everybody was concerned about the budget and about the deficit. We haven't been thinking for some years now about benefit expansions or eligibility expansions in those areas where we think there are gaps in the program. Instead the main task for those of us concerned about health policy has been to try to deflect various proposals to cut benefits, to reduce eligibility, to shift costs to the beneficiaries and to cap

Medicaid and other provisions which we think would have a serious detrimental effect on the programs. Once again this year the Administration is setting up budget proposals to cap Medicaid, to increase the Part B premium, increase the Part B deductible, increase the co-payments, institute new co-payments on home health care, delay eligibility, shift the costs to beneficiaries. All of these steps will lead to a gradual decline of the program.

One element in the decision environment was that the pressure was on to have these programs contribute to the deficit reduction effort, and this leads us to try to find less damaging alternatives to the proposals that come to us from the Administration--typically in the form of trying to enhance efficiency or productivity or eliminating waste in the program. We've done the easy ones; and it's getting harder and harder to find those kinds of proposals, those that are going to yield a substantial dollar in savings, or have a substantial impact on the program. So that was the first and most important thrust of the decision environment. We are making budget policy not health policy.

Second of all, these issues are being resolved in the context of some large, omnibus package, which includes most, if not all non-defense spending provisions and typically includes taxes. This means that if any particular piece of the large puzzle becomes a problem and becomes a serious sticking point, it can lead to an unraveling of the entire package. At one point last year, it looked as if this would happen on the issue of the physician freeze under Medicare; it seemed as if the entire package was balancing vicariously on the outcome of that issue. Another important aspect of the fact that we are deciding these issues in the context of an omnibus package is that it allows only limited attention to any given idea--there just isn't the time and energy to devote to each and every item in the large package.

A third factor in the back of our minds last year was that reform of Medicare rules for the payment of capital was already on the agenda by reason of the 1983 Social Security Amendments to the perspective payment legislation, and we had set a date of October 1, 1986 to have that issue resolved. So presumably it was going to be on the agenda for 1985, although I can't assure you at this point that it will, in fact, be resolved this year. Presumably the resolution of that issue would deal with the concerns that I outlined in the beginning. We are also aware that there are a great many other factors and considerations that will bear on the decision to buy or sell a facility, aside from Medicare and Medicaid reimbursement. Taxed provisions and other considerations will also play a major role.

The final language in the statute evolved over time. In the beginning, there was no provision on the House side and the Senate had adopted a provision in their deficit reduction package. Interestingly that provision was far more restrictive than the final language that emerged. Essentially, in the Senate language, the buyer would have stepped into the shoes of the seller. Not only could he have not increased the valuation of the assets, but he had to take the book value, the historic value minus depreciation.

Apparently, when the Senate passed the provision, they didn't give serious consideration to the recapture provisions of the Medicare rules; so that while people are arguing whether or not Medicare was buying a facility more than once, the Senate provision appeared to resolve in Medicare buying it less than once.

On the House side, there had been hearings by the Ways and Means Committee on the issue, and a good deal of interest. So we went into conference with considerable interest, developed particularly through respect for the Medicare program. At this point, most of the discussion was about the Medicare program and about hospitals.

The committee that I'm with--House Energy and Commerce--has jurisdiction over the Medicaid program and Part B of Medicare. The House Ways and Means Committee does not have jurisdiction over Medicaid but shares jurisdiction with us over Part B of Medicare. On the Senate side, the Finance Committee has jurisdiction over both parts of Medicare and Medicaid.

At the closing of the conference the discussion had less to do with whether it was a good idea to adopt a provision on limiting the revaluation of assets, which was taken as a given, than with how we should do it.

So when we turned to the Medicaid piece of this, we decided that we should not simply pick up the Medicare language and simply insert it verbatim in the Medicaid statute. Instead we did several things that were intended to give the states considerable discretion in how to deal with the problem.

One of those was to switch to talking about payments, not about the valuation of assets per se. Medicare provision talks about evaluating assets which is the basis for payment; in the Medicaid provision, we didn't talk about evaluation of assets, but about the bottom line payment.

In addition, the focus was not on payments, but on payment methodology. The state, we thought, would be able to come in and talk methodology and not payment amounts.

Thirdly, we thought this would all be done in the context of the state providing satisfactory assurances, meaning whatever the Secretary said was satisfactory. There would be a good deal of choice there on the part of the Secretary and our expectation was that it would not be a very close scrutiny.

Finally, we said that there will be increases in Medicare reimbursement in order to give the states some range in which to move. As it turns out, it may well be that the last motion, that increases can't exceed what they would be under Medicare, may have wound up undercutting whatever flexibility we were giving to the states with our first three notions--payment, payment of methodology and satisfactory assurances.

Because of the environment that we are working in, much depends upon the Congressional Budget Office estimates. With respect to Medicare, which is predominantly dealing with hospitals, the CBO told us that over a period of three years, they'd save about 140 million dollars, based on the assumption that about

60 institutions would change hands each year and normally there would be about 75 percent step up in the book value of the asset.

When we asked what the implications would be if we extended it to Medicaid, meaning primarily nursing homes, the answer was that over three years it would yield 115 million dollars in savings. Later in October of last year, CBO did some rethinking and re-examining of the assumptions and changed that estimate to 195 million dollars over three years.

The assumptions were that capital represents about 12 1/2 percent of payments for nursing home care--it's a little over seven percent for hospitals-- that about one-eighth of the nursing home capacity will turn over each year, and there will be about an 80 percent step up in the book value of the asset.

TOM FOX I will share with you the legal analysis which I followed in attempting to interpret Section 2314. In looking at Section 2314, the appropriate analysis which immediately came to my mind was two-fold. One, in interpreting a statutory provision, the first thing you look at is the plain language of the statute, attempting to derive your interpretation on that basis. If the statutory language is not clear, it is then appropriate to utilize the legislative history, and to use that legislative history as some aid construction in interpreting the language of the statute. So with that in mind, I broke Section 2314 down into two parts, the changes to title 18 and to title 19. Title 18 is of the Social Security Act section 1861, and title 19 is of the Social Security Act, section 1902.

The change that was made to the Medicare statutory provision 1861 (v)(1) was to add a new subparagraph (O) which did several things. One was to state that in establishing an appropriate allowance under Medicare for reimbursement of providers for depreciation and interest on capital indebtedness for a hospital or nursing home that goes through a change of ownership, certain limitations would apply under Medicare.

One of those limitations was that there would be definite rules as to how the acquisition cost would be computed, and there would be certain exclusions from those acquisition costs in arriving at the cost to the purchaser in the acquisition-- those are set forth in the conference report.

The other limitation was that there would be a continuation of the recapture of depreciation as to the purchaser, and that the acquisition cost would be reduced by certain amounts such as attorneys' fees, accounting fees, feasibility studies, and the like.

The legislation also stated that the Secretary would be expected to continue the depreciation recapture provisions as they existed under Medicare in the past. The conference report also indicates that there will be the need for the Secretary to address sale and leaseback transactions.

The last part of the limitation imposed by this section was the language in the statute that they would apply to Medicare reimbursement for capital assets following a change of ownership that was obligated on or after July 18, 1984.

We will now look at the other amendment that was accomplished as a result of 2314 which was to change title 19 of the Social Security Act, specifically Section 1902(a)(13). Here, the statutory language doesn't mention any of the limitations which I previously have discussed relating to Medicare. It simply says that the states must now provide assurances to the Secretary that its payment methodology cannot reasonably be expected to increase solely as a result of a change of ownership in excess of the increase that would result from the application of the limitations in the amendment to the Medicare statute--section 1861 (v)(1)(O). This actually only represented a type of upper limit or overall cap that would be applied to evaluate the reimbursement that the states would be paying under Medicaid for property.

Another significant aspect of the section amendment 2314 was that there is another effective date for the amendment to 1902(a)(13), and here it indicates the effective date, insofar as Medicaid is concerned, would be October 1, 1984 or later--if a state would be required to enact legislation, changing its Medicaid payment methodology in order to be in conformity with the section 2314 amendment.

Having looked at the plain language of the statute let us now look at the legislative history. As you look at the statutory language and the legislative history on the Boren amendment, there are several principals which emerge, which have to be read in harmony with any interpretation that would be given to this most recent change. There are essentially four:

1. The legislative history of the Boren amendment indicates that states must have flexibility and discretion in establishing a payment methodology without regard to the Medicare principles of reimbursement.

2. The states must be free to establish Medicaid rates on a state wide basis, geographic basis, class basis, or an institutional basis.

3. The states must also be able to include incentive allowances to encourage cost containment or to include incentives to attract investments.

4. Lastly, for purposes of this Medicaid reimbursement provision and the discretion that would now be extended and given to the states as a result of the Boren amendment, there will still be application of the Medicare upper limit that is provided by Section 1902(a)(30)(A). But in doing this, it would simply be an aggregate test, that is, the state must in the aggregate not exceed in its Medicaid payments what it might have paid under Medicare.

Those four principles were important as a result of the Boren amendment, and I will now discuss the legislative history of the Deficit Reduction Act of 1984, specifically Section 2314.

When you review the conference report, you will find at least four strong points which emerge:

1. One is, and this is also expressed in the Boren amendment, that the revaluation of asset provision was not intended to limit the discretion that the Boren amendment had given to the states.

2. The conference report acknowledges the congressional awareness at the time that a number of states had adopted alternative methods of payment--other than the Medicare principles of reimbursement or the Medicare system of payment--for both operating costs as well as property costs. It also acknowledges that a number of states had adopted limitations on capital costs and other payment areas.

3. In the conference report it specifically mentions an exclusion from the Medicare limitations to any state that adopted a fair rental system of reimbursement for property.

4. The next item in our search of the legislative history is to examine the letter that has been written by Senators Dole and Durenberger, which is dated the 7th of September of 1984. There is a very persuasive argument that can be made for having to review and to read this letter as being part of the legislative history. First of all, Senator Dole is chairman of the Senate Finance Committee and Senator Durenberger is chairman of the Health Subcommittee.

It appears to be rather well accepted and established principles of statutory interpretation that any explanations that are given of legislation by a chairman that might be responsible for that legislation are considered supplemental to committee reports and entitled to the same weight that you might give in the statutory interpretation to a formal report, such as a conference report.

With that background on the legislative history I've arrived at several conclusions. First of all, I find no statutory authority either in the plain language of the statute or in any of the legislative history for the Health Care Financing Administration's interpretation that's taken in the October 1984 transmittal that for both Medicare and Medicaid reimbursement purposes, the section 1861 Medicare limitations apply to all changes of ownership obligated on or after July 18, 1984.

When you read the legislative history and the statute, you find an entirely separate set of limitations; depreciation recapture, computation of acquisition cost and lease purchase requirements, all of which arise out of section 1861 of the Medicare statute, but do not apply to the section 1902 amendment to Medicaid.

The second point that I would make is that there is nothing in this language or legislative history which would require the states in any way to follow the Medicare recapture of depreciation provisions, to compute acquisition costs for purposes of Medicaid, such as now exist in the Medicare provisions, or to adopt any of the lease purchase regulations that the Secretary's office may come up with.

Thirdly, it is apparent from an analysis of this statute that the states are not prohibited from increasing reimbursement for depreciation, interest and any return on equity capital, so long as that increase in the aggregate is not in excess of what would occur under the Medicare provisions--solely as a result of change in ownership. There is no prohibition in section 1902 that would prohibit the states from increasing reimbursement for depreciation, interest and equity capital to a level that would at least equal what those Medicare principals would yield in a particular situation.

The legislative history also gives a rather accurate analysis or perspective on what congress intended to be covered or affected by Section 2314 and what not. The conference report is very clear that the fair rental system was not intended to be affected by this.

The Dole and Durenberger letter indicates, acknowledges what they knew to be the various reimbursement systems in the states--those systems that impose limitations on what are described as facility capital costs or overall payment limitations that cover capital cost increases.

In looking at that, the only way that any weight or consideration can be given to what Senators Dole and Durenberger have said in the letter is to look at those states which have some type of limitation on capital costs. Those are such things as flat, fixed, class, or negotiated rate systems. I would also include in that category states that limit reimbursement on construction costs, depreciation or interest, with some fixed dollar or percentile limitations.

What HCFA had to say regarding Section 1902(a)(30) was that the states should be free to develop, as they were allowed to previously, their own methods for determining what the upper limits should be for purposes of determining compliance. When you analyze that same legislative history, what you find that it says for purposes of an upper limit test is that the state should have broad discretion; there should be no data collection requirements beyond those which currently exist, which at this point are minimal; and no additional administrative duties beyond those that are currently required. In conclusion I would look at this amendment to the Medicaid statute in much the same way for the assurance question that the Department has looked at the types of assurances that it would accept or require for purposes of reimbursement.

Last year, we called this the "postcard assurance process." What that entailed was that the postcard would be sent in by the state indicating that the state assures that its payment rates are sufficient to reimburse efficient and economically operated facilities; and that constitutes the assurance process. I would submit that the Department need only add an additional sentence to that postcard which would say that we assure that the rates which we are paying for property meet the statutory limitations of Section 1861(v)(1)(O), and that should end the inquiry.

Our next speaker will be David Curtiss, and David, as I indicated at the outset, is a vice president of Newman and Associates and he will present the financial community's perspective on this change in the legislation.

THE FINANCIAL COMMUNITY PERSPECTIVE

DAVID CURTISS In a word, the financial perspective of the freeze on the revaluation of assets is--it's just more bad news.

Let me give you some general background about how the financial community perceives the long term care industry. Generally speaking, the industry is perceived as being largely dependent on debt. Up until last year most of that dependence was upon tax exempt debt; but, last year's tax laws precluded most nursing home operators from access to the tax exempt debt markets. The large chains have exceeded their forty million dollar IDB limit; the small operators now have to compete with other projects in other industries for limited statewide allocations of IDB funds.

The rules for obtaining conventional taxable financing are much the same as they were under obtaining IDB financing. Project feasibility is the test for the issuance of debt. Whether debt is issued as an unrated IDB, whether debt is issued in the form of an FHA insured mortgage, or whether debt is issued under some form of credit enhanced debt, the test is still project feasibility.

Simply said, the amount of debt available to a project is determined by the cash flow that that project generates. Thus in an acquisition transaction, the revaluation freeze is going to decrease the cash flows that are available; and therefore, it's going to decrease the project feasibility.

There are two aspects that I want to stress on the revaluation freeze. Obviously, you lose reimbursement from the depreciation, and you also lose interest expense which is related to the revalued part of the asset. There's an example in the text that shows that on the average you could lose perhaps $50,000 in a typical acquisition. $50,000 is enough to make a project unfeasible in this industry.

The general market perception of the nursing home business from a debt-issuer's point of view is that it's fairly risky. There are several reasons for this. The biggest reason is the dependence on the Medicaid reimbursement. Somewhere around 50 to 60 percent of patient days, nationwide, are Medicaid days. Constant changes in the Medicaid reimbursement laws cause concern about the ability of the program to maintain a constant cash flow stream to individual nursing homes.

Varied formulas in the different states for determining reimbursement confuse the issuers and the purchasers of nursing home debt. The capital markets question whether constant cash flow streams can be maintained in the face of regulatory changes such as the subject of our panel today. This is somewhat extraordinary in the credit markets because usually a government subsidy or some form of government backing for a program is considered a real plus in determining whether to issue debt. In this case we see the government program as being a deterrent to the ability to issue debt.

In addition to the dependence on the Medicaid program, the credit markets have found other reasons to regard the nursing home business negatively. There has been a checkered history of business failures and successes, and it's hard to separate the failures from the successes at the inception of a project--the projects all seem too similar.

Nursing home assets are viewed as single purpose structures. Debt to equity ratios are high in comparison to other industries. Obviously, the high degree of risk as perceived by the credit markets translates into high interest rates.

There are traditional credit enhancements that are available to other industries, such as letters of credit, collateral pledges from savings and loans, and surety bonds. However, these credit enhancements are not easily applied to the nursing home business. The wariness that characterizes the credit markets, also characterizes the issuers of credit enhancements.

There's a vicious circle in all this. Rating agencies are reluctant to rate nursing home debt; and therefore, they prevent the nursing homes from access to the institutional markets. The institutions are only going to buy institutional quality debt, which is debt rated BBB or higher. Nursing home operators must then seek credit enhancement (which is largely unavailable to the industry) or issue non-rated paper. Non-rated paper trades at prices that yield high interest rates, supposedly because of a high degree of risk. Nursing home credits become associated with the non-rated market, because there are no alternatives, and must pay high-risk interest rates. The high-risk interest rates prompt more projects to default, which therefore confirms the prophecy that it is a risky business. It's a vicious circle.

There's also an irony of social policy in the asset revaluation phase. Acquisitions of high Medicaid homes are now going to be discouraged. Those persons who are choosing between building a nursing home or acquiring a nursing home, will now be impelled to choose to build the new home. Under the new construction scenario, the cost is going to be fully reimbursed. I think it can be reasonably said that the cost of new construction far exceeds the cost of an acquisition; therefore, one could logically argue that the revaluation limitation is in fact promoting higher costs to the Medicaid program. It's ironic, but it seems to be true.

In my text I have suggested several potential remedies to the credit problem, and I encourage you to look at them although I really don't expect any of those potential remedies to occur in the near future. One idea is, if the Medicaid laws and the Medicare laws could be stabilized, perhaps that would give the credit issuers some reason to believe that the industry is more stable, that the cash flows would also be more stable.

I've argued that perhaps the federal government could see some advantage to insuring mortgages of nursing homes--something akin to the HFA 232 program. I don't expect that to happen, but it would make sense. If the government could charge premiums based on expected risk, adjust those premiums periodically, and charge an origination fee. Perhaps a mortgage insurance program would make good economic sense, and it would result in reduced capital costs passed on to the Medicaid programs. With a federal guarantee or a federally insured mortgage, institutional credit markets could be accessed, probably saving 300 basic points on interest costs every year. But again, I don't expect that to happen.

I think capital costs could also be reduced by bringing back tax exempt debt, however unlikely that seems. Generally, tax exempt debt would be priced 150 to 200 basic points below comparable risk taxable debt. It would make sense for this particular industry to be able to use tax exempt debt where the federal government or state governments end up paying well over 50 percent of the load anyway.

One of the things that perplexes those of us who are faced with trying to find a way to finance new nursing home beds is the expectation that there will be 1.2 million to 1.5 million new beds needed by the year 2000. We're asking, "How are we going to finance them?" The credit markets aren't good right now and there's still the nagging wariness about the nursing home debt. The revaluation freeze doesn't do anything to help that particular problem. The markets regard the revaluation as further evidence of the government's being fickle, and changing the programs; it is tough for credit markets to see a constant cash flow stream and a constant source of repayment.

One certain outcome of the need for capital in the future and of this revaluation law is that there will certainly be a harder look at the equity markets. The industry has been very dependent on debt. Now the question is, "How can we avoid debt if we're not going to be reimbursed for the additional cost of issuing it?"

In the equity markets there are essentially three areas. There is venture capital, which doesn't make much sense for the nursing home business because those people who provide venture capital tend to ask for 50 percent of your business back.

There are also equity syndications, a good idea for this business, although at the present time, the usefulness of this idea is clouded because of the treasury department's tax simplification laws, which propose to take away most of the tax advantages of syndications. The cash flows, alone, from the industry aren't strong enough to make syndications a good idea. Syndicators and the investors in syndications expect to be able to reap the tax benefits that would normally accrue in a real estate investment.

Thirdly, there is the stock market, a great source of capital for major chains all two dozen or so of them. It's not a good source for the small operator because it takes enormous funds to access that source. For the operator who wants to finance one or two projects, or perhaps three or four projects, it's just not feasible to go to the stock market to raise the money for it.

One of the results of the revaluation freeze is that there will be a definite advantage to the large chains who seek to make an acquisition. Because the large chains are the only ones with the access to the stock market, they can obtain funds without having to incur the interest rate penalty. Thus acquisitions would be more advantageous to the large publicly owned chains than to smaller operators.

This isn't to suggest that the chains are free of penalty in all this. Obviously they will lose reimbursement for depreciation too, but to the extent that they can substitute equity for debt, the full blow of the asset revaluation freeze is somewhat less to the chains than it is to the small operator who doesn't have access to any capital markets other than the debt market.

In summary, we say that the asset revaluation limitation is another financial setback for the long term care industry. The credit markets have been the primary source of capital for the industry and in all likelihood will continue to be so.

From the perspective of the financial community, it would make sense for the reimbursement programs to tackle the long term problem of reducing the cost of capital to the providers. Such an undertaking is particularly important as the industry braces for the financing of 1.5 million new beds by the year 2000.

The significant reduction in the cost of debt to the industry could be achieved through the federal guarantee of mortgage debt, and revitalization of tax exempt financing opportunities. Also opportunities to acquire or rehabilitate existing structures should be encouraged, not discouraged, as a lower total cost alternative to building new beds. At least half of all cost savings, from whatever source, will revert directly to the government.

The nagging question in financing long term care condenses to this: how can reliable and low-cost credit markets open up to an industry whose major customer is viewed at this time, more as a threat than as an ally? Given the dependence of the industry on credit markets and the apparent bent of the reimbursement programs toward reduction of payment, those of us who finance long term care projects are perplexed over how we're going to finance roughly 45 billion dollars in new construction over the next fifteen years. Without some relief from the major payer for the long term care services, capital project finance will never escape the painful interest rates exacted by investors who invest in risky credits. Financially the asset revaluation limitation is a step in the wrong direction.

THE INDUSTRY PERSPECTIVE

TOM JAZWIECKI I will discuss the industry perspective, and then tell you a little bit about how I think state reimbursement plans are going to be impacted. First I will point out some of the problems with Section 2314; what I would call the paradox situations caused by such public policy and the actual implementation of that policy.

PROBLEMS WITH SECTION 2314

As far as our industry is concerned, Section 2314 is a devastating piece of legislation because of its impact and the way it appears it will be implemented.

While the legislation affects both Medicare and Medicaid providers, it has a serious effect on the Medicaid program and the Medicaid provider. When you realize that two out of every three patients in a nursing home are dependent, to some extent, on Medicaid, the legislation has a tremendous impact on not only the Medicaid population, but the operational structure of an industry. Public policy was targeted at least in one sense, at a single cost center, i.e., provider capital costs. Congress is addressing a specific program cost element but it didn't look to the overall reimbursement or payment levels in the Medicaid program, which are quite frankly, fairly low throughout most of the states.

As a rule of thumb, the average cost that is recognized in the Medicaid program today is approximately one-tenth of what the average cost is in a hospital. Section 2314 affects both profit facilities and non-profit facilities. It makes no difference between the two. While some may view my position as a proponent of the proprietary industry, the American Health Care Association represents a significant portion of non-profit facilities in the country today.

The legislation affects a provider more seriously, the greater that provider participates in the Medicaid program. If a provider is totally private pay, the legislation has no impact at all. If a provider is 100% Medicaid, it has all the impact in the world.

In reviewing the congressional intent behind the Section 2314 legislation, I want to point out several paradox situations that may develop.

The legislation was intended to stop trafficking. That's a very laudable goal and, after having worked a few years ago in government, I can understand that goal. But the legislation also has the potential to actually increase the potential to sell a facility. If you reduce the economic base of the industry--if you decrease the value recognition of provider assets, the obvious incentive is to get out of the industry. Thus, the incentive to sell is increased under Section 2314.

There was strong congressional concern over the trend towards mergers and acquisitions. It is common for people who talk in terms of mergers and acquisitions to think of corporate giants, large corporations. Ironically, this piece of legislation impacts most devastatingly on the small provider; the provider who's been in the system for a period of years and the type of provider who likely participates to a great degree in the Medicaid program.

There was hope that the legislation would lead to a decrease in the overall rate of growth in program expenditures by limiting provider capital cost increases. Yet I'd like to point out that this objective could actually backfire; it can lead to increased program costs, and let's ask ourselves why. In terms of capital cost, the level of capital expenditures in the Medicaid program are related to capital financing costs to providers. The greater the risk perception by lenders--the people who actually generate the private investment necessary in this industry--the greater the borrowing cost. By significantly reducing the asset value recognition of nursing homes, you adversely affect the equity base of the long term care industry, thereby preventing or at least reducing the ability of a provider to collateralize debt obligations; again, something that could lead to higher borrowing costs in the future. And when you consider that, in terms of what Medicare and Medicaid spend for capital costs, the majority of such expenditures are for interest payments on new or newly acquired facilities, higher interest rates result in higher program capital costs. It's not unlikely that, during the first several years, 90 to 95% of the total capital costs recognized by either program is interest. The greater the interest rate, the greater the interest expense, and the greater the cost to the program. If we were to take a look at a typical 30-year mortgage arrangement at 12% interest--during the first five years of debt amortization--almost 100% of the debt service payment is interest. For the first twelve years, 90% or more of the payments are actually interest. So a very significant portion of program capital financing costs are related to interest expense which is related to market interest rates. This is something that lawmakers and regulators have to be aware of when developing public health care policy. For example, let's assume a facility was purchased or acquired six years ago for $2.5 million. Suppose that that facility today, without the 2314 impact, was worth $3 million, and was to be sold, and the going interest rate could be 12% if it were mortgaged properly. Suppose that because of the asset revaluation provision, lenders actually perceive a higher degree of risk in the industry and charge a premium on the interest and the borrowing cost. If that premium were a 3% differential, the program actually picks up almost three-quarters of a million dollars more in cost for that particular facility, financing a $2.5 million asset at 15% versus a $3 million asset at 12%.

That's a tremendous increase in financing cost that's passed through to the Medicare and Medicaid programs, solely because of a change in interest rates. And even if we were to adjust for reduced depreciation allowances because Medicare and Medicaid are not recognizing the increased asset valuation, the programs would still experience about a quarter-million dollar increase in capital financing costs over that thirty year period. So the additional costs to our public programs could be significant as a result of Section 2314 if the market perceives the industry to have a greater inherent risk and charges a high borrowing premium.

There was congressional concern with paying more than once for a facility. Yet, the Medicare principles of reimbursement do not actually pay the historical cost of a facility when you consider the time value of money. Without getting too technical, I will relate that principle to inflation. If we consider a 5% factor in terms of time value of money, meaning that a dollar today is worth a lot more than a dollar forty years from now, and add up all the depreciation cash flows using this 5% factor, the value of all those depreciation cash flows over a 40 year period would be about one-half of what the facility actually cost. At 10%, it's about one-quarter the historical cost of the provider. There is a significant amount of difference in terms of the value of the depreciation cash flows versus what actually gets paid. When Medicare or Medicaid contends it does not want to pay more than once for a facility, the time value of money relative to those depreciation cash flows must be considered. There is a significant difference in the value of the depreciation allowances versus the actual historical cost when consideration is given to the time value of money.

The provision applies to hospitals and nursing homes, but the question then arises as to whether hospitals and nursing homes are indeed comparable. Congress has directed HHS to study capital reimbursement for hospitals and has given them a 1986 target date to develop a new reimbursement methodology. There is no similar piece of legislation directed at nursing homes. We basically are stuck with Section 2314 as it impacts on Medicare and Medicaid providers.

When we look at the hospital industry, we see overbedding. The average occupancy in hospitals is approximately 77% nationwide. For small hospitals-- less than 50-bed hospitals--the average is roughly 50%. Yet, when we look at nursing homes, the average nursing home today is experiencing approximately 95% occupancy. In many pockets throughout the country, the average is closer to 100%. Currently, because of the excess capacity of hospitals, there is no reason to build additional hospital beds in this country. But when we look at the nursing home side, independent estimates project that roughly 1.2 million beds are needed by the year 2000 just to keep pace with the current level of long term care service capacity that is provided for our elderly today. The cost of that 1.2 million nursing home beds is projected to be around $60 billion, almost twice what we pay today for all of long term care today.

There is language in the conference report that indicates many states will not be affected by Section 2314. However, there are many states which believe this to be a fine piece of legislation, one that has given them the excuse to actually freeze property cost reimbursement to nursing homes and use the federal legislation as the implementation vehicle. We took a survey of the number of states that have actually modified their plans, and to the extent of our survey ability, thirteen states have actually implemented the freeze since the enactment of this act. A quick look at various factors affecting those particular thirteen states would indicate an overall concern over the commitment of funds to the Medicaid program. Just about every one of these 13 states is faced with either a large Medicaid population, a very large aged population, or a very large rate of growth in the aged population. Coupling that with various fiscal and budgetary restraints on Medicare and Medicaid that have been implemented or are being proposed by the current administration one can at least partially understand why these states considered implementing a capital freeze. Many other states are in the process of modifying their current Medicaid reimbursement plans. Again such states are attempting to come into conformance with what they perceive to be federal requirements.

Section 2314 was intended as basic program reform. Yet it has a major devastating impact on the very type of providers Congress may want to keep in the system--those which have been there for a long period of time and those who participate very heavily in the Medicare and Medicaid program. In essence the federal government has told such providers that the value of their facility is not worth very much. For a small owner operator who's dependent not only on the operational income generation of that facility but also on the equity buildup in the assets of that facility and who wants to retire at some point in time, that equity may no longer be there.

IMPACT OF SECTION 2314 ON STATE MEDICAID PROGRAMS

Let's take a look at the impact on state Medicaid programs. Congress indicated that many states would not be affected. Yet many have already changed their plans; at least thirteen have instituted a capital freeze. If we were to look at Medicaid reimbursement systems throughout this country today, I would classify Medicaid capital reimbursement approaches into five broad categories: (1) fair rental states; (2) class rate states; (3) states that have caps or limits on the capital cost center itself; (4) states that have overall caps or limitations on the overall rate level; and (5) states that adopt the Medicare principles of reimbursement.

Several states are either using or contending they're using a fair rental approach to reimbursement for capital costs. A fair rental system is not all that complicated. A fair rental system just replaces one or more of the accounting oriented elements of depreciation, interest, and return on equity, with some type of rental allowance. The allowance is basically predicated on the value recognition given the facility.

At present there are approximately eleven states which have or plan to have a fair rental system in place; three of these states are Maryland, West Virginia, and Montana. Five states fall in the category of class rates--California, Arkansas, Louisiana, Oklahoma, and Texas. Another state, North Carolina, has a flat rate state for the indirect portion which includes capital cost and therefore can also be considered a class rate state for capital purposes.

In a class rate state the individual behavior of the actions of any one particular provider do not in essence affect or influence the payment level. The rate is basically a composite action of all provider cost structures. A class rate is derived by arraying all provider cost structures and selecting a target level for reimbursement.

States with limitation on capital cost items probably make up the largest group of all the states. The limitations include percentile or other types of statistical measure which limit individual capital cost centers, construction cost per bed, overall capital recognition, depreciation definitions that are different from Medicare, and various step-up restrictions. Many states use occupancy factors, which may lower the payment rate on the amount of capital reimbursement. Medicare has no such comparable counterpart.

Kentucky used to have a requirement that there would be no step-up allowed to a new owner unless the old owner held the facility for twelve and a half years. It was roughly a pro rata increase based on two-thirds of 1% per month. It may have been a reasonable approach in not recognizing the constant turnover--or turning--of facilities for the state of Kentucky. Yet, because of Section 2314, Kentucky felt it was required to revise its methodology and model it after the federal statute. It basically froze the payment rates. Ohio has a per-bed limitation. It runs anywhere from $2.50 a day to approximately $7.50 a day depending on when the provider was actually licensed.

From a practical standpoint it seems that Congress intended that at least two areas should not be impacted, the fair rental approach and the class rate approach. And it will be prudent for government to assess each of the various other state methods to determine whether or not they actually can be cost effective, in the long run.

Some Medicaid officials interpret HCFA's position to require an almost verbatim adoption of the Medicare principles of reimbursement. Such interpretation would include not only the asset valuation issue, but depreciation recapture rules and depreciation methods. We do not believe from an industry standpoint that this is actually the Congressional intent.

Pennsylvania for years had considered implementing capital freeze. After passage of the Section 2314 on July 18, 1984, it took the state less than a month to adopt a capital freeze.

The state of Connecticut had a fair rental approach. It allowed a step-up, but only in very restricted areas. Upon the death of an owner, when an owner was terminally ill or when he retired after the age of 65,--these appear as somewhat reasonable limitations. However, when 2314 was passed, Connecticut did away with these allowances and simply said no step-up period.

Washington state has a proposal to implement a fair rental system on October 1, 1985. The system basically incorporated some factors which are common to fair rental approaches. It also was attempting to refrain from revaluing facilities every year. It only wanted to revalue those facilities once every ten years and only upon the sale of a facility. Yet the HCFA has formally notified the state of Washington that even such a limited proposal is not acceptable because of the step-up that will occur, but only after ten years.

The HCFA reponse to Washington state is cause for concern because the industry has worked for several years with the state legislature to develop a reimbursement system that is equitable to both the state and the providers. The federal statutes thwart those efforts and could result in a more costly approach being adopted.

Interestingly, eight of the thirteen states that have adopted capital freezes are now at least in the discussion stage of looking at fair rental approaches as a more reasonable alternative. Three states in Medicaid had a capital freeze before Section 2314, however one of those three adopted a fair rental system, and another is developing a fair rental approach at this point in time.

In summary, the congressional intent of the legislation was to emphasize state flexibility, but this intent has yet to be expressed by the Health Care Financing Administration. While there is current congressional discussion concerning action to mitigate the adverse effects of Section 2314, the message the states are getting is that anything short of a Medicare methodology would not be acceptable. Some states are using the federal statutes as an umbrella under which to implement a capital freeze where they couldn't have done it before. Let me end by stating that there was a rationale behind Section 2314. There was a public policy concern, yet, the way the policy is being implemented will have an adverse impact on both this industry and the future cost into the Medicare and Medicaid programs. Reasonable alternatives to Section 2314 exist. These alternatives, including fair rental systems, need to be explored.

Chapter 3

Innovative Financing and Delivery Options for Long Term Care

Speaker: Robert A. Streimer

What I would like to do today is discuss with you some of the very urgent concerns that led to the development of the recent HCFA conference at which were discussed a variety of initiatives relating to the financing and delivery of long term care and then briefly outline the major initiatives that were presented at the conference. I will first focus [through a slide presentation] on the demographic trends in the nation and the current financing dilemma surrounding long term care.

DEMOGRAPHIC TRENDS

Long term care requirements are determined in large part by the size and composition of the population 65 years and over. The elderly population has doubled in the thirty years from 1950 to 1980 having increased at a faster rate than the U.S. population in general. In 1980, one in nine of the U.S. population was 65 or older. It is projected by the year 2030 that nearly one in five will be 65 and over.

Life expectancy has been increasing steadily since the beginning of the 20th century. Most of the increase in the first half of the century is attributable to the reduction of the mortality risk from infectious diseases and to reductions in infant and maternal mortality. Recent increases in life expectancy stem from reductions in mortality associated with chronic diseases.

From 1965 to 1977, life expectancy at birth increased 4.3% while life expectancy at age 65 increased 11.6%. There have been substantial reductions in heart and cerebro-vascular mortality rates during this period. We can expect significant changes in the mean age of individuals who comprise the 65 and older population. In the decade from 1980 to 1990 the age group from 65 to 74, which were known as the young olds, will increase at about the same rate as the general population, while the 75 to 84 year olds and the 85 and older, or the old olds, will increase at twice the rate of the general population. In the next two decades, 1990 to 2000, and from 2000 to 2010, the 85 and older group is expected to increase far more rapidly than the younger population 65 and over.

Counting the long term care population is very difficult, and the aged are only one segment of that population. They are not necessarily identified with a particular diagnosis or condition but with the need of supportive services over an extended period of time. People with mental or physical conditions can be part of the long term care population also. Supportive services are services that address health, social, and personal care needs. Most prominent among the personal care needs is the assistance with eating, toileting, transferring, bathing, dressing, meal preparation, cleaning, shopping, supervision, monitoring, and education of various kinds.

Persons needing personal care are those requiring assistance with the activities of daily living, many of which I just mentioned--bathing, dressing, transferring, toileting, and eating. Service needs increase dramatically as age increases. In the age group 65 to 69, only 2.6% need assistance with personal care. By age 85 and over, 31.6% of the population need such assistance.

Of the total long term care population, 29% reside in an institutional setting, 71% in the community. With regard to the nursing home population, about 89% are 65 years of age or older. It is estimated that for every person aged 65 and over residing in a nursing home there are nearly twice as many people, requiring similar levels of care, residing in the community.

The probability of having ADL dependency rises with age, reaching 35% by age 85. The probability of residing in a nursing home for ADL dependent aged persons also rises sharply as age increases. At age 45 to 64, only 24% with ADL dependency are residents in nursing homes. By age 85 and older, about 60% of the population with ADL dependencies reside in nursing homes.

The 1977 National Nursing Homes Survey showed that 1.3 million persons were residents of nursing homes. Under the assumptions of growth of the aged population by specific age groups, the nursing home residents will increase 54% over the next 20 years, and 132% to almost 3 million by the year 2030.

The public sector's ability to finance increased long term care needs arising from the aging of the population is not likely to increase. In 1965, when Medicare and Medicaid were enacted, there were four workers to each Social Security cash beneficiary in the retirement and disability program. By 1980, the ratio fell to 3.3 to one. It is projected that by the year 2010, the ratio will fall to 3.1 to one.

Since the advent of the Medicare and Medicaid programs, long term care expenditures have grown dramatically. In 1965, the year before the implementation of Medicare and Medicaid, the nation spent just over 2 billion dollars on nursing home care, or 5% of the total health care outlays. By 1982, nursing home care spending came to 27.3 billion dollars, or 8.5% of the total health care bill. Excluding the special ICF/MR category for the mentally retarded, spending for other nursing home care has more than doubled between 1976 and 1982, growing from 11 billion to 24 billion dollars.

The Health Care Financing Administration administers the Medicare and Medicaid programs. And Medicare and Medicaid play the major role in financing health care for the elderly and the poor. Medicare protects the elderly against the costs of large hospital and medical bills, while Medicaid finances the majority of the health care needs of the poor. These programs have gone a long way toward providing access to needed care for the aged and the poor.

In 1982, over 27 billion dollars was spent on nursing home care. The federal government paid nearly 29% of the bill. Most of the federal spending was through the Medicaid program; that is 25.3%. State and local Medicaid spending came to another 23.2%. Thus, the federal and state spending came to 55% of the national nursing home bill. Direct payments from individuals on an out-of-pocket basis came to 43.6% of the bill. Private health insurance covered less than 1% of the total nursing home outlays.

The aged in nursing homes often spend their income and become needy. It is estimated that approximately half of the people Medicaid pays for in nursing homes were not initially poor, but spent their income and assets as a result of catastrophic nursing home bills. Medicaid strength in financing care for the poor is diminished by the pressing long term care needs of the aged. In 1982, 44% of the Medicaid budget was devoted to paying for nursing home care. If we exclude care in ICFs for the mentally retarded, the figure is 32%.

For a long time, there has been a labeling of the aged as a homogeneous population. This packaging of the aged is not only unfair, but diverts our attention from potentially promising solutions to the problems that face us with regard to long term care financing and delivery issues. In truth, the aged ranged tremendously in health status, in income, in preferences, in interests, and in their social setting. There are two requirements for solving the complex financing and delivery problems in long term care. First, we need a clear delineation of the problems and the issues. Second, we need to develop a better understanding of the aged population, including a deeper knowledge about the range in their health status, in their income, their preferences, as well as a better understanding of their social setting, and relationship with family and the community.

THE HCFA LONG TERM CARE CONFERENCE

There were five major issues that the long term care conference focused upon. The first was the need to find ways to prevent unnecessary institutionalization. The substantial spending on nursing home care has not necessarily contributed to the satisfaction and well being of the elderly. For many people, nursing home care is appropriate, but for many others, it is not. Most aged persons with functional limitations prefer to remain in the community as long as possible. Thus, we need to find better ways to help the aged maintain their independence as long as possible.

The second issue was to find solutions to the lack of financial protection for the catastrophic expenses for long term care. It is essential that we find better ways to finance long term care. If third party coverage were available for long term care, Medicaid's role in health care financing could be better directed towards the poor.

The third issue focused upon the need to find better and more efficient ways to deliver services. The long term care population requires a broad range of services that address the health, social, and personal care needs of the functionally limited persons. It is of the utmost importance to find better and more efficient ways to deliver these services rather than to continue to rely on the costly medical model.

The fourth issue focused upon the significant role that housing plays in the well being of the aged. We need to find new approaches to appropriate housing for the aged. This would include better coordination between housing and long term care delivery systems, especially as the elderly strive to maintain their independence with ever advancing age.

The fifth issue we focused on was the importance of the family in support systems towards the well being of the aged. It is the family and others, including friends and neighbors, who provide the majority of personal support and assistance through informal care, and it is important to find ways of easing the burden of those who provide continuing care for the impaired elderly.

The conference proceeded by having experts in a range of various fields present what they had been doing relating to these issues, as well as what the research was showing. I would like to synopsize the eight major topics that were discussed at the conference.

LONG TERM CARE INSURANCE

The first topic discussed was long term care insurance. Only 1% of the payment for the nursing home bill is from long term care insurance. The American Health Care Association has a number of projects underway looking into long term care insurance, and I expect that over the next several years, we are going to see much progress in this area.

The average aged person in the nation faces financial ruin if he or she requires long term care services. The feasibility of long term care insurance rests upon two facts. In any one year, the probability of requiring long term care services is relatively low for the population over 65, because the majority are in good or excellent health. And second, the range in income among the aged is relatively large. An analysis of that income range indicates that a sizable proportion could afford to pay for insurance premiums for long term care insurance.

A prototype policy was presented which included a deductible feature of 90 days, but which also included coverage for home health care. The latter is a very important feature needed to counteract any bias towards institutional care that might tend to be built into a long term care insurance plan. The cost of the prototype policy was estimated to be in the range of 450 to 550 dollars per year, an amount not necessarily affordable to all of the aged, but clearly affordable by many.

One of the presenters at the conference was the chairperson of the long term care task force of the Health Insurance Association of America. They and all of their members have been looking at long term care insurance quite actively. He viewed the feasibility of long term care insurance rather pessimistically, and the basic problem that he presented was the openendedness of long term care needs and the difficulty associated with premium costs for that kind of openended proposition. He also questioned the market for long term care insurance, observing that the availability of Medicaid for individuals who spend-down their income mitigates very heavily against consumer interest in long term care insurance.

The second presenter in the area of long term care insurance was the executive of an insurance company that has the most experience in selling long term care insurance, that's the Fireman's Fund. He described their very favorable experience in a rather sizable but controlled growth market. They are primarily in California and they are marketing to a several county area. Their growth rates have been rather impressive over the last several years. He stressed the importance of an indemnity type of policy, rather than a service benefit type of policy as probably the most significant way to contain costs of long term care insurance. Additionally, it is very important that any insurance policies for long term care have cost-sharing provisions built into them to deter over-utilization of services.

LIFE CARE COMMUNITIES

Most life care communities have been developed within the past five or ten years. Today there are about three hundred of them in existence and they have up to 100,000 residents. The life care community is a financially self-sufficient residential community for the elderly that combines residential living with the availability of medical and nursing services in specialized premises on the facilities. The characteristics of a life care community can be broken down into three components. The first is the design phase on a major apartment complex and the various skills necessary to finance and manage that complex were skills needed to be brought to bear on developing life care facilities. The second major piece of a life care community is the dining and activity facilities, and the various sort of expertise that is required for that kind of a program and that would also be brought to bear in developing a life care community. The third element is health care; all life care communities would need to have a health care center that could provide regularly to its membership at three levels: a skilled level, an intermediate level, and some assisted living unit type of level.

The life care community is one alternative available for assuring adequate access to housing and health care services for the elderly. A lifetime contract is established between the resident and the community that defines each party's financial and service obligations, the underlying concept of which is one of pooled risk to provide a lifetime continuum of care. The resident pays a lump sum accommodation fee prior to occupancy, and a monthly fee thereafter. The average entry fee as of 1982 was $35,000, although a wide range in entry fees exists. The average monthly fee in 1982 was $550. Again a wide range of monthly fees exist. The average age of entrance to the individuals that join life care communities are people in their seventies. In the past many of the life care communities guaranteed free total health care to all the residents. Several bankruptcies occurred when these promises were not fulfilled.

The second speaker that spoke about life care communities was actually the president of one and he related some of his experiences. He felt that, to prevent failures and abuses, that there needed to be a new knowledge basis, self-assessments, accreditation and the development of life care community associations to share their knowledge and experience with one another. There is a serious actuarial challenge to determine the nature and manner of health care services that can be provided to the resident without causing the resident to incur substantial additional charges. Most persons connected with managing life care communities are actually in favor of regulation at the state level with regard to disclosure, certification, accreditation, regulation of financial status, protection of rights of residents and the legal structure of the community. It is indeed unusual to hear from a private sector health care institution that actually wants to be regulated.

HOME EQUITY CONVERSION

The next item that was discussed was home equity conversion, the general premise of which is the converting of assets in home equity into a lifetime stream of income. Three out of four elderly-headed households own their own homes and over eighty percent of those have paid off their mortgages. Within the past few years, there has been a growing national effort to develop ways for older persons to use some of their home equity while they remain in their homes. The presenters concluded that home equity might be used to relieve some of the substantial economic and emotional strains faced by the aged with long term care needs, while at the same time being responsive to their strong preference for the individuals to remain in their own homes. The stream of income could be used for better nutrition, rising utility costs, home repair or other personal care or long term care needs. Two other speakers discussed their actual day to day experience with home equity conversions. While the number of home equity conversions has only been in the hundreds so far, a nonprofit organization known as the National Center for Home Equity Conversion has been established in Madison, Wisconsin to provide consultative and planning services for financial institutions, for groups of retired individuals, and for individuals who desire to look into these kinds of arrangements.

There are several possible models of home equity conversion that were discussed at the conference. One of the two most commonly discussed was the reverse annuity mortgage, where the individual continues to own his or her home while the equity decreases. The other was a sale leaseback model where the individual sells his home but continues to live there. The speakers noted the importance of sound legal advice and financial counseling as key elements of any decision to convert home equity into cash. While the market is likely to be small at first, home equity conversion can grow and flourish in the future, if the initial experiences are favorable.

THE SOCIAL HMO

The next area discussed is the social HMO, also known as the SHMO. The SHMO endeavors to provide solutions to the separation between financing and delivery of services and the separation of the delivery systems for acute care, institutional chronic care, and community based social support. There are four essential features of the social HMO: (1) a sponsoring agency takes responsibility for bringing a range of acute and chronic care services into a single system, (2) the social HMO serves a membership that is representative of the community, enrolling both disabled and able-bodied elders, (3) the social HMO is paid on a pre-paid capitation basis by both individuals and third parties, and (4) a social HMO is at risk for the service cost. Thus, the social HMO endeavors to consolidate the system on many levels: provider, population, finance, and risk. Financing for site planning and development has been raised privately, primarily from foundations. Four sponsoring sites have been set up: the Metropolitan Jewish Geriatric Center in Brooklyn, New York; the Kaiser Permanente Medical Care Program in Portland, Oregon; the Ebenezer Society in Minneapolis; and the Senior Care Action Network in Long Beach, California.

The next speaker who spoke about social HMOs was the director of the site in Brooklyn. In the Brooklyn area there is a very large elderly population and they are very concentrated geographically. That works very much to their behalf. Within a very small radius, there were 80,000 persons residing who were over 65 years of age. The knowledge about the feasibility, cost-effectiveness, risk-pooling concept, and viability awaits actual demonstration at these four locations, and the government is moving to fund these four major projects in terms of actually providing the range of care.

STATE AND FEDERAL TAX MODIFICATIONS

The next item that was discussed was state and federal tax modifications, both those that exist and those that would be desirable for the future. Most modifications were looked at as ways to assist the aged to maintain their financial independence and to assist families who provide assistance to the aged. A review of state and local income tax laws and other tax laws shows that 42 states provide tax breaks on real estate and 39 states provide tax breaks on income taxes. There are only four states that furnished tax breaks for people who spend money to care for aged relatives. A review of the federal law showed there are several tax provisions that are also favorable to the aged: (1) the personal exemption doubles at age 65; the new law that taxes social security benefits only taxes those benefits for the higher income aged, (2) capital gains from the sale of a home after age 55 are not taxable for gains up to $125,000 and (3) IRAs and other pensions which delay taxes until retirement when income is lower is also a tax advantage. Several modifications to the tax law are possible and need to be studied further. There could be greater tax breaks to the elderly and the aged but at a later age. Currently tax breaks begin at age 65 or earlier. Deductions for relatives who provide long term care services at their own expense could be added to the tax laws. Establishment of two separate IRAs, one earmarked specifically for long term care, is another thought that was presented at the conference. Tax treatment was further discussed by a state representative from the state of Idaho, which is one of the four states with a law that was recently enacted which specifically provides deductions for relatives who provide long term care services at their own expense. This law does not provide much incentive in Idaho because of the low tax structure in the state. So apparently it is very easy for the state legislature and the state budget office to go along with this tax break since it didn't apply to many people. But it's a step in the right direction--a point was being made. Idaho has also recently established a voluntary account program in which citizens of Idaho voluntarily contribute to a fund earmarked for medical assistance. And strangely enough the fund is actually beginning to receive quite a few contributions. Idaho has recently also enacted a family responsibility law. Adult children, parents and spouses are responsible for payment towards medical assistance. A maximum of $250 per month or one quarter of the Medicaid payment. In the first year of this program, 30% of the families were exempt because of their income, while for the remaining families, the average payment required was $42 per month.

FAMILY CARE

The next group of speakers discussed family care. While we recognize that private and public initiatives in the financing of long term care are of vital importance, the quality of life and the sense of well-being for all of us and for the aged, especially if they become frail and impaired, depends upon the social setting of family, friends, and neighbors. And in the final analysis, it is the society we live in that gives pleasure and meaning to our lives. Most older people in need of care are found living in the community, not in institutions. The ongoing care needed is often not medical but personal care in the form of assistance in the activities of daily living--shopping, cleaning, and meal preparation, and most is provided by families. While the amount of help needed by the elderly living in the community varies greatly, estimates of the proportion requiring some supportive services is about one-third of 8 million people. About eight to ten percent are bedridden or home-bound and as functionally impaired as those in institutions. The dissolution of the family and the isolation of the elderly is a myth. Study after study has destroyed this myth. What has emerged instead is a picture in which the social support system of the elderly increasingly involves an amalgam of informal assistance by family and by significant others, such as friends and neighbors, as well as services provided by organizations supported privately and publicly. About 60-85 percent of all impaired elderly are helped by the family in a significant way, often at great personal sacrifice. It's important to observe that the elderly themselves provide substantial assistance to their children and other family members in the form of financial assistance and, if their health is good, in the form of child care and housework. The amount of help parents receive from children is related to the level of frailty of the parent and the paucity of income. That is, as older people become more vulnerable, children respond with more assistance. The extent of informal support provided to the elderly does not vary much by social class, but there are some special problems. One-third of the elderly are without children, or with no children nearby. And women, the very group who provide most of the informal social care, are increasingly in the labor force. Yet they continue to provide informal support and care to their parents. The overview presentation ended on this note. If informal support was to continue to be a principal mode of social care for older people, consideration must be given to methods of assisting families, friends, and neighbors in their efforts.

HOUSING

The seventh topic area that was discussed was the area of housing. There is no single plan or living arrangement suitable for a person simply because he or she is old. Important variables to be considered are health, social and economic requirements. Today there is a new generation of the elderly that is better educated, more affluent, more mobile, and better able to afford appropriate housing. Housing has a significant impact upon an individual's behavior, life-style and well-being. As older people require some support services, the goal is to maintain individuals at their maximum level of independence in the least restrictive setting. The island approach of the life care community provides an excellent, unique and worthwhile service for a small portion of the market. Congregate housing is similar to an apartment hotel and is essentially individual housing units, generally an efficiency or one bedroom unit, with a common room for dinner. A variety of other supportive services are generally available such as transportation, social workers services, classes, and enrichment activities. Many of the congregate facilities for the elderly that are in existence today are assisted by HUD funds, including development funds and subsidization of monthly rental fees for the residents. The major problem today regards ongoing development of congregate housing without governmental assistance. While we know that congregate housing works well with federal assistance, we have still not found the answer for private market forces in the area of congregate housing. A market rate like that in private congregate housing today is very expensive to develop; the fee for an average unit in the Washington, D.C. area would be upwards of a thousand dollars per month. Few middle class elderly will move to private congregate housing at that price unless they really need the supportive services that are available there. Thus, they will begin to resemble the nursing home population. Ideally, it would be better if the community of residents in congregate housing was more diverse with a range of independent as well as dependent elderly as exists in the publicly subsidized facilities.

VOLUNTEERISM

The final area that was discussed was the subject of volunteerism. And an overview of the concepts of volunteerism was presented by a speaker from St. Vincent's Hospital and Medical Center of New York. Volunteerism could play a much larger role in the personal and social support needs of the elderly, and could also offer the promise of substituting free services for services that are now paid for privately or through insurance. Yet, in order for this to happen, imaginative new volunteer programs need to be designed. For example, individuals could earn credits for volunteer services, much like we do now for blood donors. And they could use those in the future. Some programs are experimenting with stipends for low income elderly volunteers which provide services for considerably less money than ordinarily paid services. There is a great deal of evidence about the beneficial aspects of volunteerism, including the personal satisfaction of the volunteer in providing support to families who are assisting their elderly parents.

Stipends in volunteerism raises the issue of below minimum wage, and conflicts would possibly be created with unions. Volunteers must also be trained to provide a training to understand and be responsive to the psychological and supportive needs of the elderly.

The conference closed on a very positive note, since what was presented was a very useful framework to begin to discuss a much broader range of long term care needs for the elderly population. Some things will probably be developed at a much faster rate over the next three to five years.

I'd like to get your thoughts on the feasibility of the social rights home movement.

Well, there has been a great deal of controversy over it, and the government is committed to fund the projects for the poor. I was very impressed with the speaker from the Brooklyn project, and I sometimes wonder whether the Brooklyn situation is not incredibly unique where within a very small radius of several blocks you can enroll virtually your entire apartment-living population. I think we will not know for four or five years from now whether these projects are financially viable and whether the system is set up to capitate the care of the individuals. Since the success of these projects is unsure, the entire venture is a risk. The financial support for taking the risk is not coming from the government, the government is really capitating them for the entire benefit package and then also embracing within that the cost of the social services.

(Inaudible question).

There are a number of technical concerns about the actuarial activity of setting premiums and assuming risk as any insurance company would. In order for long term care insurance to be a successful proposition, you have to enroll a very broad base of the over sixty-five population. That included the young olds, and you had to enroll those in great numbers because the concept of insurance is spreading the risk. If all that you were able to enroll were those likely in need of long term need services, it would be a losing proposition to the insurance company which was very nervous about adverse selection by those who would enroll in long term care insurance. This pessimism stemmed from an uncertainty about being able to enroll the elderly population over a much larger base to spread the risk.

What is being done to help seniors to develop a wellness attitude toward aging, which I think, if promoted, would save a lot of money?

Those individuals that tend to have gotten their health care through organized settings, like pre-paid health plans and HMOs and certainly that's one of the foundations of the social HMO, have had more exposure to education and promoting wellness in promoting better health habits. However the population that interacts with the traditional fee-for-service medical system does not get that kind of education. I'm not aware of anything that's being done to promote it except for the populations that are enrolled in comprehensive programs of one kind or another.

Chapter 4

Health Care in the 1990s

Speaker: Donald C. Yesukaitis

This chapter is based on a study that we, (Arthur Andersen and Co.) together with the American College of Hospital Administrators (ACHA), decided in 1983 to put together concerning health care in the 1990s to determine potential trends and strategies. The study took approximately 8 months to complete and was released in August 1984 at the American Hospital Association (AHA) convention in Denver. We undertook the study because of the dynamic changes that have taken place in the industry, and because we wanted to find out if we could form a consensus of opinion among people who are considered to be the experts in the health care industry as to what they envision health care in the 1990s to be.

The study concentrates principally on the hospital, although there are sections that are relevant to the long term care industry. Also, whatever happens in acute care is going to have some effect on long term care as well as on suppliers, attorneys, consultants, accountants, investment and commercial bankers, and others who participate in the health care industry in the United States.

METHODS

The type of method used is called a delphi technique; it is a forecasting technique used principally to study rapidly changing industries. It is not a statistically valid study. However, over 1,000 health care experts participated in this study (Gallup, for comparison, normally uses a sample size of between 1,100 and 1,200 people to forecast a presidential election, in which 50-60 million people may vote), which is an acceptable sample for using a delphi technique in this environment. Our firm has used this technique in other industries, such as the investment community, telecommunications, financial services, and the automotive industry.

49

The technique involves gathering a group of panelists from across the country, assuring them complete anonymity, and having them fill out a questionnaire. The questionnaire was developed by our firm and the ACHA and was then reviewed by a panel of advisors. The advisor from the long term care industry was Jack McDonald from Beverly. The questionnaire was then sent out to all the participants, who answered it and then sent it back to us.

We then quantified the results, printed those results in a second questionnaire, and sent it back out to all who participated, giving them an opportunity, if they so desired to reassess or change their opinion. The questionnaires then came back to us. We then went through the results to determine whether we did or did not have consensus, and we reviewed the various comments that were written in on the questionnaires, and at the conclusion of the study, we and the ACHA came up with what we consider to be the potential implications and strategy recommendations resulting from the study.

The panelists included hospital and other health care administrators, physicians, legislators and regulators, suppliers, insurance executives, and representatives of other groups. The hospital representatives included people from executive management as well as members of the board at various institutions across the country, including all types of acute care hospitals as well as specialty hospitals. Physicians covered virtually every medical discipline or specialty, including research as well as teaching. The other providers on the panel included people from long term care facilities and health maintenance organizations (HMOs). Legislators and regulators included people from Washington, from the states, and from municipalities and county government. Approximately 60% of them were from county, state, and local government; the other 40% were from the federal level, including people on Capitol Hill as well as at the Health Care Financing Administration.

Suppliers included investment and commercial bankers, attorneys, and supply companies that sell directly to the industry. Payors included executives of Blue Cross and Blue Shield, the other major commercial insurance companies in the United States who are active in health care, as well as preferred provider organizations (PPOs) and business coalitions.

MAJOR FINDINGS

Several main themes came through as a result of the study. First, the overriding concern of management representatives who participated in the study was the continued financial viability of their institutions. Second, there will be growth--in fact, that there will be increased growth to the exclusion of growth on the inpatient side in the various outpatient and ambulatory care areas. Third, government, regardless of the type of regulations and legislation that may come out, will continue to be the largest purchaser of health care in the United States. This is true whether we will be dealing with a competitive environment--that is, with a more conservative approach--or with a liberal, proregulatory approach, with state rate setting and initiatives of that nature. As a result, our panelists predicted that Medicare's share of total health care expenditures in the United States will continue to grow, from approximately 16% in 1982, which was our base year, to 19% and possibly more by 1995.

Another principal message is that social philosophy will shift, and in fact it is currently shifting with respect to health care access. This addresses some of the tougher issues that we will be facing through the rest of the 1980s and going into the 1990s.

Another key message is that ownership and affiliations are going to change. There is in fact going to be a proliferation, our panelists believe, of merger activity and possibly networking, in the sense of a traditional nonprofit community such as a Catholic chain or a Voluntary Hospitals of America (VHA), for example; there will be more affiliations and more networking of hospitals and possibly other providers in the field as a result of this as we move into the 1990s. One of the principal reasons for this is that payment systems are the main thing currently driving the change in the health care industry today.

Providers, principally hospitals but extending eventually into the long term care market, will face ever-increased competition from each other, from noncompeting providers in their area, from physicians, and from new entries into the market. The new entries are the entrepreneurs. They are the ones who feel that there is still an opportunity for them to get a reasonable return on their invested dollar by going into the health care market. The market they are talking about is not the acute care hospital but the long term care or ambulatory care market. How long that feeling will prevail--whether 5 years or 10 years-- probably in part will be dictated by what type of payment mechanism will emerge from the Medicare program as well as the Medicaid program in the various states.

Our panelists predict that the skills required by individuals in the health care field will have to change. The composition of boards will change, subject of course to state laws. In West Virginia, for example, a state law was recently upheld in the courts that allows the state to dictate what the composition of the hospital board will be. In all areas, the composition of boards will change over time. In fact, they are changing already, becoming comprised more of people who understand the industry and who understand business, cash flow, return on investment, and the bottom line. As a result, the traits of a chief executive officer will change. It will still be important to be a good public relations person and one who understands physicians and can get along with and motivate them. However, the new chief executive officer will also either have the abilities or recognize the need to bring to his or her management team, people with skills in strategic planning and financial planning, and who understand the business of health care and the current environment.

Physicians will also experience change. Our panelists predicted that physicians at some point in the 1980s or early 1990s will be in a position where they will accept mandatory assignments, and in fact over 85% of physicians agree that they will have to accept assignment. The panelists, including the physicians, agree that their average compensation will decrease over the next 5 years, and panelists as a group and physicians specifically also agreed that they have to improve their business skills.

With regard to strategic planning, cost and productivity, or the ability to manage costs effectively and properly and offer productive and efficient care, will be among the key determinants of success through the rest of this decade and into the 1990s. Marketing is going to be critical.

There was movement, for example, in the last Congress--and there will be again in the present Congress--to provide consumer information. This is aimed principally at the acute care field so that people will have an opportunity to determine who is rendering their care in the least costly manner. It is debatable whether one can produce that information or whether it will be meaningful without taking into account severity of illness and so forth. However, the trend is there to provide information to the buyer about the operation.

SOCIAL AND ECONOMIC ISSUES

In 1965 and 1966 when the Medicare and Medicaid legislation (titles 18 and 19) was passed and implemented, we opened the floodgates to an extent that the federal government never anticipated. As a result, for the last 20 years we have been providing in this country the best health care in the world to more people than probably any other country in the world, and we provided access to almost everyone. The one group that has had problems is the uninsured, and this will be a topic of debate as the present Congress moves forward.

However, if one accepts the premise that the system is now being driven by economics or by payment systems, we are now in a balancing act. Can we in fact continue to provide the access of care that we have in the past, at the quality level that we have in the past, if we as a people may not have, or may not choose to make available the financial resources to render that quality and provide that access?

As a result, we wanted to know whether our panelists felt that health care in this country was still a right. Overwhelmingly, they said yes. Everyone in the United States is entitled to a minimum level of health care. The key there is "minimum," because when we asked the panelists whether everyone is entitled also to the same level of health care, the answer was no. This response was heard as well from the regulators and the legislators in the panel. Although they felt more strongly that everyone should be entitled to the same level of care, there was still consensus among that group that in reality we are going to have a multitiered health care delivery system in the United States. Therefore two of the key issues today and as we go forward are going to be accessibility and the quality of care that will be issued.

As a result of those answers, we wanted to know which groups the panelists felt would be most affected by the access, quality, and economic issues. They indicated that those people who have the dollars attached to them will in fact have the highest the quality of care and will have continued or greater access to care. The private-pay patient who has the ability to pay will have increased quality and enhanced access. There will be little change for those who are beneficiaries of Blue Cross and Blue Shield or the other commercial insurers. Ninety percent of our panelists believe that the uninsured indigent will have a rather dramatic decrease in quality as well as access, and 70% believe that the same will happen to the Medicare and Medicaid beneficiary through the rest of this decade and into the 1990s.

On an issue related to quality and access, the panelists believe that there will or should be legislation passed that will give either the patient or that patient's proxy the right to deny heroic measures or heroic medicine--to give the physician the opportunity, the option, the right, or the permission to allow nature to take its course.

This relates to the concept of living wills, a recommendation of the Bowen commission, which was set up in 1983 to make recommendations to the president on ways to remedy the solvency crisis of the Medicare Part A Trust Fund. Another way to look at this is that, in the minds of some, Congress will define life and death. That may never happen politically, but it does give an indication as to what people are thinking, and perhaps the coverages at some point will change which may get us to this point.

Health care expenditures in the United States from all sectors now stand at a little over 10% of gross national product. Our panelists predicted that by 1995 that figure will go up to 12%. That prediction is not out of line with what the Health Care Financing Administration has predicted. Regardless, then, of what we see in the way of legislation and regulations, health care is still going to be a big ticket item in this country and a big player with respect to economics.

In fact, if we look at the federal government today, there are four major items that fairly soon will consume total revenues collected in the United States at the federal level: defense, Social Security, interest on the national debt, and Medicare. Therefore, health care is going to continue to be scrutinized at the federal level. At the state level, the health and welfare budget, on average, is the largest single item in any state budget across the United States. Therefore, health care will continue to receive attention on a state level. Probably that interest will be exacerbated depending on what happens on the federal level with respect to budget freezes or program cutbacks, reductions, and so forth.

LEGISLATION AND REGULATION

Because health care is still going to be an important area for the federal government, we asked our panelists where they thought the government was going to take us, either legislatively or by regulation, with respect to health care.

They did not perceive that there is going to be any national health insurance. They also did not believe, however, that there will be any mass movement to replace the currently existing systems across the country with a state rate-setting system applied universally. The panelists also believe, however, that there will be regulations to restrict expansion or replacement of facilities across the country and that there would be a limit eventually on coverage, or total dollars to be spent by the Medicare program for the extension or the continuation of life of the terminally ill, aged individual. They also believe that antitrust--the Federal Trade Commission (FTC)--will become a bigger player in the game.

MEDICARE COVERAGE

Our panelists believe that Medicare will expand into the ambulatory market; they foresee increased coverage by Medicare in skilled nursing facilities (SNFs), home health, hospice, as well as rehabilitative services. This may become even more acute if the increase in the population over age 84 continues at its current level.

With respect to payment systems, the panelists believe that Medicare will in fact expand the PPS. Whether this is DRGs or not we did not ask, because DRGs are a methodology, whereas PPS is a system unto itself. The experts believe that the government will in fact expand PPS to SNFs, home health agencies, and hospices, to psychiatric and substance abuse, as well as to physicians. On the agenda for the Office of Research and Demonstration (ORD) for the years 1985-89, for example, are the following items to be studied and possibly pursued further: DRGs for hospices; development and refinement of specific case mix measures for subacute care and SNFs; a DRG system to incorporate acute and long term care; and possibly a PPS or competitive bidding or vouchers for SNFs and intermediate care facilities.

Senator Durenberger, Chairman of the Health Subcommittee of the Senate Finance Committee, has indicated that he would very much like to get a PPS for SNFs, home health agencies (HHAs), and hospices in the current session of Congress.

Since DRGs are the subject of much current discussion, we wanted to know from our experts whether they thought DRGs were going to prevail. They feel that DRGs will in fact prevail at least on the federal level through 1990. However, they do not believe as a group that they will prevail by 1995. They also believe that Medicaid would implement DRGs by 1990 and that the commercial insurers and others involved will probably adopt some sort of a PPS, but not necessarily diagnostic related groupings. In fact, not only is ORD, for example, looking at vouchers, competitive bidding, and long term care, and so forth, but they are also looking at vouchers with respect to acute care. In one term, capitation may be where the thrust is going to be, at least with the people who are currently in charge.

COMPETITION

If we talk about the bottom line--about dollars, payment systems, coverages, and so forth--the emphasis will be placed on extended care. Among our panelists, 98% expect an expansion of extended care facilities in our country as we move into the 1990s. They also project a greater need for rehabilitation as well as substance abuse facilities. They do not foresee a change in psychiatric needs, and they expect a decrease in needs for children's hospitals as well as respiratory institutions.

We wanted to know how successful the experts thought some of the competitors to the acute care hospitals were going to be. They said that hospitals can expect to face stiffer competition, at least over the next 5 years, from ambulatory care facilities, diagnostic centers, physician-operated clinics, and so on. They also told us that freestanding outpatient clinics were going to be the most successful from a profitability standpoint. However, they also felt that home health and ER centers were going to be next in line. While they felt that hospices would be successful, they did not hold up as much hope for their relative profitability.

The groups that the entrepreneurial community is most interested in are home health care and the DME (Durable Medical Equipment) markets. These are the two areas where they are presently looking to invest their dollars. Therefore, you might start seeing more competition from that segment of the market.

Consumer awareness is going to become ever greater. We see a definite trend in the country away from first-dollar coverage and toward more co-payment and higher deductibles on the part of the employees. We have seen the advent of HMOs, which are showing rather remarkable growth, and PPOs. Once the individual pocketbook is directly affected, people are going to be more concerned about where they go for care. This may not be an overnight revolution, but over time people will become more sensitive to costs if it is their dollars that are being paid. As a result, and if consumer information legislation eventually passes the Congress, this trend will be exacerbated, and the buyer will become, our experts think, over time a more prudent and more discriminating buyer.

The group that is anticipated to grow most quickly is the investor-owned hospitals, which are expected to increase their market share by at least 60% by 1995. Eventually, at least on the hospital side, they will be involved with approximately 25% of the market. As a result, our panelists believe, there will be a rather dramatic increase in multihospital systems, whether for-profit or nonprofit systems. They could be informal or formal affiliations, mergers, or acquisitions. The point is that multihospital systems or large providers are going to control, manage, lease, or own over 53% of the nongovernment hospitals in the United States by 1995.

The group of hospitals that was anticipated to decline was in fact government hospitals. We also asked our panelists what they thought was going to happen with the level of charity care in this country. They told us they felt that the for-profits would decline--that the not-for-profits would probably decline somewhat in the free care that they render, and, of course, there would be a rather dramatic increase in the amount of free care that would be rendered by the government-owned hospitals whether it's federal, state, or local.

If you combine the fact that if their predictions are correct--that we're going to be dumping patients into the government side--with the fact that they also predict that that's where the greatest decline in number of hospitals is going to be, and if you also combine that with the fact that their prediction or their feeling in this case is that the lowest quality care is given in government hospitals, we could be marching to a rather ticklish situation in the next 5 years or so with respect to that element of the population. Free care, while not a topic that is going to be solved, for example, by the U. S. Congress in this session, is something which is elevating in priority on the agendas of several key players in Washington.

RESTRUCTURING AND REORGANIZATION

There was a wave of hospital restructurings across this country several years ago. The second wave is upon us now and is probably being increased because we now have a PPS, and people see that if they are going to change, they want to start changing now.

We asked our panelists whether they thought these restructurings were in fact beneficial and they felt that they were. They gave them the flexibility they were looking for from the regulatory side. Remember that in the first wave of restructurings, when people talked about regulation, the main thing was trying to use the retrospective reimbursement rules that we had and to restructure around that. It took some of the cost centers that were nonreimbursable and gets them out of the hospital side, while keeping the reimbursable overhead in the hospital. The panelists also felt that these restructurings provided increased access to capital, principally through the use of for-profit subs in a lot of these restructurings. Again, although there was not the absolute consensus we had on some of the payment policies and social philosophy issues or regulations, still a good majority expected a continuation of reorganizations and restructurings through the 1990s.

BUSINESS VENTURES

Business ventures are expected to increase greatly. This is not a phenomenon that is going to take place in the next 5 years; it is here now. It is being done at least in the hospital sector, to help diffuse the risk and to help hospitals protect or expand their service area. The Congress has for a number of years considered abolishing Health Systems Agencies (HSAs), and they have used a continuing resolution to keep them going. The administration continues to push to get rid of health planning. As an aside, the state of Utah recently phased out its certificate of need (CON) review program and in fact will not even have a section 11(22) review program. A number of other states have done the same thing or at least have allowed their own CON review programs to be phased out.

If health planning is eliminated, the ability to maintain market share through a regulatory structure is going to decrease for hopitals at least and presumably to a certain extent for long term care providers also. However, the panelists believe that it will also allow them to improve their access to capital, and that will be a key issue in the future. Assuming we are not as successful as we hope in getting the federal deficit under control, and that rates therefore continue at a rather high level, the hospital or any health care provider may no longer be looked at simply as a health care provider. They will be in more competition with the other people in the other markets or sectors of our economy who are going for those dollars. If your trend is not as favorable and if you are a greater risk, it is going to cost you a lot more money which could be prohibitive.

With respect to finance, our panel believes that hospitals' share of national health care expenditures in 1995 will be where it was in the late sixties: down to about 38% of total national health care expenditures. The most rapid increase will be in the area of nursing home care, or long term care. Physician services, other personal care, and other health spending are expected to continue at present levels.

As mentioned above, the primary concern of our respondents was the continued financial viability of their institutions. The next two areas of concern to hospital executives and their boards were access to capital and the decline in their admissions and the reduction in the average length of stay. AHA recently released their trend data, which indicate that, overall across the United States, the average length of stay is 6.6 days. Our panelists had predicted that that level would not be reached until 1990. However, the AHA figure may be a short term aberration.

WINNERS AND LOSERS

We wanted to know who our sample felt were going to be the winners and losers in the health care market. They responded that anyone affiliated on either a nonprofit or for-profit basis with a chain or some other big group has the greatest chance of success, because of pooling of resources, access to capital and management talent, and so on. The losers will be the freestanding hospitals, whether for-profit or not. The smaller the bed size of the institution, our panelists indicate, the less its chances for success.

Changing relationships will be seen between the long term care community and the acute care community. Many in the nursing home industry may have already been approached with rather attractive proposals for keeping beds open or available for hospitals. HCFA has issued a policy with respect to these contractural arrangements between hospitals and long term care providers.

The responses from our sample indicate that there will in fact be failures, notably among hospitals with fewer than 50 beds and those with 50-100 beds. Most at risk are hospitals that are away from the major urban areas, or a little farther out than a lot of the population base. If we start to see a number of failures or a decrease in services, or an acquisition of these smaller hospitals by bigger chains, that could have a ripple effect on the availability of a market, for those who have homes in those affected areas.

IMPLICATIONS

A lot of what happens in the future will depend upon the mood of the country. Will the public and its leaders eventually feel that 12% of GNP for health care is too high and should be reduced? Or, on the other hand, should it be 13%?

Again a personal opinion--what I think is an implication with respect to what's going to happen in the nineties in long term care. Principally the people in commercial insurance have provided something like 1% of the total revenues to the industry in the last several years. Can they, will they, and should they be a player in the field? Will employers eventually recognize the need to provide long term care coverage? We do not know yet. If I were in the long term care market, I certainly as a businessman would try and start to do something in that area to educate people as to the need for that coverage as they move out.

Another factor, which may be the stickiest of all, is, with both husband and wife working in most households today, who will take care of their elderly parents? Health care expenditures in this country are going up, and the population is aging. The fastest rising group is those 84 and over. Will or should we eventually start providing legislative incentives for people to stay home to take care of elderly relatives, or are we willing instead to pay to institutionalize them? This is an issue that is going to recur as we go through the rest of this decade.

Equity conversion is one option being considered. Senator Specter put in a bill last session. The basic concept is that the elderly person, in one scenario, would have the ability to sell his or her home to a younger investor. The younger investor would then have the tax advantages as long as they exist and then have capital gains treatment and so forth on the sale.

The seller would have the opportunity either to get the cash equity out of the home or to get it paid back through an annuity, but also have the right to remain in the house until both husband and wife either pass away or are permanently institutionalized. They would also receive favorable tax treatment on that conversion.

Finally, anyone in the nursing home community, investors as well as operators, must carefully analyze what it really costs to operate. Productivity is a very ill-defined term at times, but if you are not starting to take a good hard look at it, the opportunity to expand your profitability is greatly diminished.

Chapter 5

The Institute of Medicine

Speakers: Robert E. Burke
Patricia A. Butler
Joel M. Hamme

The Institute of Medicine put together a committee to study the regulation of nursing homes in the fall of 1983. This occurred as a result of congressional and public concern over changes that were proposed by the Secretary of HHS in what are called the Subpart S Regulations--the set of federal standards that govern the survey and certification system for Medicaid and Medicare nursing homes.

The conditions of participation that are the underlying quality standards for Medicaid and Medicare nursing homes have been in effect for over ten years now. In June of 1978 the Secretary of HHS proposed some changes to those standards and in 1980 published a proposed rule that would have made three significant changes. First, it would have raised the resident's rights from a "standard" to a "condition," which has an importance in terms of enforcement because when a "condition" is found out of compliance, decertification action can proceed, but as a "standard" the violations of patients' rights have a lot less weight in an enforcement action. The second change would have been consolidating what are now the SNF conditions of participation with ICF regulations into a single set of standards. Thirdly, a new condition of participation would be added, called Patient Care Management, that would have required a more in-depth assessment of each resident's condition and time limits for updating that assessment, required interdisciplinary care planning and care evaluations, and would have tied that whole system into the survey process.

In December of 1980, the secretary signed a proposed regulation into law that would have elevated residents' rights to a condition, but it would not have made the other two changes. The regulation was withdrawn when the new administration took office in January of 1981. No changes at all have occurred since then.

At a parallel track at this point in 1980, the Secretary was also looking at the Subpart S Regulations and held public hearings throughout the country. In

1982, a notice of proposed rulemaking to make about six specific changes in Subpart S was published. These changes constituted the genesis of the Institute Committee: (1) to allow nursing homes that meet JCAH standards to be automatically certified for Medicare without further surveys by the Secretary or the state health departments which are contracted with the secretary for that function; also allowing states to "deem" JCAH accredited facilities for Medicaid if they chose to do so, (2) to delete the quarterly staffing reports that are now required and which are considered by some an unreliable check on quality of services, (3) to delete on-site surveys that follow the plan of correction to determine whether compliance has been achieved, (4) to delete what is now a 12-month requirement for contracts, which actually follows from changes in the Omnibus Budget Reconciliation Act that do delete 12-month time limited contracts for Medicare, and which would have extended that provision to Medicaid as well, (5) to delete the automatic cancellation clauses that are in current contracts so that, if cited deficiencies have not been corrected, there isn't an automatic cancellation although enforcement actions could proceed at that point, and (6) to delete the current requirement for annual surveys and allow what was called a flexible survey cycle, so that some nursing homes might go as long as two years between surveys.

In response to public outcry about these proposals and some congressional inquiry, a six-month moratorium was adopted on any changes in the nursing home regulation process in 1982; that was extended to ten months later on, so that these proposals were essentially tabled.   At that same time a bill, the National Nursing Home Standards Act of 1983, was introduced in May of 1983, and it proposed that an Institute of Medicine study be commissioned to look at the whole issue of nursing home regulation. In June of 1983 before that bill got very far, HCFA officials agreed with Representative Waxman, who was one of the authors of that bill, not to change nursing home regulations pending a final study by the Institute. And so that bill essentially also got tabled. The Institute of Medicine then, in September of 1983, contracted with the Health Care Financing Administration to do a 22-month study for about a million and a half dollars for a report that would become available in August 1, 1985.

The Institute of Medicine routinely works through volunteer committees which are composed of people with expertise, background and broad perspectives in the particular area of public policy concern. And the National Academy of Sciences staff actually does research and works closely with the committee members but the committee members closely direct the study and develop the recommendations.

The Institute committee is composed of twenty members, and includes physicians, nursing home providers, nurses, social workers, state survey agency directors and academics. I happen to be the only lawyer.

The committee organized itself into four subcommittees initially to look at different aspects of the issue of nursing home regulation; and has now reassembled in order to share our knowledge. Most of last year was devoted to working in subcommittee activities. These four subcommittees are looking at: (1) the definition of the quality of care and quality of life, how those terms are defined, how they can be measured, and an evaluation of the current conditions of participation as well as comments on the new federal tax instrument, the so-called "patient-care and services" (PaCS) instrument that is now being tested in a couple of states, (2) the current regulatory system defining state and federal roles as they now exist, questions of effectiveness of the current system, and strengths and weaknesses, (3) the whole range of non-regulatory activities that have an impact on quality of care, such as demography, bed supply reimbursement and case mix and their impacts on quality, and in possible not financial, non-regulatory incentives that could be provided for improving care, and (4) how consumers can be more involved in nursing home policy and in the regulatory process, how other public groups and consumer representatives such as families and visiting groups' ombudsmen can be involved in the regulatory process.

As the subcommittee began their work, it was decided to include yet a fifth group dealing with enforcement, which has met to study the question of how the legal system throughout the country interfaces with the survey certification system, what federal policies might be changed to improve the interface, what intermediate sanctions might be applicable for changes in federal law that would enhance the ability of the enforcement system to assure quality, and what changes in current federal policy regarding the survey process could be applied to enhance enforcement of nursing home standards.

The committee has undertaken a whole series of research activities; first, it held a series of five public meetings to get input from a variety of individuals, and received comments from over 140 people in about half of the states. A series of focused workshops have been organized with theme papers and very rigid agendas, involving issues such as reimbursement, the consumer role in nursing home regulation, enforcement and management incentives to improve nursing home quality. The staff has undertaken a series of original research projects: detailed case studies in several states, a survey of state survey and licensure Agencies, and literature review and background papers.

Throughout all of the committee's deliberations, some basic underlying concepts have become evident: the goal of nursing home regulation should be to assure quality of life as well as quality of care, something which has not been explicitly recognized in the standards at this time; also, since residents are the very reason for existence of the regulatory system, they should be involved in both the study, and they have been, and in the nursing home regulation activities.

Following are some major areas of the committee's research. One is the question of whether the focus of regulation ought to be on residents or facilities. A more controversial topic is whether regulation ought to focus on outcomes as much as possible or on "structure" and "process" measures, the way the current system is designed. We're also looking at residents' rights, the issues of residents' roles and surveys, definitions of quality of care and quality of life, the whole set of issues around frequency and timing of surveys, the issue of time limited contracts and the predictability of surveys, the question of the fragmentation of the current enforcement system, the fact that the survey certification system doesn't usually interface with the personnel licensure and "inspection of care" systems in states, the whole issue of the SNF-ICF level of care distinction and the somewhat technical question of consolidating SNF and ICF standards into one set of standards, the effect of reimbursement and bed supply on quality, and qualifications in training of staff, particularly aide training which has continued to be an issue of major public concern. Staff-to-resident ratios will also be considered, as will the physicians' role in nursing homes and the nursing home's legal responsibility for physician behavior.

STATE AGENCY SURVEY

ROBERT BURKE In order to answer questions relating to the relationship between enforcement and quality of care, it was decided to survey the health facility licensure and certification directors across the 51 political entities in the United States. They were asked to respond to a questionnaire that was about 22 pages long. All the items revolved around the principal questions, "does enforcement make any difference whatsoever?", and "why is enforcement a necessary but not sufficient component of quality?" In order to address those types of theoretical issues, we were asking specifically, "do the current enforcement practices differentiate among states and if so, what tends to explain those differences?" The focus of the study then, was to try to determine from data that we could not find in any other data system currently available what was happening primarily in eight areas. This survey was the only primary data collection effort that was done on this specific project. Of the 51 respondents in our study population, 47 states have responded. Of those 47 states whose responses we have in our computer, about 38 consistently completed most of the items.

There are two explanations as to why only 38 fully completed questionnaires have been received. One is that the agency, in other words, the state director of licensure and certification, does not keep that data that we requested in on enforcement actions and budgets. Secondly, the data systems that we were trying to tap into don't exist in all the states. For example, we were planning to look at changes in resources, meaning both staffing and budgetary, from 1980 to 1983 or 1984, depending upon which was the most recent data that were available. What we found out by and large was that the 1980 data were just not consistent. That is the budget categories differed between the years or the data were not archived in an easily retrievable manner and were not forwarded to us. We were expecting there to be a problem with 1983 or 1984 data but this was not the case. We only have 1980 data for 30 states. Therefore with limited 1980 data analyses of changes over time are also limited.

SOME FINDINGS

Following are some interesting preliminary findings: (1) of the 47 people that responded, the licensure in the Title 18 and 19 certification surveys are done by every single agency and two out of three of those agencies also conduct the Life and Safety Code; (2) there are also 17 who conduct in addition, the inspection of care; (3) however, very few of these agencies make certificate of need determinations and only two reported that they had any direct input into the determination of the Medicaid nursing home reimbursement rate or payment system; (4) the majority of the agencies are responsible for licensing and certifying activities for other types of health facilities; all but three of them also license and certify acute hospitals, and all but two handle home health care agencies, hospices, and most are also responsible for licensing boarding care facilities. The picture that we start to see is that the licensure and certification agency staff are very busy people.

There is also a great deal of variation among state agencies in the size of their budget and the staff that are available per nursing home. We found that the percentage of total survey resources allocated to nursing home-related activities, whether it be any of the above (licensing, certification, inspection of care,) just about 50% of their time. In other words, 50% of the surveyor's time is used in looking at other types of facilities. The range though, is very broad. For example, in one state they are able to devote 91% of their effort to looking at nursing home-related activities. And in another state they're only allowed 13% of their time to look at nursing home activities. The median, however, is about 55%, so using the law of averages, you could say about half the time are they looking at nursing home activities. We also found out that the state survey agencies vary tremendously in the amount of money that is allocated to regulatory activities per nursing home. When you divide through the agency budget by how much time was allocated to nursing home activities, the amount varies from a minimum of approximately $1300 to a maximum of almost $40,000. The middle or median ground is about about $4700 per nursing home. The number of nursing homes per surveyor ranges from the low of 0.8 to a high of 42, with an average of about 13 homes per surveyor.

There is also great variation in the different aspects of the survey process. All states report that they conduct both licensure and certification surveys, licensure being the state component. Roughly three-quarters of those states responded that they always conduct combined licensure and certification surveys. The remaining only combine the surveys when it is convenient for scheduling. Of the seventeen state agencies that reported that they also perform the inspection of care review in addition to the licensure and certification, nine indicate that these reviews are done by the same team at the same visit as the certification survey, while the others do it a different time and usually with a different team.

The length of a certification visit also varies widely by state and by facility classification, between skilled nursing facilities and the intermediate care facilities. We ask specifically for the individuals responding to think of a nursing home of average quality, however they defined average quality for their state with about the average size; the average sized facility nationally is 102 beds for facilities, so we told them about 100 beds. We asked them to think through how they would allocate their staff for the length of time it would take to do that average facility. The combined licensing and certification surveys for the average turned out to range between one person day and 12 person days for ICFs, with a median of around six; and from one and a half to 18 person days for SNFs, with a median of seven. The post certification follow-up surveys ranged in time between half a person day and four person days effort for an ICF, whereas for an SNF it ranged from a half a day to six person days. A great deal of difference was found between complaint visits which vary by state but didn't vary whether or not they were going into an ICF or an SNF. The average visit is about two person days of effort and the shortest is less than a half a person day. The median for that group is one person day.

Thirty-three states have also responded that some major component of the licensure or certification procedure has changed in the last three to five years. Seven states indicated, for example, that they're currently using an abbreviated survey and this may result in why some of the variables of length of time are lower. One of the sacred cows that we've often heard as we've been doing work on this study is that most states never do a hands-on/direct assessment of any of the patients' residents that are in nursing homes. We found to the contrary about three-quarters of the states responded that as an integral part of their licensure and certification there is an element of a hands-on survey. We asked them also to compare the state licensure requirements with the federal standards and found that about 50% of the respondents judged that their state licensure requirements for ICFs are more stringent than the federal government and in addition, one-quarter thought that their state was far more stringent, and about one-quarter said that their ICF standards were less stringent. Looking at the SNFs, we find that there is an equal split. One third say that state standards are about as stringent as the federal government, one third say the state is more stringent; the remaining third reported the state is less stringent. We were also very interested in looking at the specific elements of enforcement.

Through review of the past five years of developing literature on intermediate sanctions, we developed a list of fourteen different types of intermediate sanctions that are currently available to states. We asked the states to respond as to whether or not they have the specific sanction; if they have it, does that agency have the deciding authority to use it, or do they have to pass it on? If the sanction has been used in the past year, how often has it been used? It was found that 44 states report having the authority to revoke a facility's license, 40 have the authority to decertify a facility, 37 have the authority for injunctions against a facility, 36 have the authority to relocate residents from substandard facilities, 35 have the authority to issue conditional licenses, 32 reported having the authority to suspend all new admissions, and 26 reported having the ability to impose administrative fines.

When we asked to look at the application of how states were using these intermediate sanctions, we found that in 1983: 15 states have revoked the license of at least one facility, 15 report having suspended admissions to one or more facilities, 14 reported having issued conditional licenses, 13 reported that they have issued at least two fines.

We also surveyed training activities in the states. We were often told that many surveyors never get training in the actual enforcement process including topics such as how to be good witnesses, so states were asked explicitly if they had training programs, and if they had used them within the past year. Thirty-three states reported that they do have a special surveyor training session on enforcement topics each year. The specific range in hours of special training per surveyor varied widely. The median value was about eight hours of training per surveyor.

Another question related to whether the states with the enforcement training components for surveyors had higher enforcement actions. The survey showed that those states without a training program for surveyors used, by and large, only four different types of intermediate sanctions, while those who had the training generally used nine types of sanctions. Furthermore, the states with the special training reported in 1983 pursuing over 1700 different enforcement activities while the other states only reported 34 enforcement actions. Obviously the difference is so great that there's a need to look at budget and bed-size constraints, but we have not done this yet. Also, one of the major issues that we investigated was with inter-agency enforcement cooperation. Since state attorneys may reside in the health department, or may reside in a district attorney's or attorney general's office, how is interagency cooperation achieved; who is helping whom? What we found was what is called in survey jargon a classic case of response set. What was reported was that except for the resident advocacy groups in the state, there is *always* interagency cooperation.

In summary, the survey pointed up the fact that states that encourage the enforcement system have developed training programs for their surveyors and also have developed a larger series of sanctions that are available to use. Furthermore, they seem to use them far more often. A more important question, though, is whether this affects quality, but we can't yet answer. We've learned several things, however. We thought the agency director was going to be the key informant for policy issues and a source of facts. We've now found quite clearly that he or she has only one piece in the puzzle. It seems that the decision to cite an element, standard, or the conditions as out of compliance rests with the surveyor. So perhaps additional surveys need to be conducted that are targeted at the surveyeyor. Another of the many shortcomings in the survey is that we did not directly survey the legal system and we perhaps should. If the survey agency has more visits to a facility, we have found that they're more likely to use a sanction. We've also found that if the survey agency's budget for nursing home is higher than the average, then they're likely to use more sanctions.

Whatever socio-political environment that causes states to be active in other health and social programs also works for their long term care programs. For example, if the state licensure requirement for a number of nurses per day is higher than the mean, which is about eight hours per day, the total number of sanctions applied is higher. Again as a major point, another important element we were looking at was the discussion of what are classified as "key" citations. Certain elements within the certification form are considered key. We found that compliance with key citations has no relationship to the number of enforcement actions that are taken in a state. The clearest finding that we have right now is that the more sanctions that are available to a state in a state, the more often that they're going to be used by the survey and certification team and the more likely they are to have a positive action within the legal system.

SMITH VS. HECKLER CASE

Litigation Review

PATRICIA BUTLER Following is a very brief background description of the *Smith* litigation. I was one of the attorneys for plaintiff in that case at the pre-trial stage and actually, between changes in the attorney general's office and legal aid in Colorado and changes in the general counsel's office in HCFA and in the Justice Department, I think there are probably as many lawyers in this case as you usually find in an antitrust action.

The case was originally filed in 1975 in the federal District Court for Colorado on behalf of a group of young nursing home residents who were severely disabled--in particular, for violations of patient's rights; the complaint alleged that the facility was failing to provide the necessary nursing and rehabilitative care that was required by federal law. Evidence produced at the early stages of the case illustrated serious problems with care in a particular individual defendant facility: there was theft of personal needs fund; retaliation against residents who were attempting to communicate with their counsel; overmedication of psychotropic drugs and other chemicals; decubiti; the punitive use of cold showers; serious inadequate nail and skin care that led to open wounds; inadequate bowel assistance; and sanitation problems such as cockroaches in the food. These are typical scandalous nursing home problems; and even the state health department's own survey confirmed the problems and said the residents were being warehoused.

The named plaintiffs sued two groups of defendants: one was the nursing home owners, individually seeking damages under a whole series of theories; and that case has been severed from the case against the federal defendants, with several pre-trial motions pending.

On behalf of a class of all the residents in the state was the second set of claims which were against both the state health and welfare agencies and against the department of at that time HEW, now HHS. The claims against the government defendants, which are the ones that have subsequently been litigated, were under the Medicaid statute. The plaintiffs alleged that they were being deprived of needed health care services, partially because the federal survey process was looking not at whether they were getting care that they needed, but at the facility's capability to provide care. It's the old process-versus-outcomes kind of anomaly that has been recognized as a major problem of the SNF and ICF conditions for some time. Furthermore, given that set of facts, the plaintiffs were arguing that it was the Secretary of HHS's duty to establish a system of quality assurance and a process for survey and certification that actually assured that facilities were rendering services to meet resident needs. The case was based on a whole series of provisions in the Medicaid statute and its legislative history.

In 1978 the state agency defendants took the unprecedented position of switching sides and joining the plaintiff residents against the federal government under the theory that the federal nursing home survey system was inadequate and incapable of making sure that residents received care that they needed, and that the state was forced to use this inappropriately focused system and not allowed to use another. Furthermore, budgetary and other limitations forced it into the federal survey process exclusively. That is one of the areas where if the case now came to trial, this would be a harder position to accept because the federal government has more recently allowed quite a bit of flexibility on the part of state agencies in designing survey systems and granting some limited waivers to get around some of those limitations. But that wasn't true at the time.

The state and the resident plaintiffs began two years of depositions and documentary discovery and, among other things, learned about the PACE project, a resident assessment project into which the federal government had poured millions of dollars in the mid 1970s, and which then just disappeared. It looked at one point as if there had been sort of a conspiracy to dump that project, one which had, at least in the eyes of some of its project officers in HCFA, been partially designed in order to fit into Survey and Certification and not just be an assessment tool. It looked to the plaintiffs at that point as if PACE might have been the answer. Yet it was nowhere in evidence.

The case was almost settled in the summer of 1980, when regulations were proposed that would have, among other things, adopted a patient care management system which was designed to focus facilities' attention on what residents needed and whether they were getting that care. Part of the settlement discussions were that either Subpart S regulations themselves or some internal agency guidelines would connect up that PCMS approach to the survey process. However the only regulation that was actually published was the residents' rights condition at the end of 1980 and that was withdrawn by the current administration.

So the attempted settlement failed and the case went to a three-week trial in May of 1982. Shortly thereafter, the district court issued three factual findings and a seemingly fatal legal conclusion. The court found that there were serious deficiencies in at least some nursing homes including the one in the case in particular. The court went so far as to label nursing homes ''orphanages for the aged'' based on the evidence in the record. It also found that the current survey system is facility-oriented rather than patient-oriented and that it is feasible for the Secretary to require the use of a patient care management system that would look at the assessment of resident needs, the development of care planning, and provide a system by which care delivery could actually be monitored and could be tied into the state agency review system.

The court however then went on to find that the Secretary of HHS has no duty to develop such a system because the Medicaid Act is a cooperative state-federal program to finance care and does not provide an explicit federal duty to establish any sort of a monitoring system. It is significant to know that, related to this case, the state had been penalized earlier by the federal government for not completing its inspections of care on time. The state had made some rather creative but unsuccessful arguments in that case and had litigated the matter in front of the same judge, and about two months before he issued the *Smith* opinion he wrote an opinion challenging the state and rebuking it for what he thought was a frivolous appeal. The judge therefore may have felt that the state's becoming involved in the *Smith* case was partially because it had been negligent in performing other duties and was trying to deny responsibility under related federal regulations. The District Court's opinion in *In re Estate of Smith v. O'Halloran* is reported at 557 F. Supp. 289 (D. Colo. 1983).

Nevertheless the plaintiffs appealed the case and in October of 1984, the Tenth Circuit reversed the district court's order holding and ruled that the Medicaid statute imposes upon the Secretary of HHS a duty to establish a system to adequately determine whether facilities receiving federal money under the Medicaid program are satisfying the requirements of the Act, including providing high quality patient care, and including a system which has the capacity to monitor whether care that's actually needed is actually provided.

The court went further and said that mandamus relief was appropriate in the case and that the Secretary had totally failed to discharge her duty, and therefore mandamus should issue; it has remanded the case to the district court which will be holding a status conference in the near future. The Tenth Circuit's decision in *In re Estate of Smith v. Heckler* is reported at 747 F.2d 583 (10th Cir. 1984). [Since this presentation occurred, HHS decided not to appeal the Tenth Circuit's decision to the U.S. Supreme Court.]

FURTHER IMPLICATIONS

One of the underpinnings of the Tenth Circuit's opinion was the change in the recent federal Medicaid amendments, where Congress reaffirmed what it claimed was always its intent and said that specifically it was the Secretary's duty under Medicaid to establish a system of nursing home standards and enforcement adequate to protect the health and safety of residents. The Tenth Circuit referred to that in a footnote. In general terms, the case comes at an interesting time, given that the IOM committee report is also forthcoming since a lot of these same survey process and enforcement issues are going to be examined by the committee. It is going to take quite a bit of time once the Secretary comes forward with a plan--which I assume is what this district court will order--for people to evaluate that plan.

It may be very helpful to the court in evaluating the plan and fashioning a judicial remedy that the Institute's background papers and report become available. Furthermore, existence of the court's jurisdiction over this whole area of the federal survey process may give added weight and credibility to the Institute's report and provide an opportunity for the plaintiffs and the Institute committee to work together.

JOEL HAMME I am not a member of the Committee conducting the Institute of Medicine study, nor do I currently represent any of the parties in the *Smith* case, but I have had extensive experience representing hospitals and nursing homes, with regard to the certification and decertification process. The *Smith vs. Heckler* case is somewhat like an antitrust case in the sense that there are an abundance of lawyers involved, and because antitrust cases are notorious for the fact that they are not decided quickly, but once they are, frequently no one knows exactly what happened or what was decided.

The decision of the Tenth Circuit involved issuance of mandamus relief. Mandamus is something that's very difficult to obtain, requiring a government official to have a clear nondiscretionary duty to do a particular task and a finding that that particular official failed to discharge that duty. That is exactly what the Tenth Circuit, surprisingly to many people, found in *Smith vs. Heckler*--that the Secretary of HHS had failed to discharge a clear nondiscretionary duty to monitor and evaluate nursing homes in the Medicaid certification process, and to insure that there was, in fact, high quality care being given. If you take a look at the ruling, the Tenth Circuit says that, although the Secretary has broad discretion as to how to go about enforcing those standards and conditions of participation, she must in fact enforce them; she must assure that there is high quality care, and the Tenth Circuit concluded that she had not done so, and she had not promulgated regulations that insured she was going to do so.

One of the interesting things about the Tenth Circuit's ruling is the fact that it made clear that its decision does not in any way invalidate any of the conditions or standards of participation. At the very outset of the opinion, the court indicates that the plaintiffs are not contesting the legality or the appropriateness of the conditions or the standards of participation. What they were contesting, according to the court, is the surveys forms and the survey process. What that seems to suggest is that this may be a case in which no regulations may have been invalidated. Ultimately, regulations may or may not be published but what the Secretary and her agents are going to be required to do is to change their survey forms and the way they look at nursing homes when they certify them for Medicaid.

The most notable aspect of this portion of the case was the fact that the plaintiffs suggested that the survey forms that HHS and the states used for Medicaid certification had over 500 questions in them and that fewer than 6% of those questions focused on patient care or on talking to the patients about the care that they've received. It is very possible that the plaintiff will get a large portion of what they want, perhaps survey forms that focus somewhat more on observations of and discussions with the patients about their care and a look, not so much at paper compliance, but at whether facility policies are being implemented and how they affect the patient, and whether the patients are receiving good and high quality care.

The Tenth Circuit's decision in *Smith vs. Heckler* case is interesting in several other respects, one of which is that, although the case deals with the Medicaid certification process for nursing homes, there is going to be some impact on Medicare certification of skilled nursing facilities. The process is and has been very much the same, if not identical, in both types of facilities. There will also be implications for the certification process for other types of institutional providers such as hospitals forcing answers to the question of whether the certification process for those entities is patient-care related and if the same problems and dilemmas exist with the survey forms for those providers. Again, the Tenth Circuit's ruling doesn't require that any changes be done in that respect, but as a matter of academic interest and perhaps ultimately as a matter of practical implications, the agency may have to look at that as well.

As for the next step, the case will go back to the District Court, and the results of the upcoming status conference will have to be analyzed. Whether rulemaking will occur or whether the case will be decided at the District Court level without any real changes in the regulations remains to be seen.

INTERMEDIATE SANCTIONS

PROBLEMS WITH DECERTIFICATION

Decertification as a weapon in HHS's and the state's arsenal is a very black and white proposition--you're either in the program or you're out of the program. For many years, there were no alternative sanctions or less stringent sanctions that could be applied to facilities that may have been close to, but were not entirely, in full compliance. What was found in the decertification process was that one weapon in an arsenal really isn't enough; whenever you have only one weapon, it's not going to be used properly.

There are a great many cases in which HHS and the states, not through any explicit conspiracy but through conspiracies of silence, would not decertify providers which clearly deserved to be decertified, but which as a practical matter could not be because they were either government-operated providers that had huge patient censuses, or they were providers that were in areas where there was no other place to put the patients. So when decertification is the only remedy available for quality of care problems, it's not going to be used properly or judiciously--something which was discovered by the states, by HHS, by the provider community, by advocates who represent patients, and by patients themselves.

In addition, the decertification process raised a whole slew of legal issues about the rights of patients and facilities. There were frequently disagreements between the federal government and the states as to whether or not somebody should or shouldn't be decertified and the timing of the decertifications. There was plenty of litigation concerning the rights of facilities, patients, and the states, and one had to wonder what all of this contributed to the quality of care that was supposed to be rendered at these facilities.

Perhaps the reason why HHS lost the *Smith* case can be illustrated by the fact that over four years ago Congress gave HHS the authority to impose intermediate sanctions. HHS still has not issued proposed regulations about what the states can do in terms of intermediate sanctions, what the parameters of that power will be, and how they're going to exercise their look behind authority. It has taken over four years to even go through the development of the proposals within HHS. [Shortly after this presentation, HHS issued proposed intermediate sanction regulations. 50 Fed. Reg. 7191 (Feb. 21, 1985)].

Although it is useful to conduct studies to determine whether the use of alternative sanctions enhances quality of care, it is also crucial to look at the interrelationship of patient care and the reimbursement that is being given to nursing homes. It's probably true that you could shower money on most providers around the country but that would not necessarily insure good care. Yet the great bulk of providers, if they're paid a fair rate under a fair system, will provide good care. In some instances, the lapses in patient care, the inability to provide the care that's supposed to be provided under the regulations have been due to the fact that the Medicaid program was not paying rates that are equivalent to what should be paid in order to provide quality care. Thus, what happens in these circumstances is that you get a dual track system of care; one system of care for the Medicaid patients and another system for private pay patients. Alternatively, you may have a system in which both private pay and Medicaid patients receive the same levels of care and the private pay patients become indignant because they are paying fifteen or twenty dollars more per day than the Medicaid patient, and they don't think they're receiving better care.

One of the things that the state of Minnesota is now finding out about rate equalization is that many of the providers of that state have gone to deluxe service wings to provide more care or different forms of care--services that are not covered by Medicaid. While Minnesota's rate equalization statute was designed to end up with a situation in which everybody received the same quality of care, it is inadvertently having exactly the opposite ramification; many providers are being forced to think about going toward an explicitly dual track system of care in which private pay patients who want to pay more than Medicaid in that state will receive more, and maybe even be housed elsewhere from Medicaid patients. The Medicaid patient will receive care that meets certification standards but it may not be the same level or the same quality as what the deluxe wing patients are receiving.

> *Two questions, I guess. In light of the findings that you were relating about the fact that, concerning state Medicaid directors, you find that it's really the surveyor that is making most of the determinations in terms of conditions or standards, can the Institute include in its list of recommendations, some that would look at some kind of training and/or educational qualifications for surveyors as already exist for nursing home administrators and apparently you're suggesting for nurses' aides? The second, for those of us who don't have a law degree: what is the significance of the change in wording from the current wording in terms of the secretary's duties "adequate to protect the health and safety of residents" to the wording now required--to insure that nursing homes are providing high quality care? That seems, as a layman, to be a significant leap in terms of obligations. What is your opinion of the matter?*

PATRICIA BUTLER In answer to the first question, the issue of surveyor qualifications has come up. In light of the number of technical issues we're going to be exploring, I can't promise that that's going to get a lot of prominence in the final report, but it did come up last week and it will certainly be at least in the background information. And it's an area that the survey agency directors are really concerned about. They recognize the importance of higher quality people in their agencies and recruiting and professional development and retaining good people is a major survey agency managerial problem.

JOEL HAMME In answer to the second question, if I may quote from the Tenth Circuit's opinion--the court says that the plaintiff's contention was that the secretary had violated the statutory duty to assure that federal Medicaid monies are paid only to facilities which meet the substantive standards of the Act; the facilities which actually provide high quality medical rehabilitative and psycho-social care to resident-Medicaid recipients. So the Tenth Circuit at least uses the term "high quality" at one point, I guess if you read through the opinion it's possible at some point they use a different term to describe that.

I guess that's my question. It seems that the standard previously was "adequate to protect the health and safety of residents." Is there now a new standard that is "high quality care" based on the Tenth Circuit opinion?

JOEL HAMME Well I think the term "adequate to protect the health and safety of residents" is in the new amendments to the statute, the amendments which clarified the Secretary's duty; that is, that the system has to be adequate to protect the health and safety of residents. What the court has said is that the health and safety provided have to be of high quality. I don't think that those are necessarily inconsistent but the issue that you're raising is how high the quality has to be. That's exactly what the plaintiffs and the Secretary will be arguing about when they have a new system put out before the courts to examine.

Evidently the Medicaid statute at least at one point does use the term "high quality" because, again, referring back to the Tenth Circuit's opinion, the court talks about the descriptions of standards and methods the state will use to assure that medical or remedial care services provided the recipients are "of high quality." And then it cites Title 42 of the U.S. Code, Section 1396(a)(22)(D). So the "high quality" term is in the Social Security Act and the Medicaid Act in particular.

I think this would be more of a comment. I'm involved in the survey process and we sometimes conduct dual surveys with two separate teams simultaneously. To ensure correct survey procedures, we have begun to use miniature computers. Many times we've found that when a surveyor checks his forms after the fact, it seems that what is written down is not essentially what you were told regarding deficiencies at the time of the survey. We've also agreed to consulting information that we could have survey participants run the information on their own computers. This is seen by the staff as a much less negative type of survey.

PART 2

FINANCIAL CONCERNS:

Contracts, Financing, and Insurance

Chapter 6

Sale/Leaseback as a Financing Technique

Speakers: David S. Houghton
John K. Sutherland

The sale leaseback is a transaction in which the owner of a property sells that property and then leases it back from the new owner. The question we will discuss is, when should the owner of a long-term care facility consider a sale leaseback arrangement. Essentially, the "why" of a sale leaseback, in most situations, is that an owner of a facility will have used up his or her depreciation, so that all future operating income is going to be net income; the owner wants cash and has only two choices: either to enter into a sale leaseback or to go into the mortgage market. The choice will depend upon the cost of mortgages at that time. Choosing to refinance avoids any tax cost, but there remain the costs of financing: substantial interest payments and loan origination fees. These must be measured against the costs of doing a sale leaseback, which include the tax cost of the sale and any capital gains, only a portion of which will be reportable and taxable because it is a true capital gain in most situations. There might also be recapture of depreciation, an additional tax cost that can only be calculated on a case-by-case basis.

Generally, one chooses the sale leaseback route when mortgage interest rates are quite high; when the mortgage rate was 20%, there were a tremendous number of sale leasebacks. When the mortgage market returned to a somewhat more reasonable level, more straight refinancings were seen.

The sale leaseback arises in two contexts. One is a true sale leaseback in which the owner-operator is seeking liquidity, is willing to absorb the tax cost, but wants to continue managing the property. The owner simply sells the property, leases it back for some reasonable period of time, and normally retains some right of first refusal or an option to repurchase. The other context is a little different. It is a kind of sandwich deal in which the operator needs cash to expand, perhaps into a new facility or to take another one over--this may apply to a small chain or to a single facility that wants to grow. In that situation the owner can sign a contract for a new property, close on that new property, immediately sell it off to a passive investor, and then lease it back. Here one is not simply getting cash out of an existing facility but is getting cash out of a new property as well, because if you buy and immediately resell, you are going to do so at a profit so you can get some working capital. Another option is simply to sign a contract on a new property and then sell the contract for cash, on the agreement that the passive investor will lease the property back to you. This is not a true sale leaseback transaction, where an owner-operator wants to get cash out of something he or she has already operated, but a lot of the same concerns apply: What do you look for in the purchase? What kind of terms must you have to satisfy a limited partnership or some other form of passive investor? What about rent adjustments, options to repurchase, rights of first refusal?

THE ACQUISITION

One of the reasons the sale leaseback arrangement has become a very popular method of financing an acquisition is that it is often difficult for a nursing home to obtain a conventional loan--to convince savings and loan associations or mortgage brokers that this nursing home is going to be a good investment on their part; they're looking at an operator. This is especially true for new or expanding operators. Without any track record, it is virtually impossible to get conventional financing. Even with a track record, if an operation is expanding into other parts of the country, very often its previous lenders will not want to go along.

As a rule, the representative of an operator seeking to buy a nursing home wants to buy assets only, not stock. However, when negotiating the purchase of the nursing home or homes, do not overlook the possibility of a stock purchase. Despite all the well-known problems, there can be some attractive benefits if the right protective provisions are written in; for example, arranging a stock purchase by a subsidiary set up solely for that purpose and then dropping down the assets to the investor, with a leaseback to the operator, can be a desirable way to deal with a potential seller.

INITIAL CONSIDERATIONS

What then are the special considerations in an asset purchase involving a sale leaseback? First, the operator has to know who the investor group is, what kinds of information they are going to want, and ultimately what kind of lease considerations are involved. The operator wants to know how much the investors are going to be able to pay for a facility, without having a solid contract or having the lease actually signed. One thing operators can do to protect themselves is to extract from the investor group an offer to purchase. If I enter into a purchase agreement, they offer to purchase my purchase agreement, or they offer to purchase the assets that I get as a result of that purchase agreement. That binds them to me. At the same time, the operator should ask for a lease agreement stating the terms of the lease. This agreement can be appended to the offer to purchase. There are essentially two ways to execute an acquisition. First, the operator can negotiate the purchase agreement and then assign that purchase agreement to the investor, who actually comes in and does the closing and simultaneously enters into the lease with the operator. Second, the operator can actually take possession of the title and simultaneously transfer title to the investor group with the leaseback; this arrangment would constitute a truer sale leaseback.

There are obviously different kinds of considerations with the latter method. The only time the operator should be in the chain of title is when it is done as an accommodation to the investor group. The only legitimate reason is usually when there is some layered financing--either seller financing or third-party financing--and the investors do not want to be on the notes personally. The operator is willing to be on the notes corporately and sometimes personally, and when he or she then sells to the investor group, the investor group merely takes possession subject to those encumbrances and that indebtedness. The purpose of this is to sell some protection and some tax benefits as an accommodation to the investor group. There are a lot of risks to take into account, however. For example, if the operator actually takes title and goes on the notes, make sure any obligations under the lease to pay the lease rentals are contingent upon the investors' payment of the underlying debts. Otherwise, if the investors go bankrupt, the operator can be obligated to pay the lease payment to a bankruptcy trustee and still be obligated to pay on that mortgage, because the operator is on the mortgage. Make sure that you only have to pay the banker--the holder of the first lien--and not some bankruptcy trustee. There are other difficulties when the operator enters the chain of title that can impact on the ability to transfer title later and cause untold confusion to title agents and title insurance companies.

BROKERED ARRANGEMENTS

The operator cannot always identify the principals. Very often an operator will be dealing with a broker who is going to put together an investor group. The operator may not even know if the investor is going to be a partnership or a group of tenants in common; you are dealing with one individual and so your contract is going to be in that individual's name and/or that of his or her assignee.

It is important for the operator to designate one spokesperson who will be responsible for all communication, especially when brokers are involved. When more than one person from your side starts talking to more than one person from the other side, there is no way to do any planning. More than one deal has taken substantially longer than it should have because an unauthorized person made comments or offers on behalf of a seller, or even on behalf of an operator.

Secondly, it is very important that the operator and his or her counsel get him to fix on the desired end result. The negotiations will involve a lot of details, and without some clear goal in mind you can lead your client astray.

IDENTIFYING ASSETS

Naturally, in an asset purchase, all of the assets must be identified. When dealing with an investor group, questions arise about who owns some of the assets. The investor group is primarily concerned with the hard assets--the real property and sometimes the personal property. However, the intangible assets must be identified as well as the hard assets. Who, for example, is going to get the goodwill? Who is going to get the trade name or trademarks? Who is going to get the name of the facility and who is going to register it--the lessee, the operator, or the landlord? These issues must be decided in advance, because if the landlord later evicts the lessee, he or she may well want to retain the trade name.

Most buyers' counsel draft the broadest possible assets clause. On the other hand, you can draft an assets clause so broad that you take things you do not want--for example, contracts. Do not obligate yourself to take any contracts before you know what is there; they may have several sweetheart contracts and you could end up getting assets you do not want. Be very careful in drafting the assets clause to stipulate that you will only take contracts that you approve.

ACCOUNTS RECEIVABLE

Of course you also need to deal with accounts receivable. This is not a problem in a true sale leaseback, but in an acquisition it is necessary to identify and address accounts receivable right up front. Those are difficult negotiating sessions, but they are better done a month in advance of closing than on the day of closing.

TITLE INSURANCE

The normal kinds of things with respect to real property are going to take place at the closing, except that operators, for some reason, are not always concerned with title insurance. This usually varies in direct proportion to the length of time they have been in the business and their size. It is very difficult sometimes to get people to talk about title insurance; however, in a sale leaseback, the investor group is going to require it, and you need to make sure in your purchase agreement that you address their demands. In fact, it is expedient to send the investors' attorney that portion of the draft which shows title requirements for tentative approval. Do they want the survey exception, for example, or do they want a survey of the property? They are the self-proclaimed real estate lawyers, so let them handle as much as that part of the transaction as they will. They are the ones whom you have to satisfy, so in the sale leaseback it is to your advantage to let them help you draft that particular clause.

LIABILITIES

Naturally, liabilities have to be addressed because the investor group is going to require that the operator assume all liabilities. The investor will expect an indemnity from you for any potential liability. To protect the investor and to protect the status of the prospectus or the offering circular, the acquisition contract must specifically state that the operator will have paid all federal, state, and local taxes due and owing at the time of closing--not just that the operator is going to pay them or has filed returns.

The same thing is true with respect to Hill-Burton obligations, although they are seen infrequently. You may want to include a provision on section 1128(a) on civil penalties.

OTHER DOCUMENTS

In the disclosure, what things will be required of the owner? Obviously, the document is going to provide financial statements, cost reports, mortgages and liens. On the very first contact ask for copies of the mortgages, and liens, any lease agreements, contracts, licenses, union agreements, and insurance. You have the obligation to make that information available to the investor group so that they can review it. They are going to be relying on your contract to do that.

Finally, address the accrued employee benefits like sick leave and vacation, because that will come back to haunt you. Always ask for surveys if they have them. It is also important to ask for appraisals. If there is a fairly recent appraisal, it may show that the facility is worth only 80% of what you are offering. You need to obtain these documents and give reasonable access to the investor group.

THE CLOSING

How does one address closing in the purchase agreement? While you may stipulate a "fall apart" date, the closing date must be left open-ended because you do not know who the investor group is going to be or how long it is going to take them to get up and going. In many instances you are not familiar with how long it will take to get the state approvals that are required. When your investors come to the closing, they will bring with them a sum of money that they think will be sufficient. In the purchase agreement you need to address transfer taxes, sales taxes, and use taxes. This is a clause that can be drafted as broadly as possible, so that you will ferret out local provisions about which you are unfamiliar--you don't want to get "hometowned," so get it in the contract and draft that particular provision as broadly as possible to avoid any traps.

INDEMNITIES

The agreement will undoubtedly have a provision on indemnity in which the purchaser indemnifies the seller for anything that happens after the closing date and the seller will probably indemnify the purchaser for anything that happens prior to the closing date. That provision should be sent to your insurance agent, as well as a copy of the seller's insurance, to find out if you are protected. This is doubly important because not only are they going to sue you, but they are going to sue your landlord, and that lease is going to have in it your obligation to defend them in any litigation and hold them harmless from any liabilities.

ASSIGNATION

The provision needs to say that the parties and interests--this is normally boilerplate in your contract--inure to the benefit of the seller and the buyer or their successors or assignees. That provision will not be difficult to get in most cases. It may be desirable to add a provision that states specifically that the buyer has the right to assign all rights, title, and interest into this contract and/or their obligations incurred under this contract in whole or in part that are freely assignable. That is something you will have to negotiate.

The seller may say, "I want to know who I'm dealing with," and at that point you may have to make some disclosures. Some of the representations and warranties are going to run to the operator, and some will run to the landlord. If you cannot sign the whole contract, you will want to make sure that some of those representations and warranties protect you and not just the landlord, so you don't end up out of privity.

In a contract involving passive investors the last thing you want to do is rankle them. Send them the documents every month that they request, but avoid getting them involved in any litigation.

You need to give special consideration if the seller is involved in financing, or if the operator is going to actually obtain no financing and get in the chain of title, and then transfer the property subject to that financing.

FINANCING ARRANGEMENTS

When structuring the financing package, if the seller is going to do any financing, you must very carefully stipulate who the parties are, who is responsible for payment, and who the guarantors are going to be so that you can make the seller comfortable on that portion of the financing. Very often one of the best reasons for doing these deals is that the seller is willing to do some financing of the obligation. However, there should be protection against the bankruptcy of the lessor, no matter how remote the possibility may seem.

THE LEASEBACK

PARTIES

The parties in a sale leaseback are straightforward and noncontroversial. You have a landlord and you have a tenant. The tenant used to be the owner but is not the owner any longer. There is also a third party, the guarantor. This is one area in a sale leaseback where the operator may perceive a great deal of inequity. If the investor is a limited partnership, there is a very special rule that many people are not familiar with. By way of background, a limited partnership, which will be the typical investor vehicle, allows each partner to take a depreciation or write-off--that would include the interest deductions--to the extent of the basis in their partnership interest. The basis of a limited partner and his or her partnership interest, generally speaking, is the amount of cash the partner paid. However, under the tax law, there is an ''all or nothing'' rule, under which a limited partner gets to include in his or her basis not only cash invested but a pro rata portion of partnership debt if all partners are personally liable on that debt or if no partners are personally liable on that debt.

The debt in this case is the mortgage against the property. If the limited partnership is to be personally liable on that debt, then the limited partner's write-off is going to be limited to the cash he or she has invested in the deal. That is not acceptable. Limited partnerships cannot tolerate recourse financing. Recourse is not an issue in a general partnership or if you have a group of tenants in common. However, that is a relatively rare way of doing these things because passive investors want to be passive and nonliable for anything. The limited partnership entity is therefore *the* most useful way of doing a leaseback. You certainly are not going to do it in a corporate form, because to do so would throw away all the tax benefits. The investors are interested in this deal for two reasons: one is cash flow and the other is tax benefits. In most of the sale leasebacks that are structured either as a sandwich deal or as a true sale leaseback, the tax benefits are quite substantial even though the deals are structured to produce some cash flow. Most deals are set up to make economic sense, but to add on tax benefits from the start, you need nonrecourse financing.

How does that relate to the parties? While the limited partners do not want to be personally liable, they want to make sure there is somebody personally guaranteeing the lease. If someone is not personally liable, then there must at least be a corporation with some significant assets acting as guarantor. A corporate guarantor can empty out its assets pretty quickly by way of dividends, or unconsented-to dissolution, but there is a tremendous tax cost to that. If you have a corporate guarantor, you can be fairly certain it will remain as an entity.

PREMISES AND SUPPLIES

This is going to parallel your purchase and sale agreement with real estate, personal property, supplies, business records; those are things you must make sure are parallel. It is always advisable to have your client buy the personal property, because there is a 5-year write-off on that property, and so that is a good component of the depreciation.

In the purchase contract it must be determined whether or not you are buying all the supplies at the current level, or only the state minimum supplies. If all the supplies are purchased, do you then have to pay extra for everything that is above the state minimum?

In describing what is included in the premises, you will have to deal with the issue of what happens on termination of the lease. Does everything automatically go back to the landlord? Are there state minimums again? What condition is the facility going to be in?

TERM OF THE LEASE

The term of the lease cannot commence until you obtain the appropriate licensing. In a limited partnership with a passive investor, only the seller knows exactly what is going to have to be done and possibly the operator. That's an area where all of the parties are going to have to cooperate to make sure that the licensing and the qualification to do business occur at the same time, that is, at the closing. In some states, to qualify to do business in that state, you have to be licensed in your name. That is when the lease term is going to commence.

The operator will want a lease term that is as short as possible and with as many options as possible; a 5-year term and five 5-year options. The landlord is going to want a 25-year term, or at least a 15 or a 12-year term. The basic idea is that on most seller financing, even with a 25 or a 30-year amortization, you will have a 12 or a 15-year due date. The buyer wants to make sure that the lease extends a reasonable enough time beyond the balloon date on the financing so that when it is time for new financing, the lender will not say, "Why would I refinance? This lease is up in a year. I have no idea if the tenant is going to renew, I have no idea what the market value of the property is. I do know it's a single-use property and that if it's vacant for a day, we have some serious problems and possibly the requirement to get a new certificate of need." Make sure that if you have a 12-year balloon date, your lease is 17 or 18 or 19 years, so you have that cushion to be able to get new financing.

RENT

Do not state in the contract that the rent will be as the parties agree; it's not enforceable. There is no option to renew if that is what your agreement is. There must be a formula--a fixed amount. Get an appraisal as to fair market rental, plug in the initial base rent, plug into that some kind of reimbursement rate adjustment or Consumer Price Index or some other formula, but make sure that there are external factors that will determine that rent without the parties having to agree upon it.

On the rent itself, obviously, most rents are paid in advance whereas mortgages are paid in arrears. The landlord will want some kind of late payment charge if a payment is missed. The two alternatives on late payment charges are a late payment charge a given number of days after the due date or having the tenant pay rent within a certain number of days after notice that of default. I have occasionally agreed to the second alternative and deeply regretted it. I strongly prefer late payment charge if rent is not paid when due, or within a certain number of days after the due date, because I do not want to have to give a notice. Every time a client of mine has to give notice it means expenditure of funds, and the operator ought to know when the rent is due without having to be notified.

The question of when rent adjustments will occur is probably every bit as controversial as what formula will be used, because if there is a rent adjustment every 5-10 years, it means that the operator has that much longer to run the property at the old rent even though the income from the property could be increasing. It used to be that the Consumer Price Index was used all the time. That is a great way to go, except that it will bankrupt tenants if we have high inflation again. There have been situations in which it was voluntarily agreed to abandon the Consumer Price Index because it would bankrupt the tenant, and if the tenant is bankrupt, you do not have a property.

Another possibility is to base adjustments on the reimbursement rates from the state. This is a little risky from the owner's point of view because it is so highly charged politically. Also, it doesn't work very well if you have all private-pay or a lot of private-pay patients. Still another possibility is percentage rent whereby the landlord gets a percentage of the gross or a percentage of the rates that are being charged by the tenant for a particular bed. Under such an arrangement, however, the landlord is going to have some problem policing it. It has been said of restaurant leases, which almost always have percentage rents, that there has never been an honest rent paid. It is very difficult to prove what gross receipts are. Generally accepted accounting principles give some flexibility, and it is very easy to hide income and very expensive to audit. Also, if you decide to go on the basis of the rates being charged by the tenant operator, you will have to decide whether to wait it over the year depending on whether they have had a certain number of patient days at public and private? Do you determine what the waiting is on a particular day so that they jam in as many public-pay patients on that one day as possible and then try to get rid of them if they possibly can?

Make sure that, beyond the right to audit, the tenant operator maintains accurate books and records, because without those, even an audit will not produce the right answers. Obviously, in any kind of a sale leaseback, whether a true sale leaseback or a sandwich deal, the tenant pays all other operating expenses: real and personal property taxes, assessments, insurance premiums-- everything else is additional rent to be paid by the operator.

The one area where the tenant has some flexibility is real estate taxes. Make sure you have the right to protest the assessment, because in a lot of situations, the assessment is wrong or the rate is wrong. Without the right to protest, the tenant would simply have to pay and the landlord would not voluntarily let the tenant protest it necessarily unless the tenant gave the landlord some of the money saved.

The other question regarding rent is whether there will be a rent abatement for fire or other casualty. Generally, I allow abatement on a fire only if there is renter interruption insurance or business interruption insurance that continues to pay the rent from some other source.

SECURITY DEPOSIT

The security deposit is an issue in every lease. It is unusual to see it in a true sale leaseback; you do see it relatively rarely in a sandwich deal. Usually in a sale leaseback you are providing either the means of acquiring a new facility, in which case you want the operator to have some working capital, or you are doing it in order to provide your seller, who then becomes your tenant, some cash to go buy something else. A big security deposit merely reduces the benefits of the transaction.

INSURANCE

There are some fairly minimal insurance requirements that I would impose on an operator. I would require all-risk insurance. All-risk is better than the alternative, extended coverage, because all-risk covers everything that is not specifically excluded, whereas extended coverage covers only what is specifically mentioned.

I would also require full replacement value, or at least 90% of replacement value. The operator is going to be responsible for maintaining property. He or she nevertheless is not going to want full replacement value necessarily because the insurance premiums will cost more. The owner will probably want 80% replacement value, or some limit that is equal to the mortgage that is still on the property. If you get any insurance that is less than 90%, you the operator in effect become a co-insurer, that is, you will have to come out of pocket with some cash to fix any kind of casualty. If money comes out of the operator's pocket to pay a casualty, it means he or she has less money to pay the owner and the owner wants to make sure that the operator has all the cash readily available to pay the rent. Therefore, the owner will want at least 90%, preferably 100% replacement value. The owner will also want a reasonably small deductible for the same reason.

The owner will want the tenant to have liability insurance--as broad a coverage as possible--and to make sure that the owner is named insured. The policy must cover products liability and professional liability, and motor vehicle usage by the employees.

Obviously there is other insurance as well: business interruption, rent interruption, worker's compensation. If you have a situation in which one person is particularly important, make sure that there is key person insurance, because if that person dies or becomes disabled, then you have a facility with nobody to operate it.

The owner will obviously want some control over the form and the contents of the insurance: who the insurance company is, whether it is qualified to do business--that is all fairly routine. As with any other lease, the owner wants to be indemnified for anything that could possibly happen on that property. The one problem is that there is no valid indemnification--in the states I am familiar with--for punitive damages. In such a situation, the landlord may be assessed as well; that is simply a risk that the landlord must live with because one cannot insure around it.

The landlord will probably ask for impounds--meaning that every month or every quarter the landlord will receive the taxes and insurance money. The tenant will likely protest, and there may be a compromise: you will pay impounds if you breach the lease or fail to make your payment on time once or twice so that I only require impounds if I feel insecure for some reason, and usually it will be for an objective reason, such as missing a rent payment.

USE OF THE PROPERTY

On the use of the property my tendency has been to restrict the tenant as much as possible to the specific category for which it is licensed at the time of purchase. There are other possibilities. The lease may state that the property may be used for any lawful purpose. I do not want that expansive a use clause because I have made representations in my offering circular as to what the property will be used for. The landlord will want the right to make the tenant seek permission to change the license category at all. That is for the landlord's protection, not only because of my representations but because there are some operators who like to change uses because they think that some other use is a little better, whereas if they thought it through a little more they would realize that what they have is best. The landlord will want the opportunity to have some input on that.

MAINTENANCE AND ALTERATIONS

Maintenance and alterations are fairly straightforward. The landlord will say "Maintain it in good condition." The landlord will be required to say, for tax reasons, "ordinary wear and tear accepted." Otherwise the landlord will not be able to take depreciation, and the tenant can point out to the landlord that if the property is not allowed to deteriorate through ordinary wear and tear, depreciation is not allowed.

There may be some conflicts over maintenance--what happens if the boiler breaks down a year before the lease is over? The landlord will want the boiler replaced with like or better equipment. The tenant will want to patch it. You can prepare for that ahead of time as best you can but often you will not come up with anything that is agreeable to both parties, and that unfortunately is something you are going to have to live with until the 24th year when something happens. Regarding alterations, obviously the landlord wants the tenant to get his or her consent.

LAWS AND REGULATIONS

The landlord will require the tenant to comply with all laws and all deficiency notices. The landlord wants the tenant to do everything to operate that facility in the best manner possible, both for the landlord's personal satisfaction and for the willingness of the investors to reinvest because they are proud of what they own, and also because a better-run facility is better business.

REPORTING REQUIREMENTS

Reporting requirements is an area where I get some real resistance from operators, but investors will want these things reported to them because they want to know if things are going sour with the business. The kinds of reports that the owner wants are the inspection reports--that is, public knowledge (although sometimes it is hard to get the operator to tell the right person to send them out)-- cost reports, operating statements every year, and financial statements every year. The owner wants to know every year how things are going. He or she wants the tenant to make a fortune so that the tenant can pay the rent. Alternatively, if things look bad, the owner will need that money to pursue his or her remedies.

The owner will want a right to audit and will want the tenant to call if somebody is going to decertify the facility or put a hold on its reimbursement funds. It's acceptable for operators to have financial problems or to run into deficiencies. What matters is that the communication is there. Also, if the tenant ever wants to buy another facility for the chain to grow, there has to be a lot of cooperation in sharing of documents and knowledge.

EVENTS OF DEFAULT

Events of default are rather obvious: tenant fails to pay the rent or maintain the property properly. The question is, must the landlord give notice to default, or is the tenant automatically in default and can the landlord simply start the eviction proceeding. That depends on your individual negotiating situation.

The question then becomes what kind of remedies does the landlord have? Obviously, the landlord will have the right to terminate the lease and the right to collect the rent as it comes due to and sue for it. The landlord will always insist on the right to accelerate future rent and collect it now. The landlord will want the right to a receiver. Receivers are court-appointed. In some states, the law is that you can take property yourself as your own self-appointed receiver. That is extremely dangerous for a landlord to do and I think an operator can fairly safely assume that no one is going to come and seize possession. The landlord will want a right to cure the tenant's defaults when the tenant fails to pay the insurance premiums, and will want repayment with interest at the maximum rate permitted by law. The landlord will want reimbursement for expenses, for lease commissions if the property must be re-leased to somebody else, and for the cost of repairing the facility if the tenant has let it run down.

If the tenant is also providing the seller financing and has failed to pay the rent, the landlord will want the right to offset, that is, to stop making mortgage payments if the tenant has stopped making rent payments. This is a much more difficult provision to get. It is almost impossible on a sandwich deal because the seller financing is being provided by someone other than the operator. There is a bankruptcy issue here; that is, if you are the mortgagee and the tenant, can your bankruptcy trustee cancel the executory portion of the lease and get you out of that obligation, and *not* cancel the executory portion of the mortgage, and therefore leave the landlord still liable for it? Or will the offset provision take care of that? Nobody knows the answer. There is no case law on this matter.

BANKRUPTCY LAWS

You can write into your remedy section that tenants can have the remedies the bankruptcy court permits. Bankruptcy courts, from what I have seen, are filled with bleeding heart pro-tenant types, so they will let me have the property back when they think that the rent has been delinquent long enough. Unfortunately, this is an area of the law in which the federal legislature has seen fit to completely tie our hands.

ASSIGNMENTS AND SUBLEASES

Assignments and subleases is an area where there may be some very substantial disagreements. The law of most states appears to be that the landlord cannot unreasonably withhold consent and must look at the assignee to see if the assignment is reasonable, not at whether the assignor is making rent payments. In any event, the tenant should make sure or at least request that the landlord consent for an assignment or subleasing. The landlord, on the other hand, will want some personal undertaking by somebody or some entity with assets in order to allow an assignment, and will make sure the contract is specific in defining an assignment. Under California law, for example, there is no assignment if a corporate tenant sells all of its stock. There are specific cases saying that that is not a lease assignment, unless you define assignment that way. Therefore the lease should specifically define assignment to include dissolution, merger, sale of stock, and all of those kinds of things.

REPURCHASE

The final issue is the repurchase rights. Obviously, the tenant will ask for the minimum--the right of first refusal. There will not be much resistance to that.

The tenant will also want an option to purchase at some time. The landlord will not allow that earlier than about 7 years, because 5-7 years is the holding period for which the landlord is going to want the property.

In about 5 or 6 years, depreciation will be gone; all rent income will be taxable as ordinary income. The landlord will be starting to pay principal amortization on the loan and will want to unload the place simply because it will be a good source of cash income. It will no longer provide the write-off that some other investment with an equal amount of cash will provide. At that point, the landlord would consider giving an option to purchase, probably based on fair market value in accordance with an appraisal. The tenant, however, will probably want to use some other formula such as a multiple of the rent then payable. Sometimes one sees a formula based on the Consumer Price Index with a ceiling on it. That, however, can be a real risk both for rent and for repurchase rights.

Could you be more specific about what is acceptable on the right of first refusal?

Why is it acceptable?

No. Be more specific about what terms are acceptable to both parties.

Oh, on the right of first refusal all that's going to be is that, if I want to sell the property--two alternatives: one is, that I'll offer it to you on the same terms I'd offer it to someone else, or I'll offer it to you on the same terms I receive in some other bona fide offer. My preference is for whatever I'd offer it for, not in accordance with an offer I had received. I have a little more control that way. The problem, of course, with the right of first refusal from the tenant's point of view is that they can be manufactured so easily.

I've never heard anything like that.

Which only points to the problem--proves my point, I think.

From a business point of view, where does section 2314 cut across all this?

Well, we talked about this last night. I think from a business point of view, it's one thing that has to go into the mix. But John's still going to be concerned with whether or not cash flow is going to cover the lease payments--current cash flow.

He's going to have to make some assumptions that things like the Wisconsin cases, where they tried to cut the rates, are not going to happen, or at least you are going to have to build enough cushion that he's happy with that. But these deals still make sense. There still are passive investors out there and I think it's one more thing John has to worry about and he's going to change his rent increase adjustment--going to have to be a lot more sensitive to the problems of the operator as a result of it--but we'll still see these deals. We're still going to do them.

What's going to happen is, when my client is looking at the viability of a deal, he's going to make sure in that nursing home that the initial rent is going to run somewhere between 14% and 16% maybe of the then gross income. You sort of have to play with those numbers and play with the down payment, and play with what the market value is on a per bed basis to come up with numbers that work. But they've got to work as with the numbers as of the reimbursement rate, as of closing. You don't assume an increase when you're seeing whether it will work, and you cross your fingers for no decreases.

Those numbers are pretty standard with all investor groups that I've come across--somewhere in that neighborhood. Basically what the deal is is that, instead of paying interest in points, you're going to give a certain return on a cash investment, and you're going to fix it basically like interest. You'll say, "I'll give you a 10% return on your money," and they're going to say, "Drop dead." You're going to say, "I'll give you 14% on your money," the money being cash down plus in most situations the front end load for that partnership that's been set up. So let's say I pay $100,000 down and I pay $10,000 in up-front fees, you're going to have to give a return on $110,000, and you're going to figure that out after awhile, and they're all pretty standard. Either they've got front-end load fees or they've increased the interest rate, or they put in a real estate commission. One way or the other, you're going to give a certain return on the cash that the actual investors have put in.

My question was, are you seeing problems now because of that section--somebody's purchase acquisitions not having enough income now because they're not getting reimbursed?

I see more problems from operators that grossly overvalue their properties. So it's a shortage of product, not a shortage of reimbursement increases. I don't see that as a problem because most investor groups are going to want a pretty strong showing of private pay.

And to that end, that section may well have the impact of causing sellers to come more in line with what makes economic sense, rather than having buyers go out and pay inflated prices.

What kind of a private-paying ratio do you normally look for?

As big as possible.

Is there a minimum?

I would guess a minimum would be--we've done a third. We've done less than that. It depends on what you're doing. It depends on how much you're going to pay. If you're going to pay $9,000 a bed, certainly you're going to get all public-pay. If you're going to pay $30,000 a bed, there sure better be an awful lot of private-pay patients there, unless you're in the Northeast where prices are insane. They're crazier there than I think they are in California.

Are either of you familiar with anything being done with the new tax laws, where you've got a tax-exempt operator wanting to do a sale leaseback?

Yeah, I've done a whole lot of research on that and it's a problem. The other problem that's come up is that the tax law that was just introduced says that any partnership that has more than 35 partners will be treated as a corporation. And what that's done is that it's guaranteed that the large public offerings that are buying nursing homes can't be made because they can't represent; they'll be traded as a partnership. So it's basically confined as a tax vehicle to the smaller, Reg-D offerings--you're probably talking about 150 beds maximum-- unless you get some real heavy-hitter investors.

I just want to make a couple of points in sort of rebuttal just to highlight for you--I won't go into them. On business records in the lease, make sure you don't violate any state laws with respect to privacy of the records by granting to them carte blanche business records. In fact, in many states you can't sell the business records, and you don't want to be leasing back business records that you're generating and you have some obligation. So you need to make sure that is looked at pretty carefully.

The other important one I wanted to comment on, although I had several that I wanted to get up and rebut on, was the assignability--you're just going to have to arm-wrestle that out. Assignability is a problem and you just need to get the best deal you can get. There are some good reasons why John's first draft is not a good one for you. He ought to come away from that. Be careful about things like 100% replacement value and replaced property--new property on the premises. Don't let him stick in there anything that's found on the premises that's his, because if you computerize later on, he may be getting a real windfall.

What Dave is talking about is additional property you're adding in, not a replacement of something that's there.

That's right. But you have to talk about the replaced property as well. The other thing that I think you need to do just as a practical matter for your clients--this doesn't happen in other cases but there are so many requirements--Let me say something about the reporting requirements. John is the only lawyer that I deal with where his clients ask for all of that. All the other people really are passive, but if dealing with John, you're going to get all those records requirements. You need to outline for your client the operator, what's required, when it's required, because if John gets irate with you and he gets upset with you, your client is going to be mad with *you* for not reminding them. They're going to see that as your obligation to set up and organize some sort of tickler system of what's required and when it's required under the lease.

Chapter 7

Contractual Concerns in Acquiring, Managing, and Selling Long Term Care Facilities

Speakers: K. Peter Kemezys
Frank S. Osen

In your materials, there is an outline and a sample agreement. We will look through the agreement, and then refer to the outline. The form of the agreement that you have contemplates a situation wherein a buyer has been leasing a facility on a long term lease, and now desires to go ahead and purchase the facility from the seller. One of the reasons we chose this example is because it is rather "clean." In this instance, the buyer will have been responsible for the day-to-day operations of the facility, for filing cost reports, for the employees of the facility, and a lot of the representations and warranties typical to the sort of agreement where a purchaser is essentially locking in cold, and buying a facility from a seller who has been operating that facility. A lot of those representations aren't contained in this agreement, but they are set forth in the outline and we will discuss points which are in the outline but may not be in this particular agreement.

Another reason for using the example of a lessee-purchaser is because if a lessee has a lease that was entered into prior to the effective date the amendment placed a freeze on the step-up, and that lease contains a detailed and specifically enforceable option to purchase the facility, the purchaser may be able to get around the deadline for the freeze in the step-up. The lessee-purchaser, if he purchases the facility pursuant to the terms of the purchase option contained in his lease, may be able to argue, under 2314(c)(1) that the freeze does not apply because he had a specifically enforceable agreement (i.e., his purchase option) entered into prior to the date of the freeze, and that it therefore does not apply to his particular transaction.

STRUCTURE OF THE TRANSACTIONS

Asset revaluation legislation will probably have no effect on acquisitions of nursing facilities. The long term trend is that there will probably be more centralization within the long term care industry.

When we talk about long term care centralization we do not necessarily mean one or two nursing home providers selling out to one of the chains. It also means a local provider buying out another local provider. You are going to find that somewhere down the road, your client who may have one or two nursing facilities, has been talking to his competitor across town, and has found out that his competitor wishes to sell, for whatever reason. The seller is going to want to sell to a local interest, and if your client has the resources, he is going to ask you to structure this maneuver.

Insofar as the structure of the transaction, several types of transactions can occur. In a stock purchase form of a transaction, not only can you cover all of the points necessary for a typical stock purchase, but you also include all of the points necessary as if it were strictly an asset purchase.

Asset purchases are far more simple, in that they benefit both parties better than stock purchases. However, there may be situations, perhaps Certificate of Need laws, or restrictions in certain financial documents, that present an asset purchase. Those particular restrictions, mainly affect a stock purchase, but you should be aware that even when there is a stock purchase, it will take on the characteristics of an asset purchase.

With respect to the preparation of the offer, of the agreement in principle, in most cases we are talking about initiating your first document after your principals have gotten together and worked out the broad strokes of the acquisition. They then come to the attorney, and want to get something in writing. Generally, the vehicle for doing this is called the letter of intent. The letter of intent memorializes, it records the purchaser's intention to go ahead and purchase the facility, and it will usually contain the general terms, the purchase price and any contingencies in the deal. Obviously the purchaser is going to want the closing of the transaction to be contingent upon getting his CON.

LETTER OF INTENT

A letter of intent should always specify that it is not binding until the parties have received the approvals of their respective boards of directors, or in the case of a partnership, of the general partners, and have committed their agreement to a definitive written purchase agreement. If you include that caveat, an attorney may point out that a letter of intent is not really binding. If you really get into the legalities of it, it is not. But often a letter of intent will afford your principal a degree of comfort that he would not have otherwise. If you are trying to get a definitive agreement negotiated, having that written signed letter of intent from the other party gives him at least a degree of comfort that the transaction will be finally reduced to a comprehensive agreement.

IDENTIFICATION OF THE PARTIES

After the letter of intent, we go into the agreement itself. And virtually all agreements begin by reciting who the parties are, and detailing what sort of legal entity each party is. If it's a corporation, you are going to want to call the Secretary of State of your state or the state that the other party is located in, and verify that, in fact, this is the name of the corporation, that it is a valid corporation in good standing. You are going to want to verify the entity holding title.

RECITALS

After establishing the legal entity, the recitals are basically the narrative; they detail the circumstances of this transaction. In this transaction, as I said, we have a buyer who is a tenant in the facility, pursuant to a lease. If that lease contains an option of purchase, reference it in detail. This is necessary because if you do have a valid option in a lease that was executed prior to the freeze on the step-up, it may get you around the deadline. Make it clear that this purchase is taking place pursuant to this option in the lease.

IDENTIFICATION OF THE FACILITY

You also need to identify the facility. Do this in general terms, noting the number of beds, specifying that it is certified, because your seller is going to be signing this agreement, and you want to verify that they have a Certificate of Need for that number of beds. And then you reference Exhibit A which will contain your detailed legal description of the facility. You will later verify the legal description in the title report, against the one that you have as Exhibit A, and make sure that there's no variation. In addition, you need to detail the real property, the structures, fixtures, aiding, surfacing, and improvements.

PERSONAL PROPERTY

In a lease context such as the one in our example, there may be little, if any, personal property being purchased, because the operator here will have been leasing the facility. He may have all his own equipment in there, and may just be buying the physical plan, the structure, the real property.

But in the event that there is personal property that will be acquired, the standard vehicle for doing that is a bill of sale. You attach a bill of sale as an exhibit to the agreement, so that when it comes time for the closing, and you ask your seller to sign that bill of sale, he will already have agreed to the form by which he is giving you that personal property.

You also need an itemized schedule of all the personal property, which the buyer operations people will have to verify and work out with the seller. You don't want, for example, to find out from the seller that there's an automobile at the facility that is included on that inventory, of which you were not aware; you may have an understanding that that was not going to be part of the personal property that was conveyed. But if it ends up on that inventory list, when the seller executes that bill of sale, he has sold it.

So both sides are going to want to pay particular attention to that inventory list. But there is a school of thought that it is preferable not to include a list of personal property that is going to be conveyed along with the facility since if you miss something on that list, arguably, you are not going to get it. I think that on the whole, one should list the personal property, and if there is an error in that list the purchaser is still protected by the phrase "that is located in and upon the premises."

If there are architectural plans to the facility, the buyer will want to have those; it's a good idea to specify that if any as-built plans or surveys exist, that the seller will also agree to turn those over to the purchaser.

LEASES/MAINTENANCE CONTRACTS

The next paragraph addresses the leases or the maintenance contracts that may be in existence. This can be done several different ways. The buyer may want a provision that the seller will provide to him copies of all maintenance contracts or he may restrict it to copies of all such contracts, service contracts or maintenance contracts, that are not cancellable within a certain period of time, say upon thirty days notice. That way, your buyer will know, and you will have a chance to look over these contracts and provide a mechanism whereby if the buyer doesn't want to be stuck with a particular contract, he can have the seller arrange to terminate it prior to acquiring the facility.

LEASE/PURCHASE DETAILS

You also want to detail in the text how you are going from a lease to a purchase. When the buyer leased the facility, in addition to first and last months rent, or pre-paid items of rent, he may have been required to provide a security deposit. If so, you want to provide that this is credited against the purchase price. You will want to set forth the amount of the purchase price, and explain how it's going to be paid. If you have an all-cash deal, let me caution you that, with respect to recapture, both Medicare and Medicaid have a right to go back and assess recapture penalties.

Let me give you the example of an all cash deal, where the seller has taken his money and moved to Florida, and you have no note or anything of that nature from which to withhold payments. If the assessing agency wants to come back and assess penalties for recapture, it will not matter to the state that the buyer has a wonderful contract that provides that the seller is responsible for all recapture prior to the acquisition date.

The state is not going to care about that. As far as it's concerned, it can easily get its money by stopping payment on the checks that it's writing monthly to the facility, or it can chase the seller down to Florida. I leave it to you as to which method the state will more likely adopt. So, if you have an all cash deal, I would caution that you will want to think about escrowing a portion of the purchase price for that window period, during which recapture penalties may be assessed. If not, if you have a note, as you do here, you will want to include a provision in that note, that in the event of any assessment, or recapture penalties, the payment can be offset or withheld to make that good.

With reference to recapturing, a third alternative is to just insert in the contract, and make part of your agreement, that the seller agrees to go to the state and get a determination prior to closing of just what the recapture situation looks like. There may be a lot of reasons why you don't want to do that. That may be stirring up a nest of vipers, but you do want to be sensitive to that recapture issue.

In a provision with respect to the note, the buyer may assert for his benefit that the note may be pre-paid without penalty. Whether or not that the seller is going to agree to this depends on the circumstances of your particular transaction.

I can't think of an acquisition we have made, even if it involves one facility, where there wasn't at least a nominal escrow. And I think that most parties appreciate the uncertainty surrounding reimbursement, so that they will agree some escrow is necessary. You will be arguing for quite a while as to how much is necessary, and the duration of it, but I think almost any seller will agree some escrow is necessary. Even if you have a small one-facility agreement and particularly where you are dealing with unsophisticated principals, an escrow is very beneficial. I would caution you when you have a purchaser who is going in cold to purchase a facility, that you use the services of an escrow.

The adjustment to the purchase price is also something that is specific to this example, because it is a situation where you have a lessee changing from a lease to an ownership position. Obviously, if you had a new purchaser, you would have certain adjustments to the purchase price, and you would pro-rate property taxes, insurance, and things of that nature. So, the adjustment to the purchase price provision is specific to this particular circumstance.

CLOSING AND EFFECTIVE DATES

The reason that you have a difference between the closing and the effective dates is that your closing may be extended because it is dependent upon several conditions precedent. You may agree on a certain date, but when it comes time for you to close, the buyer may have had a hang-up getting a CON. The seller may be trying to get permission from one of its mortgagees, and may not have been able to get written consent. So you have a provision in here where the parties can extend the date of the closing. Regardless of that, in the vast majority of instances, it will be easier if you have an effective date, as of the first of the month, for your accounting purposes, and for Medicaid purposes. It just is a lot cleaner, if you have a first of the month effective date.

There's also a provision to the effect that if the closing has not taken place by a certain date, the parties may agree to terminate the transaction. This benefits both parties. The seller is not going to want to have this facility tied up, while the buyer can't get his CON, or makes dilatory attempts to do so. So, it prods the buyer to get his act together. The buyer may want to have as long a period on this as possible, and the seller would prefer to have a shorter period. So what you end up with is going to be subject to negotiation.

CLOSING--SELLER'S OBLIGATIONS

The next provision addresses the seller's obligations at the closing, and it simply details the various documents the seller is going to have to get together, and either bring to the closing, or execute at the closing: a warranty deed, which conveys the property itself; a policy of title insurance, preferably with the survey; the bill of sale, which we've already discussed; and assignments of any of the maintenance contracts or service contracts the buyer will be assuming. It is also better practice to make an exhibit to the agreement wherein the seller states, in effect: "I give to you, buyer, all my interest in all of these maintenance contracts, and all of these service contracts." This is done before the signing in order to avoid the problem at closing where the seller may say, " I did not agree to the form of this assignment." Then you have another set of problems in trying to get an assignment drafted that will meet with his approval.

LEGAL OPINION

Both sides are going to be asked to provide an opinion of counsel, which essentially states that to the best of counsel's knowledge, the representations included on behalf of his particular party (be it the buyer/seller in this agreement) are true and correct, that his party does have the ability to enter into this agreement, that it's a valid and binding obligation, and that he has reviewed the necessary documents.

You'll note between page seven and eight, we have paragraph A at the bottom of page seven, which refers to the seller as a corporation. Paragraph B at the top of page eight, refers to the seller as a partnership. This is done merely by way of illustrating that, depending on what entity you have selling the facility, you'll have different representations with respect to the legal opinion. In the case of a corporation, you are going to want to see a certified copy of the Board of Directors' resolution, authorizing that corporation to enter into the transaction. In the case of a partnership, you will want to see a copy of the partnership agreement.

In areas where we're buying from a partnership, we insist that all partners sign the purchase agreement. If there is a limited partnership involved, quite obviously, we will insist that the general partners sign. We will also insist on some documentation that the transaction has the approval of the limited partners. We certainly don't want to get involved in a tug-of-war between the general partner and the limited partner, even though the limited partner's agreement gives the general partner the right to do everything under the sun, including sell the first-born son of the limited partners. So we will want some assurance the limited partners in the partnership agreement agree to the transaction.

If there's a corporation involved, in addition to the opinion of counsel, we will also ask for an officer's certificate. If we are dealing with a one-person corporation that is obviously superfluous. But often, you will be facing the situation where there may be three or four major shareholders, say with 20% interest in a corporation, so we'd like an officer's certificate indicating that the person is signing on behalf of the corporation, and that all of the warranties and representations contained in the purchase agreement have been complied with, basically somewhat similar to the officer's opinion you see here.

The final paragraph of that legal opinion states that in rendering its opinion, the counsel may rely on certificates that have been furnished to it as to factual matters that are not independently verifiable by that counsel, but to the extent that the other counsel does rely on certificates, you are going to want to know.

Most opinions of counsel will be couched in language indicating the counsel or someone under his direct supervision is familiar with the transaction and has taken a look at those documents he considers to be important. On the basis of the foregoing, he gives his opinion. Quite obviously, an opinion of counsel is not a 100% guarantee that something is true. If there is a reference to the fact that your opinion is based upon certain documents you have reviewed, that you feel is necessary, a purchaser has the right to say, let me see what documents you have relied upon. Any attorney who does give an opinion of counsel that does not contain that type of limiting language is an idiot. I think you really have to have that type of language in an opinion of counsel. You cannot give a 100% guarantee.

There is sometimes a situation wherein certain documents or acknowledgements might not get executed at the closing. Say your seller is down in Florida with this money, or there are bad feelings between the purchaser and the seller, you are going to want to provide some sort of mechanism whereby the seller agrees to execute, acknowledge, and deliver further documents or assurances, or instruments that may be required in order to reflect the transaction as contemplated by this agreement.

You are also going to want to assure to the extent you can, that if it is necessary to get the seller to join in or to assign any right that it may have to prosecute any sort of claim on behalf of the facility, that you get this permission from the seller. Sometimes you may not have gotten the right to use the name of the facility in a transaction, and so you may want to provide that the seller will assist you in prosecuting any claims in its name if it is necessary that you have the seller along with you to do so after the closing.

CLOSING--BUYER'S OBLIGATIONS

The next section gets into the buyer's obligations at the closing, and obviously the buyer is going to deliver the cash, that's what the seller is mainly interested in. In this case, it's by check. The seller may want to stipulate that the buyer provide the money by wire transfer, in which case, the money will be automatically wired into either the seller's account, or into a trust account, and this gives your seller a little extra margin of comfort to know the cash is there and waiting at the closing.

If you are the counsel for the seller, you have a duty to advise the seller that he should not accept a check, but he should accept current funds. The reason for that is if you accept the check, you may in effect be losing a day or two of interest. If you are talking about a three million dollar deal, a day or two of interest is substantial.

From the buyer's standpoint, if you get the wiring instructions set up early enough, you can usually contact the wire transfer officer at the bank, and arrange to have the money invested and have the interest that's accruing prior to the closing, or prior to the transfer from buyer to the seller, accrue to the buyer's benefit. It's important that you get the complete wiring instructions as quickly as you can, get a transfer number, obviously a bank account, a bank address, and get that worked out on the front end.

One other caution. If you are closing on a Friday, make sure that you have your wiring instructions in by 9:00. If you wait till 12:30 on Friday afternoon, there is a reasonable chance that your bank will never get that money that particular day. So if you are going to close on a Friday, particularly if you are dealing with one of the larger banks, make sure that the wire gets in early in the morning.

LEGAL OPINION

The buyer will also be asked to furnish a legal opinion of counsel. One other thing which is not in this agreement, but which title companies will want in order to record, is a certificate of good standing on behalf of the buyer. It is important that counsel for the buyer, before the closing date, arrange to have someone get a certificate of good standing from the Secretary of State's office. In Washington, D.C. you can do this quickly, but in another state, where you are not close to the state capital, or if you are closing out of state, you will not be able to do this quite so quickly, so you are going to want to address well before the closing.

If your Secretary of State's office will cooperate, you can set up a telegram to the place of closing, indicating that that corporation is in good standing as of the date of closing. Most Secretary of State's offices will cooperate.

The representations that the buyer's counsel is asked to make are essentially parallel to those the seller's counsel has made in his legal opinion. The seller will want to know that this is a valid and binding obligation, and the buyer's counsel will want to look at the documents that were used to form the basis of the legal opinion.

REPRESENTATIONS AND WARRANTIES

The representations and the warranty section which begins on page eleven is perhaps the most important section of the agreement from the buyer's standpoint, and it's also one to which you will have to pay particular attention, in order to tailor it to the specific circumstances of your transaction. This agreement contemplates a situation where a lessee is going to purchase a facility. If you have a purchaser going in cold, purchasing from a seller who has operated, who's been responsible for cost reports, who has his own employees in the facility, who may or may not have dealt with the union, then you must tailor the representations and warranties, so we will probably be referring to some of the more comprehensive representations in the outline here.

If you are buying one facility or fifteen facilities, you should always have a due-diligence search. You should not rely upon the warranties, and the representations solely of the seller. Before you sign the purchase agreement, you should have taken a look at the articles of incorporation, partnership agreement, cost reports, the census, the patient funds, and the daily rates that the nursing facility has charged for the past three years.

Your client may have made the deal without you, especially if the other party is a friend or an acquaintance; they may have shook hands and dismissed the need to see all of the pertinent documentation. The buyer may therefore not know that two years ago, the census was at 48%. Counsel must therefore conduct a due-diligence search, and if there's anything that you find out of the ordinary, quite obviously, the seller should be made to explain it.

Don't rely upon the warranties and representations. They are very important, but two years down the road when a dispute arises your client may wonder why you did not discover a certain problem at the outset. A due-diligence search is designed to avoid such problems and if there are any skeletons in the closet a reasonable search should reveal them. Even if you are purchasing one facility, a due-diligence search should be made.

Tailoring the representations and warranties to your specific situation is important; it is a way of telling your seller on the front end, look this is the sort of thing my client the buyer is concerned about, and this is the sort of picture he has of what he's buying. Now if this is not the case, we want you to come forward with the documents to show what the situation is.

You will want to know, for example, that there are no leases in force, that there's no mortgage, or encumbrance outstanding on the property. If there is, obviously you are going to want to take a look at it. If it contains a due-on-sale clause, or if it contains some sort of acceleration provision, or requires the consent of the lender, you are going to want to make sure that your seller has the permission of the lender, or that your buyer has gotten the permission of the lender to go ahead and purchase the property and assume the mortgage.

The representations that are in here essentially track the exhibits with respect to setting forth the equipment leases. You will want to know that there are no encroachments on the premises, or no encroachments from the premises onto other property, and normally your vehicle for determining this will be your title report and survey. But it never hurts to have an extra set of suspenders, so you want to build in comprehensive representations despite your due-diligence search, and despite what your operational search of the facility has been.

You want also to provide that you will get a title report in order to see what is affecting title. And your buyer will want the option either to require the seller to fix anything that may be a cloud-on title, or if the seller cannot fix it, your buyer will want the option nevertheless to waive that provision in writing, and go ahead and purchase the facility. He may want the opportunity to have an adjustment made to the purchase price to reflect that, however.

Representation H deals with brokers' or finders' fees. If a broker or a finder has been involved, you will want to include a specific representation to the effect that there are no brokers' or finders' fees or commissions which are payable, except the obligation of seller or buyer to XYZ Realty, or to certain individuals. Get a representation that there are no others, and you will want an indemnification from the other party. Many times brokers come out of the woodwork after the deal has been completed, or the deal is set to close. A broker may show up at the escrow company, or send a letter to one of the parties claiming that he has a right to a commission. So you will want this representation included for protection in this respect.

You also want representations with respect to zoning, legal description, the seller's ability to convey the property, and as to whether or not personal property is subject to any sort of security agreement or conditional sales contract. You'll request a UCC search; that would essentially provide the back-up for the representation you are requesting here.

Make sure you get the exhibits in plenty of time prior to closing. If you wait until closing, the following may occur. The seller will furnish you with a number of exhibits, and with copies of the documents that are noted in the exhibit. You start taking a look at the documents, and most of which will refer to other documents not included in the exhibit, ones you have never seen before. A one-day closing can sometimes become a three and four day closing while your seller scurries for a document that was executed years before. If you get the exhibits thirty days beforehand, you can go through them. If the documents that are part of the exhibit refer to other documents, you can have the seller try to locate them. That way you will have a smoother closing. Don't wait until the day of closing, or even a day or so before closing to take a look at the exhibits that are going to be the exceptions to the reps and warranties.

Representation N is essentially a catch-all, stating there is no agreement in existence materially adverse to the business properties of financial conditions to the sellers. If you were the seller's counsel, I think you'd leap on that one right away.

If you take a look at the reps and warranties that are contained in the outline, you'll see that some, such as the financial statements, pertain basically to stock transactions. If you are buying assets, you are not necessarily worried about the financial statements of the seller. If you are buying stock, you are, and the same goes for his tax returns. Depending upon whether it's an asset or a stock transaction, you should tailor your reps and warranties. In a stock transaction, we normally prefer that all of the reps and warranties you see on this asset transaction be contained and, in addition, the reps and warranties that apply solely to stock transactions. That's why I indicated previously that stock transactions take on many of the characteristics of an asset transaction.

I will now briefly describe some of the representations and warranties contained in the outline that are not in this agreement. When you are dealing with a situation in which the buyer has not been an operator of the facility, you will want to include some of these items. If you are buying a seller's facility, and the seller has been operating it, and has been employing the employees at the facility, you will need a representation and an exhibit with respect to all employee benefit plans. This would include all pension and profit sharing, all accrued vacation, a list of the employees, a schedule of their salaries, any labor agreements in effect, and whether there has been any labor controversy or labor activity of any nature. Another thing you will want to note, in either an asset or a stock context, is absence of any changes between the date you signed the purchase agreement and the date of closing. You don't want the seller selling off something you may consider material to what you are buying, by stating that it is not material. An absence of change clause effectively puts the seller on notice that there should not be any changes during that interim period without the buyer's prior written consent.

One of the things we found to be a frequent problem, is patient personal funds. It's surprising how many facilities maintain the last three years' patient fund records on three-by-five cards, not in alphabetical order, nor in any order, and if you wait until the day of closing, they're really going to be fouled up. You need an indemnification and warranties strictly for patient funds. It has become evident that some states understandably feel very strongly about nursing providers enriching themselves through embezzlement of patient funds. They don't quite realize you are not going to be rich on $25 a month, and it is very difficult to convince the state that you inherited the problem; you did not cause it.

By the same token, if the seller is representing a warranty to the buyer that he is handing over accurate patient trust funds and that this is in fact an accurate accounting of those funds, and an accurate statement thereof, the seller will want in return a representation from the buyer that from and after that date, the buyer is going to handle those funds properly, and will account for them as required by the practices in the state.

On page 17, item C, this provision states that the buyer is covenanting to use its best efforts to obtain licensure and authority to operate the facility, and to get certification and provider agreements. The seller, by the same token agrees to cooperate with the buyer in this respect. The buyer doesn't want an uncooperative seller when he is attempting to go to the state agencies and to secure the required certification and licensure. And again, there is a parallel representation in here that the representations which the buyer has made in this agreement will be true and accurate as of the closing date.

SELLER'S OBLIGATIONS PENDING THE CLOSING

The next section deals with the obligations of the seller pending the closing. The seller agrees that it will not do anything to change its operations at the facility prior to the closing. You certainly don't want to sign an agreement and have the seller decide to start transferring all of the key employees over to his facility ten miles away. The purchaser wants to tie the seller down, and make sure the picture that he has of the company as it's reflected by the due-diligence searches is going to be accurate, as of the closing date.

Insofar as the covenants of the seller during this interim period, when you are buying stock, you will require a couple of things not necessary in an asset transaction. One is declaration of dividends. You don't want your seller to declare a dividend three days' prior to closing. You also don't want any change in the organizational structure of the facility you are buying.

These provisions essentially provide that the seller is not going to execute any new service contracts or leases; is not going to encumber the property by taking out a mortgage on it; is not going to institute any novel methods of purchase, sale, lease, management, accounting, or operation that will materially vary from what it has done in the past; or amend any contracts; and that its representations and warranties will be true as of the closing date. The buyer will want to set forth conditions so that it is clear at the time you execute the agreement that unless certain things are done, the buyer will have the option not to proceed with this contract, because the buyer is obviously going to want to be satisfied that it can get a CON and licensure, and is going to want to satisfy itself that the reps and warranties are true. Again, there is a catch-all in here. Item C, that no action, suit or proceeding before any court or governmental body is not exactly a catch-all, but you are going to want to insure that none of the regulatory authorities having jurisdiction over your particular transaction has stepped in and said, "I'm sorry buyer, you can't buy this facility; we are not going to license you." In the event that happens, you are obviously going to want an out.

There's one caveat to this, if the buyer is assuming any debt that your seller is going to remain contingently liable for. Make sure that there is a rep and warranty that the buyer will not breach those liabilities that he is assuming; that he will not convey his interest of those liabilities to anybody else; and also, if he does assume some liabilities, you are going to take back a security interest second deed of trust, or whatever. You should also demand that there be a rep and warranty by the buyer that he will maintain adequate insurance upon the building.

On page 22, item I, is a provision for the benefit of the buyer to the effect that the buyer will be able to satisfy itself on the closing date; that there has been no proposed or actual material changes to the Medicaid reimbursement system in effect in that state prior to closing. That was engendered because of the change of the law last year. The buyer should be able to assure himself that this still is a deal that makes sense, from a reimbursement standpoint.

The conditions precedent to the seller's performance essentially parallel some of those of the buyer's conditions precedent. The seller will want to ensure that the reps and warranties of the buyer are true and that the buyer has complied with all its obligations under the agreement. And similarly, the seller will not necessarily want to proceed with the transaction if the suit or injunctive preceding has been instituted by any of the regulatory authorities.

Another thing you will want to include is a division of revenue clause in there.

Concerning the indemnity clauses, we have the basic indemnity, essentially the one that both parties agree to. The seller is responsible for his representations under the contract, anything with respect to the facility that's attributable to his period of ownership. The buyer is responsible with respect to his representations and warranties and for anything that's attributable to the facility after the period of transfer.

CLOSING COSTS

With respect to the closing costs, those are also subject to negotiation. They vary just as title insurance costs vary state to state. Many purchasers, particularly larger purchasers, do not pay for title insurance. It's an item they expect the seller to pick up, but I would caution you that wherever you're dealing business and if you do business in different states, the custom varies. You can go to your local title insurer for a book which sets forth the title insurance practices state to state and the allocation of closing costs, because they do vary. In fact, in

California I know they may vary whether you're doing a deal in northern California or southern California, so it's important to know that because you can normally negotiate something based upon the local practice.

With respect to the legal expenses, one provision not in here that you may want to consider is an arbitration clause so that if there is a dispute and the parties want to arbitrate it, each side can pick an arbitrator and those two can agree on a third, or specify AAA arbitration. That's an avenue you may want to consider. A purchaser may also want to restrict his seller's ability to compete with him either by proximity within a certain radius of the facility that he's buying, or for a certain period of time.

FACILITY'S NAME

You may also want to consider whether your buyer wants to use the facility's name. Make sure that it's specifically in there that the buyer can use the specific name. Make sure that the seller warrants that he in fact has the right to use that name. Otherwise two years down the road someone in another city could claim they have trademarked that name since 1960 and then you're stuck. So, have the seller warrant not only that you can use the name but that the name is legally used.

BULK SALES

Regarding bulk sales, most attorneys would rather not deal with that question. I think that it is a reasonable attitude to take that bulk sales does not apply.

PUBLICITY PROVISION

The last thing I'll touch on just in passing is the publicity provision. Depending on the sensitivity of the negotiations or the competitive atmosphere in the particular market, you might want to think about a provision such as this so that you don't have your seller announcing that the deal is going to take place until it in fact has done so, and that you agree on the substance of any sort of press release.

> *Assuming that you represent the purchaser and I represent a seller that is a limited partnership, and I represent the limited partners if that's different--maybe it's the same. If you asked me to have my limited partner sign an agreement in sending*

you the sale, am I derelict as the attorney for the limited partners, by doing that, in breaching their limitations under the Uniform Limited Partnership Act?

Well, I don't think so, because you're not being asked to execute the document. You're not being asked to do that, and that's a duty that is reserved for the general partner. When I said you want some assurance that the buyer is not caught up in a dispute between the general partner and the limited partner, why do you want the limited partners to acknowledge (1) that they are aware of the transaction, and (2) that it is not contemplated that there is any litigation between the general and limited partners concerning the transaction? And so you're trying to get around that particular limitation . . .

But I'm concerned about ruining or depreciating the immunity from liability that the limited partner has by being involved in the management of the business which will depreciate.

But once again, you're not being asked to execute the agreement; you're not being asked to do anything except to make a statement that you're aware of the transaction. There's no contemplated litigation concerning the transaction, so you're not even being asked to give an opinion concerning the fairness of the deal. I think that you probably don't have a problem.

The Uniform Act had a provision that action by a limited partner on approval of the sale of substantially all of the assets is not a management; at least it is here in Tennessee; I don't know that other states have that particular provision but I understand it's fairly uniform.

How can you say that the DEFRA provision regarding the evaluation of assets may not apply to the exercise of an option to purchase contained in a lease when the statute specifically refers to the owner of record as of July 18, 1984?

If your buyer can tie it specifically to a valid and enforceable lease agreement containing an option which was in existence prior to the enactment, then the argument is that Section 2314(c)(1) applies to exempt the lessee-purchaser because he can claim a change of ownership of assets ''pursuant to an enforceable agreement entered into before the date of the enactment of the Act.'' The rationale is that the purchase option constitutes an ''enforceable agreement'' within the meaning of section 2314(c)(1).

Chapter 8

Conventional Financing

Speaker: Alan S. Goldberg

In any transaction involving financing, an experienced attorney can soon tell whether lender's counsel wants the deal to go through or not. At that point, usually about a third of the way through the deal, everything changes--people, personalities, reactions, relationships. A nursing home deal is the easiest for lender's counsel to kill, and borrower's counsel is defenseless in that situation.

This chapter is about how to make a conventional financing arrangement for a long term care institution and what I consider good lender's counsel procedure, and how other attorneys, businesspersons, accountants, architects, and other advisors should deal with lender's counsel.

The approach I use in these deals is to draw up a very comprehensive commitment letter which may be 20-30 pages long. This approach is based on the assumption that the more people are told up front, the more they are alerted ahead of time, the more they realize what lender's counsel will be looking for, the more they understand the half-pound of documents necessary, i.e., the mortgage, the note, the loan agreement, and the security instruments, the better they will be able to prepare. Too often the contrary occurs: lender's counsel belatedly presents a ton of documents with all sorts of camouflages issues that the other side just cannot deal with effectively within the time frame allocated. The commitment letter therefore should try to set out as many of the things that borrower's counsel should prepare for, as many of the opportunities that you should take to preclose a transaction as possible.

The reason nursing home deals are among the most difficult and the easiest to find frailties in is that they involve many uncertainties as to the reimbursement system, and licensure system, certification, and so on. Most lenders that have not handled many health field-related loans are very anxious about all of this and enter these deals very tentatively.

Generally they get in because a mortgage banker or other colleague, associate, or correspondent they have been involved with has done a health deal previously. They are not quite sure what nursing homes really are, and they miss the major points and focus on the minor points more heavily, and that is what scare them. For example, they may concentrate on zoning, not realizing that a comprehensive zoning opinion like that used in a traditional financing situation is much less likely to be necessary in a nursing home transaction, given the many levels of evaluation that nursing homes have to go through for licensure and approvals. By the time a nursing home is ready to be financed, particularly if it is a refinancing, the likelihood of zoning being a problem is quite remote. Health financing deals often go bad because lender's counsel simply did not understand or would not illustrate to the people involved at the lending desk that zoning is not the critical feature.

On the other hand, lender's counsel should pay attention to the health law and regulatory aspects, where the lender really should have full protection.

As in so many transactions involving health institutions, the critical ingredient is not location, location, location, but management, management, management. Management in turn rests on the regulatory scheme and on the ability of good management to continue, and on the reimbursement efforts of management: the best managers know how to make the complex reimbursement system work for them. Occasionally when lender's counsel gets involved in these arrangements, the deal has not yet fully been struck--that is, the terms, the note interest rate, the duration of amortization, prepayment provisions, and the like have not been fully determined. Good lender's counsel stays out of the deal at that juncture. Borrower's counsel can tell whether lender's counsel is going to be a problem if there is the sense that lender's counsel is negotiating the deal. However, unsophisticated loan officer might look to counsel to help them in negotiating these business terms. Be wary if this happens, because like most lawyers, lender's counsel will be aggressive and try to carve out and cut back many of these business terms. That is generally not their role, and if they do get involved in that way, borrower's counsel may appropriately object. It is preferable to get the loan officers to negotiate their business deal first, and then give it to the lawyers. Negotiating a business deal falls outside the profession and experience of most attorneys, and most do not want to be placed in a position of losing credibility with the other side.

The arrangement described here is structured about a general partnership, not a limited partnership. Many of the deals involve limited partnerships, and the same commitment letter can be used for these as well, although there are certain differences and distinctions with regard to taxes.

RATES AND PAYMENTS

Many nursing home loans are now structured as balloon arrangements, and in fact in some cases the interest rate is targeted to float with a bond index, using any number of floating mechanisms, for example, Treasury bills. Different lenders use different mechanisms, depending as much on their regulators as their own business sense. It may be to the borrower's advantage to negotiate a ceiling on a floating rate, but lenders will want a floor if they are giving a ceiling. Again, lender's counsel is well advised to stay away from those negotiations.

Other issues involved are the reimbursement consequences in the particular state, dealing with reimbursement of interest and ability to get bases back on principal. Lender's counsel should have some understanding of those issues, so that lenders unsophisticated about the law in a given state can be told before they come in that structuring a deal in a certain way may not be feasible in that state, that it may ruin the borrower's economic viability, and that is not in the interest of the lenders. Thus, lender's counsel should also provide help at least in meeting the terms of the state reimbursement mechanism, without necessarily dictating the terms of the transaction.

PREPAYMENT AND PENALTIES

Prepayment, privileges, penalties, and the like are common and customary to most real estate transaction. There is no reason why they should not apply in long term care financing, and often they do. A rather onerous provision that may be included (and negotiated) deals with acceleration of payment in the event of occurrences over which the borrower has no control. For example, if an eminent domain procedure is threatened, or if there is a loss of some reimbursement base or other aspect of the reimbursement mechanism, a prepayment may be required. The prepayment penalty might be 0.5%, or more or less, and borrower's counsel might want to negotiate to get those provisions loosened up. They sound like force majeure situations, and prepayment penalties may be in fact unenforceable in situations in which the borrower has absolutely no control over the circumstances.

COLLATERAL

The collateral security that forms the underlying basis for a nursing home loan consists obviously of land, fixtures, and the like. Good lender's counsel will try to smoke out more. On occasion borrowers may not disclose to a lender, particularly an out-of-state lender, all the property owned in the particular area, or the opportunities that the borrower has in terms of other determinations of need or other interests in facilities, be they nursing homes or hospitals and the like. Lender's counsel should determine very early whether a given borrower has other interests in the area. In a shopping center loan one generally looks for exclusives or restrictions, and there is no reason not to do the same in a transaction involving a health facility. Do you want a competitive operation to open up across the street? Do you want to know that his borrower owns a vacant lot, next door or up the street, that has not been disclosed and is not subject to the mortgage, that would have been tremendously beneficial to the lender, if a foreclosure does not ensue? Nondisclosure is becoming more and more common, particularly as properties have greater value because of the ability to expand into their health operations. Good lender's counsel will try to uncover any such properties, and good borrower's counsel will advise the borrower that full disclosure on that score is certainly a wise thing to do to stay on good terms with the lender.

Lender's counsel should look at the application and at the appraisal. I generally do not look in detail at the plans and specifications. I do look at the financial statements, again not as a businessman, but often I find some footnote or some indication of something that makes me more sensitive and more concerned about what the documents for loan purposes should contain.

As borrower's counsel, therefore, never turn things over to the other side until you have looked at them yourself. Many borrowers turn things over immediately to the lender for evaluation without their attorney looking to these things. Even if the attorney is not going to be looking at them as a businessperson, look at those things, because the lender and the lender's counsel will as well and you want to be alerted to any potential problems.

Forethought, preplanning, and prethinking are the watchword in all of these deals--no surprises, no situations involving shakeups, but rather total credibility and the understanding that there is full disclosure. Regarding fixtures and personal property, there is a lot of equipment leasing currently for tax reasons and a lot of trusts set up for children. Even after the change in the tax laws, it is still not totally inappropriate or inadvisable to set up 10-year trusts and the like, and occasionally you will want assignments of leases. Lender's counsel should try to be understanding of the estate planning needs of borrowers and try to work out with borrower's counsel mechanisms for explaining them to the lender.

Recourse

Recourse/nonrecourse is an unfamiliar aspect of the loan transaction to many unsophisticated borrowers, and many nursing homes in the Northeast and elsewhere, not to mention the West, are still owned by the proverbial mom-and-pop operators. Borrower's counsel should be concerned about that and alert the borrowers before they apply for their loan commitment that they should be asking for nonrecourse provisions in the mortgage note. As lender's counsel again, be alert to the fact that, when the commitment letter comes out, it may not be inclusive of all the issues to be concerned about in a recourse/nonrecourse deal. In many states, as well as at the federal level, rather substantial penalties are imposed in transactions and situations involving fraud for recapture, issues involving hazardous waste, and the like, which in many states are becoming very significant. For issues involving misappropriation of funds, fraud, and abuse-- things of that nature--generally, we advise lender to try not to have nonrecourse paper, but to include some personal liability, not because you want anyone to pay, but because you make the borrower a lot more sensitive and concerned in terms of personal liability. They are less concerned, oddly enough, about being liable to the government, and more concerned about being personally liable to the lender. Lenders should sensitize unsophisticated borrowers to the fact that there may be personal liability for wrongful appropriations or other kinds of situations over which they will have substantial control and, if there is such liability, that the lender is going to seek personal liability for repayment of the loan.

When representing the borrower, however, be very careful not to ruin your tax advantage. In a limited partnership where one is trying to spread cost basis, for purposes of tax depreciation and the like, any deviation from total nonrecourse financing opens the window a crack toward the Internal Revenue Service asserting that it is a recourse deal, that the general partners have some personal liability, and then you lose your spread of basis. There are some current rulings and some current law on those issues, and one still has to be pretty careful. As long as you are dealing in these very sophisticated and unique situations, not involving direct liability from indebtedness primarily, but involving liability for repayment of certain sums on account of fraud and abuse and the like, you probably do not ruin your tax advantage. Again, however, lender's counsel should be understanding of borrower's counsel's motivations. Lender's counsel does no good by hurting the borrower's tax deal if the borrower's counsel is unsophisticated and knows nothing about the Internal Revenue Code, as, unfortunately, a number of lawyers who purport to have total expertise do not. You have accomplished nothing if you know that in that circumstance the borrower is not going to be able to repay the debt. In fact, if you help the borrower you make a friend, you make a better deal, and you do a lawyer-like thing, which is to be decent and honorable and not hide from people what is obvious to you as an expert.

CERTIFICATIONS

Certifications often create a lot of trouble in the commitment process. These are very complex issues, involving life and safety codes, state requirements, departments of public safety, and federal and state regulations. We use a form for certifications from both the bar and/or the architect and a consulting engineer. Here, in my view, you cannot be careful enough. Lender's counsel has to do everything possible to be assured of things involving structural integrity, compliance with life safety codes, and issues that might involve waivers and survivorships of waivers if there should be a foreclosure.

When there is a transfer of ownership life safety code waivers do not necessarily survive. As borrower's counsel, at least alert the lender to that and not have someone ask the question later in the process.

ZONING AND LOCAL ISSUES

Zoning and issues involving local laws, subdivision control, and the like are a real problem. There are two ways to approach it. With nursing home chains often the lenders are unconcerned about zoning and never in many deals even require zoning opinions. Being lender's counsel for a prenegotiated deal like that is obviously a delight because they do not involve reading or evaluating those opinions. On the other hand, as borrower's counsel you have a real quandary. You may not know whether or not a zoning opinion will be required, and sometimes it is not carefully set forth in the commitment letter. In a complicated state zoning scheme such as is encountered frequently in the Northeast, you can spend 3-5 weeks and $3-5,000 of legal time to come up with a zoning opinion, and then you have to take a qualification. The process tends to be easier in the West and South. On the other hand, if you do not have to present a zoning opinion, you save a lot of money. Most nursing homes are zoned properly--if anyone were going to create a problem, they would have done so already, and the period of time beyond which you cannot raise a claim has generally elapsed.

Zoning either makes or breaks a deal depending upon whether the lender is sensitive to it and whether the borrower is prepared. If a zoning opinion is a requirement, and the borrower says he or she will cause counsel to give a zoning opinion, lender's counsel must try to be helpful, and tell the other side what he or she requires.

Occasionally a borrower's attorney will sign any agreement you propose, without examining it carefully. Lender's counsel should resist the temptation to take advantage of such a situation, however, because all one gains is a claim against that attorney's malpractice insurer. They haven't researched every law and contract and every section. Every state has its variations to the basic law. One state, for example, has a specific certificate of compliance that has to be reaffirmed every 2 years and must be obtained through an inspection. Good lender's counsel will inform borrower's counsel of these provisions well in advance of the closing. Borrower's counsel should not be expected to provide total assurances for everything, and likewise lender's counsel should not request and opinion that he or she would not be prepared to sign.

Many zoning codes, particularly in the Northeast and particularly those that are 5-10 years old, will have relatively sophisticated zoning provisions dealing with nonconformity. For example, if a nursing home is built at a time when nursing homes are permitted, but the zoning bylaw is later changed, what generally happens is that the nursing home is declared to be a validly existing, nonconforming use and structure. However, if there is damage by fire or casualty, there may be an imposition of a constraint, restriction, or impossibility of rebuilding, and if you cannot rebuild, then the location may be worthless for anything except single-family housing. In such cases, lender's counsel should discuss with the other side how to get around the problem; for example, some further change in zoning may be possible, or there may be some indication that that provision is not applicable. There may be an insurance way of getting around the problem, or it may be a safety issue, such as a sprinkler in the nursing home. Take extra care to be sure there are some protective features involved. It is a matter of creativity and genuineness of intent to make the deal close.

ENVIRONMENTAL ISSUES

Matters involving environmental controls, regulations, flood hazard area, and the like should be familiar to borrower's counsel, and lender's counsel may well ask for a very sophisticated environmental law opinion. This is less common in the South and the West, but in the Northeast 20-page opinions on environmental issues are often rendered. Nursing homes are as suspect as any other activity, particularly now that many states have hazardous drug acts that require disclosures to employees and the like because of hazardous waste and dumps.

AS-BUILT SURVEY

Borrower's counsel should certainly read the survey, and be aware that astute lender's counsel will read the survey as well. Borrower's counsel should get the best certification possible on the survey, so that when it is given to lender's counsel it is a done deal and understood.

INSURANCE

Insurance is an extremely complex matter, and even insurance professionals disagree on issues involving insurance.

Attorneys are best advised to involve themselves in the insurance aspects as little as possible. Lender's counsel should have the insurance documents sent to the lender's insurance advisor, and at the closing should check to be sure the names are right but get no further involved. Insurance is not generally a legal issue unless there is a validly existing, nonconforming use issue or some other builder's risk problem involving new construction.

LICENSES, PERMITS, APPROVALS, AND REIMBURSEMENT RATES

Some commitment letters provide that if there is a change in reimbursement base, or in the reimbursement mechanism in terms of a setoff or right of recapture, the loan is automatically called. This is the toughest approach, but sometimes the lenders want it. They are concerned about the income stream, the reimbursability, the basis, the Medicaid and the public versus private census.

THE ADMINISTRATOR

The lender will want control over who the administrator is. This is tough again, what you want here is a particular kind of administration. The lender may not necessarily want approval rights over the individual, but does want to know that the management is not being furnished by some other company that may not be as astute and capable. Many lenders want the so-called mom-and-pop equity owner management, whereas some are prepared to take absentee management.

TITLE

Good borrower's counsel will initiate a title search as early as possible, or at least when the commitment letter is issued. Do not expect the lender's counsel to initiate anything. Sit down with the title examiner's representative, and sit down with the title insurance company, if you will be buying title insurance, and tell them what the nature of the transaction is, so that when they frame the commitment, it does not go from the title company directly to lender's counsel without your reviewing it. There may be an error, or there may be something that's misleading or a problem. You should be able to go through those documents and make a presentation to lender's counsel, which will always be appreciated and will make the job more efficient and easier.

LEASING

The standard commitment letter is not intended to deal with sale leaseback arrangements, but obviously it can be amended to cover such deals.

DOCUMENTATION

The commitment letter should also contain a list of documents which is specific as to the kinds of terms and conditions that they will contain, particularly the more onerous ones, in terms of what the borrower might expect. Much of the documentation tends to be fairly standard and routine.

Due-on-Sale Clause

The due-on-sale clause provides that, if the borrower sells the nursing home or hospital, or transfers interest in the partnership, loan is automatically called. There is thus no opportunity in that transaction to sell subject to the mortgage loan. Of course, the prepayment penalty may apply there, and is something borrower's counsel should explain to the borrower.

Active Participation

Many facilities are financed solely on the reputation, integrity, and evaluation of the individuals managing and owning the home--it is not the real estate appraisal that makes the deal to an astute lender. If the commitment letter does not provide some means to restrict any transfer, there is some exposure for the lender. In fact, some commitment letters include a life insurance provision, on the life of the operator. Life insurance is relatively inexpensive and is tax-deductible, but it will help both the lender and the borrower.

Medicare Receivables

There is a federal statute in the United States Code dealing with Medicare and Medicaid, that states that medicaid and Medicare receivables may not be pledged as collateral without certain special procedures being followed. In many cases, otherwise sophisticated counsel are unaware of this provision and have not qualified their enforceability opinions on the Medicare and Medicaid receivables.

Use of the Facility

An obvious provision in the commitment letter is that the facility be used as a nursing home or as a hospital, depending on what the particular facility is. If the owner ceases to use it as such, the property rally has no value, if the original appraisal was based upon a going business.

Anyone dealing in the financing of a hospital acquisition or anything involving acute care should be aware of the Hill-Burton recapture rules, and if there is any Hill-Burton recapture, determine the consequence it will have on the financial viability of their operation.

Miscellaneous Documents

As lender's counsel, be prepared to give borrower's counsel the form of opinion you'd like to get. The borrower does not always have a good form of opinion, and probably will be better able to deal with the battle of the forms if lender's counsel sends their forms first, because the lender knows what is required. Always be prepared as lender's counsel to justify why it is you want what you want, and if you cannot justify something, do not ask for it. Explain that a particular form is required for the auditing procedures of the state insurance authority or because of federal regulations or whatever the reason is.

Unions

The commitment letter may contain a provision regarding labor union involvement at the facility. Good lender's counsel is going to be very concerned about unions in health facilities.

Medicaid Census

Often lenders will try to stipulate that the facility will maintain a 30% or 50% census of private-pay patients. Many states, however, have discrimination laws involving Medicare, Medicaid, and public assistance patients. With these laws it can be very difficult to determine compliance. The best thing is to tell the lender that it might be acceptable to require a certain percentage of private-pay patients at the time of closing, but certainly you may not require in many states a continuing percentage as a condition of the loan. That may be deemed conspiratorial action or an implicit violation of the law. Even if technically the lender is not involved, in some situations the lender might be looked at askance in the community for imposing those kinds of conditions. It is very important to have private patients in a long care facility, but it is very tough to require that they be there. Lenders should have a clause put in the loan documents that gives total protection against discrimination claims, both federal and state.

Medicare and Veterans Administration contracts are often involved. Lender's counsel should look at the provider agreement, the last certification survey, and the deficiency sheets, and should call the Department of Public Health to find out if there are any patient abuse allegations. Borrower's counsel should do the same, but sooner, so that if any issues are raised, you can respond and deal with them.

CONCLUSIONS

In summary, the keys to a successful financing arrangement are preplanning, not being unreasonable--not asking for things that you would not give yourself, acting cooperatively and not surprising people, and establishing your creditability early on as someone trying to make the deal succeed.

In some states, they don't issue some of the licensing documents until after the closing etc., etc. As lender's counsel, you understand that and if it's brought to your attention, obviously you can't ignore it.

Good point. I will see commitment letters and loan documents often say the facility must be licensed as a long term care facility in the name of the new owner before closing. In some states, it's impossible--you can't do it. Why put it in there? Why make people look foolish, if you know it can't happen? In some states, to the contrary, what happens is, on the date of the closing, you apply for a license and that results in automatic licensure for a period of time. That's what lender's counsel should say: "On the closing date you shall apply for the license." We'll look at the license or package, and then I ask for the opinion from the borrower that, if this package is filed, if the documents are proper, if the normal procedures occur, borrower knows of no reason why the license shouldn't issue in ordinary course. Nothing unreasonable there, but you're right, often you cannot get instant certification. It's impossible generally to get certification as of the day of closing. What do you get? You get a no-felony certificate as I've indicated here. Many states are looking much more carefully at suitability. Many states now will come in, totally without any reason, and investigate and find if someone has a felony conviction or whatever it is, they're going to pull their license. So what you do is get a due-diligence certificate originally that says, "I have not been convicted of a felony." Sounds silly, doesn't it? Just your luck, again I had a deal like that. The guy was convicted of a felony and we couldn't do the deal because they were unsuitable, but no one told anybody because it was never inquired into due-diligencewise. So the answer to your question is, by all means, if it's impossible to be done as lender's counsel, don't ask for it. If you're borrower's counsel, prepare to deal with it with an alternative suggestion, because lender's counsel may not have done a nursing home deal before and may not know what certification is. Believe it or not.

We got a one-and-a-quarter-page commitment letter from a major western commercial bank, and when it came down to the documents they were very surprised and had more to be discussed. Under those conditions, what is your position in terms of the commitment being made?

The only time I've had that come up is before the commitment fee went down. I'll even show them the draft of the commitment letter before they give up the money, and before they sign it. Again, I don't want to take anybody's money under false pretenses. So I generally don't get into that problem. But in that issue, in shopping center or commercial deals you have a real problem, because there is good law establishing the propriety of a lender keeping a commitment fee, assuming it is not a penalty or a forfeiture, and you have to deal with those issues. But I've seen those issues taken to court. I think we may have done one ourselves, as a matter of fact, and you can win, representing the lender. It's awfully tough to fight those deals, and frankly, again, for a borrower the problem is, do you want your borrower to get a reputation for suing First Bank & Trust Company, which is one of the three major banks in the city. Tough issue. Well, okay, there may be a reason for doing it.

We negotiated for no personal liability and then the documents came up in full recourse.

I guess there you're asking me something different--you might have the misrepresentation issue. Remember, verbal representations of attorneys can often form the basis for an excellent action, which name I won't describe, but I think in your situation, frankly, it sounds like you may have good cause of action. Remember, in many states, a lot of people don't realize that these are applicable--again, another hopefully worth the price of admission--consumer protection acts. That doesn't sound like a lending transaction, does it? It does; in some states there are unfair and deceptive trade practices acts, and you haul off with a complaint and I don't know whether your state has it or not. The treble damages and attorney's fees under unfair and deceptive practices rendering a commitment letter that's misleading and having a representation that's inaccurate, boy, you're going to get their attention and they may well say, "Hey, we don't want this contingent liability on our books--we'll give it to you back." See, as long as the lawyer's fee is paid, as long as the time and effort and overhead of the institution is paid, an astute institution, they're going to give the money back in most cases. If they don't, then there may be something going on here you don't fully understand and no one's prepared to tell you. I'm a little surprised. It sounds like rather sharp practice. Good lenders aren't in the business of taking commitment fees and not making deals. I mean, again, you get an early sense in many deals that the lender is pushing the money out the window.

Chapter 9

Contract Arrangements

Speaker: Michael H. Cook

There have previously been certain limits placed upon hospitals and upon costs that public programs would cover, yet essentially hospitals were encouraged to provide more and more care for each day and to keep the patient in the acute care setting for as long a period as it was medically appropriate to do so. However, in April of 1983, Congress dramatically altered the method by which hospitals would be reimbursed for in-patient care. Instead of paying whatever costs a hospital incurred in caring for the patient, Congress established in advance a price that the government would pay for Medicare patients, irrespective of the costs of caring for those patients. Now there are some exceptions to that--extremely long term stays and extremely costly stays which are known as outliers--but essentially hospitals receive a fixed price dependent upon the patient's principal diagnosis upon admission to the hospital. This system became effective with each hospital's cost reporting period beginning October 1, 1983.

In addition to providing a tremendous incentive to hospitals to upgrade the qualifications of the medical records staffs, it also provides a significant incentive to hospitals to eliminate unnecessary stays and to discharge patients at the earliest point in time that their medical condition allows. There has been a substantial degree of speculation in the health care industry, that the advent of this prospective payment system may result in greater competition between hospitals and long term care facilities, as hospitals look for alternative placements for their patients by either acquiring or building long term care facilities, or converting acute care beds in the hospitals to long term care beds.

But there's also been a substantial degree of speculation that long term care facilities presently in existence will be the beneficiaries of the prospective payment system; because now hospitals that wish to place their primary emphasis on doing what they do best--namely, providing acute care services--are going to have an economic incentive to discharge their patients and transfer them to long term care facilities as soon as it is possible to do so. This speculation is so prevalent that the General Accounting Office has initiated a study on post-

127

hospital, skilled nursing facility, and home-health agency care, and the effects of PPS on this care in six cities across the United States.

The pressure on the hospitals to discharge patients early is likely to increase rather than decrease, as the prospective payment system is phased in over a three year period. Essentially at the beginning of the system, a hospital receives a blend of its own hospital-specific costs trended forward, and the regional and national average rates for caring for a particular type of patient. In the beginning of the program, the blend is weighted heavily towards the hospital's own historic costs, whereas at the end of the three year period, it's weighted more towards the average regional and federal rate for caring for a particular patient. By 1987, most hospitals in this country are going to be receiving the average national rate for caring for a particular case.

Also, although the system is supposed to be budget-neutral--meaning that overall federal outlays are supposed to be the same at least during the three year transition period as they would have been if there had been no prospective payment system enacted--because of the budget deficit, it appears at least to many people in the industry that the Department of Health and Human Services is using, shall we say, creative actuarial figures to ratchet down on the prices that they're paying hospitals under the DRG system. So even if you haven't heard from your hospitals yet that they feel economic pressures to lower their lengths of stay, I guarantee you that in the future, you will be hearing that. I'd like to discuss today several of the opportunities that the PPS system creates for cooperative action between your facilities and hospitals.

The outline that I've prepared refers to two generic types of arrangements that provide incentives to long term care facilities to accept hospital patients. I'll spend the bulk of my time discussing these arrangements. I'd also like to discuss a couple of joint-venture type arrangements that seem to make a great deal of economic sense and that probably haven't been discussed much if at all.

INCENTIVE/TRANSFER ARRANGEMENTS--BONUS PAYMENT AND BED RESERVE AGREEMENTS

Incentive or transfer arrangements are novel, and you should be aware that the government entities that regulate the Medicare and Medicaid programs are not terribly conversant in these agreements. The United States Department of Health and Human Services is giving us some answers slowly, but nevertheless, there are still going to be questions that haven't been answered to date. Therefore it is incumbent upon us to make our clients aware of the legal risks involved in each of these agreements.

In addition, because of the different laws in each state, you will find that many state Medicaid agencies aren't aware of these agreements yet, and you're probably going to have to wait for some time before you're going to know for a fact, how the Medicaid agencies are going to treat these agreements. Because of the permutations, you're likely to find that no one boiler plate contract is going to be able to cover every situation, and that the way that you structure these contracts can make a difference as to the legal and economic viability of the arrangements.

The two most prevalent types of agreements being discussed are what are referred to as the bonus payment concept and the bed reserve agreement. The bonus payment is a payment that is targeted to specific patients that the long term care facility accepts. An example of a very simple bonus payment arrangement would be a hospital's agreeing to pay a long term care facility $10 a day for each patient that the long term care facility accepts. A hospital may calculate that its marginal costs are $30 a day for caring for that patient, so it may be economically viable for the hospital to enter into such an arrangement.

The bed reserve arrangement is one in which the long term care facility agrees to reserve a certain number of beds for hospital patients for an established payment. A simple arrangement of this type would be one in which a long term care facility agreed to reserve ten of its beds for the exclusive use of hospital patients for $3,000 a month. The hospital would make this payment irrespective of whether the beds were utilized.

There are a number of permutations to these agreements. For example, the payment by the hospital could either be monetary or in-kind. Perhaps the hospital might agree to provide for long term care facility patients, radiology and pharmacy services, laboratory services--either free or for a discount--or training for the long term care facility's nursing staff.

PRINCIPAL LEGAL QUESTIONS

The most significant legal questions that are raised by these arrangements result from two provisions of the Social Security Act that, under certain circumstances, prohibit providers of services to Medicare and Medicaid beneficiaries from receiving payment for services from anyone other than the public programs. The most troublesome section is Section 1909(d) of the Medicaid Act. The provision is referred to as the Anti-Supplementation Provision and is part of the Anti-Fraud and Abuse Amendments of 1977. Section 1909(d) makes it a crime to charge for any services provided to a patient under the state Medicaid plan, money or other consideration at a rate in excess of the state Medicaid payment level; or to charge, solicit, accept, or receive--in addition to the state payment rate--any gift, money, donation, or other consideration, other than philanthropic donations, as a precondition for the admission of a Medicaid patient or as a requirement for the patient's continued stay.

A violation of this provision is a felony that carries penalties of up to a $25,000 fine or five years' imprisonment for each violation. The statute obviously was enacted to prohibit your clients from charging a family, a friend, or the patients themselves, a fee for services or a fee for admission or the right to stay in your facility. Since the prospective payment system was not even a glimmer in anyone's eye in 1977, it's almost certain that no one in Congress ever imagined that an independent entity such as a hospital would have an economic incentive to pay for the care for Medicaid patients. Nevertheless, the words of the statute are broad and you've got to be very careful if the patient transferred under this agreement is or could become a Medicaid patient, not to run afoul of this provision. You've got to structure the agreement so that the incentive payment does not look like it's a payment for services.

Your task in determining how to draft this agreement is complicated somewhat, because the Inspector General's Office of the U.S. Department of Health and Human Services--the arm of HHS that recommends prosecution under Section 1909(d)--doesn't issue legal opinions on this provision. The reason for not doing so--at least the public reason--is that they're concerned that they can't bind the agency that actually does the prosecution, the Justice Department, by their advice. Also, they are concerned that they'll render a legal opinion with only limited facts, then discover that someone will try and bind them to that opinion in a case where there are other facts that they weren't aware of. Nonetheless, we've gotten informal opinions from the Inspector General's Office staff that in their mind, you can draft a pure bed reserve agreement that will not violate the provisions of Section 1909(d), while they believe that it would be very difficult to construct a bonus payment arrangement, where the payment is targeted to the admission of a specific patient, that would not violate Section 1909(d). But again I caution you that this advice is non-binding.

Written advice from HHS regarding the application of another provision that governs payment of services for Medicare patients, gives you a little more comfort in both areas. Section 1866(a) of the Medicare Act, and also your Medicare Provider Agreements, prohibit Medicare providers such as hospitals from charging anyone other than the Medicare program for services provided to Medicare beneficiaries.

There are, however, certain exceptions to this prohibition; for example, coinsurance, deductibles, and services that aren't covered by the Medicare program. But by and large, your clients aren't allowed to charge anyone other than the Medicare program, for services to Medicare beneficiaries that are covered under the program.

Nevertheless, the statute is broadly worded and if you run afoul of the statute, your Medicare provider agreement can be cancelled by the Secretary. So draft these contracts to eliminate or minimize any possibility that you're going to violate the agreement.

Because of the potential impact here, as long ago as February of 1984, industry representatives wrote HHS seeking advice generally on whether the bonus payment concept or bed reserve agreement would violate this provision. Acting with all deliberate speed, HHS provided the industry some answers in July and September of 1984.

HCFA basically stated in a letter that Section 1866 and Medicare provider agreements prohibit bonus payment arrangements but that these agreements do not prohibit bed reserve agreements. Essentially HCFA makes the distinction because it construes Section 1866 to prohibit hospital payments that are related to the provision of services to specific patients. HCFA views the bonus payment arrangement to be a payment for patient services because again, the receipt of the payment is conditioned upon either the admission or provision of services to a particular patient. On the other hand, HCFA views the bed reserve agreement as not being a payment for services in general because the payment under the arrangement is made irrespective of whether services are provided and irrespective of whether the bed is occupied. Most HCFA staff will refer to this distinction as "patient specific" and "non-patient specific" payments under the agreement.

This advice provides you comfort in two areas. First of all, it obviously gives you some comfort in the absence of contrary instructions from HCFA with respect to the application of Section 1866. You can draft a bed reserve agreement since it passes muster under that provision. Secondly, it gives you some comfort under Section 1909(d). Sections 1866 and 1909(d) place similar, albeit not identical, restrictions on providers with respect to receipt of payments for the Medicare and the Medicaid programs. Although the language and the penalties under the two sections aren't identical, and although different agencies enforce those provisions, I think it would be unlikely that Section 1909(d) could be enforced successfully in a manner that differs from the Health Care Financing Administration's construction of Section 1866. But again, because the Inspector General doesn't issue binding opinions and because it's the Justice Department that prosecutes violations of Section 1909(d), there will always be some risk that either the IG or an overly aggressive Assistant U.S. Attorney may attempt to prosecute your clients under Section 1909(d), even for a bed reserve agreement. At least you've got to be aware of the possibility, as unlikely as it may be.

You should also be aware that there are probably similar restrictions to the Medicare provider agreement restrictions in your Medicaid provider agreements. States enforce those agreements so you probably ought to clear with your state Medicaid agency again whether a bed reserve agreement violates Medicaid provider agreements. You will probably find that the state Medicaid agency will interpret its provider agreement very similarly to the way HCFA interprets Section 1866.

A third legal issue, and the one that hasn't been resolved conclusively to date, is the manner in which the Medicare program will treat the payments that the hospital makes to the long term care facility. This centers upon the issue of whether the payment is considered to be patient-care related, and affects the economics but not the legal viability of the agreement.

The issue is largely irrelevant to hospitals since those that are reimbursed under the prospective payment system are going to receive a set price for the care that they provide, irrespective of whether they make this payment to your clients or not. And those hospitals that aren't under PPS aren't going to have any incentive to enter into these arrangements.

On the other hand, long term care facilities are reimbursed under Medicare on a reasonable cost basis. If Medicare treats these payments as patient care related, the program may offset against your Medicare payments, all or a substantial amount of what you're paid under the bed reserve agreement. This means that you could lose a substantial portion of any benefit that you get under these agreements. The issue is under serious debate at HCFA. Although the agency is considering issuing written instructions on the matter, these instructions have not been formally issued to date. We understand that the agency is leaning toward not offsetting the revenue that you receive under these bed reserve agreements, nevertheless it's still an open issue until or unless instructions come out.

The arguments are basically these. For bed reserve arrangements, the arrangement could be characterized as an independent, non-patient care related venture in which the long term care facility accepts the risk of insuring that a bed will be available for hospital patients. If you view the transaction in this manner, it could be viewed as any other non-patient care related activity such as for example, when a hospital owns a McDonalds or a medical office building; traditionally the Medicare program has neither shared in the profits nor the losses of these non-patient care related ventures.

Alternatively, there are certain types of activities that aren't directly related to patient care under which the program does offset revenues for the activity against what are called allowable costs. An example of such a situation is where the hospital operates a parking lot. Under the cost reimbursement system, Medicare reimburses the costs of operating and/or owning a parking lot, and offsets against those costs any revenues that the hospital takes in by either charging staff or by charging visitors or patients who park in the area. They are, in essence, looking for the true costs. So if Medicare were to consider these types of arrangements to be essentially standby costs of providing patient care, then you could construct an argument that the bed reserve payments should be used to reduce the otherwise allowable costs.

Frankly, I think that as a matter of policy, it would be ludicrous for HCFA to offset revenues received under these arrangements. From the hospital standpoint, the program is structuring its reimbursement system to encourage hospitals to discharge patients at the earliest moment and to place them in the least acute care oriented setting possible, and yet they'd essentially be drying up one of the areas and one of the avenues under which the hospitals could transfer patients. From the viewpoint of the long term care facility, the Health Care Financing Administration would be drying up one non-governmental related source of revenues to the facility that could be used to offset the costs of caring for heavier care patients that you're likely to see under these transfer arrangements, and also to compensate for what usually is a substandard rate that the facility receives under the Medicaid program. But again, I caution you that although we understand that HCFA is leaning in the direction of not offsetting these revenues, no official policy has been issued yet.

You should also try to ascertain how your particular state Medicaid agencies are going to treat these payments. Most likely they're going to follow whatever HCFA does. But check with the agency, especially if you've got a high Medicaid patient load and therefore could have a high percentage of these costs offset against your Medicaid reimbursement.

Regarding the bonus payment arrangements, it seems that even if HCFA reverses its position and allows these types of arrangements--something I doubt that you'll see--nevertheless you'd probably encounter a revenue offset under that situation.

OTHER LEGAL QUESTIONS

I've also listed in the outline a number of other federal and state statutory and regulatory provisions that could affect whether your client enters into one of these agreements, and also how you structure the agreement. A few states have enacted statutes that preclude long term care facilities from discriminating against patients that they accept by source of patients--basically known as "first come, first serve" statutes. Also states and the federal government have enacted statutes that prohibit anti-competitive behavior. Additionally, the Medicaid Act, and implementing regulations, place prohibitions on the limiting of providers from whom a recipient may receive services. These are known as freedom-of-choice provisions.

Federal regulations also provide for the termination of a Medicare provider agreement if the facility places restrictions upon the admission of a Medicare patient that it doesn't place upon all other patients. Federal criminal provisions also preclude facilities from offering or receiving remuneration in return for the referral of Medicare and Medicaid patients.

Finally, there are risk management considerations if a long term care facility accepts, pursuant to a bed reserve agreement, patients that it couldn't otherwise care for.

Now other than for those of you whose clients' facilities are in states that have enacted "first come, first serve" statutes, I don't think you're going to have any real difficulty with these other provisions. They shouldn't be deal busters but you should be aware of them and you should structure the agreement to avoid running afoul of the provisions.

LEGAL VIABILITY

So what does that tell you about the legal viability of these agreements? First, they're novel and some of the questions haven't been answered yet. Secondly, it appears that you can probably draft a bed reserve agreement that will be legally a viable agreement, and you're probably going to run into trouble if you draft a bonus payment agreement. But how do you tell whether a particular type of arrangement is a bed reserve agreement or a bonus payment?

The staff with whom we've spoken at HCFA and the General Counsel's Office used the words "patient-specific" and "not-patient specific." If a given payment is triggered by the placement of a specific patient in a facility, I think there's a strong possibility that HCFA will look at that agreement as a bonus payment arrangement. On the other hand, if the payment will be made irrespective of whether a patient is placed in the facility, then I don't think you're going to have any trouble. HCFA also considers in-kind payments to be payments that at least trigger provider agreement considerations.

To give you a feel for how this can be applied and also for understanding the agency's train of thought, I've included in the outline several hypotheticals. These hypotheticals were presented to HCFA in correspondence, and while they haven't been answered officially yet, we've gotten some informal answers and I think this is what HCFA is going to be settling on. Again, think in terms of patient-specific.

The first hypothetical is where the hospital reserves ten long term care facility beds for the exclusive use of hospital-discharged patients, and the long term care facility receives $75 for each day in which one of these reserve beds is vacant. The payment stops when a patient enters the bed. It appears that HCFA will not consider this type of payment to violate the Medicare provider agreement because there are no payments being made whatsoever when there's a Medicare patient, or any other patient, in the bed.

The second hypothetical is the hospital reserving ten long term care facility beds for the exclusive use of hospital-discharged patients, again, at $75 a day when the beds are vacant. But when the beds are filled, the hospital will pay the difference between the third party payment rate and the private pay rate. HCFA tentatively considers this to be a violation of the Medicare provider agreement because you're using a different standard of payment that gets triggered when a patient enters the bed. So they consider that differential between the private pay rate and the third party rate to be a payment for services.

The third hypothetical is where the hospital reserves ten long term care facility beds for hospital-discharged patients. The hospital provides one full-time registered nurse at any time when there's a hospital patient in one of these beds. HCFA would consider this also to be a violation of your Medicare provider agreement because the payment triggered when a hospital patient enters the facility.

Now you take that same situation except that the hospital provides a full-time registered nurse irrespective of whether there's a hospital-transferred patient in the bed. HCFA would *not* consider that to be a violation of the Medicare provider agreement.

The next hypothetical is where the long term care facility agrees to provide the hospital priority consideration for admission to up to five beds. The hospital provides laboratory and radiology services to all of the facility's patients and also provides a 30% discount for pharmacy services. Again, HCFA doesn't consider this to be a violation of the Medicare provider agreement because it's not related to whether a patient is in the bed. It's not related to a specific patient. However, on an agreement like this, you've got to be very careful about how the hospital and the long term care facility designate those payments on their cost reports. You've also got to look closely at the illegal remuneration provisions of Section 1877 of the Medicare Act.

The fifth hypothetical is where the long term care facility agrees to provide a hospital priority admission for complicated care patients. The hospital provides free in-service education programs for the long term care facility staff. Again, no violation exists because the in-service education is provided whether or not there are hospital patients in the facility.

Finally, the hospital reserves a number of beds for the exclusive use of the provider for a specific payment, and there's no difference in payment whether the beds are utilized or not. Again, that would not be a violation of the provider agreement.

As I mentioned, careful drafting of bed reserve arrangements can also minimize concerns in the non-third party arena. As an example, to minimize risk management concerns, the parties may wish to specify as clearly as possible in the agreement the types of patients who can be admitted to the facility, and those who cannot, by the type of severity of condition. Or you may wish instead to provide the long term care facility with the right to refuse to accept any patients that it doesn't believe it can care for medically, or for whom it cannot provide psycho-social care that's necessary.

The agreement should specify who has the right to decide when the patient can be discharged from the facility, or when the patient can be transferred back to the hospital if necessary. I'd suggest to you that it makes good sense to reserve this right for the long term care facility, and I'd suggest that you ought to spell it out in the contract.

Also, the parties to any reserve agreement should consider spelling out in the agreement, the point at which the patient--who is admitted under such an agreement--no longer occupies a reserved bed. For example, suppose a patient enters your facility under one of these arrangements and stays for a year. How long is that patient to be considered to occupy one of the reserved beds? Is it the first ten days or is it for the whole year's stay? Again, you may want to spell this out in the contract so that you don't have future disputes.

The parties should also consider specifying what constitutes an available bed. Does that mean that the long term care facility can't utilize that bed for anyone at any time other than a hospital patient, or does it mean that the hospital simply reserves the right to transfer up to 10 of its patients--or a specified number of its patients--to the long term care facility by giving the facility a certain number of hours or days advanced notice. If you enter into the latter type of agreement, what's the penalty if you can't make the bed available? Again, you may want to specify this in the contract to avoid future disputes.

Obviously, the most critical element is the compensation. I think that you'll find for these agreements to be viable, they've got to benefit both the hospital and the long term care facility. Most importantly, your clients should have a firm grasp on what the client needs to make this contract viable. Don't do it because it's a fad; do it because it's going to be good for you; because you're going to get some money out of it.

You should also spell out in the contract that it is not a contract for services, but rather a contract for the risk of being able to provide an available bed. Also, specify in the contract that the long term care facility has the right to bill third parties. You want to do whatever you can to make sure that this agreement does not look like a payment for services, and that's one way of doing it.

Another primary concern affecting compensation is whether the hospital will share in the cost of caring for transferred patients who either become indigent or have no source of payment, or for whom the third party retroactively decides not to make payment. Many of you may have had clients who complained that Medicare fiscal intermediaries deny coverage of services on a retroactive basis for reasons that don't seem to make any sense whatsoever. This has become much worse in the last two years since the intermediaries have received instructions from HCFA to make coverage determinations "more accurately."

Under what are referred to as "Waiver of Liability Provisions," your client may have no recourse against the patient whatsoever and your provider agreements may prohibit your client from receiving payment from anyone for this patient. In determining the compensation, you can probably structure compensation for these denials into the agreement by determining how much have you lost in the past on an average from retroactive coverage denials, and building it into your rate.

You may also wish to place in the contract provisions for some kind of sharing by the hospital and the facility for retroactive coverage denials where it's permissible to charge someone else, or for patients who become indigent with no patient payment source whatsoever.

The agreement should also obviously specify the term during which it is in operation and the circumstances, if any, under which it can be terminated. Since the agreement should be one that benefits both parties, and since it's one on which you're going to have to work cooperatively, I'd suggest that you may want to simply place in the contract a provision that the contract can be terminated for any reason with 30 or 60 days' notice.

That does not cover every provision that you ought to include in a contract, nor have I answered every legal question that will arise for every contract whatsoever. But I hope I've left you with the thought that the advent of the prospective reimbursement system does provide possibilities for arrangements that would allow the infusion of capital from non-governmental sources into your facilities, and also that these arrangements could be economically beneficial to the facilities.

PURCHASING/LEASING OF VACANT HOSPITAL WINGS

There are also several types of arrangements that have not been discussed prevalently, but that I believe make a substantial amount of economic sense. It may be possible for companies that operate long term care facilities to purchase or lease vacant wings of hospitals, or manage vacant hospital wings that are converted into long term care beds from hospital beds. This may be done under a strict management contract or under a joint venture.

Initially, it would seem that hospitals would be totally unreceptive to this idea. Yet hospital occupancy rates are declining dramatically across the country, because of the incentives of the prospective payment system and also because of the emergence of outpatient surgery centers that eliminate less complicated surgical cases from the hospital setting. In some areas it's not unusual to find hospitals running 40% and 50% occupancy. While at this time some of these hospitals can still remain economically viable with those occupancy rates, if the occupancy rates continue to decrease, the economic viability of these institutions is unlikely to continue. Also, the budget deficit is causing HCFA and Congress to reevaluate their present posture of paying for vacant bed space.

Right now the Health Care Financing Administration is looking at the possibility of adding to the DRG rate a 6.2% adjustment to cover interest and depreciation. This means that in the future, hospitals may not be reimbursed for vacant bed space whatsoever. In a number of states, Medicaid also reimburses hospitals on a fixed per diem that is based on a prior year's rate trended forward for inflation. In these states, fixed costs were determined for a patient day based on a time period when those costs were spread over more patients. As the occupancy rate declines, and it's declining for Medicare, Medicaid, and private pay patients, these fixed costs are not being fully reimbursed under the Medicaid program because they're being spread out over fewer and fewer patient days. This means that if hospitals in your states haven't felt the pressure yet, they will feel the pressure shortly to get rid of some of this vacant bed space.

The topic of conversation with virtually every hospital administrator that you speak to turns almost immediately, or at least at some point, to the decline in occupancy and to the expected further decline in occupancy. On the other hand, you hear daily about the graying of America, especially as the baby boom generation gets older, and you hear about the need for more long term care beds. Now it seems to me that it's going to be more economically viable to use existing vacant space than to construct new beds.

In terms of a sale or a lease of a wing from a hospital, you're probably not going to run into the same problems that the freeze on re-evaluation of assets has created for the purchase of existing long term care facilities, because hospitals are going to need to get revenue to cover their fixed costs of maintaining presently vacant space--the interest and the depreciation. They're not going to need to make a profit on that space.

The next question logically will be why won't hospitals simply start their own long term care facility? Some may, but I suspect that if you're persistent at approaching hospitals, and if you're patient in explaining to them what it takes to run a long term care facility, they'll discover that your client can operate these facilities more economically than can the hospitals. Also, the hospitals will discover that the care is quite different from the type of care that they're used to providing. You're used to running your facilities by economizing on a very micro-economic basis--essentially, looking at each and every purchase. Although hospital personnel are operating their facilities more efficiently, they are not used to running facilities on the same micro-economic level.

Additionally, they're not used to providing psycho-social services to patients. They're used to the more acutely ill patient and the medical model of care. This isn't to say that your clients are going to be able to convince your local hospitals to convert acute care beds into long term care beds tomorrow, or to bring your clients into the operation of conversions of space that the hospitals continue to own. You've still got some hospital boards that believe that the 50-70% utilization that they're experiencing is going to turn around tomorrow. In another year they're not going to believe that.

When you're talking about non-profit hospital boards, there's also a certain reluctance to turn over the control of the operation of any part of the facility to an outside group. If there is a possibility of tax-paying entities operating the long term care portion of the facility, there's even a greater reticence. In addition, many hospital personnel are not aware of the maturing of the long term care industry in the past ten or fifteen years.

Issues such as certificate of need issues also need to be addressed if you're going to convert beds, but it is likely that you will find at least some receptiveness to that idea from your state health planning officials. These folks are bureaucrats; they are judged on statistics, and I suspect they'd be happy in many instances to make a trade-off of getting rid of excessive hospital beds in an area in return for the conversion to long term care beds. They'd be killing, in essence, two birds with one stone as long as there are long term care beds in the inventory that need to be parcelled out. If nothing else, I suspect you'll get preferential treatment.

Also, many non-profit hospitals have bond financing and you will need to determine whether it is possible and how to get permission to enter into one of these arrangements. However, the bond trustees often have some flexibility, and if it would be economically profitable to the facility, there's at least a decent chance you can convince a bond trustee to allow the conversion.

You're also going to have to watch out if you joint venture with a non-profit hospital for the possibility that you'll endanger the 501(c)(3) status of the facility. Again, you'll have to structure the transaction carefully, but this concern shouldn't be a deal buster; and you'll also have to watch out for anti-remuneration provisions of Sections 1877 and 1909 if you're going to joint venture with a hospital in this area.

Despite these potential obstacles, I think it will be possible to structure workable agreements wherein you can assist hospitals in utilizing this excess bed space, or where you can purchase that space from them. I think your clients should consider approaching hospitals and beginning a dialogue in this area. While you may encounter resistance today, George Washington University has solicited from proprietary hospital corporations bids to purchase its hospital. The same marketplace considerations that led George Washington University to turn to the private market for capital also provide incentives for other hospitals to turn to long term care companies to help them utilize their vacant bed space.

> *There is a lot of upset in the nursing home industry regarding the swing bed conversion problem, particularly in a small community. Are you suggesting, instead of "fight 'em, join 'em"?*

Yes.

> *Even in the case of some of the facilities that are already converted?*

I don't think it's a bad idea whatsoever. I think it makes a lot of sense. You've got a lot of excess bed space out there, and I think that many hospitals can't run these facilities, or don't want to run these facilities.

Chapter 10

Commercial Insurance for Home Care and Nursing Home Care

Speaker: Mary H. Michal

My interest in commercial insurance started a number of years ago with a public interest law firm which specialized in issues affecting the elderly and disabled. Principally I was working on Medicare and Medicaid as they relate to private insurance, and found many problems in the long term care area, both in terms of consumer understanding and the lack of products to choose from. That led me to the Insurance Commissioner's office where I spent a number of years as a regulator, looking at the same issues from a different perspective. Now I'm in private practice, still working on some of the public policy issues that affect how we can establish a financing mechanism that's going to address the problems of long term care which we're seeing increasingly as our elderly population grows.

Last fall, U.S. Senate Committee on Aging held a special hearing entitled "The cost of caring for the chronically ill--the case for insurance." This was a very elementary first step; those people who testified at the hearing and submitted statements all said essentially the same thing: there's a problem and we want to work on it. Nobody had any really substantive solutions to offer.

OVERVIEW OF LONG TERM CARE

What is long term care? We have to start with the premise that long term care is not just nursing home care, but that it covers the whole range of basic living services including meals, chores, transportation, and personal care such as bathing, eating, and dressing. In terms of how many Americans need long term care, the figures are startling: it is estimated that almost 1 in 4 of the 28.8 million older Americans will need either nursing home or substantial home care. In terms of cost, it is sufficient to say that long term care is extremely expensive and out of the reach of most elderly people, which leads to the question: What kind of coverage is now available?

We know that Medicaid, while it does cover a big chunk of long term care, is needs-based and problematical from that perspective; that Medicare, since it is tied almost exclusively to acute and post-acute care, doesn't begin to consider this issue. Medicare supplement, because it's tied into the Medicare program so significantly, also doesn't offer much. Only 50,000 individuals throughout the country are currently covered by individual long term care policies, and these policies mostly cover nursing home care. There are many nursing home policies on the market, but they don't begin to cover the full costs of nursing home care. They do provide some kind of indemnity benefit, but it is usually very limited in scope.

Home health care, while it is more extensive than the nursing home benefit under Medicare, is problematical too, because it requires that the individual be home-bound. That creates a disincentive to getting necessary support services for those individuals who are not necessarily home-bound, but who may need some assistance in maintaining themselves in the home. Some of the major exclusions in both Part A and B of Medicare for home health care are drugs and biologicals, Meals On Wheels, housekeeping services, transportation required to take the housebound individual to the hospital and so on. All those things that are non-medical in nature, that don't fit nicely into the insurance model, are excluded under Medicare.

Medicaid is for the very poor. In addition there is a tendency nationwide to cut back on covered services under Medicaid. With the federal prohibitions against divestment, those individuals who might have qualified in the past for Medicaid are increasingly going to be turning to private funding mechanisms. The challenge is to meet that need for people who don't qualify for Medicaid or who aren't getting the assistance they need under the Medicare program and Medicare supplement policies, and the situation is exacerbated by the fact that now divestment is not nearly so much of an option as it used to be in the past.

PRIVATE INSURANCE AND MEDICARE

That brings us to the question of private insurance and Medicare supplement policies. Medicare supplement coverage is governed by minimum standards set forth in Public Law 96-265, which is normally referred to as the Baucus Amendment. Before its enactment, there were many policies on the market that were being sold under false pretenses, that didn't cover the kind of things they said they covered, and that were being called Medicare supplement policies when their benefits may have been extremely minimal. As an effort to counteract some of these consumer protection problems, the federal government enacted the Baucus amendment, which in essence sets minimum standards and gives the states the opportunity to set their own minimum standards. If the states failed to act, then the federal government would move in and set up a panel system, where they would evaluate each policy sold in any particular state that didn't have minimum standards and basically give it a "Good Housekeeping Seal of Approval."

In almost all cases the states elected to act on their own, feeling that federal intervention in this area was not the best route to take. Consequently, most states now have minimum standards for Medicare supplement policies. However, these standards do not relate very much to benefit levels; rather, they relate more to disclosure, to loss ratios in the particular policies, to duplication of benefits, and to prohibitions. They don't address very clearly the issue of what has to go into a Medicare supplement. The federal standards allow the insurance company to tie benefits in with Medicare, so that companies are still not required to provide meaningful compensation for long term care.

NAIC

To their credit, the National Association of Insurance Commissioners (NAIC) promulgated the Minimum Standards Model Act which a number of states have adopted in one form or another. The National Association of Insurance Commissioners is a voluntary organization of all of the state's insurance regulators, who meet quarterly to form task forces which deal with various aspects on insurance regulation.

The NAIC model regulation contains a definition for convalescent nursing home, extended care facility or skilled nursing facility which says that a definition of such a home or facility shall not be more restrictive than one requiring that it (a) be operated pursuant to law, and (b) be approved for payment of Medicare benefits or *be qualified to receive such approval*. This is significant because in those states which have adopted this model regulation, Medicare supplement may not tie itself solely to a Medicare certified facility.

It is important though, to look at the specific policy provisions also. First of all, if the definition is tied into Medicare there may be a violation under that state's insurance regulations. If the definition is not tied in with Medicare, then what is it, and is it consistent with actual claims administration?

Other than that provision regarding the definition of the facility, the model regulation isn't really that helpful. The rest of the requirements are that the facility primarily be engaged in providing skilled nursing care, be under the supervision of a duly licensed physician, provide continuous 24-hour a day nursing service under the supervision of an RN, and maintain a daily medical record for each patient. But the provision in the model regulation goes on to say that the definition of such a facility need not include any home used primarily for rest, any home which is for the care of drug addicts or alcoholics, or a home which is used primarily for the care and treatment of mental diseases or disorders, or custodial or educational care. Neither the federal Baucus Amendment nor the NAIC model offer any real assurance that long term care is going to be covered, except for that one provision which seems to say that if the home is not Medicare certified, but could become Medicare certified, then that should be acceptable in terms of a definition of a skilled nursing facility. While many of these policies do offer extended benefits beyond 100 days, there's little actual coverage, given skilled care limitations.

STATE MANDATES

State mandates are another issue. In Wisconsin for instance, there is a mandate that any time a person is in a hospital, the policy must provide 30 days of post-hospital skilled nursing care. It's a much less stringent definition than Medicare's and it does provide an additional benefit which is not only available under Medicare supplement policies, but under any disability policy sold in the state of Wisconsin. State mandates however, are currently under a lot of scrutiny, which is going to diminish their popularity as well as their power as challenges under an ERISA (Employee Retirement Income Security Act) become more prevalent.

There is a case in the Supreme Court now regarding insured employee welfare benefit plans, in which the state of Massachusetts is attempting to force insurance companies to include in their plans the state mandate for nervous and mental disorders. The insurance companies who brought the case to the Supreme Court are arguing that even in insured employee welfare benefit plans, ERISA preempts the state from deeming those plans to be insurance for purposes of state regulation. This case would basically wipe out all state mandates, if the Supreme Court decides in favor of the insurance companies. Nevertheless, currently there are a number of states that have mandates that affect long term care--not only nursing home care but also home care. It is important to examine your state statutes to determine whether there are some additional mandates, because the provider community is not always completely aware of these mandates. There is probably under-utilization and not all the claims that could be validly filed are filed because of a lack of awareness.

Moving away from Medicare supplements, indemnity plans are those which cover an amount per day, regardless of actual cost, and they are very prevalent for nursing home care. These coverages are often limited to skilled nursing care, so we still have the same problem; in any instance where lower levels of care are available for intermediate or custodial care, the benefits may be severely limited.

A typical skilled nursing home policy from 1980 listed these various benefits: For the first 20 days in the nursing home the benefit was $6.60 per day, or you could choose plan 2 which was $13.33 per day. After the 21st day up to 4 years the benefits went up to either $10 per day or $20 per day. You will see this type of coverage with these kinds of benefit levels, there are more restrictions in the fine print. There is a benefit for home confinement which pays $3.32 per day, and one for custodial care which also pays $3.32 a day.

What was the premium?

About $200 per year in 1980, and the definition is very restrictive. Skilled nursing home facility is defined as a facility which meets the requirements of either Medicare or Medicaid. This definition excludes homes that are primarily custodial.

BLUE CROSS OF NORTH DAKOTA NURSING HOME PLAN

An example of a plan worth scrutinizing is the Blue Cross of North Dakota Nursing Home Plan, where the key elements are a high deductible and waiting periods after nursing home care begins of ninety days or more. In addition, one of the positive features is that they usually try to trade off benefits to encourage lower levels of care if that is appropriate, so that in a comprehensive plan you might get 2 days of nursing home care for every unused hospital day, or 3 days of home health visits for every nursing home day that's left over. Some of these plans are trying to develop ways in which utilization in higher level more acute facilities can be substituted with utilization in less acute care facilities. This is another incentive to get people into what may be a more appropriate, but less intensive care situation.

It is my understanding that the Fireman's Fund provides up to 4 years of payment for either skilled or intermediate care after a 90-day deductible.

That is a very standard approach, and similar to the one taken by Blue Cross in North Dakota, and some of the other plans cropping up around the country; there are some options in terms of benefit levels, and there is a cut-off in benefits--4 years is standard.

With the $40 per day plan would that be paid to them, and then they could have their social security or their own resources pay the difference?

Correct, that is how it would work. There have been some plans that are not indemnity, and the UAW plan is an example of that. Mark Meiners goes through all the various plans that are being developed and if you are in a situation where you want to look at some of these possibilities for your clients, his overview is very good. He made long term care his issue. "The State of the Art in Long Term Care Insurance" is his article, which is about a year old, in which he lists the various models that are currently being explored.

Another model is one with a limited PPA (preferred provider arrangement) where providers who opt into the plan are given some incentive to do so at lower costs. Blue Cross of North Dakota is a good example of that. Skilled and intermediate care are covered for the 101st day through the 730th day, and then there is an option to increase coverage to the 1000th day. In terms of the provider relationship, Blue Cross of North Dakota enters into an informal agreement with participating nursing homes to make a one-time payment of $20 per bed into a reserve fund, and Blue Cross agrees to provide prompt payment.

If an individual goes to a preferred provider, one of the nursing homes in the plan, the individual gets full coverage up to the benefit maximum. If another provider is chosen, Blue Cross pays only 80%; there is a 20% copayment. There's an incentive on the part of the consumer to go to one of the preferred providers. There have been some problems with consumer acceptance in the North Dakota plan, but the fact that they have tried to do some cost containment, from the standpoint of bringing in preferred providers and making it really beneficial for those providers to come into the plan, is an interesting concept.

With regard to adverse selection, some of these plans do have open enrollment but then have waiting periods. The rates are significantly lower for those people who enroll as early as age 55. The problem of adverse selection is certainly a substantial one unless there is a long waiting period and some kind of underwriting. It is a matter of looking at each of these models to determine how they work, because some have more stringent underwriting than others, and some try to counteract the adverse selection problem by having longer waiting periods.

Has there been any compensation to the hospital on the trade-off system you described in low cost for higher quality?

There are a lot of arrangements now between hospitals and nursing homes, and to the extent that commercial insurers become part of this effort to contain costs the number of joint ventures or contractual arrangements between hospitals and nursing homes will probably increase.

The major limitation in most of the policies that are still on the market has to do with coverage for nervous, psychotic, and psychoneurotic disorders or deficiencies without demonstrable organic cause; nearly every policy seems to have that exclusion. With all the focus on Alzheimer's disease right now, it's a serious problem if policies are going to exclude on the basis of no demonstrable organic cause.

Other common limitations and exclusions in different policies include limitations on covered levels of care. Many policies are limited to skilled nursing care, or if not limited to skilled nursing care, the benefits for intermediate or custodial care are very minimal: $3.33 a day is not a significant benefit. Another limitation is prior hospitalization. In almost every policy you will see that if the care is rendered with no prior hospitalization, it won't be covered. Maximum payouts of course, are standard. Pre-existing condition limitations very often will stipulate a 90-day waiting period for pre-existing conditions, or the policy may not be issued at all. One of the real abuses in the marketplace occurs when the agent "clean-sheets" the application and writes down that the individual's health is perfect when in fact that is not the case. This causes a problem later on in terms of collecting benefits. The insurance company says, "Gee, you had a heart condition and we are not going to pay," when in fact it was the agent who clean-sheeted the application.

Advertising problems have been well-documented in this area, and there have been numerous congressional hearings, state hearings all over the country, and inquiries by the National Association of Insurance Commissioners. Besides the clean-sheeting that goes on, another problem involves replacements. There is a big incentive within the insurance industry for agents to go out and collect their first year commission, which could be a 70% commission on the premium, and then the next year turn around, go with another insurance company, go back to the consumer and say, "Well, I'm with a better company now, and you'd be much better off buying this policy," collecting their first year premium on the new policy, and so on.

There are a lot of abuses like that in the system, both in terms of advertising and the kind of techniques that are being used among agents. This may not be the norm, but it is happening, and it is one of the reasons why we are seeing some of these regulatory developments. Only two states, Wisconsin and North Dakota, have specifically regulated nursing home insurance but if you're having trouble collecting claims that you feel ought to be paid, one place to look for satisfaction is the unfair claims settlement provisions under most state laws.

REASON FOR FAILURES

In terms of reasons for current market failure, there are several. One is the availability of Medicaid: as long as Medicaid is a fallback for people, it is going to be difficult to establish a sound financing mechanism in the private sector for long term care. It is necessary to somehow mesh public and private funding to create incentives that currently aren't there. A second reason is adverse selection and moral hazard. Up until now the industry has been very fearful of establishing any kind of plan that provides meaningful benefits, because they are afraid that only those people who really need immediate extensive coverage will buy it. That may be true of a high premium high pay-out plan, so we have to build something into this system to prevent that adverse selection from occurring. And if we have a plan that provides extensive benefits for long term care, including home care, to what extent will people use covered services that they would otherwise either not utilize or pay out of the pocket? The industry is also nervous because they don't know how to rate these policies and they don't fit very nicely into their medically oriented system.

Other reasons for problems in the market have to do with the existence of high cost regulation and the difficulty of making insurance claims within the current system. The key under the current system is the skilled nursing definition; so often there isn't a clear definition in the policy. Insurance claims procedures should be carefully examined. Failure to follow contract language or internal claim-handling procedures may constitute unfair claim settlement practices.

In cases where violations appear, you should consider not only litigation, but also complaints to the State Insurance Commissioner. Each Insurance Commissioner's office has some mechanism for recording complaints from consumers, from advocates, and from providers. If there is a problem in terms of claims administration or in terms of language in the policy, that should be brought to the attention of the Insurance Commissioner. The whole area of Medicare supplement and insurance for the elderly is usually considered to be a high priority.

Bad faith in insurance contracts is illustrated by the *Poling v. Wisconsin Physician Service (WPS)* case. It involves Alzheimer's and Parkinson's, and it is a case in which the insurance company did not have adequate internal claims-handling procedures.

At trial WPS indicated that they had relied on their medical report in making the determination that this was non-skilled nursing care. It later came out that the medical report was not even filed with the insurance company until after the claim was initially denied. From the standpoint of a consumer, in those situations where the claims may not be particularly large, the issue of bad faith and punitive damages is going to be a big issue in terms of whether there is a case there to be pursued.

THE FUTURE PROPOSALS

There are existing policies which cover more than skilled nursing home care that have interesting features such as cost containment mechanisms and high deductibles at the front end, with some really meaningful benefits levels for a period of several years. There are proposals for fee for service and indemnity coverage, as well as Medicare supplement add-ons like catastrophic long term care coverage. Mark Meiners has also developed a prototype; it looks like the Fireman's Fund policy is modelled on that.

The Meiners prototype which includes home care, is based on some very detailed assumptions regarding utilization of benefits, and the premium is reasonable. Depending on the monthly payout, it is possible to get a reasonable policy for $500-$600 a year. However, in terms of a really extensive long term care package, it may not be feasible to fully finance that package through current premiums, and other proposals are being offered in addition to the Meiners prototype which challenge the idea of funding long term care through premiums.

One idea is home equity conversion. I'm very attracted to this idea as a funding mechanism, but apparently a lot of older people are not. As things change, as other funding sources become less attractive, as Medicaid becomes less attractive, perhaps attitudes about home equity conversion will also change. There has been quite a bit of study regarding this and since the majority of elderly people, even the poorer elderly, do own their own homes, it's something that deserves continuing attention. Ken Sholen, who runs the National Center on Home Equity Conversion in Madison, Wisconsin, has studied existing mechanisms and attempts to utilize home equity conversion as a funding mechanism. According to Sholen, 75% of seniors own their own homes and two-thirds of these are held mortgage free, so we're talking about 500 billion dollars in home equity among senior citizens.

In different proposals home equity conversion could take the form of either a loan or a sale. Reverse mortgages are those situations where there is a monthly loan advance from a lender to a homeowner and repayments don't become due until either the end of the term of the loan, the sale of the home, or the death of the borrower or the homeowner. There are several models that are being tried throughout the country. The Century Plan is one of those. It is the first long term reverse mortgage loan, developed by a New Jersey corporation called American Homestead. One problem is acceptance among the elderly community. Another problem is acceptance among the lending community and that may be even more serious; a lot of lenders just don't want to get involved in this.

> *One of the problems with home equity conversion is that an elderly person at home sees the home as the anchor and says, "This is all I've got left, this is all I have." Maybe it needs to be tied to some kind of premium base so that they feel they've got something else to hang onto besides the house.*

You're right that this is the crux of the problem. The idea of finally having your house mortgage free and clear and then suddenly owing money again, flies in the face of everything that people have worked for their whole lives.

The life care contract is another option which needs to be examined. Even though there have been problems with life care contracts from a consumer protection and financial stability perspective, the idea of paying an endowment up front for the assurance of a broad range of services later provides another type of model.

Some of these continuing care contracts are not truly life care however. Basically, they provide an independent living unit for a monthly charge with perhaps some medical or personal care services, and an option to purchase more. When we're talking about life care, it's important to determine what we're talking about; are we really promising to take care of that person for life or not?

Life care is moving away from its original concept into small endowments and smaller promises. Large endowments and total protection for the future is probably unworkable, as it is in the area of long term care insurance. The Meiners proposal in comparison offers relatively smaller, less comprehensive protection for long term care coverage, but there is some ability to assess the risk and to avoid adverse selection.

Facilities in Wisconsin offer continuing care in some form or another, but they are not really life care. Some of these facilities have in fact, required comprehensive health insurance as part of entry; that's a first step.

Another important possibility is social HMOs. While they have a lot of problems, they also have a lot of potential, and as Medicare risk contracts become accepted, we're going to see a lot of HMOs developing, whether they be risk contracts or cost contracts or wraparounds. A lot of HMOs are not ready for the risk contracting, but just the fact that the federal government has agreed to it has forced them into reviewing whether they should be offering a wraparound; that is, absolutely no contract with the federal government, but accepting assignment for Medicare and then adding the additional benefits to make some kind of comprehensive package for the elderly, which may include drugs and biologicals, and which may go well beyond the standard Medicare supplement that's been available in the past. If you're going to offer coverage to the elderly for medical care, the next step is to try to prevent this costly hospitalization by providing Meals On Wheels, chore services, and personal care services in the home. You can probably keep this person in a more independent environment, and do more prevention at a lower cost. Very gradually we will see, even in traditional Medicare supplement HMOs, a movement toward including some personal care type services even without calling it a social HMO.

Social HMOs (SHMOs) have some potential for long term care and there will be more discussions between long term care facilities and social HMOs, and even traditional HMOs, as the

HMOs begin to see that they can contain their costs by utilizing long term care services.

Aren't HMOs exempt from Certificate of Need (CON) regulations?

In Wisconsin HMOs are exempt from Certificate of Need regulation and they have considerable flexibility to contract and to set up their own mechanisms.

There are a number of social HMOs that are just starting up: Metropolitan Jewish Geriatric Center in Brooklyn, Ebenezer in Minnesota, Long Beach Geriatric and Keyser Permanente. The Health Policy Center at Brandeis, and of course it was Brandeis who really came up with the SHMO concept, has been following these four projects that are just now becoming operational. They published an article on the subject of social health maintenance organization demonstrations in July of 1984.

They also published another article in August of 1984--"The Social Health Maintenance Organization: A Vertically Integrated Pre-Paid Care System for the Elderly" which you can get through the Brandeis Health Policy Center. They offer a good description of how the plans are working; each model is a little different.

The biggest concern about whether social HMOs can work is that they involve two separate entities that operate very differently. When a medical-model-oriented HMO adds the social services component which may be visiting nurse service or a network that is providing personal care, then the question is: Who's going to be in control? Who's going to be the case manager? Everybody likes the idea, but everybody wants to have control.

A period of time is needed for adjustment and to determine how to get case management into the system in a way that everybody can accept. There will be major changes as these Medicare supplement HMOs recognize that they can do the job much better from a prevention orientation if they utilize services that have traditionally not been a part of the insurance model, such as the personal care and chore services.

Referring to the Boren-Long amendment and the prohibition on transfer of assets in two years, our state, Rhode Island, has a one-year prohibition. It seems like what they're doing is in contravention of the federal statute.

That's possible.   From an advocacy perspective, there are problems with a number of state statutes. Wisconsin had a law that was in contravention before Boren-Long, which was much more restrictive than federal requirements, and there were constant challenges and maneuverings.

The fact that under Boren-Long you still have the exemption for the homestead certainly makes it very difficult to consider home equity conversion.   As long as Medicaid is a fallback, there will be problems pulling together private funding mechanisms, because people will find it unpalatable to give up the house prematurely if they don't have to.

It is a creative possibility to combine private *and* public funding; we can't just look to the private sector to fund long term care because it is such a mammoth issue. Unless we look at ways to integrate the private and the public funding mechanisms, it is going to be difficult to create a really comprehensive package.

PART 3

ADMINISTRATIVE ISSUES:

Legal and Ethical Concerns

Chapter 11

An Interdisciplinary Nursing Home Audit

Speakers: Sanford V. Teplitzky
James L. Buxbaum
John H. Seyle

My name is Sandy Teplitzky and I'm a partner with the law firm Ober, Kaler, Grimes and Shriver in Baltimore, Maryland. The other panel members are John Seyle, a licensed nursing home administrator in Maryland, and Jim Buxbaum, a certified public accountant. We will give you some background about the audit, and what use we think you can make of it. Then we will discuss a number of specific categories for review and suggest an approach to conducting an audit within the nursing home. The audit itself has been developed so that it can be performed either by outside consultants or internally. Although we recommend the participation of three distinct categories of health care professionals in the audit, it is not absolutely necessary that you have all three.

What are the concerns of the nursing home industry today? The number one concern for the industry itself should be quality patient care. That may not be perceived as the top priority by the public or the regulators, but it's got to be listed in the top two or three by everybody, and certainly at the top by the nursing home industry itself.

Another concern--probably the one that some of our critics and the regulators might think is our top priority--is dollars, revenue streams. Clearly, if you're going to provide quality care, which is our top priority, you've got to insure an adequate flow of revenue to maintain the high quality of service. Through planning and review of the operation of the nursing home in advance, you can avoid many problems later on.

While you might think it takes a lot of time to perform an audit like this, or that it might be expensive to have consultants perform it, I can assure you it will be less time consuming and less expensive than addressing some of these issues on a crisis basis, when either the investigators show up because of a fraud problem, or the surveyors show up because of a licensing or certification problem, or the intermediaries or the state representatives show up because of a reimbursement problem. This is an area where time and effort spent up front could serve you well.

What are the pressures that face all of us in the industry on a day-to-day basis? Perhaps the most significant is government regulation, notwithstanding the fact there are task forces on both federal and state levels to reduce the amount of regulation the industry has to deal with. Therefore, we must learn to work within the government regulatory schemes.

Another influence is pressure from patients and families, whether it is direct or indirect, subtle or not so subtle. You are dealing with the patients on a daily basis. Most likely you are dealing with the families on a regular basis also. Many families undergo the relatively normal reaction of guilt when placing a family member in a skilled nursing facility or some other long term care facility, and they may either overreact or underreact to certain things. By periodically reviewing the operation of the nursing home, you can prepare yourself for whatever types of reactions you get from patients and their families.

Finally, whether yours is a union or a non-union nursing home, there are employee issues to deal with. These issues include not only compensation for employees, but more critical perhaps, the relationship between the employees and the patients in the facility. Employees can also have a big impact when some of those other individuals come into the home that were mentioned earlier, such as the surveyors, the auditors, and the investigators.

Why did we develop this audit? It really came about as a result of my representation of John's nursing home. John was faced with a validation survey from the Health Care Financing Administration, which is performed just to make sure everything is going smoothly. Things came up during that survey which made us think about the whole issue of reimbursement. Additionally, we realized that there were a wide range of patient-related issues that John, although he runs an excellent nursing home, decided he just didn't have the time to constantly monitor. He's not a lawyer, he's not a CPA, and he thought that maybe there were some other things I should be looking at as well. This is how we came up with the concept for the audit.

Why did we pick the three disciplines? The answer is relatively simple. The pressures from the regulatory agencies and in the area of fraud and abuse require review by someone experienced with the legal aspects of the health care industry who has more specialized experience than a general corporate lawyer. We're in a different environment these days with 60% of the health care dollar being spent in this country coming from either the state or the federal government, and it's increasingly important that a lawyer experienced in health care matters be consulted.

The certified public accountant is another obvious component because of the necessity of insuring adequate cash flow, preparing cost reports, determining what staffing levels ought to be in place, etc. Finally, and probably most important, is the administrator of the nursing home. I say administrator, not owner, because we're finding increasingly that, especially where the facility is being administered by a non-owner, it may be critical for the owner to step back and say, "Okay, somebody else look at the operation of this home and tell me what they think." This is especially true where the owner is not a licensed health care professional.

The Audit

What exactly is this document? We call it an interdisciplinary nursing home audit. It's a list of questions and areas that you ought to look at in the context of how a specific facility operates. It's intended to address the multifaceted nature of nursing homes and to uncover potential problem areas before they become actual problems. Hopefully, it will also reveal a number of areas within the nursing home that don't need any special attention because you are taking care of those very well on a day-to-day basis.

We also have intended this document, and the whole program, to react to any current pressing problem, such as a spot licensing survey or a reimbursing audit. The audit, therefore, will help you focus in on a particular problem you might be faced with. It will also help you plan for the future, with sections on health planning and marketing in the context of the health care industry and the hospital industry under prospective payment. Hospitals are seeking to develop alternative sources of revenue, and they are increasingly looking to nursing homes and home health agencies.

Preliminary Questions

How do you approach the concept of a nursing home audit? It doesn't take a health care specialist to come up with questions of who, what, when, where, how and why, but it makes some sense that before you start looking at your facility, you think of all the questions you could possibly ask if you were an outsider to the facility. (Please refer to outline on page 172.)

With respect to documents, who proposed it? Who wrote it? Who has the authority to implement it? Who has the responsibility to make sure it's being implemented? Who reviewed it when it was written? Who's going to review it down the road? Who's going to decide whether you still need it? And if you don't need it, who can decide to get rid of it? Who can or must sign the necessary changes in the document?

Look at procedures as well as documents. Very often, you'll find that you've got a policy in place in the home, but no one really remembers why it is there. Think about some of those issues when you go through the facility in this type of an audit and try to decide what you were intending to do in the first place. What does the document actually say? Does it say what you think it says? How is someone who is not in the nursing home on a day-to-day basis going to interpret what this particular document says? Does it say what it means? Does it mean what it says? These are pretty common sense type issues, but they are the kind that can be overlooked when you are responding to a specific question from a reimbursement auditor, or when a licensing surveyor is in the facility.

When was a document or procedure initiated? When was it implemented? When was the last time it was reviewed? When was the last time you reviewed the contract between you and your dietary consultants? When was the last time you reviewed some of the medical procedures on which the nursing staff bases its day-to-day care?

Most documents or contracts will eventually expire. The obvious ones are labor contracts or employment contracts, but there are other documents and procedures that have some finite life to them. You ought to be making a list of those things so that you don't find yourself two days before the end of your labor contract with the union trying to renegotiate the contract. That's at the far end of the spectrum, but you will find that you've got the same problems with other aspects of the facility.

Then there are the "where" questions, such as where is it kept? One problem I had in a home that I did some work for concerned their policy manuals. They had the proper policy manuals, but where were they? They weren't at the nursing station where the nurses could get to them; they were in a locked cabinet in the administrator's office, which didn't do anybody any good. A common sense rule is that you ought to have documents and policies and procedures located in the places where the people who need them can get to them.

One issue that's come up in Maryland concerns the location of the drug box, whether it has to be locked or whether it can be unlocked but kept in a cabinet that's locked, and where that cabinet is. "Where is it kept?" is a much more crucial question than it looks like at first blush.

Don't forget the "how" questions. How is a special procedure enforced? How does the administrator take action when he finds that an employee is being accused of abusing a patient, either physically or mentally? How does the administrator react to a new vendor showing up at the door, making a pitch for buying that vendor's products or services? How is something updated? Is it done on a regular basis or not? Perhaps it ought to be reviewed on a regular basis. It may not need updating, but there ought to be some mechanism for looking at policies periodically.

Finally there are the "why" questions. Why is it there? Why is it still enforced? Why is there a document that says what it says? And then you can react to the questions and go from there.

Following these questions, it is helpful to identify various issues and put them under the category of the individual who's going to have lead responsibility. (Refer to section of outline entitled "Assignments by Discipline.") This is not to imply that only the lawyer looks at the contracts, or that only the accountant looks at staffing analysis. Nor does it mean that the administrator should be the only one looking at such things as risk management. But rather, if you've got the ability and the luxury of having the three disciplines involved, these categories have been separated into the areas where one individual ought to be asking the questions. You may find that the lawyer is asking the accountant and the administrator the questions rather than necessarily answering them him or herself. You may also find that questions are not limited to the administrator and the accountant; for example, interviews with the employees in the facility may be quite helpful and informative.

CONTRACTS

The legal issue of contracts is certainly one area that is not limited to the lawyer. Most contracts will have tremendous reimbursement ramifications, so you'll be talking with the accountant; and certainly they will impact on administrative responsibilities, so the administrator, and in this case probably the owner, ought to be brought into play. Examine contracts that currently exist, find out where they are, get them into one centralized location, review them for when they were entered into, whether they are still effective, whether they ought to still be in place, and what to do for the future. (Refer to outline for examples of the types of contracts that should be reviewed.)

The administrator contract is probably more relevant when the owner is not also the administrator, but you're going to want to take a look at issues such as the salary reimbursement guidelines of the administrator. Do you have, both on the federal and the state level, limitations on the amount of reimbursement that can be made for administrator salaries? In Maryland the state representatives were applying the owner administrator guidelines to a facility which was administered by a non-owner and cutting off compensation levels for the non-owner administrator. In that case, reviewed by a state appeal board, we argued that the application of the owner administrator guidelines were not relevant in this situation. Where the owner administrator guidelines are set up to protect against the potential abuse of the owner giving himself an unreasonable salary, that potential does not exist when you are dealing with an administrator who is not an owner.   The appeal board agreed and we obtained additional reimbursement relating to the administrator's salary.

The medical director's contract is significant when, because of improprieties on the part of the medical director, either ethical or professional, you find yourself in the position of having to release the medical director. Can you do that under the contract you've got in your facility? First of all, do you have a contract with your medical director? If you do have a contract, do you have the right to terminate the privileges of the medical director? Is there some hearing procedure so if you do terminate privileges, or the contract itself, the individual can't sue you on the basis of breach of contract? If you do terminate the contract of the medical director, how does that effect the patient's freedom of choice of physician, especially where, as a result of being medical director, the physician obtained patients who weren't his or hers initially, but became so upon admission?

Admissions agreements need also to be reviewed. These agreements received wide publicity and review in Maryland recently and will probably get similar attention elsewhere in the future. In one portion of these agreements, commonly referred to as the private pay provisions, individuals entering the nursing home as private pay patients agree to remain on private pay status for some period of time of up to one year. It is argued that such provisions violate the federal and state nursing home patients' bill of rights, by prohibiting patients eligible to receive Medicaid benefits from relying on those benefits to pay for their care in the nursing home. If your state health department doesn't deal with this issue administratively, then either the federal or the state government may act legislatively with respect to private pay agreements.

Another issue involving the admission agreement is the scope of the guarantor provision. Most admission contracts require the signature of a guarantor. What does that mean on your contract? Does it mean the individual signing as a guarantor is going to be responsible for consentual issues or financial issues or both? We have found increasingly in Maryland that individuals from the State Office on Aging are unwilling to sign as guarantors where they interpret that to mean that they're going to be financially responsible for the care of the patient. This is something that you can take a look at ahead of time and resolve.

Medical consent may not only involve contracts but may also require specific consent forms. What is the law in your state regarding living wills?

Management agreements should be documented as to their reasonableness both in terms of amount and duration. Have you demonstrated through the documentation that it was an arm's-length transaction? Have you demonstrated that you considered other alternatives besides the management agreement that you entered into? It's sometimes as important for the background documentation to be in place as it is for the actual contract to be correct. If you are a non-profit facility and your management agreement provides a percentage of the net payment as a management fee, do you realize that you may be jeopardizing your tax exempt status? Tax questions may come into play, and by reviewing the management agreements you can address them up front.

Finally, examine your hospital transfer agreements. Can hospitals pay nursing homes to reserve specific beds, so that when the hospital finds itself at the tail end of the DRG permissible stay, and has decided for a medically sound reason that it's time to transfer the patient, there is already an agreement worked out with the nursing home for the transfer to be made? Is there some requirement that the hospital continue payments once the patient is in that bed? In other words, is the payment going to continue whether or not that bed is being used by a former hospital patient?

Agreements may also go the other way, that is, when you've got a patient who's come from the hospital, can there be agreements which provide an easy way of moving that patient back to the hospital if medically necessary? These are just some of the issues that the legal part of the audit should be dealing with under contracts.

THIRD PARTY REIMBURSEMENT

One of the reasons we prepared this interdisciplinary audit was because we found on too many occasions--especially in the third party reimbursement area where the accountant and the lawyer usually deal exclusively with one another-- that we were always being brought in at the appeal stage. Had we been involved at the beginning or in the planning stage, however, many problems could have been avoided without involving the auditors or a formal appeal process. In third party reimbursement, a small change in your planning can make a significant change in your reimbursement. Some of the following examples are items which you might be aware of, but they are significant enough to bring to your attention.

(Refer to outline section entitled, "Third Party Reimbursement," presented by Jim Buxbaum.)

Many of you are familiar with distinct parts, that is, possibly having 100% of your Medicare beds certified and then decertifying a portion of them. Let's say you have a wing or a floor of your facility that you can designate as a nursing home within a nursing home--all you do is allocate cost from one area to another, especially if you have your heavier care patients in this one designated area. For example, if you have three patients and you increase your reimbursement from sixty dollars to eighty dollars purely because, let's say, your laundry and staffing costs are higher in that area (and you can document it usually by time and motion studies or segregation of the payroll), those three patients would represent about one thousand patient days a year, times your twenty dollar differential, which equals $20,000 on the bottom line. Nothing was done differently other than allocating costs which were already expended from one area to another area.

Another example involves the issue of related parties. You should know that being considered related parties may involve both advantages and disadvantages. An entity which owns real estate may find it advantageous to create a related party situation with its lessee operating company if, for example, the Medicaid structuring in the state for capital reimbursement can give you greater revenues.

Financing arrangements is another area where pre-planning can pay off. In putting together a new project, expanding a facility, or adding additional services, financing is going to be required. Proper planning can often greatly increase reimbursement for the capital expenditures and poor planning may be disastrous.

I would estimate that 50% of the adjustments that we get on a Medicare-Medicaid audit are due to lack of documentation. This is another example where simple documentation procedures can, and should, be implemented to avoid negative adjustments in your cost report.

To summarize our approach to third party reimbursement, we look at it in terms of planning, actual cost report preparation, the audit and exit conference, and the appeal. In cost reporting, proper treatment of costs is critical. Generally, it's a matter of whether you put them in one place on the cost report or another. In one instance, there was a cost report that had $100,000 worth of interest income or investment income that was assigned as unrestricted. When we took a closer look at it, we saw that it should be restricted. The $100,000 could be recovered against about $1,000,000 worth of total interest expense on the mortgage, so essentially, we saved $100,000 by reassigning it to restricted funds investment income.

I can't emphasize enough the diligence that you should take in dealing with the auditors, doing the audit, and at the exit conference. Try to attack the adjustments that are being proposed at that stage, not at the appeals stage when you can wind up spending unnecessary legal expenses to take care of something that could have been handled from the very beginning.

Capitalization versus expensing is another area where an item which is really very simple, such as the $500 rule, can confuse people. Many of you are still under the impression that if you buy multiple items of $500 or more, you have to capitalize them. That's not so. You can expense them whether it's multiple or single. A good example of capitalization versus expensing concerns a $40,000 roof repair which we were at first going to capitalize. Instead, we treated it as a repair. Although the state's auditors proposed a negative adjustment by requiring the cost to be capitalized, the state appeal board upheld our position, resulting in a $20,000 increase to the provider's reimbursement.

In this case it was difficult to convince the hearing officer, whose entire house cost less than $40,000, that a $40,000 expense with respect to the roof was really a repair, and not a brand new roof. But if you take a look at the rules governing expenses and capitalized items, i.e., whether it increases the productivity or the useful life of the asset, the argument made was that the roof was not going to last any longer than the rest of the building and if you had a great roof, that wasn't going to increase the useful life of the entire facility. Also we obtained a number of estimates on what it would cost to put up an entirely new roof and they came out to about $100,000. When you're dealing with these situations, it's important that as you fill out your cost report, you place these things in the areas where you think they belong and accumulate adequate supporting documentation in the event an appeal is necessary.

This is not to say that you put in items which you *know* don't belong in certain areas, or you *know* don't belong in the cost report. With respect to an item such as the roofing repair, where you believe that it belongs in expensing rather than capitalization items, you put it in the cost report and you flag it; you put on the front of the cost report that you are putting it in that category because you believe it belongs in that category and that will avoid the potential for fraud and abuse. The thing to keep in mind is if you don't put it in the cost report the way you want to get it, you won't ever get it that way. You may not anyway, but you can't get it if you haven't put it in. What you're doing is preserving your appeal rights, and that's one of the other things to keep in mind in the third party reimbursement area.

One last issue relating to third party reimbursement is the requirement for an access to books and records clause in any contracts you have with subcontractors. The rule is that where you have entered into a contract for the provision of services for the facility, and where the cost or value of those services is going to be $10,000 or more over a twelve month period, you have to include what's known as an access clause in the contract. This clause must provide that for four years after the provision of that service, the books and records which will support that service and the cost of that service can be reviewed by the Medicare people or the Comptroller General. Keep in mind that the penalty that's applied in this area is not for refusing to turn over documents, but for failure to have the access clause in your contract. What's the penalty? The penalty is disallowance of any costs incurred with respect to that contract. Two services which the federal government have specifically identified are contracts for insurance and contracts for leases. Both of those have been designated as service contracts. Those are pretty significant dollar amount contracts, so make sure the access clause is in there.

THE ADMINISTRATOR'S ROLE

The role of the nursing home administrator in conducting an interdisciplinary audit will be discussed by John Seyle.

When you're communicating with auditors, you need to decide early on (and it should be spelled out somewhere in your policies), who is going to talk to the auditor and about what and under what circumstances. You don't want auditors wandering around your facility, talking to any and everybody and asking questions. Even though it might be an honest mistake, the wrong person answering the wrong question is unnecessary and can be prevented if you make sure that the auditors are supervised, and if you plan ahead.

At the exit conference you have more decisions to make. The person who prepared the cost report, whether it's the accountant or the administrator or the bookkeeper, certainly needs to be there to defend the report. You have to decide whether anybody else needs to be there, although you should limit the types and numbers of people who attend the exit conference to those who are responsible for the cost report and who can respond to questions raised at that time.

As a general rule, you're much better off keeping lawyers away from the exit conference for a whole host of reasons. Perhaps the one exception to that is where you've got a specific area of cost that you've been told during the audit is going to be disallowed. If that issue is going to be determined eventually on the basis of some legal argument, it is helpful to have the lawyer at the exit conference. In fact, if the auditors seem to be wavering but not quite agreeing to your position, ask the lawyer to submit a mini-position paper so there will be something formal on the record. We have found in dealing with bureaucrats and pseudo-bureaucrats that the longer they're permitted to hold to a specific position, the tougher it's going to be to get them to change. So to the extent that you can work with them up front, you should be advised to do so.

The next topic I'd like to talk about is responsibility and authority in general. Basic legal authorities stem from the federal laws and rules for skilled and intermediate care facilities, and most of you are familiar with those. State facility regulations are in most cases either an adoption of or an extension of the federal facility rules, and professional licensing regulations are required for certain health occupations, such as the facility administrator.

You should review the chain of federal rules which define the responsibilities for the administrator and director of nursing as well as the medical director or principal physician. Further, review the standards for other types of health professionals such as RN's, LPN's, dieticians, physical therapists, etc., who, although they are not federally certified, are licensed by the state and must meet those state licensing regulations in order to operate within the nursing home.

For example, federal rules state that there must be a licensed administrator responsible for the day-to-day operations of the nursing home. That individual must meet certain qualifications. The state facility regulations normally spell out in more detail the role that the administrator plays and the responsibility he has on a day-to-day basis. The administrator's licensing regulations go a step further. While based on federal law, they differ from state to state as to educational requirements, continuing educational requirements, and the amount and type of training required to be an administrator operating in the state where the facility is located.

Having determined that the administrator is licensed and meets all these other requirements, the auditor should review the role that the administrator plays in the facility. Does he have a contract--a management contract? If so, what does the contract say? When was the last time it was reviewed? What is its duration? How much authority is granted under the terms of the contract? Is the authority granted under the contract sufficient to allow the administrator to carry out his duties as required by state and federal facility licensing regulations?

> *How much should owners and administrators rely upon the fact that some of these people are licensed, and therefore the state has stamped them as appropriate people to be administrators or directors of nursing; to what extent do you think the owner and administrator have to watch over the quality of work being performed by those individuals?*

Well, in the case of the administrator, I think the owner should
have a very close working relationship with that individual. I
don't think an owner can be in Florida all the time, for
example.

One situation dealt with a facility which hired a director of nursing who was
licensed by the state. The owners of the facility, neither of whom was the
administrator, were later told that they were out of compliance with a number of
licensing and certification rules because their director of licensing was no good.
Some problems have been created with respect to relying upon the fact that
someone has a license, and the moral is that the owner or the administrator ought
to be looking at and talking with these people on a regular basis to assure
themselves that the individuals are in fact performing adequately.

The responsibilities of the management type staff people--the director of
nursing, the administrator, the business manager--certainly need to be spelled out
in some detail in policies and procedures, and to the extent that they are, the staff
person can be held accountable. There are however, cases where people take on
responsibility or authority which may not be granted them in policy and
procedure. And this is where your audit has to be careful.

For example, your director of nursing may have been buying food for the
past twenty years because she always did it that way. The administrator may
have allowed that to happen even though the food service person is responsible
for buying food. You as an auditor are not going to see that unless you ask the
proper questions; unless you get in there and see the real relationships between
staff members. Without guidance from the policy and procedure manual a
facility can get into trouble. One of the things that can happen is that people
accept or take on responsibility for which they were not authorized to accept,
which under their professional licenses they should not have accepted, and which
in fact, according to their own licensing rules, they should have probably
reported to the licensing and certification people as violations of state and federal
law.

In summary, in the context of the audit, this is one area that you ought to be
looking at closely, not merely relying upon the fact that a person is licensed to
perform a certain function. Are they performing the function they're hired and
licensed to provide? Are they doing a good job? Are they doing something they
shouldn't be doing?

The auditor needs to talk to at least the management and staff people. Let
them explain to you what they see their job as. After you've reviewed the policy
manuals, the procedure manual, the job descriptions, and the contracts, then go
talk to the director of nursing and ask how that person sees that function. What
do you do every morning? Give me an example of a typical day in your life. If
you find out about half way through, she says "At eleven o'clock, I go down and
pull the time cards and take them to the business office," then your next question
is, why? You can pick up a lot simply by talking to staff people and determining

areas where people have picked up responsibilities or taken to themselves tasks which they really shouldn't be doing. Then you can build your recommendations to the facility on these findings.

A major focus of the audit should include a review of the manner in which communications are carried out between the staff members. Are there regular staff meetings? Who talks to whom? When do they talk to each other? What do they talk about? How well do they communicate? You need to determine whether there are areas where there is no communication. Does the director of nursing not talk to the office manager because they had an argument six months ago and they haven't spoken since? That's a breakdown that can really be costly. These are the kinds of things that you've got to look at and keep an eye on, as an auditor and as a manager on a day-to-day basis, to make sure the operation is running smoothly.

Another important topic is a staffing analysis to determine how many people you need, and what types? (Refer to outline section entitled "Accountant's Functions.")

This is another area involving direct patient care and where a lot of money can be saved or made, by trying to coordinate your patient mix with your staffing. With nursing salaries making up somewhere between one-half to two-thirds of your overall salary structure, if you're operating at 2.5 nursing hours per patient day or 2.6 versus 2.2, those 0.2 and 0.3 hours of nursing per patient day can make a significant impact on your bottom line.

In the state of Maryland, the nursing "cost center" is reimbursed on a prospective payment basis and thus the need to quantify staffing patterns. To carry out this task, develop a profile of your patient mix over a period of time; your actual profile is certainly going to change from time to time. Quantify it and then try to coordinate with your staffing of nurses, whether it be aides, RN's, LPN's, or other licensed personnel. Too often we find a mix which might require maybe 2.1 or 2.2 hours of nursing care, or what we feel should require that much, and the provider might be staffed at 3.0 or 3.3. We're not saying that it's an exact science or that the staffing and the patient profile should match one another perfectly all the time, but they should be within the same ballpark. There are measurement tools available so that over time you can establish a patient mix which you feel is proper for your facility.

To give you an example, in Maryland a heavy special patient is one which requires assistance in the five activities of daily living which are required, plus other services.

If you normally provide care for that kind of patient, can you tell a hospital, "I won't take this patient because I've got too many of them?"

The answer is yes. You can say your staffing will not allow you to take that patient and you're better off if you can prove it. One of the charges you're going to hear later on concerns the discrimination issue, that is, you're not taking enough of the heavy care patients. If you can say to the hospital or to the certification agency or to the ombudsman, "I've got ten tube feeders; and I've got four who require decubitus ulcer care, and they're all on this one unit and I've staffed that unit to four hours of care. I simply can't take another one because it would require me to staff at five, and I can't afford it, or I don't have the available staff to provide adequate and appropriate care for that individual,'' you have blunted the argument that you're not taking care of enough heavy patients.

There is literature available relating to staffing levels. The Maryland system has a measurement tool, and George Washington University has one, which is the basis for the Maryland approach. Those are two which can give you an idea of the types or levels of care and a comparative minutes-of-care per activity, so that you can base your staffing on a rational system.

Get a feel for your patient mix and profile your patients so you can staff accordingly. Sometimes the administrator and director of nursing are not even close in their estimation. For example, a predominantly light care or moderate care patient might require 2.0 hours of care, but might be staffed to 3.5. To correct this over a period of time, put into action a program that will help you to be more realistic. While you might not necessarily be cutting staff, you might realize that with the staff you've got, you can properly take care of patients with heavier care needs.

I have a question as a practicing attorney: Once you undertake this process, do you in some way tend to limit your own personal liability?

You always attempt to limit your own liability.

What am I exposing myself to if I miss kickbacks, rebates, and bribes?

Perhaps ''audit'' may have been the wrong term for what we're performing. ''Audit'' is viewed with quotation marks around it, as a formalized effort by a number of people who are going to, at the end of the audit, have a specific finding that people will rely upon. The final product of such an ''audit'' may be a formal opinion letter. What we're really talking about here is performing an in-depth review of the operation of the nursing home in an attempt to improve patient care, perhaps increase reimbursement, and to avoid significant problems at a later point in time. Of course you can't review kickback arrangements that your client didn't reveal to you. I certainly am not going to issue an opinion letter at the end of my review of a nursing home's operations and say, there is no fraud and abuse going on in this place. I may not even be issuing a formal report at all. I may just be sitting around in a room with the people from the facility, talking about the things that I found.

How do you know going in, what you're going to look at?

You can't go into the audit cold; instead, you spend some time talking to the people at the facility. Very few of these audits will consist of all of the categories mentioned. Most of the time the administrator or owner has some specific concern, and by talking to him or her ahead of time, you can narrow down what you're going to be looking at as you go through the audit.

FRAUD AND ABUSE

There are certain guidelines for fraud and abuse that I want to discuss because it is a delicate subject. I very seldom review specific documents in relation to fraud and abuse. Instead, I sit down with the person or even write them a letter as to what the parameters are in this area--what types of things you can do, what types of things you better not do, and what types of things fall somewhere in the middle. I have to rely upon the person from the nursing home to tell me there might be a problem, which then permits me to look at it. It really has to be a team effort--talking to the people in the facility, seeing what their concerns are, and giving them some guidelines. I do not issue a formal opinion letter upon which all kinds of ramifications could result later on.

Fraud and abuse is a critical area for review. I'm certain that each of you in this room is saying to yourself, well why do we have to spend any time on this topic because I'm running my facility--or the facility I represent--is being run properly, and I don't have a problem. Unfortunately, the prohibited practices may be so widespread and the applicable laws are so broad, that seemingly innocent normal business practices may be suspect. For example, a representative from the federal Office of the Inspector General once defined abuse as the "utilization of loopholes or vagueness in regulations to achieve maximum payment or reimbursement which is not clearly prohibited." I don't know if you have any problem with that, but I do, and so do some of my clients. It's good for my business; it's not so good for my client's business. I don't think that that's the definition that's being applied on a day-to-day basis, but you ought to realize that the mind-set of some of the investigators is: There's fraud and abuse going on out there in the industry and we're the good guys who are going to clean it up. I'll grant that they're the good guys, but I won't grant that fraud and abuse is rampant.

A document issued a couple of years ago to Medicare fiscal intermediaries, which has been distributed to state fraud control units, provides a list of fact situations, which if encountered, are to be referred for investigation. According to this document, Medicare intermediaries--and read for that your state Medicaid auditors--are to report for investigation whenever they find the following things. There's a list of about twenty-five. I'll just touch upon a few:

- Recording of personal expense items as provider cost for patient care.

- Billing for services not furnished.

- An ineffectual board of directors and/or audit committee.

- Indications of personal financial problems of administrators.

- Significant changes in business practices--for those of you who have dealt with corporate restructurings, one of the things that they look for is a complex corporate structure, where the complexity does not appear to be warranted by the provider's size.

- Frequent changes of legal counsel; frequent changes of key financial officers. This is an industry where there's a lot of movement, and movement to some of the investigators means trouble.

What are the other sources of investigations? Beneficiaries receive a form like the Blue Cross/Blue Shield form that says, "This is not a bill," but which tells you that payment was made for these services on your behalf. Because of the older population being served in nursing homes, many people will not remember that they had three X-rays instead of two, or that a specific doctor came to see them. At the bottom of that form is a phone number to call if they've got any questions. That phone number is not the phone number of the facility that they're currently residing in; I can assure you of that.

Other sources of information include: validation surveys; disgruntled employees--perhaps more appropriately, disgruntled ex-employees who have an ax to grind; the Inspector General has been kind enough to insert a toll-free hotline number in Washington, D.C. that you can call if you want to report a problem. Competitors are a prime source of investigations. So, it's not just the person who's paying for his boat by running it through the nursing home that may have a problem in this area. The organizations who are out there investigating fraud and abuse include:

- The Office of Program Validation of the Health Care Financing Administration.

- The Office of Investigations of the Office of the Inspector General.

- The U.S. Attorney's Offices.

- The FBI.

- The State Attorney General Offices.

- Medicaid Fraud Control Units.

- The Treasury Department.

- The Secret Service.

- The Postal Inspectors.

- Undercover Agents.

I would submit to you that there are more people looking for fraud and abuse than committing fraud and abuse. But I can tell you right now that those people have to have something to do, and one of the things to do is to investigate. That doesn't necessarily mean there's going to be an indictment or a criminal trial. But think for a minute what it's going to look like when you wake up on Sunday morning and you get the newspaper, and on the front page it says, "XYZ Nursing Home Has Visit from FBI Officer About Medicare and Medicaid Fraud." That has a direct relationship to your potential admissions over the next couple of months. When the investigation doesn't pan out, what happens? It certainly doesn't show up on the front page of the paper.

Part of the problem we encounter in this area, is that in any other industry in this country that provides goods and services, it is a common business practice to have sales people who are paid on a commission basis. If you do that in the health care business and you get Medicaid or Medicare referrals, you're guilty of a federal felony punishable by five years in prison and a $25,000 fine. It is illegal to pay money for a Medicare or Medicaid referral. Not only can you not pay cash for the referral, but the law also prohibits payment "in kind"--that means discounts on services, etc.

The issue of what is a referral is a difficult one. If someone goes to the hospital to help with discharge planning, and tries to encourage the hospital to suggest your nursing home as an appropriate placement for the patient, is that person--who's on your payroll by the way--creating a referral source? In the marketing of nursing home services, with joint ventures with hospitals becoming much more important because of the prospective payment system, these are issues that are going to come into play.

In the Inspector General's manual for investigating nursing homes it states that rebates are okay even where they're used to encourage future referrals, if they're properly accounted for. I wouldn't take any comfort in that statement because I've seen a lot of fraud and abuse investigations which were based on a rebate having been made.

The federal government issued a document entitled Intermediary Letter 84-9 last September that deals with the subject of kickbacks. In effect, it states that if you have an agreement with a therapist who refers a patient to your nursing home, and then who provides valid occupational or vocational services for that patient which will generate a fee (not from you but from the patient), the fact that you entered into an arrangement with that therapist and provided for an opportunity for the therapist to generate a fee, is a kickback under the fraud and abuse amendments.

The position adopted in that document may not withstand a judicial challenge. However, you ought to have somebody in the facility looking at whatever arrangements you may have with therapists, with durable medical equipment suppliers, with home health agencies and make sure that you're not paying for something "inappropriate" like a referral. If you're not worried about the criminal aspect of this issue, let me refer you to something called the Civil Money Penalties Law. Each time there is a submission of a false claim--and false claim is defined somewhat hazily as either knowing or having a reason to know that it was false, the agency can, without going through the criminal arena, apply what's known as a civil money penalty. These penalties include $2,000 per false claim (and they've identified each line item in a cost report as a separate claim), and double the amount of the claim as a penalty. If you submit a bill for $100 and it should have been $90, it's not double the ten dollars, as it is in other civil penalty laws; it's double the amount of the claim--double the $100.

In the civil money penalty area, the burden of proof is, in legal terms, "a preponderance of the evidence" rather than "beyond a reasonable doubt," as in the criminal context. You may end up wishing they did bring a criminal action because you may find it's a lot tougher to beat the administrative sanction, and you can see that it won't take too many "false claims" to run up so much money that the facility is going to have trouble staying in business.

Also, under the regulations implementing the Civil Money Penalties Act, the Inspector General is specifically authorized to use statistical sampling to determine not only the number of false claims, but the amount of those claims subject to civil money penalties. There's also a possibility of suspension from the program.

There are a number of areas which generally create problems, such as payments for referrals over misutilization of services and billing inconsistencies and improprieties. One area where you can be very helpful to the nursing home is to help the administrator devise a mechanism for what happens when the investigator comes to the door. Who answers questions? Who talks to them?

Who makes copies for them? Don't wait until the investigator shows up on your doorstep to decide that you need to implement that type of a process.

Unfortunately our time is up and we haven't even scratched the surface of this review or this audit. Hopefully the document will give you enough of the other areas to give you an idea of what you ought to be looking at, asking the questions that we've talked about, and hopefully a little time spent up front can save you an awful lot of trouble down the road.

SUPPLEMENT TO CHAPTER 11

INTERDISCIPLINARY AUDIT/OUTLINE

Our experience shows that all too often the nursing home lawyer, accountant or other consultant is called upon to resolve a matter that either has assumed crisis proportion or resulted in substantial cost to the nursing home. In most cases, the matter was of a nature that could have been anticipated and the adverse impact avoided or substantially lessened. It is with this in mind that we have developed the concept of an interdisciplinary audit of the nursing home.

Our audit is not designed to be an exhaustive analysis of every facet of an institution's corporated existence and operation. Rather, through interviews with nursing home financial and administrative personnel and a review of certain documents, it is intended to be an inquiry into, or evaluation of, those aspects of the nursing home's operation which our past experience and present concern (such as health planning, third party reimbursement, and fraud and abuse) suggest are the most likely sources of difficulty.

If inquiries do not produce any information that suggests corrective action is necessary, unless the nursing home personnel raise some related issue not addressed in this outline, no further inquiry should be made as to that particular subject. Often such discussion will trigger nursing home concerns about matters related to those listed in the outline. These should be raised and resolved at the time of the interview.

When potential difficulties are discovered, an audit can be expanded to obtain sufficient information upon which to base an evaluation of the problem and recommendations as to the resolution. At that point, the nursing home will be in a position to determine what it wishes to do as to such matters.

In those instances where the nursing home has private legal counsel or other consultants, the nursing home administrator should be encouraged to advise them that such an audit is to be performed and to share with them any findings and recommendations by the audit team. This is particularly important where the recommendations involve recurring matters that require continuous monitoring.

AUDIT INQUIRIES

A. Who
   1. Proposed it?

    2. Wrote it?
    3. Implements it?
    4. Reviewed it?
    5. Is affected by it?
    6. Can change it?

B. What
    1. Is intended?
    2. Does it say?
    3. Does it mean?
    4. Does it affect?
    5. Is required to change it?

C. When
    1. Was it written?
    2. Was it implemented?
    3. Was it reviewed?
    4. Will it be reviewed?
    5. Will it expire?

D. Where
    1. Is it kept?
    2. Is it posted?

E. How
    1. Is it enforced?
    2. Is it reviewed?
    3. Is it updated?
    4. Can it be changed?

F. Why
    1. Is it necessary?
    2. Is it still enforced?

ASSIGNMENTS BY DISCIPLINE

LEGAL	ACCOUNTING	ADMINISTRATIVE
I. Contracts	I. Third Party Reimbursement	I. Responsibility and Authority
II. Fraud and Abuse	II. Staffing Analysis	II. Personnel Management

LEGAL	ACCOUNTING	ADMINISTRATIVE
III. Patients' Rights	III. Data Processing and Accounting Systems	III. Federal and State Regulations
IV. Third Party Reimbursement	IV. Cash Flow Management	IV. Marketing
V. Labor	V. Long Range Planning	V. Policy Manualization
VI. Organizational	VI. Tax Planning	VI. Risk Management

LEGAL

I. Contracts

A. Employees
1. Administrator
2. DN
3. Medical Director
4. Management Employees
5. Medical Staff
6. Labor Contracts

B. Patients
1. Admission Agreement
2. Medical Consent

C. Vendors, Consultants and Contractors
1. Supplies
2. Ancillary Services
3. Legal and Accounting
4. Leases
5. Management Agreements
6. Construction

D. Third Party Payors
1. V.A.
2. Medicaid
3. Medicare Intermediary

    4. Other Insurers

  E. Other
    1. Partnership
    2. Joint Venture
    3. Stockholder
    4. Hospital Transfer Agreement
    5. Financing (i.e., HUD, Hill-Burton)

II. Fraud and Abuse

  A. Goods and Services
    1. Kickbacks, rebates, and bribes
    2. Payments for referrals
    3. Over- and misutilization of services
    4. Billings
      a. double
      b. false
      c. services known not to be covered
    5. Exclusive purchase agreements

  B. Patient Related
    1. Contributions as prerequisites for admission or continued stay
    2. Patients' funds
    3. Supplementation
    4. Quality of care

  C. Reporting and Disclosure
    1. Guideline 32 involving filing of cost reports
    2. Purchase of personal goods through nursing home and inclusion in cost report
    3. Disclosure requirements
    4. Phantom employees

III. Patients' Rights

  A. Preadmission
    1. Admission Agreement
    2. Contribution as prerequisite
    3. Payment status
    4. Discriminatory practices

  B. Patients' Bill of Rights
    1. Right to privacy

    2. Right to treatment and DNR
    3. Increase in rates
    4. Informed consent
    5. Issues of competency including responsible parties
    6. Financial affairs
    7. Family and visitor responsibilities
    8. Access to non-patient areas
    9. Provision of non-routine services
   10. Delinquent accounts while still in facility

  C. Transfer or Discharge
    1. Reason
    2. Timing

IV. **Third Party Reimbursement**
(See Accounting)

V. **Labor**

  A. Attempts to unionize
    1. Employee contacts
    2. Educational activities

  B. Dealing with union

  C. Attempts to de-unionize

  D. Non-union employees

  E. Contract Negotiation

  F. Contract Implementation

VI. **Organizational Issues**

  A. Structure of Facility
    1. Goals
    2. Participants
    3. Liability of Participants
    4. Tax

  B. Documentation
    1. Incorporation
    2. Partnership

3. By-laws
4. Annual review

C. Tax Review

ACCOUNTING

I.   **Third Party Reimbursement**

A. Prospective Planning
   1. Distinct part
   2. Related parties
   3. Financing arrangements
   4. Expansion of services
   5. Salary considerations (i.e., P.T., Administrator, Executive Director)
   6. Management agreements
   7. Preopening
   8. Documentation
   9. Prior approvals from intermediary

B. Cost Reporting
   1. Classification
   2. Allocations
   3. Home office
   4. Capitalization vs. Expensing
   5. Procedure with Medicare intermediary
   6. Tax vs. cost reporting
   7. Choice of fiscal year

C. Audit
   1. Communication with auditors
   2. Participation at exit
   3. Follow-up

D. Appeals
   1. Timely filing
   2. Timely communication with attorney
   3. Legal Emphasis
   4. Precedent of specific issues

II. **Staffing Analysis**

A. Current Staffing Review

    1. Current staffing for a particular period of time
      a. wages by category
      b. hours by category
      c. FTEs by category

  B. Goals
    1. Nursing area as profit center
    2. Legal aspects
    3. Patient mix

  C. Efforts to Achieve Goals
    1. Comparison of actual vs. standards vs. budget
    2. Analysis of Medicaid reimbursement vs. costs

III. **Data Processing and Accounting Systems**

  A. Availability of information
    1. Management
    2. Cost reporting

  B. Internal control

  C. Checks and balances, e.g., accounts receivable and third party billing

  D. Automation considerations
    1. In-house
    2. Under arrangements

  E. Third Party reporting, e.g., maintenance of proper logs

IV. **Cash Flow Management**

  A. Accounts Receivable Maintenance
    1. Collection policy
    2. Billing policy: private and third party

  B. Accounts Payable Maintenance
    1. Purchasing policy alternatives
    2. Payment policy

  C. Investment of Funds

V. **Long Range Planning**

  A. Goals

      1. Higher profitability
      2. Expansion of services
      3. Alternate revenue sources

  B. Alternatives
      1. Status Quo
      2. New Facility
         a. CON
         b. financing
         c. types of beds
         d. location
         e. layout
      3. Expansion of Existing Facility
         a. 10% rule
         b. CON
         c. replacement vs. additional beds
         d. financing
         e. layout
      4. Acquisition
         a. structure of new entity alternatives
      5. Delicensing or Closure

VI. Tax Planning

  A. Form of Entity
      1. Corporation
         a. Regular corporation
         b. S corporation
      2. Partnership
      3. Proprietorship

  B. Credits Available to Facility
      1. Targeted Jobs and WIN Credit
      2. ITC
      3. Section 179

  C. Accumulated Earnings

  D. Tax Status
      1. Exempt
      2. Non-exempt

ADMINISTRATIVE

I. Responsibility and Authority

  A. Responsibility

      1. Legal
         a. federal facility regulations
         b. state facility regulations
         c. professional license regulations
      2. Contractual
      3. Delegated
      4. By Default

    B. Authority
      1. Explicit
         a. scope
         b. limits
      2. Implicit
         a. assigned
         b. assumed
      3. Lines of authority

    C. Coordination and cooperation among executive staff

II. Personnel Management

    A. Hiring
      1. Finding applicants
      2. Application
      3. Interviewing
      4. Reference checks
      5. Paperwork

    B. Employee Relations
      1. Compensation
      2. Scheduling
      3. Evaluation
      4. Discipline
      5. Grievances
      6. Probation Period
      7. Applicable Laws
      8. Education
      9. Personnel Manual
      10. Dealing with unions

III. Federal and State Regulations

    A. Prospective Compliance
      1. Federal and State Laws

          a. similarities
          b. differences
          c. reconciliation
      2. Federal and State Regulations
          a. similarities
          b. differences
          c. reconciliation
      3. Obtaining Waivers

   B. Reactive Compliance
      1. Analysis of statement of deficiencies
          a. nature and materiality
          b. cause
          c. correction
          d. prevention of recurrence
      2. Responding to citing agency
          a. denial
          b. plan of correction
      3. Appeals
          a. basis
          b. procedures

IV. **Marketing**

   A. Goals
      1. High occupancy maintenance
      2. Patient mix
          a. source of payment
          b. level of care required
          c. cost/benefit determinations
          d. staff capabilities
      3. Public relations
          a. community
          b. medical
          c. social structure

   B. Implementation
      1. Advertising
      2. Personal contacts
          a. other providers
          b. patients and families
          c. local nursing programs
      3. Networking
      4. Monitor competition

V.   **Policies and Procedures**

   A. General and Business
      1. Employees
      2. Purchasing
      3. Billing/Collections
      4. Visitors/Guests

   B. Patient Related
      1. Nursing Care
      2. Medical/Ancillary Services
      3. Emergency/Disaster
      4. Medical Records

   C. Disclosure
      1. Licensing and Certification
      2. Other Government Agencies
      3. Public

VI. **Risk Management**

   A. Insurance
      1. Needs
      2. Coverage
      3. Costs/benefits

   B. Operating Approach
      1. Safety precautions
      2. Employee instructions
      3. Property maintenance
      4. Preventive measures
      5. Emergency and loss procedures

Chapter 12

Ethical Issues in the Nursing Home Setting

Speaker: Judith A. Johnson

The provision of nursing home care for the elderly appears to be a growing industry in our society. A recent article in *Healthcare Financial Management* offers these insights: At the end of 1984, approximately 11% of the population of the United States, or 26,000,000 people, were age 65 or older. It is estimated that by the year 2000, 13% of the population, or approximately 35,000,000 people, will be age 65 or older. Even more significantly, the number of people older than 85 is expected to more than double between 1980 and the year 2000, with approximately 5.1 million individuals falling into that age bracket by the year 2000. While at the end of 1984 approximately 1.4 million individuals were being cared for in approximately 23,000 nursing homes, by the year 2000, this figure could rise to 2.6 million patients. The cost of providing such care is, and is expected to continue to be, high. The national expenditure in 1982 for nursing home care was approximately 27.2 billion dollars. Using a conservative growth rate, by 1990 expenditures could reach 90 billion dollars.

The sheer increase in the number of patients to be cared for coupled with the cost of such care could be expected to give rise to difficult ethical issues, including issues of adequate staffing, quality of care, and "rationing" of available health care resources. In addition, public interest in the ethical aspects of all types of health care appears to be growing. For example, based on the real or perceived abuse or neglect of handicapped newborns, extensive attention has recently been focused on protecting their rights. Evidence of this interest includes the judicial proceedings involved in the "Baby Doe" and "Baby Jane Doe" cases, the promulgation (and invalidation) of the "Baby Doe" regulations, and the passage of compromise legislation, the Child Abuse Amendments of 1984. A number of the issues highlighted in the "Baby Doe" debate are issues that could as well arise in connection with elderly patients being cared for in long term care settings. For example, nursing homes must also confront the question of whether it is ever justified to withhold treatment from an impaired elderly patient based on the prognosis that she will never return to cognitive, functioning life, or based on quality of life considerations, or based on the cost and burden to a family or to society of caring for such an individual. Treatment issues surrounding "Granny Doe" are similar to, and as troubling as, the issues involved with the "Baby Doe" case.

Perhaps the primary distinguishing feature between the impaired elderly and impaired newborns, which in my mind at least makes the ethical issues concerning the elderly even more poignant, is that society tends to approach newborns, even those who are disabled, with the expectation that, if properly treated, they may have a reasonable life expectancy. Newborns are seen as helpless and lovable, and attract many champions to their cause. In contrast, the elderly may be perceived as individuals who, no matter what care is rendered, are approaching the end of their allotted life span. Their care, or lack thereof, may arouse less public concern. As a result, if there is a "cutting edge of the law" in terms of ethical issues, I would suggest that it lies in the law's response to questions involving the care of those who are perhaps our most defenseless, the impaired elderly, and that society and the law will in fact be most sorely tested in their approach to decision-making in regard to patients in long term care settings.

There are many ethical-legal issues raised in the nursing home or long term care environment. Because there is insufficient time to address them all, I would like to focus on an issue that has very recently received national attention, the withholding of artificial means of supplying nutrition and fluids. This issue will, I believe, continue to arise, particularly in the nursing home setting. Modern medicine can sometimes cure or control conditions that were formerly fatal for elderly, incompetent patients. These seriously ill individuals, with primitive mental functioning, may be kept alive by artificial procedures which provide nutrition and hydration. The question will arise, as it has in regard to other life-support systems, as to when such procedures may legally and ethically be omitted. Emotional issues surrounding food and "water", and concerns in regard to euthanasia, will make resolution of the question particularly difficult.

Three major legal cases have recently addressed issues surrounding nutritional life-support systems. These cases provide insight into what appears to be an evolving judicial response to this difficult, ethical-legal question. The most recent decision, issued by the Supreme Court of New Jersey, suggests that at least in certain circumstances, special legal protection in this area may be appropriate for nursing home patients.

BARBER V. SUPERIOR COURT OF LOS ANGELES COUNTY

Although the first major case, *Barber v. Superior Court of Los Angeles County (147 C.A. 3d 1006, 1010 (1983))*, decided in October of 1983, did not involve a nursing home patient, it probably produced the most controversy since it arose in a context much different from other "right-to-die cases"--namely, in the context of a criminal prosecution of two California physicians for murder.

Initially, a magistrate, after a lengthy hearing, ordered that a criminal complaint brought by state prosecutors against the physicians be dismissed. A trial court ordered the magistrate to reinstate the complaint. A court of appeals then addressed the issue, and ultimately issued a writ of prohibition, restraining the trial court from taking any further action against the physicians.

In the *Barber* case, the patient, Clarence Herbert, suffered cardiac-respiratory arrest after uneventful surgery. He was placed on life-support equipment, but within the following three days was determined to be deeply comatose and in a vegetative state. His physicians felt that this state was likely to be permanent. The family requested the withdrawal of life-sustaining equipment. After the ventilator was removed, Mr. Herbert began to breathe spontaneously. Two days later, after consultation with the family, the physicians ordered removal of the IV lines, and Mr. Herbert died, principally from diffuse encephalomalacia secondary to anoxia, but also in part due to pneumonia and dehydration. (*California v. Barber and Nejdl*, Municipal Court of the Los Angeles Judicial District, County of Los Angeles, No. A 025 586, Magistrate's Findings No. 10.)

In analyzing whether the charge of murder should be dismissed, the appellate court first noted that the decision had to be made in light of legal and moral considerations only recently brought to public attention, and not yet adequately addressed by the legislature. According to the court, the criminal law was not adequate to resolve some of the troubling issues raised by modern medical science. Application of evolving legal principles in regard to treatment, and developing moral precepts, was necessary.

In applying these principles, the court rejected the notion that cessation of life-support measures is an affirmative act; instead, it is the failure to provide further treatment. " ...each pulsation of the respirator or each drop of fluid introduced into the patient's body by intravenous feeding devices is comparable to a manually administered injection or item of medication." "Disconnection" of an IV line is akin to withholding of an upcoming injection. Thus, the court found logical grounds for rejecting the distinction between withholding treatment, and withdrawing treatment once begun, a distinction which had previously led to a concern that treatment might not be started on some patients, for fear it could not be withdrawn, and which had seemed to some practitioners to elevate form over substance. Finding a rational basis for rejecting the distinction was an important step in the *Barber* court's analysis.

"Further [said the Court], we view the use of an intravenous administration of nourishment and fluid, under the circumstances, as being the same as the use of the respirator or other form of life support equipment." The California court specifically rejected the prosecution's attempt to distinguish between respirators and IVs--finding it based more on "emotional symbolism" than reason. Consistent with the thinking of some ethicists and physicians on this subject, the court stated that medical procedures to provide nutrition and fluid are more similar to other medical procedures than to typical ways of providing nourishment; therefore, the benefits and burdens ought to be evaluated in the same way.

Once the issue was characterized as a treatment decision, involving omission rather than action, the question became simpler: Did plaintiffs have an affirmative duty to continue this particular form of therapy? As expressed by the court, the purpose of the IV therapy was to sustain biological functions in order to gain time to address the patient's underlying pathology. In regard to Mr. Herbert, the physicians had reasonably concluded that he was comatose and that meaningful recovery of cognitive brain functioning was unlikely. Therefore, according to the court's analysis, there was no duty to continue IV therapy once it became futile or of no reasonable benefit to the patient.

Rejecting the "ordinary-extraordinary distinction", the court advanced, as a more rational approach to deciding whether treatment is required, the determination of whether the treatment is proportionate or disproportionate in terms of the benefits to be gained versus the burdens caused. The decision as to whether a particular therapy is of reasonable benefit, and must be provided, depends on the unique facts of each situation. However, there is some consensus, said the court, that the focal point of the decision-making process where the possibility of recovery is virtually non-existent should be the prognosis as to a reasonable possibility of return to cognitive and sapient life, as opposed to forced continuation of vegetative existence.

In regard to the procedures to be followed in arriving at a decision, the court noted that in the absence of legislation to the contrary, failure to institute guardianship procedures prior to accepting the decision of a surrogate did not itself render the physicians' conduct unlawful. In this case, the wife was the proper surrogate and would have so qualified had court proceedings been instituted. There was no legal requirement of prior judicial approval before carrying out her decision, made in concert with the physicians. The surrogate's decision should be based to the extent possible on the patient's desires as expressed when he was competent. In the absence of such knowledge, the patient's "best interests" should govern. The court indicated that in performing the best interests analysis, the surrogate could consider the "quality" as well as the extent of life. However, the court did not explain this term. In the context of the case, it may well refer to the fact that the patient was in a comatose or vegetative state.

While the *Barber* case arose in a criminal setting (and is, of course, binding only in California), it did offer useful guidelines for decision-making in regard to the withdrawal of artificial means of supplying fluids to incompetent patients whose prognosis is similar to that of Mr. Herbert. While acknowledging the emotional component of a decision involving food and fluid, it suggested a framework for analyzing these cases which was basically consistent with a framework which had been developing in a number of states over the years in regard to other treatment decisions. Although the facts of each situation would continue to be determinative as to the outcome, a model for decision-making had been made available, in which a benefit-burden analysis could be applied to all forms of medical treatment in order to determine the existence of an affirmative duty to continue specific therapies. Utilizing this model, certain family members, in appropriate circumstances and in consultation with physicians, could reach decisions without necessarily seeking judicial intervention.   It should be remembered that the necessity for judicial involvement will depend on state law. In certain states, a judicial determination of incompetence, appointment of a guardian, and authorization for discontinuation of treatment may be required. Furthermore, some state courts may not feel comfortable authorizing the removal of IV lines or similar support systems in any circumstances.

Several major issues were not, of course, addressed in *Barber*, including the withholding of treatment (1) from elderly, incompetent, nursing home patients (2) who were not comatose or in a vegetative state.

In The Matter of Mary Hier

In the Matter of Mary Hier (18 Mass. App. Ct. 200, 200-203 (1984)), a case which did involve an elderly nursing home patient who was alert although incompetent, was decided by the Massachusetts Appeals Court in June of 1984. The court's major premises in approaching the question of artificial means of providing food and fluids were consistent, in essential respects, with the premises adopted by the California court.   Consistent with prior Massachusetts cases, however, the emphasis was on "substituted judgment", with the benefit-burden analysis subsumed as part of that judgment. The procedural history of *Hier* was significant in that it highlighted the importance of the underlying facts of each case and dramatized the difficult ethical issues that may arise even when a rational decision-making model is applied.

In the *Hier* case, the patient was a 92-year-old woman, who suffered from severe mental illness and had been hospitalized for at least 58 years, with her care being paid for by public assistance. She had been treated with thorazine which apparently reduced her extreme agitation, although she disliked the injections. In addition, because of a physical malformation, she had, in 1974, undergone a gastrostomy and was thereafter fed through a tube surgically implanted through the abdominal wall. She had allegedly removed the tube repeatedly and had undergone a series of reinsertions. In April of 1984, after removing the tube several times, she was transferred from the Beverly Nursing Home to the Beverly Hospital. While it might then have been possible to reinsert the tube without surgery, she apparently refused. Because no family member was available, the hospital petitioned for appointment of a guardian and ultimately asked the court to authorize the guardian to consent to administration of thorazine (as required by state law), but not to request consent to surgical reinsertion of the tube.

A guardian ad litem and counsel were appointed for Mrs. Hier, and they advocated surgical reinsertion of the tube. Applying the substituted judgment test, which has long been the standard applied in Massachusetts treatment cases, the probate judge decided that if Mrs. Hier were competent, she would refuse surgical intervention. The guardian ad litem appealed, espousing the theory that failure to supply nutrition to a patient not brain dead, comatose or vegetative and not facing imminent death, cannot be justified by the right to privacy or on any other grounds.

Like the California court, the Massachusetts Appeals Court rejected the argument that nutrition should be differentiated from "treatment," and the right of choice confined to "treatment" only. While not indicating which, if either, decision it approved, the court distinguished Hier's situation from the Superior Court decision in *Conroy* (see following case) and from *Barber*--but the distinction, said the court, was *not* between terminating a procedure (as in *Barber* and *Conroy*) and commencing it, but between supplying nutritional support with only modest intrusiveness and supplying it through the use of highly invasive surgical procedures. In weighing the intrusiveness in Mrs. Hier's case, the court looked at Mrs. Hier's particular circumstances and considered the following facts which were peculiar to her situation:

1. The complications presented by virtue of her prior operations and scar tissue, and the burden of the proposed operation on an elderly person in a physically debilitated state;

2. The inability to evaluate the complications beforehand, due to her condition;

3. The relatively high risk of surgery due to her age and other complicating factors; and

4. The need for restraints after surgery.

According to the court, these factors taken together made the proposed operation more onerous and burdensome for Mrs. Hier than for a younger, healthier person.

The Appeals Court approved the probate court's application of the substituted judgement test, noting that the court properly took into consideration:

1. That Mrs. Hier had repeatedly and clearly indicated her opposition to procedures necessary to introduce tube feeding (both gastric and nasogastric);

2. That the benefits to be realized from performing the gastrostomy were diminished by her repeated history of dislodgments;

3. That such dislodgments could probably not be prevented except by the use of physical restraints;

4. That physicians who had seen Mrs. Hier and evaluated her condition were making thoughtful recommendations that surgery was inappropriate in her case, and, in footnote, that

5. Mrs. Hier's religion (Roman Catholicism) would not impose ethical constraints on her treatment choice.

The Court also examined other possible interests that might outweigh Mrs. Hier's and found no third parties to be protected; medical ethics did not require surgery; and the state's interest in preventing suicide was not implicated in a decision to forego major surgery.

Citing an earlier decision involving hemodialysis treatments for an incompetent patient (*In the Matter of Spring*, 8 Mass. App. Ct. 831, 845-46, 380 Mass. 629 (1980)), the court said:

> "The general state interest in the preservation of life--most weighty where the patient, properly treated, can return to reasonable health, without great suffering, and a decision to avoid treatment would be aberrational--carries far less weight where the patient is approaching the end of his normal life span, where his afflictions are incapacitating and where the best medicine can offer is an extension of suffering."

Somewhat surprisingly, the Appeals Court decision was not the end of the matter. The guardian ad litem persuaded the probate court to authorize transfer of Mrs. Hier to another hospital for evaluation as to whether she was an appropriate candidate for hyperalimentation. After evaluation of Mrs. Hier at St. Elizabeth's Hospital in Boston, counsel for Mrs. Hier moved the probate court to reopen the evidentiary phase of the hearing. New evidence revealed (1) Mrs. Hier's voracious appetite, (2) less agitation after treatment with thorazine, (3) no attempts by Mrs. Hier to remove the IV, (4) evidence Mrs. Hier wanted to live and felt she was getting better, (5) medical testimony that reinserting the gastrostomy tube would be good medical practice, not excessively burdensome, and would offer reasonable hope of benefit, (6) medical evidence that the procedure was relatively simple and that there was little scar tissue, and (7) medical evidence that the risk of mortality was approximately 5%, and that without the surgery, Mrs. Hier would die. (*In the Matter of the Guardianship of Mary Hier*, Additional Findings of Fact and Order, Probate and Family Court Dept. #84-0818-GI (July 3, 1984), pp. 1-8.)

The probate court found there was a substantial change in circumstances, that Mrs. Hier now acquiesced in the surgery, and that the new evidence was "overwhelmingly contradictory" to the previous evidence in several key respects. A new-guardian was appointed with authority to consent to the surgery.

The revised order of the probate court was not based on a rejection of the analytic model initially used by the probate court and subsequently approved (and expanded upon) by the Appeals Court. Instead, it was based on substantial new, and different, testimony in regard to the risks of treatment, and Mrs. Hier's state of mind and wishes (due, perhaps, to the administration of thorazine). The results in *Hier* emphasize the sensitivity of the outcome in treatment cases to the facts presented to the court. Because medical experts may have different views as to a patient's condition and prognosis, and because a patient's condition may change rapidly, careful monitoring of each situation is important from a legal and ethical standpoint. Growing sophistication on the part of the courts in regard to medical treatment issues, and in some states at least, 24-hour access to the courts for adjudication of treatment cases, should facilitate this monitoring process.

In The Matter of Claire Conroy

The *Conroy* case (486 A.2d. 1209, 1216-17 (N.J. 1985)), which was reviewed at three levels of the New Jersey courts, presented a fact pattern which is, I believe, one which will be addressed more and more frequently, namely, appropriate treatment for elderly, senile, physically debilitated nursing home patients.

Ms. Conroy was an 84-year-old patient suffering from organic brain syndrome, as well as a variety of serious physical ailments, including necrotic decubitus ulcers, urinary tract infection, arteriosclerotic heart disease, hypertension, and diabetes. Evidence at the probate court level, including direct observation by the judge, revealed that except for minor movements of her head, neck, arms and hands, Ms. Conroy was unable to move. Although she was not comatose or in a vegetative state, she did not speak, but lay in bed in a fetal position, occasionally following the movement of visitors with her eyes. She moaned when moved or touched upon some portions of her body, but medical testimony was inconclusive as to whether she was capable of experiencing pain. She had lost the ability to eat independently or by hand-feeding, and was being kept alive by means of a nasogastric tube. There was no reasonable expectation that her condition would ever improve. She had no close family members involved in her care, although a nephew had shown consistent interest in her well-being.

The patient's nephew, who had been appointed her guardian, felt that if competent his aunt would refuse continued treatment with the nasogastric tube that was keeping her alive. The nursing home was reported to be "neutral" as to the outcome, but the physician would not "consent" to removal. Therefore, the nephew sought judicial intervention.

SUPERIOR COURT, CHANCERY DIVISION

As had the court in *Barber*, the first New Jersey court to hear the *Conroy* case rejected the distinction between extraordinary and ordinary treatment (*In the Matter of Claire Conroy*, 457 A.2d.1232 (Ch. Div. 1983)). Instead, the focus, said the court, should be on the patient's present condition and reasonably predictable future condition. If the clear prognosis is that she will never return to some meaningful level of intellectual functioning and comfort, and that her life has become and is likely to remain impossibly burdensome to her, then active treatment could be withheld. Where life is impossibly and permanently burdensome, prolonging life is pointless and probably cruel.

Based on Ms. Conroy's medical condition, including the fact of her extremely primitive mental functioning and her variety of physical ailments, the court concluded that her life had become impossibly and permanently burdensome to her, and authorized discontinuance of the nasogastric tube. In a moment of candor, the court acknowledged that such an action would lead to death by starvation and dehydration, and that such death might be painful. The court also acknowledged some misgivings as to the impact of the decision on other individuals who were senile or retarded. While acknowledging the difficulties posed by these situations, the court sought to give some guidance by distinguishing between individuals with virtually no intellectual functioning, who were unable to love or respond to love, and individuals who maintained that capacity although senile or retarded. The court also cautioned against premature or wrongful withdrawal of treatment. While rejecting the need for judicial involvement in all similar cases, the court noted that judicial involvement may be appropriate when the patient, prior to competency, has not given any indication as to her wishes, when family and/or physicians disagree, or when the patient is in a nursing home which does not have an institutional ethics committee to provide protection for the residents.

SUPERIOR COURT, APPELLATE DIVISION

On appeal, the Superior Court in *Conroy* (464 A.2d.303 (N.J. 1983)) considered whether, given the circumstances of the case, the decision to discontinue the nasogastric tube represented a correct application of the balancing test established by prior case law in New Jersey (*Quinlan*), i.e., whether Ms. Conroy's right to privacy outweighed the state's interest in preserving life. The appeals court based its decision that withdrawing the tube was *not* justified on a number of factors. First, Ms. Conroy's condition and prognosis supported a greater state interest in treatment. While she was "confused", she was not vegetative or comatose. She had some capacity to relate to the outside world. Her conditions did not appear to be fatal. Basing a decision to withdraw treatment on Ms. Conroy's low level of intellectual functioning, which precluded her from enjoying a meaningful quality of life, was, the court felt, a dangerous precedent. The court also disagreed with the Chancery court's characterization of the "treatment"--not only was the nasogastric tube not invasive, said the appellate court, it was also not even medical treatment. "In truth, Conroy was little different from the many other ill, senile or mentally disabled persons who are bedridden and cared for in nursing homes."

In addition to basing its reversal of the lower court decision on its application of the *Quinlan* reasoning, the court also stated that the result was dictated by the ethical considerations inherent in the case. While acknowledging some controversy as to whether food and fluids can be withheld under any circumstances, the court stressed that ethical considerations mandate the provision of food and fluids for all patients not comatose and not facing imminent and inevitable death.

> "If, as here, the patient is not comatose and does not face imminent and inevitable death, nourishment accomplishes the substantial benefit of sustaining life until the illness takes its natural course. Under such circumstances nourishment always will be an essential element of ordinary care which physicians are ethically obligated to provide." According to the court, to remove the tube would constitute euthanasia, based on unacceptable quality of life considerations.

SUPREME COURT DECISION

The Supreme Court of New Jersey, in overturning the decision of the appeals court, indicated that its opinion was limited to the question of withholding life-sustaining treatment from "incompetent, institutionalized, elderly patients", who had formerly been competent, whose condition involved "severe and permanent mental and physical impairments", and who had a "limited life expectancy" (death within one year). (*In the Matter of Claire Conroy*, 486 A.2d. 1209, 1216 (N.J. 1985)). As the court noted, large numbers of aged, chronically ill, institutionalized persons fall within this general category.

While disagreeing with the Superior Court in regard to the legal standards for withholding treatment, the Supreme Court found that the factual record was insufficient to justify a decision to withhold treatment in this case.

In reaching its conclusions in regard to the specific issue it had framed, the court first summarized the basis for its conclusion that if Ms. Conroy were competent, she could refuse to accept treatment with the nasogastric tube. The goal of any decision-making in regard to her care, said the court, should be to determine and effectuate the decision she would have made, if competent.

According to the court, the guardian of an incompetent patient may arrive at a decision as to what the patient would have decided, if competent, based on one of three standards. When there is sufficient evidence so that it is "clear" that the patient would have refused treatment, a purely subjective test should be applied in reaching a decision. If it is not "clear" what the patient would have wanted, one or two "objective" tests may be used. Under the limited objective test, treatment may be withdrawn when there is some trustworthy evidence that the patient would have refused the treatment, and the decision-maker is satisfied that it is clear that the burdens of continued life with treatment outweigh the benefits to the patient. Treatment in these circumstances would merely prolong suffering.

In the absence of any trustworthy evidence of the patient's wishes, or even any evidence at all, life-sustaining treatment may be withheld from a patient like Ms. Conroy only if a "pure objective" test is met. Under this test, the net burdens of the patient's life with treatment should clearly and markedly outweigh the benefits derived from life, and furthermore, the pain resulting from continued treatment should be such as to render treatment inhumane. Treatment should not be withheld even in these circumstances, however, if the patient, when competent, expressed a wish to be kept alive in spite of pain and suffering.

The tests set forth by the court in *Conroy* are stringent, and the court further emphasized that before consenting to termination of treatment, the surrogate decision-maker should be "manifestly satisfied" that one of the three tests has been met. The court also specifically rejected considerations of quality of life, which might place the defenseless, impaired elderly at risk.

Arriving at a decision for elderly, incompetent residents of nursing homes was seen by the court as particularly difficult. The court noted several major, relevant differences between hospitals and nursing homes:

1. Residents of nursing homes are a particularly vulnerable population.

2. Nursing home residents are often without any surviving family.

3. Physicians play a much more limited role in nursing homes than in hospitals.

4. Nursing homes as institutions suffer from peculiar industry-wide problems to which hospitals are less prone, including problems of abuse and exploitation.

5. Few nursing homes have "ethics" or "prognosis" committees to review the attending doctor's assessment of a patient's prognosis.

6. Nursing homes generally are not faced with the need to make decisions about a patient's medical care with the same speed that is necessary in hospitals.

Because the institutionalized elderly are particularly vulnerable, special procedures must be followed, said the court, prior to withholding treatment.

First, medical evidence should establish that the patient fits into the category of patients addressed in the *Conroy* decision. Second, there must be a judicial determination that the patient is incompetent to make this particular treatment decision, and a guardian appointed, if the patient does not already have one. Proof must be clear and convincing that the patient does not have and will not regain the ability to make the decision. If the patient already has a guardian, a determination should be made that the guardian is the appropriate person to make this decision. Extensive medical evidence should also be provided to the surrogate decision-maker for use in effecting the patient's wishes. Such facts as prognosis, intrusiveness of the treatment, and pain with and without the treatment, that would not doubt have influenced the patient, if competent, should be considered by the surrogate.

In addition, before treatment may be withdrawn, the state office of the Ombudsman of the Institutionalized Elderly would have to be notified. The Ombudsman would treat this as a notification of possible "abuse," and conduct an investigation as authorized by law. In addition to medical evidence provided by those who were involved in the case, two independent physicians should confirm the patient's condition and prognosis. In all cases in which the guardian decides that the patient would choose to forego treatment, the Ombudsman must concur before treatment can be withheld. In addition, if the guardian's decision is based on the limited objective or pure objective test, the family (or in their absence, next of kin), would also have to concur.

In reaching its decision, the Supreme Court of New Jersey, like the California and Massachusetts courts, rejected the usefulness of distinctions between passively allowing death to occur and terminating treatment, between withholding and withdrawing treatment, between ordinary and extraordinary treatment, and between artificial procedures for supplying nutrition and fluids and other life-sustaining medical treatment. The court recognized the emotional connotations of providing food and fluids. However, the court pointed out that medical procedures for providing nutrition and fluids artificially do not fit into the traditional concept of "feeding." Nasogastric tubes and other medical devices carry risks and burdens similar to those of other medical procedures. Forcing fluids into a patient who can no longer swallow, and who is terminally ill, may even result in a more prolonged and painful death. Given modern medical techniques, our concept of "feeding" must be modified.

In three major legal opinions, the courts have indicated that while cases involving nutrition and fluids may raise special symbolic and emotional issues, and while they raise serious ethical issues, they are similar from an analytic standpoint to other treatment cases.

GUIDELINES FOR DECISION-MAKING

As has been recognized by the three courts involved in the decisions discussed above, it is extremely difficult to state with certainty when it is appropriate to withdraw or withhold various medical therapies, including measures to provide food and fluids. Each case must be analyzed on an individual basis. In addition, certain nursing homes, because of religious affiliation, among other things, may have a particular ethical position in regard to treatment issues. State law will also vary. However, even though there is no single or simple answer to the ultimate question of withholding treatment, which must be evaluated in each instance, there are a series of questions which can be posed that will help gather the information and frame the issues, steps which are prerequisites to making the final decision. It is hoped that the following suggestions as to process, garnered from the three decisions summarized above as well as practical experience, may be helpful to nursing homes and their counsel.

THRESHOLD QUESTION OF COMPETENCY: THE FACTS

When the family or physician or other caregiver raises the issue of continued treatment, the first important step, sometimes overlooked, is to determine whether this decision can be made by the patient, even though the patient is not competent for all purposes. The nursing home administrator or counsel should ask the following questions: Is the patient competent or incompetent to make this particular treatment decision? How much evidence is available in regard to this question, and how reliable is it? Does the evidence clearly support a determination of competence or incompetence? Should psychological/psychiatric consultations be arranged?

THRESHOLD QUESTION: THE PROCESS

Should the decision as to competency be taken to court? Does state law indicate that a judicial finding of incompetence is always necessary? If not, is there uncertainty or disagreement in this case which would best be resolved through a judicial proceeding?

SCREENING PROCESS: THE FACTS

Assuming that a decision is reached that the patient is incompetent, then an initial screening process, designed to gather facts, clarify issues, and help the nursing home assess its obligations and understand its vulnerability, is essential. In this screening process, administration and/or legal counsel should talk to as many caregivers as possible, including the physicians, nurses and aides involved in the care of the patient, and all available family and close friends.

The following questions need answers:

1. What treatment is being provided?

2. How intrusive is the treatment? For how many hours a day?

3. What are the risks of the treatment?

4. What are the side effects of the treatment?

5. What is the likelihood of success (benefits) of the treatment?

6. What is the likely duration of success (prognosis)?

7. Are there alternative treatments? If so, answer the same questions in regard to each.

8. What are the risks, side effects, likelihood and duration of success of nontreatment?

9. What is the certainty with which each question posed so far can be answered?

10. What are the recommendations of treating professionals?

11. What wishes or reactions has the patient expressed in regard to treatment? What were the patient's wishes when competent? How clearly did the patient make these wishes known?

12. What are the wishes of the family? Is there unanimity among family members? Do any family members have a conflict of interest?

13. Does the nursing home have a policy or procedure in regard to this treatment issue? Has the policy been followed? Have the procedural steps been taken?

During this initial screening process, a decision is frequently reached that, given the basic analytic framework of the major legal decisions in this area to date, withholding treatment is not appropriate. Often this result comes about because there is no clinical certainty as to the prognosis with and without treatment, and as to the appropriateness of withdrawing or withholding treatment. On occasion, the burdens of treatment may be revealed to be insubstantial, or the burdens of nontreatment substantial. If, however, a decision is reached that the patient, if competent would refuse treatment, or that treatment is deemed medically inappropriate and, in the absence of evidence of the patient's wishes, family, friends and caregivers believe continued treatment to be inhumane or contrary to their ethical beliefs, then the next question is whether the decision can be made without judicial involvement.

SCREENING PROCESS: THE PROCEDURES

Once again, in determining whether judicial involvement is required, state law must be consulted. Depending on state law, some of the factors that will be considered include the following (a number of which will already have been explored in the screening process):

1. Certainty as to incompetency and the need to obtain a judicial determination of this question;

2. Prior or on-going court involvement or prior involvement of governing agencies;

3. Availability of family members to consult about treatment;

4. Good faith of family members and others participating in decision;

5. Unanimity of views of family members;

6. Unanimity of view of those treating and caring for patient;

7. Extent of impairment of patient's mental faculties;

8. Prognosis without the proposed treatment;

9. Prognosis with the proposed treatment;

10. Complexity, risk and novelty of the proposed treatment;

11. Possible side effects;

12. Certainty of the clinical judgments;

13. Patient's level of understanding and probable reaction;

14. Urgency of the decision;

15. Clarity of professional opinion as to what is good medical practice;

16. Interests of third parties;

17. Administrative requirements of institution involved;

18. Existence of suspected malpractice;

19. Existence of advocates of treatment in all instances;

20. Costs;

21. Institutional setting;

22. Existence of ethics or prognosis committee in the institution;

23. Existence and applicability of special state laws protecting the elderly.

The information gathered in the process described above should be analyzed as suggested in the relevant state law cases, such as the *Barber*, *Hier*, and *Conroy* cases discussed above. Each of these cases, as well as other treatment cases in various states, acknowledges the importance of the ethical issues raised in these cases, and attempts to take them into consideration in suggesting parameters for decision-making. However, progress in the medical or human sciences, or particular fact patterns, may raise ethical issues that do not seem to fit within these parameters. In those circumstances, as in the past, the law will have to develop and grow to accommodate society's ethical obligations to the elderly.

FOR FURTHER READING

Kimsey, Tarbox, and Bragg. "Abuse of the Elderly--The Hidden Agenda. Part I--The Caretakers and the Categories of Abuse." *Journal of the American Geriatrics Society* 39(10):465-472, 1981.

Lynn and Childress. "Must Patients Always be Given Food and Water?" *Hastings Center Report* 13:17, 1983.

Paris and Fletcher. "Infant Doe Regulations and the Absolute Requirement to use Nourishment Fluids for the Dying Infant." *Law, Medicine and Health Care* 11:210, 1983.

Stanley, Guido, Stanley, and Shortell. "The Elderly Patient and Informed Consent." *Journal of the American Medical Association* 252:1302-1306, 1984.

Taub. "Informed Consent, Memory and Age." *Gerontologist* 20:686-690, 1980.

Willging, Kerschner, and Peres. "Long-term care: The Malthusian Dilemma." *Healthcare Financial Management* 38(12):48-54, 1984.

Chapter 13

Legal Aspects of Handling Patient Funds

Speaker: Donald W. Grimes

My orientation is that of a prosecutor; I was the director of the North Carolina Medicaid Fraud Control Unit for six years. Medicaid Fraud Control tries to assist the Medicaid program in framing guidelines to help protect the property of patients who are residing in health care facilities, particularly long term care facilities like nursing homes.

MISAPPLICATION OF PATIENT FUNDS

In North Carolina, misapplication of patient funds was a significant problem until 1979 when the Medicaid Fraud Control Unit came into being. The minute we opened our doors we had four cases involving seven different nursing homes, all of which had to do with the misapplication of patients' personal use funds.

In 1977 the Medicare-Medicaid Anti-Fraud Abuse Act Amendments to the Social Security Act were passed, which, among other things, set up the Medicaid Fraud Control program. Those federal amendments referred to patient funds, with particular attention to the fact that something had to be done to prevent the commingling of patient funds with facility funds. They also addressed the need for a standard set of guidelines regarding accounting procedures that would protect nursing home patients who tend to be very vulnerable. They used rather general language and pretty much left it up to the states to go into the particulars as to how they felt the the problem needed to be addressed.

The other thing that that particular set of amendments addressed was that the Department of Health, Education, and Welfare needed to come to grips with and to inform everyone as to which items were covered by Medicaid and which were not. Items covered by Medicaid obviously should not be charged to patients. It also said that you may not charge a Medicaid patient an admission fee or a fee to continue to reside in the nursing home.

Let me give you a few examples of misapplication of patient funds. One case involved a fairly small nursing home, a one-facility operation owned by one individual.

To his credit, he did have a patient personal needs fund or trust account in a bank. However, in this particular instance he just simply wrote checks on the trust fund account and put them into his operating account in order to get himself out of arrears. He wrote about five different checks, a total of about $20,000, and then tried to disguise what he had done.

Did he pay it back? Yes, he paid it back the day before the Medicaid auditor showed up for the annual audit, which didn't really make any difference because he had the intent to use it for a purpose other than that for which it was intended, and that is by definition fraudulent according to the applicable statute.

That provider also had a number of Medicaid patients residing at his facility who had funds in excess of the amount that made them eligible, so he was charged with failure to disclose material facts affecting his entitlement to payment.

We had another case at the same time involving a corporation that owned three different nursing homes. They were basically owned by one family. In this particular case they did not have a patient trust fund account, and had in fact commingled the patients' personal needs funds with the operating funds of the facility. At that time there was no law in North Carolina forbidding commingling so there was nothing technically illegal about it. There was from $15,000 to $25,000 of patient funds that were owed to the patients at one or more of these facilities; and ultimately, there was $54,000 that simply vanished. The facilities were sold after all the money had been spent, so we ended up indicting the management company which was managing them at the time of the disappearance.

COMMINGLING PATIENT FUNDS: PROBLEMS AND DISCUSSION

The problem with commingling patient funds with facility funds is that essentially they lose their identity.

> *In Georgia, when social security checks come in, some of the facilities deposit the checks into a patient's fund and then draw them out from there, whereas others deposit the check into a nursing home account and almost simultaneously, or within a day or two, draw out the money for the patient's account. I can't see that there's any real difference either way, can you?*

> There is if you've got a statute that says it's against the law to commingle patient funds with facility funds, which is what we have in North Carolina. In North Carolina you are guilty of a misdemeanor every time you put the patient's check into the operating account, even though it is your intention and your practice to transfer the personal need funds at a later time. So

in your state, if there is no anti-commingling statute, there probably isn't anything illegal about it, although it could be a technical violation of your embezzlement statute.

As a result of the commingling statute in North Carolina we require that you either make a split deposit, or deposit it all in the patient trust fund account and then write out a check for patient liability to the facility.

Our statute simply says that it is unlawful for a person to commingle the funds or property of a resident patient of a health care facility with the funds of the facility itself, or with any other person or entity other than a patient residing in that facility. So anything other than that would be a violation.

You mentioned in the second case that you indicted a management company. Did you get a conviction?

Yes.

Did you send the company to jail?

No we didn't, as a matter of fact. In this instance we could not show any particular person who was responsible. We didn't have any cooperation from the employees; we had no signatures on any of the checks. They were run through a machine and had just a signature stamp. We ended up indicting and fining the management company and making them pay the money back.

Do you have a state statute that allows indictments against corporations?

We have common law or decisions of the courts that have held that you can do that. But in this case we required as a condition of the plea that the principal owner of the corporation personally guarantee the payment to prevent him from dissolving the corporation the next day so there wouldn't be any assets. As a matter of fact, when we finally went to court the management company was not even in business, so they really didn't have any assets at all.

In North Carolina we also have a requirement that funds--the personal funds of nursing home patients--be held in a bank in North Carolina, and that any records pertaining to the accounting for those funds also be in North Carolina--actually physically within North Carolina. The main reason we did that was because we had a case where the nursing homes were located in North Carolina but they were owned by a company in Virginia. The funds were being kept in Virginia, and the transactions resulting in drafts against the patient trust funds which went to the parent corporation actually took place in Virginia, although the patients lived in North Carolina. So as a result, the regulations in North Carolina do require that the funds be physically within the borders of North Carolina.

We also had another case involving a rest home where about $20,000 was borrowed by the owner of the rest home in order to make some capital purchases and he actually drew up a promissory note and had a repayment schedule. It was all done very nicely by his own accountant but of course, none of the patients knew that their money was being used in this manner; but we had to give him credit.

At least from the beginning there was an apparent intent on his part to pay the money back. The problem was that one of the administrators died and no more payments were made after he expired, so about $6500 didn't get paid back. They brought in another administrator who was the son of the owner who had borrowed the money. He couldn't figure out why the patients were owed more money that was actually in the account. So he started a new ledger sheet and just put in an amount that, if you totalled up the entire amount, would be equal to what they actually owed at the time. I guess you could call that writing it off. He made it appear that there was a different amount owed so that it would all add up. He committed what is referred to in North Carolina as "common law forgery," so it didn't help him very much. He ended up probably getting in more trouble than if he had just not done anything. In North Carolina, any time that you knowingly make a false entry into a book of accounts and that particular entry is capable of affecting the rights of the people whose money you're dealing with, then that is known as common law forgery. That is a felony also.

We had another case involving the petty cash account where the administrator kept the money in her desk drawer and would use it at their discretion. She was also the wife of the police chief of the local town. It shows that his kind of thing can happen in a basically reputable facility because this was part of a fairly large chain. She was just the administrator; had no ownership interest at all. She also stole about $11,000 out of the account herself and bought clothes for her children and her mother. This was a situation where her mother was actually residing in the nursing home and would take a two-week vacation in the summer, and during the Christmas season they would go to Florida. In the summer they had a house at the beach and they would go down and spend a couple of weeks at the beach, during which time the administrator was billing the Medicaid program for those days that her mother was not there.

In the other case that you mentioned you made a point that the patients didn't even know about it. If they had known, would that have made a difference?

I don't think just knowing would have made any difference. But if they had consented then there would have been a problem.

Another issue which is important to discuss is embezzlement. In the nursing home context, you have a situation where money is applied to a purpose other than that which was intended, which is solely for the purpose of the patient having some money they can spend on tobacco, or a haircut and that sort of thing. So the fact that you don't apply the money to your own personal use is not a defense. As far as what constitutes a fraudulent purpose, in North Carolina and also, apparently, generally, the definition of intent is simply that you have applied it to a purpose other than that for which it was intended. You've got a relationship of trust, so any time that you use it for something that you weren't specifically authorized to use it for, then you have misapplied it.

It is necessary to permanently deprive the person of the money. The fact that you're able to pay and in fact do pay the money back at a later time is not a defense. The idea of borrowing the money simply is not a defense to misapplication or embezzlement.

Another issue which you might want to be aware of is that to prove embezzlement one does not have to be able to say exactly when the money was taken. It's usually enough to be able to say that it happened over a certain period of time, and in North Carolina there are cases where that period may be as long as four or five years.

The biggest problem is commingling. If you don't have a statute that specifically prohibits it the risk is that you may just forget that that money is in there and that it's not yours; and once you have spent it then it's no longer just commingling, it's out-and-out embezzlement. Also, and this is true in North Carolina as well as in most other states, there is no statute of limitations on a felony. If it happened in 1978 and they find out about it in 1983, you can still be indicted and convicted and sent away.

Another thing that certainly is an abuse of patient funds is to charge the patient for things that are in fact covered by the per diem reimbursement. It's very obvious but it continues to be a problem. If done on a large enough scale, it could even be construed as embezzlement or false pretense. The evidence is particularly strong when you have a double charge--charging the patient and charging the program at the same time. How can you say you didn't know when you charged the program as well as the patient? That is something that needs to be looked at very carefully.

Did I understand correctly that patient funds may be deposited in the bank without interest?

That is correct. There is a set of proposed regulations concerning standards for certification that were originally published in 1980, which would require you to put the money in an interest bearing account, but approval by OMB (federal Office of Management and Budget) apparently has never taken place. This standard is a fairly high one. It's certainly more stringent than the one that we use in North Carolina.

Another problem we saw in North Carolina which probably still occurs, is that of patients who have no money but are advanced monies out of the patient trust fund account, which basically means that they are using somebody else's money. It's hard to imagine somebody being prosecuted for embezzlement for doing that, particularly if it was not a very significant amount of money, and certainly if the patient receives some monies later on and the other money is restored. But where patients don't have any money and they continue to be given money and it accumulates and becomes a significant amount, then at least technically that is misapplication of patient funds, which would be an embezzlement offense. It is hard to allow these people to have absolutely nothing when the other people are sitting around drinking Cokes and dipping snuff.

The bottom line is that you have to have sufficient records to keep up with how much money each patient gets and precisely identify where the money is going. You need to have a current inventory of all the property that the patient has when they are admitted, and any that they acquire afterward--just making sure that everything that's received or disbursed is itemized and kept up-to-date. If you know who is receiving the funds, the purpose for which the fund are being expended, and perhaps who disbursed the funds, that protects the nursing home. In the event that there *is* some money missing somewhere along the way, and you can actually go to the records and find out.

The hardest cases to prosecute and to investigate are, I must admit, cases where you have absolutely no records, or where the records are so grossly inadequate that you can't tell what happened at any time. But obviously if you do that, you're going to be investigated more often, too. Ultimately, you will pay the price. Unfortunately, the people who keep the best records are also the ones who are the most easily prosecuted. Still, it's better to know exactly what's happening to the money so that you can take whatever remedial action is necessary to get rid of people who are not handling the money properly.

Chapter 14

Medicaid Discrimination Statutes, DRGs, and Hospital Interest in Long Term Care

Speaker: Stephen E. Ronai

The entire field of Medicaid discrimination is in a dynamic and developing stage because of the pressures of the Medicare prospective payment system. People in the hospital field, facing a four-year phase-in of the diagnosis-related group system, are beginning to be concerned that they will not be able to save money on a prospective system unless they can discharge their patients promptly to a lower and less costly level of care, for example, long term care in a skilled nursing facility setting.

Many feel that contracting will become crucial to the success or failure of the DRG system, once the national DRG reimbursement system overtakes the local and specific DRG rates, which are now being implemented in the first year. Therefore, now is a good time to look at some of the issues that stand as obstacles to potential favoritism that might be requested by acute care hospitals for their Medicare DRG discharges. These obstacles take the form of certain federal statutes under the Medicare program, certain federal statutes and regulations under the Medicaid program, and certain state laws that impose limitations and penalties against nursing homes that discriminate against Medicaid patients.

A recent paper identifies the most prevalent types of DRG discharges that will be coming to the nursing homes and creating the pressure for acceptance of Medicare patients. They are specific cerebrovascular disorders; hip and femur procedures, including broken hip syndromes; heart failure and shock; simple pneumonia and pleurisy for persons 70 years or older; operating room procedures unrelated to diagnostic conditions; kidney and urinary tract infections for persons 70 years or older; major joint procedures; esophagitis, gastroenteritis, and miscellaneous digestive disorders for the elderly or with complications; metabolic disorders for persons 70 or older; organic disturbance; and mental retardation.

If you want a copy of that paper, it's available. It's entitled "Hospital DRGs and the Need for Long Term Care Services," National Center for Health Services Research or NCHSR, 5600 Fishers Lane, 3-50 Park Building, Rockville, Maryland. Rather than repeat that again, I have it here if you'd like to come up and get it. I think it may be important to you in your contracting efforts and identifying the nature of the problem to deal with this paper, which identifies from a medical point of view what types of patients nursing homes and hospitals would be dealing with. We are trying to take it out of a theoretical mode and put it down into a case-specific context.

The other area that deals with theory is this great panic that there will be a great need for this type of contracting. There may well be, but one of the other limitations on the resort to widespread use of contracts aside from the medical limitations, is the Medicare financing system. The resort by nursing homes to Medicare financing and Medicare third-party payment is considerably less than to the Medicaid and private payor systems. In Connecticut, for example, 63% of patients are on Medicaid, approximately 20-23% are on private programs, and the balance, which is very small, are on Medicare. These are believed to be the prevalent percentages nationwide. Medicare only pays the reasonable cost of certain types of illnesses and conditions that require care that is non-custodial. The criteria re strictly imposed, and it is difficult to obtain benefits, and because of the possibility of the nursing home being liable in the event of a non-coverage determination by Medicare under Medicare's waiver of liability provisions, many nursing homes are very wary of admitting patients on a skilled nursing care basis who may or may not be entitled to Medicare coverage based upon the potential for an adverse eligibility determination, which comes after admission. Lawsuits have been brought around the country by legal services associations on behalf of Medicare eligibles, or potential eligibles, in which nursing home associations have joined because the Medicare restrictive interpretation has prevented nursing homes from getting this category of reimbursement.

Ms. Michal's presentation on private insurance for home care and nursing home care covers the Medicare reimbursement coverage issues very succinctly, and shows that in addition to the length-of-stay limitation, which theoretically is a maximum of 100 days per year, there are severe diagnostic limitations in the definitions of skilled care, and these are barriers in the contracting process to Medicare eligibility.

A paper by Thomas Jaczwicki and Stephen Press, called "Provider Opportunities Under Medicare's DRG Base Prospective Payment System," highlights for lawyers, nursing home administrators, and fiscal professionals some of the important issues aside from Medicaid discrimination, such as potential antitrust issues, potential liabilities for inappropriate care and inappropriate transfer, freedom of choice issues, and patients' rights. These are treated in some of the cases described here.

The issue of Medicaid discrimination should lurk behind every hospital or nursing home contract that is directed to circumvent or to take account of the DRG discharge process. A hospital patient who has undergone an acute care procedure may at that stage of convalescence be a Medicare patient, and if he or she is transferred within 3 days of the hospital discharge to a nursing home, that patient is presumptively entitled to Medicare third-party payment for treatment in the nursing home. Exceptions are: (1) if the patient is an indigent patient at that time, and is ineligible for Medicare reimbursement as a result of an eligibility determination based upon the patient's condition; or (2) if the patient is exhausting private funds.

Thus, treatment under the state law of that patient's status as a potential Medicaid patient could be an impediment in your contract, and this is a determination that each party--contractors or contractees, obligors and obligees-- has to take account of. There are several statutory and regulatory provisions to be taken account of as well. Michael Cook has already treated the potential Medicare regulatory and statutory prohibitions, which under the Medicare Act, sections 1902(a)(14) and 1866(a)(1), prohibits pursuant to provider agreements anyone but the Medicare program from paying for a patient's care.

Under the Medicaid program there is a statute that all agree was never intended to provide an obstacle at this time when institutional providers of health care in the acute care context were seeking beds in nursing homes with respect to DRG transfers. That statute, section 1909(d) of the Social Security Act, or 42 U.S.C. section 1396 h(d)(2)(B) in the subsections, is treated in detail in the *Glengariff* case and in all the other cases to which I will refer. That statute provides that it is a felony to knowingly and willfully charge, for any service provided to a patient under an approved state plan, any money or any other consideration at a rate in excess of the rates established by the state under a state plan; it is also a felony to charge, solicit, accept or receive any money or other consideration in addition to the amount paid under the state plan, except for charity or other philanthropic motives, as a precondition to admitting that patient to a hospital, skilled nursing home, or intermediate care facility (ICF) or as a requirement for that patient's continued stay. If anyone does that, and if the money is not for services covered under a state plan, then that act constitutes a felony punishable by fine of not more than $25,000 or imprisonment for not more than five years or both. This is a statute that is observed in the breach, I suppose, by many providers who are uncomfortable with the concept of discrimination but seem compelled by the inadequacy of state Medicaid plan reimbursement, so this discrimination is a reality.

The same statute says that you cannot receive or charge as a condition of admitting a patient, or of a patient's continued stay, anything more than is paid to you as a provider under a state plan, in a state-approved Medicaid rate for the services that the state plan covers, i.e., for covered services. So the issue is, what are noncovered services? What services can you charge for? And what are potential payments that can be structured in the contract that a hospital can receive for so-called noncovered services? With respect to the Medicare prohibitions, those agreements with hospitals that are so-called bed reservation agreements, as opposed to bonus payments, have informally received, at least in letter form, approbation from the Inspector General of HHS. In those agreements, a nursing home pays, or a hospital pays a nursing home, a specified amount of money to reserve a block of beds on an availability basis, but that money is paid to the nursing home by the hospital for those beds irrespective of whether any patients occupy those beds. Thus, the payments are not patient-specific; they are not payments for services that that patient might be receiving through third-party payment under a Medicaid state plan. They are simply generic payments or gross amounts that tend to protect the hospital making those payments, against the risk that hospital patients will not have nursing home beds. It is simply a gross rental space reservation arrangement. These are not funds to supplement what a patient may be receiving as third-party payment under Medicare or, potentially, under Medicaid.

That kind of agreement apparently has an informal HHS approval, and the outside counsel for one of the national nursing home chains has apparently obtained approval in informal letters from the Inspector General as to those types of bonus payments. Reserved bed payments, however, which are bonus payments for specific numbers of beds, (i.e., $10 per bed or per patient) because they are directly attributable to the services rendered to specific patients, have not received the same kind of approval and are theoretically violations of the supplementation criminal prohibition in section 1909(d).

The general framework, then, is all that has been obtained from governmental agencies. The Health Care Financing Administration (HCFA) is circulating an action transmittal with respect to the scope of the prohibitions of the Medicare Act and Medicaid Act in terms of supplementation.

The case law in this area consists chiefly of four cases. We started off with a clean slate in 1965 when Medicaid and Medicare were enacted by Congress. At that time all that existed was section 1909(d) and some legislative history concerning the issue of supplementation. Supplementation is a term referred to in certain legislative history and in HCFA communications and is defined as amounts paid by relatives of patients or third parties, but not governmental contractual third parties, for the care of a patient for services that are covered by the single per diem payment made by the single-state agency for services that are covered under the Medicaid State Plan. The issue is under what state statutes, what conditions, and what contractual arrangements a nursing home may legally accept that type of supplementation or may have a contract with a third-party relative or other person to require that third person to pay the higher private patient rate for a duration or a stated period, prior to that patient making application for eligibility for third-party payments under the Medicaid program, i.e., length of stay or private-patient duration agreements.

THE *RESIDENT V. NOOT* CASE

The first case was *Resident v. Arthur Noot*, (305 N.W. 2d 311 (Minn. 1981), 1981 Medicare and Medicaid Guide (CCH) 31,029 (Minn. 1981), aff'g 1980 Medicare and Medicaid Guide (CCH) 30,515 (Minn. Dist. Ct., Feb. 4, 1980). Noot had been the administrator of nursing homes in Minnesota. Several decisions in the long term care field have come from Minnesota, and we now have a sophisticated case mix system coming out of Minnesota which may be the answer to some of the stringent fiscal problems we face in long term care Medicaid financing. The Minnesota rate equalization decision, about which many are concerned, is now being studied by legislatures across the country.

The *Resident v. Noot* decision, handed down in 1981, essentially held that a patient's daughter could voluntarily pay the difference between a $19.65 ICF rate, which was a single rate under the Minnesota state plan for ICF services, and a $40 private room rate, and that the nursing home could legally accept that payment, and further, that the additional $20.35 payment would not render the patient ineligible for Medicaid and that the payment would not be used as applied income so as to reduce the Medicaid contributions. Furthermore, on a petition for declaratory judgment brought by the resident, actually by the nursing home plaintiff, the Minnesota Supreme Court held that the payment by the daughter of some $21 would not violate the supplementation prohibitions that Congress apparently referred to in the Medicaid statute's legislative history.

Interestingly, there appears to be no mention in that decision of the felony statute section 1909(d). The decision does deal with the issue of Congressional intent, and the secretary, of course, did promulgate a regulation which at section 447.15 to 42 C.F.R. provides that state plans must require Medicaid providers to accept the amount paid by the state agency as payment in full for covered services. Congress was concerned, the Minnesota court said, and expressed it in the legislative history, that HCFA or the Department of Health and Human Services (HHS) at that time was not paying states adequate reimbursement, and in the early stages of the Medicaid program states were not participating to the full extent that Congress had intended with respect to this program that was to benefit indigents across the country. In fact, Congress recognized in some states the full cost accrued was paid by the state plan, and in others a negotiated rate was developed. Now this goes back prior to the July 1, 1976 effective date of section 249 on reasonable cost related reimbursement, to the time that you had flat-rate states and other states that were not paying on a reasonable cost-related basis.

Congress did recognize that many states did depend upon the supplementation of the state agencies rate with contribution from relatives of the needy individual. Congress thus recognized early on the limited nature of Medicaid reimbursement. As a matter of public policy, it is best for all concerned--the needy individual, his or her relatives, the state agency, and the nursing home--that the Medicaid reimbursement made by the state and HCFA represent the reasonable cost of services to the provider and the reasonable charges for comparable services without encouraging excess reliance on private supplementation. The committee went on to say that, while the states and Congress were not paying the actual cost of services some method of fair reimbursement was the ultimate objective. Interestingly, Medicaid reimbursement has not gotten any better, since that original statement and some form of supplementation is still being sought to assist nursing home providers to overcome the difficulties of inadequate Medicaid reimbursement.

In the Minnesota case the court held that, if the cost of a private room was not a covered service under the state plan, if the state plan did not define the size of a room as being a totally covered service, if a private room was not medically necessary, and if somebody wanted to pay for it, then the cost of a private room was, like a private telephone or television, a nonstandard and noncovered service, and therefore a voluntary payment was an exercise of generosity on the part of a relative and not prohibited as a legal supplementation.

THE *GLENGARIFF* CASE

The *Resident v. Noot* decision was viable for at least three year, until in 1984 three cases came up commencing with the *Glengariff* case, which is the most far-reaching and comprehensive case that deals with prohibitions against supplementation through the form of voluntary contract. The case of *Glengariff Corp. v. Snook* (1984 Medicare and Medicaid Guide (CCH) 33,605 (N.Y. Sup. Ct., Nassau County Jan. 4, 1984)) was a decision of the New York Supreme Court that arose on an appeal from a fair hearing officer's determination of whether or not a patient was eligible for medical assistance under the New York state plan. Under these circumstances, prior to that patient entering the Glengariff Corporation's nursing home, the son of the patient entered into a contract with the nursing home which provided that the patient would live out her final years in the comfort of a private room, and Robert Snook, the defendant and the patient's son, would pay $95.60 per day for a private room for a period of 18 months and the patient would be obligated to remain and to pay as a private patient and not apply for Medicaid eligibility until the expiration of the 18-month period.

The patient was admitted on July 10, 1982. After three months of residence, however, Mr. Snook on behalf of his mother, applied for Medicaid eligibility. The fair hearing officer and the single-state agency determined that that contract and the home's third-party rights to obtain private pay supplementation from the son constituted resources available to the patient and denied Medicaid eligibility. That decision was ultimately reversed, and Medicaid eligibility to the patient was granted as of November 24, 1982. Consequently, there were roughly 14 months to run on this potential private payment to the nursing home pursuant to the privately developed Snook contract. The New York Supreme Court reviewed the decision of the fair hearing officer on the issue of eligibility and said that the patient was eligible and entitled to Medicaid reimbursement, because that contract, irrespective of whether or not it was validly executed between two contracting parties, violated the public policy of the state of New York as interpreted by the court from the Medicaid statute. The statute they referred to was section 1909(d), which as discussed above, made it a felony subject to fine and imprisonment to exact a payment in addition to the Medicaid payment, for a covered service, from a patient as a condition of a continued nursing home stay. Additionally, one month after this contract had been entered into, New York had passed a statute similar to section 1909(d) making it a felony to exact a payment from a recipient or a recipient's representative for Medicaid service covered by the state plan, and although the New York statute could not retroactively invalidate the preexisting Snook contract, the court used the New York statute as an expression of its public policy. "We cannot enforce the statute and we are called upon in this decision," the New York Supreme Court says, "to enforce the federal statute, because this is an appeal from eligibility, but we are finding a patient eligible based upon the public policy expressed in the federal statute or the New York statute." That decision really put an end to private-pay duration contracting in New York, except, as I have indicated, in those states that specifically have tried to circumvent the statute by defining what services are not covered by the Medicaid payment under the state plan and allowing providers to obtain separate payments for those specific types of services.

THE *MARYLAND NURSING HOME ADMINISTRATION* CASE

Later in the year the Maryland nursing home administration case came to court. (*Summit Nursing Home et al. v. Medical Care Programs, Dept. of Health and Mental Hygiene,* 1984 Medicare and Medicaid Guide (CCH) 33,977. Decision of the Secretary's Designee Marsha R. Gold, May 8, 1984.) Maryland had a statute that did permit a nursing home to enter into a private-pay agreement or duration-of-stay contract with individuals who were admitted to the home at the time that the contract was made were still private patients. The Maryland statute permitted a duration of stay of contract for a period not to exceed one year. After lengthy litigation which commenced in federal court the case was remanded and laid the stage for the definitive decision of a hearing officer.

This final decision involved the construction of that statute, Health General Article section 19-345(c)(1)(i), and the attorney general's brief, which contended that those contracts were essentially void ab initio in Maryland, because although they could be made with a private patient, the contracts also contained provisions that if the person within the one-year period became eligible for Medicaid and the home did not have provisions or rooms for Medicaid patients, that patient or his or her representative would agree to engage in discharge procedures for the patient. The court basically held that section 1909(d) prohibited such agreements, not ab initio, upon their execution when the patient is private pay, but once the patient is Medicaid eligible, the condition of continued stay as a private patient violates the second half of the statute.

Additionally, the court reached out for a new string to its bow of prohibitions and pointed to provisions of the Patient Bill of Rights, which is incorporated into each Medicaid and Medicare provider agreement by the federal statutes regulations as a condition of participation. The section in the Patient Bill of Rights that they cited was 42 CFR 405.1121(k), which guarantees to the patient, once admitted to the facility, that he or she be transferred or discharged only for medical reasons or for his or her welfare, or for nonpayment of the stay. None of those reasons validate a discharge for the continued nonpayment of private patient charges for the duration of stay pursuant to a preexisting validly executed agreement.

There may be a contrary administrative ruling in the state of Pennsylvania, but that merely underscores the fact that each state has different prohibitions. Therefore, when contracting, attorneys must read the Medicaid discrimination statutes of their own state.

THE *DUNLAP* CASE

The Iowa decision, *Dunlap Care Center v. Dept. of Social Services* (1984 Medicare and Medicaid Guide (CCH) 34,048, Iowa Supreme Court July 18, 1984) is a sort of composite and arose in a different context. It was an affirmation by the Iowa Supreme Court of a lower court decision that upheld a hearing officer's decision with respect to an order requiring a nursing home to repay to the Iowa Medicaid agency $11,171.38, which the nursing home received from three patients' families on behalf of those patients so those patients could stay in private rooms. There was no duration-of-stay contract in this case; this was a direct payment, a so-called supplementation payment. However, the Iowa court had to deal with the *Resident v. Noot* case, which arose in a similar context in Minnesota. In categorizing these cases the Maryland and New York cases, *Summit* and *Glengariff*, deal with duration-of-stay contracts, and the Minnesota and Iowa cases, *Resident* and *Dunlap*, deal with cases of direct monetary supplementation by relatives. The Iowa court had no real trouble with the supplementation payment problem. It looked retrospectively at *Resident v. Noot* and declared the issue to be a matter of the coverage of the state plan.

In 1979 Minnesota clearly indicated that one could supplement the per diem payment if the supplementation payment was for services not covered by the state plan. The Minnesota state plan at that time made it clear that the cost of a semiprivate room was part of the per diem rate. A private room, a telephone, a television set, or even a wheelchair in Minnesota could be the subject of a separate supplementation payment. Similarly, the parties in *Dunlap* stipulated that if a relative purchases an electric wheelchair, a special bed, a telephone service, or a television for a resident, those costs would not be deducted from the facility's per diem Medicaid rate, but certainly the cost of a private room would be deducted. The case did not stress the issue of public policy but traced historically the evolving HHS policy, which said initially in 1969 that if the states wanted to allow supplementation, in order to encourage full participation by states in the Medicaid program, HHS ought to allow it. However, the *Resident v. Noot* decision did not clearly state, as *Dunlap* does, that in 1971 HCFA ordered the states to phase out supplementation by January 1, 1971.   On the eve of implementing the cost-related reimbursement system in late 1972 HCFA determined that, now that reimbursement was going to be adequately funded, no more supplementation was needed. That was a cruel joke based upon what we have learned about the stringencies of Medicaid reimbursement since 1972. Clearly, however, that was the intent of the agency having expertise in the area, and the Iowa court respected that. It also based its decision on the 1909(d) criterion, indicating that the felony statute had to be dealt with.

This decision constitutes therefore a strong basis for having contracts fall or rise on the difficulties of defining what a covered service is if you are going to do a type of non-patient specific reserve bed agreement. You do not want to have a contract be patient-specific. You also must take account of what the hospital is paying for, and that may be a real impediment in many states.

Some states have clearly recognized that this is a problem for statutory treatment and for treatment in the state plan. For instance, the state of Georgia recently enacted a regulation that indicated quite clearly that effective January 1985 the state plan "will allow supplementation by relatives or other persons for a private room or a private sitter or both for a recipient of medical assistance in the nursing home." Further, the Georgia Single State Agency was required to change its regulations in the state plan to take account of that regulation, and the money paid was not considered assets available with respect to Medicaid eligibility if it was limited to those types of services and private sitters. The Georgia regulation provided, however, that no provider of medical assistance shall discriminate against the recipient of medical assistance who does not have a relative willing and able to provide supplementation.

LEGISLATION IN OTHER STATES

Ohio and New Jersey have also legislated in this area. A very recent piece of legislation from New Jersey introduces the subject of state statutes that impede the free access to nursing home beds which hospitals seek through bed reservation contracts. These are statutes that essentially deal with Medicaid bed quotas.   Medicaid admission limitations, and the so-called "first-come-first-served mandate" statute in Connecticut, which states that Connecticut must maintain waiting lists and daily logs of all categories of applicants. Patients that are bona fide applicants must be placed on a waiting list in Connecticut, they must be given receipts, and then must be admitted in the order in which they appear on the waiting list. To the extent that you have a heavy spend-down by elderly people of their assets, and already our Medicaid population is at 62%, that statute does pose one of the most significant threats to transform the nursing home census to a potentially all-Medicaid population, and a countervailing force to inhibit access to the home by the larger private-pay population that seems to be out there, because of the greater financial resources available through retirement funds, IRAs, and other resources.

The Ohio statute provides that a facility with 80% or more Medicaid patients is prohibited from refusing to retain or accept an applicant who is or may become a recipient of medical assistance. There is an exception for religious or nondenominational homes for admission of their patients. New Jersey of course had a very complex and significant litigation in which the principal issue there was whether the requirement that each facility accept a reasonable number of indigent patients as a condition of licensure was valid. That requirement was tempered somewhat in New Jersey by an "escape clause" which provided a financial hardship exception to the mandated Medicaid census. If a facility could show that this reasonableness had to be tempered by the facility's inability because of a large Medicaid census imposed on the facility to obtain a just and reasonable return on equity, the percentage requirement could be reduced. That decision went to the New Jersey Supreme Court, was affirmed against numerous constitutional and statutory claims by the New Jersey Association of Health Care Facilities, and the Supreme Court denied certification. New Jersey just passed a statute that, while prohibiting private-pay duration-of-stay agreements, also requires all nursing homes to maintain a quota of 67% Medicaid patients as a condition of obtaining a certificate of need (*N.J. Association of Health Care Facilities v. Finley* 402 A.2d 246 (Sup. Ct. App. Div. 1979) *aff'd sub. nom. In The Matter of Health Care Admin. Bd.* 415 A.2d.1147 (N.J.), *cert. denied* 449 U.S. 944 (1980)).

Connecticut passed a statute in 1980 that dealt with admission in the order of application. That statute established a legislative policy of prohibiting nursing homes from discriminating against any indigents who apply for admission "on the source of payment." The definition of an indigent person was any person who is eligible for or was receiving medical assistance benefits from the state or general assistance benefits from a town. Duration-of-stay contracts or exacting of monies or any consideration for admission were also prohibited, and the statute required the nursing home to maintain a daily log of admissions. It was not quite clear the the waiting list would have to be maintained, but that was the general understanding by nursing homes.

When that statute was refined in 1984, it was changed to require not only a long and a so-called waiting list, but the granting to each bona fide applicant of a receipt, which would be a piece of evidence indicating that he or she did make such application. The penalty for failure to admit a patient from that waiting list in the proper order, based upon the log, the waiting list, and the receipt, was an order to the nursing home, generally by letter, that its Medicaid per diem reimbursement would be reduced. The amount of this reduction was 0.25% for the first violation and 1% for the second violation. However, that order would automatically be stayed if the nursing home took an administrative appeal within 15 days.

In the four years that the statute has been in effect there have been perhaps four cases, two or three of which are now in the courts being settled. As with all documentary cases in this area, the documentary trails are enormous. They are difficult cases once a documentary trail is provided, and this statute is intended to provide a documentary trail. However, does the statute prohibit the exercise of any discretion by a nursing home with respect to the implementation of an application procedure and patient admission standards, and can those admission standards be formulated into a contract with the hospital so as to favor Medicare DRG patients? We think nursing homes can and should, pursuant to their admissions contracts and pursuant to their policies, establish application procedures that reflect reasonable requirements that are uniformly applied to all persons seeking admission.

If you must put applicants on a waiting list, keep them on a log, and give them a receipt, and you are interested in maintaining your discretion, then there is language in the Medicaid and Medicare conditions of participation requiring you to have admissions policies and procedures and there are provisions in your licensure statutes and regulations with respect to your staffing and type of patient which you may admit which may provide exceptions to the strict waiting list receipt rule. These conditions may allow you to impose bona fide hurdles that any normal business may impose upon those seeking its services, despite the fact that you are regulated under federal and state statute. For example, you may require a personal visit, not by the applicant of course, but by someone who represents the applicant in a financially responsible manner. You may require a singed application--a telephone request from a social worker at a hospital seeking a bed for a relative may not constitute an application, and therefore that kind of inquiry need not be logged or receipted pursuant to the statute. You may and should require the submission of medical, social, and financial information prior to logging in the person on the list or issuing a receipt. Those kinds of requirements, applied uniformly, should pass muster. May a facility refuse admission for medical reasons? Obviously it can and in many cases it should. We did not think, in our interpretation in the advisory that we issued to our state association, that the legislature intended by the antidiscrimination prohibition implemented through waiting list receipts to supersede the duty of the nursing home or any health care provider to treat a patient for appropriate medical conditions.

Obviously, these requirements can be applied in a subterfuge and circumventing manner, but there are some heavy care patients that nursing homes, because of staffing, in addition to licensure may not at a given time be able to treat and handle appropriately. Refusal to admit an applicant must be based solely on the medical condition, and that medical condition standard must be applied identically to both indigent and nonindigent patients. The medical standard must be carefully documented with respect to these statutes that cause scrutiny because of Medicaid discrimination, so that, although generally documentation can cause difficulty if you are being surveyed, this in an area where documentation in terms of medical decisions for admission or nonadmissions helpful.

The difficult question is, may a facility require that a potential patient demonstrate some source of payment prior to admission? We believe that is a bona fide eligibility requirement. We don't believe, at least in our states, that the statute requires admission of people who have no source of payment. Obviously, a private patient has a source of payment. The issue is whether a pending Medicaid patient who is a bona fide applicant is an eligible patient. We take the position that it cannot be determined and that in may cases eligibility is denied because of transfer assets or the eligibility is contested. Those patients who are not eligible at the time are therefore treated in one of two ways. They may be noted as having applied, but they are generally not given a receipt because that patient at that time is not a bona fide applicant--he or she has not satisfied the facility's requirement that some source of payment be demonstrated. Pending Medicaid patients can be treated differently.

A sensitive issue is how long the list of applications or the waiting list must be kept. This list could be allowed to stretch out ad infinitum, rendering a long list of patients eligible to be admitted, and that kind of potential eligibility is an impairment to the contract with the hospital that seeks to transfer its Medicare-eligible patients. The hospital's need for preference obviously conflicts with the waiting list need for preference, probably for a predominance of Medicaid patients. There is no case law on the subject; one can be conservative and keep the list ad infinitum. We have advised that the list be updated every 30-60 days by calls by the nursing home to patients on the list or to their representatives. An alternative is to require those persons on a waiting list to reapply after a stated period of time. Both procedures are reasonable, and both I think would pass muster in our state. Both would impose reasonable requirements with respect to admission based upon the order of application.

States are likely to become more active in the Medicaid discrimination area. Obviously your provider agreement has statements in it and affirmative obligations to accept payment in full for all covered services for a patient. This is a reaffirmation in verbatim of the federal regulation under Medicaid, but it may also have an antidiscrimination prohibition, because most provider agreements have that language. As a matter of contract, the state agency has a remedy in the event of discrimination in addition to any statutory remedies that your state may enact. The states may take account of the attention being paid to hospital contracting and Medicaid discrimination and merely upgrade the language in provider agreements to deal with this issue.

Chapter 15

Punitive Damage Claims

Speaker: J. Mark Waxman

Potentially the most important topic involving long term care is the specter of punitive damage awards. While reimbursement issues can be the subject of ongoing planning with accountants and legal counsel, punitive damages may be the result of a single lawsuit, may be of significantly greater import than a reimbursement decision and are of potentially greater consequences.

CASE STUDY

One easy way to look at punitive damages in the context of skilled nursing facilities is to think of your own facility or a facility with which you are involved. Assume you are caring for the average 83-year-old nursing home patient, a total care patient who has been in your facility for approximately six years. The patient, Ms. Jones, suffers from chronic brain syndrome, and communicates occasionally by moving one arm and opening and closing her eyes.

We shall call your facility the Do Good Convalescent Hospital. It was built about the mid-1950s. You have 99 beds; you don't want to have 100 because if you do, your particular state regulatory agency will suggest that you have additional nursing supervisors on staff which is something that you cannot afford.

Since Ms. Jones' arrival at your facility, things have been going generally well. Over the last year, however, a little problem in the boiler room has occurred. From time to time surges of hot water seem to come out of the sinks. You've also noticed that the dishwasher water in the kitchen is occasionally too cold. To solve this particular problem you talked to your handyman who suggested that you hire a local plumber to go in and look at the valves in the boilers which were installed when the facility was built. The plumber concludes that there is some sort of difficulty with one of the valves and he believes that it may have been put in backwards. He turns the valve around, and nothing happens for several months. Two months later there is a hot water surge that comes out of the kitchen sink and affects the help; after that nothing happens.

The last week or two there was a hot water surge out of a shower on one of the floors during the daytime shift. A check is made of the boiler by the handyman, and there doesn't seem to be a problem.

Last night in your facility, two night shift orderlies passed Ms. Jones' room and they saw that she had soiled herself. Although they weren't supposed to, they put Ms. Jones in a wheelchair, wheeled her down to the shower, placed her under the shower and proceeded to wash her down. At some point during the course of this procedure, one of the orderlies felt hot water on her feet as they were walking in the shower with Ms. Jones. They looked at Ms. Jones and saw that the skin on her legs was getting rather red. They immediately moved her out, took her to her room, and called the night supervisor of nurses who came over and saw that blisters were beginning to form. The night supervisor put ointment on Ms. Jones' legs.

An hour later Ms. Jones' physician was called. He happens to be the medical director of your facility; no other doctor would accept Ms. Jones but the medical director did it as a courtesy to you. The medical director said he would be in at 6:00 a.m. since the situation did not sound that serious. When he came in, he suggested transferring Ms. Jones to a hospital. You took Ms. Jones to the nearest hospital, which does not have a burn unit. The hospital staff began administering to Ms. Jones, and they contacted another physician who applied more aggressive treatment. Ms. Jones died at 2:00 of acute dehydration caused by a burn.

Subsequently, one of the relatives brings a law suit for negligence as well as punitive damages. The claims which form the basis for the punitive damages allegations are several: (1) You failed to check out the boiler appropriately, and thereby consciously disregarded the rights and safety of the patients; (2) you should have been aware of burn facilities in the area given the risk to patients with poor circulation (of which you are obviously aware as a result of treating decubitus ulcers); and (3) you did not properly train the orderlies.

Your investigation reveals that on the night shift one of the orderlies involved had been at the facility for two years, speaks some English, had six hours of continuing education last year, but this year the records are blank. The second orderly does not speak English, and his only training was four hours of orientation on the job as to what a night orderly in a nursing facility does.

When the law suit starts, your insurance carrier maintains that this was an 83-year-old chronic brain syndrome patient who did not have a significant life expectancy, if any, and therefore the exposure should be in the $25,000 range, and no more. You talk to a burn specialist, because the insurance company will not, and the burn specialist tells you that in order to receive the kinds of burns suffered by Ms. Jones, it would take water temperature of approximately 135 to 140 degrees for 7 to 10 seconds for this particular patient. You start getting a little bit nervous.

The plaintiff's demand comes in: $1,000,000. Your insurance coverage is only $500,000. The insurance company says that it sees its exposure as $25,000, and asks what you are willing to contribute to avoid punitive damage exposure. You go back to the insurance company and say I will contribute nothing, until you offer policy limits to settle the action. The insurance company tells you it would not offer policy limits because the compensatory damage exposure is nowhere near policy limits.

The case goes on and as you near trial you make a formal written demand on your carrier to offer policy limits to settle. Plaintiff's counsel agrees to accept a settlement of $500,000, which coincidentally happens to be policy limits. You send another letter to the insurance company demanding that it offer policy limits because it is required under its implied covenant of good faith and fair dealing to protect you from exposure to punitive damages. The insurance company refuses, saying it does not insure against punitive damages, only compensatory damages.

Shortly before trial you go to the insurance company lawyers and say,"Have you done *a*, *b*, *c* to investigate the case?" They reply that they have done *a* and *b*, but not *c*. You make another demand to do *c*. You discuss whether you should be involved in the trial on behalf of your client. The insurance company lawyer tells you that if you have your own lawyer involved in the trial, there will be two lawyers sitting at counsel's table, and the jury will perceive that there is a dispute between the insurance company and the insured, sense big money and you will have a bigger award.

You go back to your client and say, "Here's what the insurance company is telling us, and there is merit to their counsel's position. If we sit at counsel's table, we also won't get to blame the insurance company's lawyer if a bad result occurs since we will have been there. You then go to discuss with your client whether you should be handling the case instead of the insurance company lawyer because they haven't done the job. You go to the carrier, and demand that your lawyer handle the case instead. Have you eliminated your bad faith claim? You have to work this out with your company.

The case goes to trial. Following jury instructions, and while the jury is deliberating, the case settles for $300,000. You talk to the jury and find out they would have awarded $675,000 for intentional infliction of emotional distress, of which $450,000 would probably have been in the form of punitive damages.

This case study is a representative story of the potential impact of punitive damages in skilled nursing facilities. It is rather easy to get a punitive damage award on facts like these from a jury. Simply imagine the plaintiff's lawyer holding up his hand in front of the jury and saying as part of his argument, "Ladies and Gentlemen, count to eight seconds and imagine 140 degree water on your hand and tell me that this nursing home did all they could to protect the rights of the patients." That's illustrative of the dangers inherent in an exposure to punitive damages.

What are the issues that we face as lawyers for skilled nursing facilities and owners? First, what is punitive damage exposure? Where does it come from? Second, under what theories can you be liable? Third, how do you deal with your insurer? What should that relationship be at the inception of the litigation and as you carry the matter through to trial. Fourth, to what extent can you avoid punitive damage exposure? The illustration I presented was designed to raise these issues. Perhaps as I address each of these issues, you can imagine them arising in your particular facility.

PUNITIVE DAMAGE EXPOSURE

In most states, punitive damages are available for intentional torts. In the nursing home setting you see intentional torts often in the form of intentional infliction of emotional distress. Fraud claims may also be made. Patient trust funds could be one obvious area in which plaintiff will allege fraud. Another example of where an alleged fraud may arise is as follows. Your admission agreement recites that you offer 24-hour service and treatment. A patient is raped at midnight by somebody who you don't know, and thus you haven't provided what you said you were going to. Is that a fraud?

Usually, simple negligence, a failure to act at a reasonable level, is not a basis for punitive damages. The vast middle ground between negligence and intentional torts seems to very from state to state and even within different courts of the same state. Some states may call something gross negligence instead of punitive damages where another will call it recklessness and it is really the same thing.

You must remember in viewing the punitive damages, that you're going to a jury which is looking in retrospect at what happened and they may have in mind that, as Hubert Humphrey said, "a nation is judged according to how they protect their elderly," a very powerful argument to a jury.

FAILURE TO INVESTIGATE

What are the specific kinds of acts that you need to be aware of, as you operate a facility and deal with potential punitive damage claims. Most of these come under the categories of failures: (1) failure to investigate patient complaint, (2) failure to investigate complaints of relatives, (3) failure to immediately seek to correct deficiencies seen in licensing and certification inspections, and (4) failure to supervise ingress and egress from the facility.

CONSCIOUS DISREGARD

In most jurisdictions, a single negligent act will not be enough to award punitive damages. You have to go further and show, if not intent, something called a conscious disregard of the rights of the patients. How better to show this then to illustrate that this problem has come up before. The first thing the plaintiff's lawyer will do in this regard is to ask for all your state survey and inspection reports, which will often indicate prior knowledge of this particular type of problem. (An argument that you will make on appeal is that you didn't have knowledge of that particular type of problem and therefore did not have a conscious disregard.) Your complaint file will also be reviewed. It, therefore, becomes important for you to have follow-up documentation indicating what you did to investigate the complaint. Lack of such files will indicate to the jury that you didn't care.

Another area that will be reviewed is that of employee training and discipline. If you discipline an employee, or you find that an employee had a particular problem, you must document the follow-up, the discipline imposed, the continuing education or in-service required of that employee, and that they did it. In other words, your defense must convince the jury that, in fact, you do care about the 83-year-old total care patients in your facility. You must convince the jury your facility does take those steps necessary to protect the safety and rights of your patients.

LIABILITY FOR PUNITIVE DAMAGES

The second issue is who is liable for punitive damages as they are assessed. Although the employee committing the tort is obviously liable, most employees don't have enough money to interest a plaintiff's lawyer. However, the managing company or its parent has assets which may offer a source of payment above that available from insurance. The question then becomes, under what circumstances is the employer or the parent of the subsidiary who happen to be operating that particular facility liable for punitive damages. Of particular concern is that the insurance carrier has little interest in punitive damages, because it is not covering that particular liability, only the compensatory damages from the injury itself. Whether the parent is ultimately liable for that, whether the employer is directly liable really doesn't matter to the insurance company. It assumes that it can cover only whatever that compensatory damages liability is within its policy limit, which may be as high as $500,000. Thus, you have to confront that issue at the beginning of the case, knowing what the potential theories of liability may be.

Direct liability may be imposed on employers for punitive damages for such things as their own lack of supervision of employees, and their own lax administration of policies within the facility for such things as ingress and egress. If the employer fails in these areas, that may be evidence of his conscious disregard of the rights of patients.

Although the two orderlies in my example actually wanted to help Ms. Jones by taking her down to the shower to clean her off, the plaintiff's lawyers may or may not see this as a goodwill gesture, and that will not absolve you, the employer, from liability of punitive damages on a claim that this situation involved negligence, not conscious disregard. If a plaintiff's lawyer can find several instances of this type of negligence, it seems that you were reckless, that there was indeed a conscious disregard of the rights and safety of patients.

MANAGING AGENT

An employer may also be liable for the acts of a managing agent. A managing agent is typically one who has some discretion about how to operate the facility. This will usually be the administrator or, in appropriate cases, the director of nurses.   Therefore, vigilance is needed on the part of senior management to make sure that managing agents are not ratifying or authorizing these "bad acts," in order to avoid punitive damage liability.

PARENT/SUBSIDIARY

In the parent/subsidiary context, another issue arises. A plaintiff's lawyer knows that an individual facility may not be well capitalized. Therefore, he wants to place before the jury the net worth of a deep pocket. To do that, the plaintiff's lawyer will first name the parent, and, second, prove something in the nature of an alter ego theory. To accomplish this plaintiff must show that the links between the parent and subsidiary are such that the subsidiary is a "mere instrumentality" of the parent. To you, this means that as you handle these cases, remember that the insurance company will readily parade your net worth in front of the jury. You also need to reach those whom you think may be deposed early in the investigation to make sure they are attuned to the issues-- namely, to give testimony that would indicate a separate and distinct corporate existence; to indicate that the local administrator has autonomy; to indicate that the director of nurses has autonomy in terms of hiring, firing, supervision, it must be proven that these individuals believe they have discretion to operate the facility on a day-to-day basis or the parent will be liable under some sort of instrumentality or alter ego theory.

MEDICAL DIRECTOR/ATTENDING PHYSICIAN ISSUES

Issues may also arise with respect to facility liability in relating to the liability of the attending physician or the medical director. There are some physicians who take care of the elderly who are not as diligent as we might like. What better way for the plaintiff's lawyer to show a conscious disregard to the rights of the patient than to pull out a patient chart and show that the facility didn't even call the doctor for 4, 5, 6 months to at least update the patient's chart. A blank chart is your worst enemy. If the physician does not come in, you are inviting liability because you showed a conscious disregard and participated in whatever error the physician committed. Liability, therefore, has to be guarded against both from your own employees and your physicians who may be in and out of the facility, and who may often refer private pay patients which are the kind of patients that you want.

CONDUCT YOUR OWN INVESTIGATION

When you detect any punitive damage exposure, it is important to do your own investigation early and make sure that your management employees are aware of the type of questions that will be asked in depositions and the type of answers and documentation that they should be willing to provide. Interview all the employees who may have knowledge of the facts surrounding plaintiff's injury. It is also wise to approach the relatives of the patient involved and get signed statements from them to the effect that they have been very pleased with the years of care your facility has rendered to Ms. Jones. You will thus show the jury that you show no malice or lack of care for your patients.

RELATIONSHIP WITH THE INSURER

In Ms. Jones' case, the insurance company never went to talk to the plumber involved to find out what exactly it was that the plumber did or didn't do and what he perceived the risks were. In addition, the insurance company did not interview a burn surgeon to find out precisely what the course of the burn was. Again, the insurance company wasn't that concerned which brings me to the next issue which is critical, namely your relationship with your carrier, a punitive damage claim.

COVERAGE

The first issue is does your coverage include punitive damages? In California, the courts and the legislature have determined that indemnification of punitive damages is against public policy and, therefore, they are not covered by insurance. This rule varies from state to state, and you should determine at the outset what the rule is in your state.

DEFENDING THE CLAIM

Many insurance companies send reservation of rights letters to their insureds. These letters provide that the carrier will defend the claim under a reservation of rights with respect to punitive damages. Yet many times the insurer will take the position in settlement discussions or at trial that there was no negligence, so there really couldn't be any punitive damages. To the extent that there are punitive damages, it is important to appreciate that the insurance company's liabilities go down, while your liability goes up.

In California recently, there was a case which held that you may have the right to hire your own counsel, at the insurance company's expense. What the California court of appeal pointed out is a conflict of interest at trial and during the course of the settlement negotiations. For instance, you may want an offer of policy limits to protect you from any punitive damage exposure while the insurance company wants to pay as little as possible. What we have seen worked out these types of situations is for the insured to chose a lawyer, in exchange for waiving the conflict. The carrier will pay for your counsel in order to insure that your interests are protected. You may wish to negotiate such an arrangement when you receive a reservation of rights letter. Using two lawyers may give you the best defense, but inevitably the plaintiff's lawyer is going to smell blood if the presence of two lawyers is discovered.

SETTLEMENT DISCUSSIONS

At what point can you legitimately make a demand for policy limits? The insurance companies themselves are only beginning to face this question. The demand should typically be accompanied by a letter which says the insurance carrier (or its counsel) failed to protect your rights by failing to properly conduct the investigation of the case. You must attempt to create some leverage in the process to make the insurance company appreciate that their exposure is greater than this $25,000, potentially on a bad faith claim filed by you.

AVOIDING PUNITIVE DAMAGE EXPOSURE

SOUND FACILITY MANAGEMENT

How will you avoid punitive damage exposure? The easy answer is run a good facility. This is not an easy task when you are dealing with patients who are difficult to care for, but for whom juries have unending sympathy especially with regard to the level of your care for them.

PUBLIC RELATIONS

In addition to running a good facility, you should maintain good public relations with the patient as well as their family. The family is going to include the survivors who bring this claim so you want to make sure they believe that you really have done a good job with Ms. Jones for the last six years and they don't want to sue you even if a claim is there. You do that by following up on complaints and by other public relations messages that come out not just to the patients in your facility but to the community that surrounds them. You answer threatening correspondence immediately. Another aspect of the public relations issue is to incorporate your subsidiaries to make sure that the net worth of the parent isn't displayed to the jury if you get to trial.

ARBITRATION CLAUSES

In order to avoid juries altogether, we recommend you place arbitration clauses in all admission agreements. Such a clause should specifically cover potential punitive damage claims which may arise either from so-called grossly negligent acts, or from intentional acts. Be sure it covers all claims for punitive damages, spelling out in so many words that punitive damage claims must be arbitrated. When the patient is admitted, make sure the arbitration clause is called to their attention, and to the attention of any relatives who are there with them or whom you can contact. Ask the relatives if they will sign the arbitration clause.

INSURANCE

If you are in a state where punitive damage insurance is available in one form or another, seriously consider getting it. It limits your exposure and eliminates the conflict of interest with the insurance company's lawyers. They have to defend that claim. They may not do it the way you want but at least you know if that claim hits, you've got some coverage. And the problem on the coverage on the punitive side may be significantly bigger than the compensatory side. In the example I gave you, you may well have compensatory damages of $50,000 and punitives of $500, one of which is insured, one of which is not. In summary, the two aspects that I think are the most important in all these cases are: (1) your own investigation of the facts early on to try to limit your exposure in the case and ensure you have all the relevant facts; and (2) use of an arbitration clause to avoid jury verdicts.

PART 4

PERSONNEL ISSUES:

Review of Labor Laws and Related Policies

Chapter 16

The Impact of Federal Labor and Wage Laws on Long Term Care Providers

Speaker: Diane E. Burkley

LABOR STATUTES

There are approximately 130 federal labor statutes which are handled by the Department of Labor. They cover a broad spectrum--minimum wage statutes like the Fair Labor Standards Act; prevailing wage statutes that apply to federal contracts or federally assisted contracts like Davis Bacon, which requires employers to pay a "prevailing" wage (which is a kind of average wage--higher than minimum wage and often the union rate) when you are building facilities in which there is federal funding; the Service Contract Act, which is the corollary in the service area if you have federal funding of service contracts, which requires employers to pay prevailing wages to the employees that are involved on that contract. There are also safety and health statutes like the Occupational Safety and Health Act and the Mine Safety and Health Act; pension statutes (ERISA) covering the whole spectrum of pension issues; job training; employee benefits such as Black Lung; and a whole series of civil rights statutes primarily related to federally funded contracts. The situation at the Labor Department is a somewhat unique and difficult one at the moment because a number of the major policymakers are not in place; people have left, but the powers that be don't want to put people back in these positions without having a Secretary. (Secretary of Labor Donovan is on leave from the Labor Department.) Some of the others that are there (those that run the wage and hour programs, for example) are reluctant to decide a lot of the issues until there is someone in the Secretary of Labor's slot. So at this point, they are inclined to move fairly cautiously and not take some particularly dramatic action, which is good news and bad news from the regulated industry's perspective.

THE SERVICE CONTRACT ACT TO VETERANS ADMINISTRATION

The applicability of Service Contract Act to Veterans Administration contracts is probably the major issue that has the most direct and immediate impact on nursing homes. The Service Contract Act applies to contracts with the federal government in excess of $2,500. If it does apply, the employer is required to pay prevailing wages and fringe benefits to the employees who perform work on the contract.

This is probably one of the most complicated wage statutes because of the complexity of the terminology and the number of times that it has been amended. The primary task is to decide if the contract is covered; that is, is the principal purpose of the contract to furnish services in the United States through the use of service employees? There is no real dispute that health care is a service, it is taking place in the U.S., and that there are service employees involved. The reason why the Veteran's Administration (VA) and the Labor Department got into a debate as to whether there is coverage in the nursing home situation is because the Service Contract Act does not apply if the services are being provided by professionals. Executive, administrative, or professional employees are specifically exempt from the definition of the service employee. The VA argued that what nursing homes are providing is professional medical services. Therefore, such contracts should not be subject to the Service Contract Act. Not unexpectedly, the Wage and Hour Administrator of the Department of Labor disagreed with this interpretation and an opinion in 1968. The Department, under Secretary of Labor Wurtz, came to the conclusion that VA contracts are subject to the Service Contract Act. It found that VA contracts with nursing homes are different from medical services in a hospital because the principal purpose of the former contracts is not to provide diagnostic or corrective care--the type normally provided in hospitals--but instead is mainly custodial in nature.

The VA sought in 1968 to have this position reversed by the Labor Department, and submitted some fairly cogent arguments to it which were nonetheless dismissed at that time. We think that there is now a chance to have that position re-evaluated. Before discussing why this is so, a little background might be useful interpreting the impact of the Labor Department's current position.

The determination that prevailing wages must be paid certainly has an inflationary impact as far as wage cost. The extent depends on the way you determine what wage rate is "prevailing." The prevailing rate is certainly not the minimum wage, although it theoretically could be. The term "prevailing" is not defined in Service Contract Act--in practice, it is based on a survey of wages and roughly equal to that rate which most of the employees in a given category make. Typically, if it is a unionized work force, the prevailing wage will be the unionized wage. Unionized fringe benefits will also have to be included, which can have an even greater impact. That means that no matter what you were paying before for that government contract, you have to pay all the employees involved whatever wage is designated for that category.

Even determining the category, moreover, can be a problem. If the category is nurses, you may be talking about nurses who have no experience or nurses who have 20 years of experience. The category can be broken down and typically is, but the wage that must be paid is going to depend on how well it is broken down, which varies a great deal depending on who is making the wage determination. There is a lot of variation and frequently the categories are not structured in a way which actually reflects what goes on in your particular work force, as opposed to what happens to be the database that is used.

GEOGRAPHICAL VARIATIONS AND OTHER PROBLEMS

Another difficult issue is the geographical area that is used as the basis for the wage determination. The prevailing wage is supposed to be based on wages prevailing in the "locality." You may be in a rural area and have an urban area right next door to you. If the Labor Department does not have enough database in the rural area where the wages are likely to be lower, it may go across the line into the city where wages are likely to be higher and use that data. The higher wage base then gets incorporated into the prevailing wage you must pay your work force. From a labor-management relations viewpoint this impacts on more than just the employees who are working on the VA contract. If you have to pay one person $10 an hour where you used to pay him $7.50, it is very difficult to continue to pay the person who is working right next to him $7.50, when before they were making the same amount. This guy who is still making $7.50 will say, "What's going on here? I'm doing the same work as he is."

Theoretically, you do not have to pay all your employees the prevailing wages; just the ones that are working on the VA contract. In the nursing home, however, you may not be able to do this because the nurse that works with the VA patients is not going to spend the full time with just those patients. According to data gathered by the American Health Care Association, the typical 100-bed facility has perhaps 60 Medicaid patients and only two VA patients. If you cannot segregate a small work force to work solely on the VA patients, you may well end up paying your whole work force that higher wage. In individual situations you might be able to structure it differently, but the potential is certainly there.

A similar problem can arise if you have, say, two VA patients this month and none next month. Are you going to turn around next month and reduce your employees' wages to $7.50 instead of $10? Not likely, if you want to have a happy work force. The inflationary impact tends to spiral because all of a sudden, all of the employees in that category are getting $10 an hour. Next year the Labor Department comes back; it does another survey. It looks at your database; you're now up to $10 an hour where you were paying $7.50. The other nursing home in the area may be up to $12.50, so your next wage determination goes up to $11.50. It really feeds on itself.

The other area where there is a spiraling effect is fringe benefits. Typically, temporary and part-time employees are not paid fringe benefit packages; yet under the SCA, if those employees are involved in the care of VA patients, they will have to be paid the prevailing fringe benefits. Again, you face the same problem with your other temporary and part-time employees--are you going to treat them differently? The cost impact of this can be very significant. It can also be significant in another area.

Another problem is that even if you don't have a unionized work force, if you are bidding on a VA contract under the Service Contract Act you are required to pay no lower than the previous employer paid. Basically, the union wages are put directly into the next contract. The purpose of this is to prevent non-unionized employers from underbidding unionized employers on federal contracts. This is probably the most severely criticized aspect of the Service Contract Act; in fact, even the GAO (General Accounting Office), has recommended repeal of the statute for this reason.

APPLICATIONS OF THE SERVICE CONTRACT ACT

The reason that there is now some hope of getting the Labor Department's position on applicability of the SCA to nursing homes reversed is because of a change that was implemented by the Reagan Administration in the regulations that govern Service Contract Act. This is a long and hard-fought battle and took from 1981 through 1983 for the promulgation of the final regulatory changes. They were challenged, but were upheld in the federal district court in Washington, D.C.

Under the old regulations, even if the contract as a whole was not principally for services but there was one line item that was for services, then the entire contract would be covered by the Service Contract Act. This would typically arise in the context of equipment. If you bought computer software and hardware from a manufacturer and there was one bid specification that was perhaps 5% of the cost for maintenance of that equipment, service work under the contract was still covered.

Looking at the language of the statute, this just does not make sense. The statute talks about a "contract" which is "principally for services"; this suggests that looking at the contract as a whole, you decide if it is principally for services. If it is, then it is subject to the Service Contract Act. If no, then the contract is not covered. This interpretation was incorporated into the new regulations.

What that means in the context of the nursing home issue relates back to the question of the professional employees and non-professional services. As I mentioned before, professionals are not subject to the act. The argument can be made based on the new regulations that the principal purpose of a nursing home contract is to provide professional medical services, even though some part of the contract is going to be for custodial care. The Labor Department previously focused on the custodial care in deciding that the VA contracts were covered. Under the new regulations, however, these are only incidental. That care is not the purpose of the contract as a whole.

There is recognition that the SCA is an act whose coverage, if it can be legally minimized, should be. Some members of the Administration probably would just as soon repeal it if they could. Politically, however, it is very difficult even to change the regulations. To give you one example, there is a provision in Service Contract Act regulations (it also appears in a different form in Fair Labor Standard Act regulations), that if you require your employees to wear uniforms, then the cost of the uniform is deemed the cost of doing business. This means the employer has to pay for the uniforms and *also* has to pay for their maintenance. The Labor Department had a rule of thumb where they would just add an "X" amount of additional fringe benefits--somewhere between $4 to $10 a week--that they would require an employer to pay for the maintenance of the uniforms. A proposed regulatory change concerned wash and wear uniforms. Since you can just stick them in your wash with the rest of your clothes, why should the employer have to pay for the maintenance? A provision in the new proposal therefore said that with the wash and wear uniforms, the employer would not have to bear the cost.

This became a major issue for the unions. From their perspective, it gets back to the SCA successorship provision in large measure. The unions have negotiated figures for maintenance of uniforms which can be a lot higher than $4 to $10 a week, and the negotiated provision is binding on the successor employer. Because of the union's objections, the final regulations adopted a compromise position: If a uniform gets thrown in the normal wash, then the employer doesn't have to pay for the cleaning. If the employee has to wash the uniform every day and he normally would not be doing a wash, then the employer has to bear the cost.

> *Have you seen any requests for redeterminations? I'm just wondering if you have any sense of how fast or how slow the process is, once they have a formal request.*

> Typically, it takes a while and a lot of the new procedures are just not in place. For example, the procedural regulations issued under the Service Contract Act talked about a Service Contract Act Appeals Board. It has been two years now since the rules were put in place and nobody has been named to the board; there is no Service Contract Act Appeals Board. All the procedures that deal with the Appeals Board are non-existent. To that extent, the Department of Labor is still following the old practice.

THE FAIR LABOR STANDARDS ACT

Just to briefly mention the Fair Labor Standards Act issue discussed in my outline--and I think this is another sort of classic example of the right hand not knowing what the left hand is doing--the hospice regulations issued by HCFA at the end of 1983 require the use of volunteers as a cost-saving measure. Under the regulations, HHS also indicated that the "volunteers" would be included within the definition of employees.

That provision had been included in the proposal. There was a lot of adverse comment on this provision because of the confusion that it would cause with respect to volunteer physicians--i.e., do you have to pay them wages--quite frankly the proposal did not make sense. HHS went forward with the proposal notwithstanding these comments. The problem that is created from the labor side by the proposal is if you have a true volunteer, you don't have to pay them wages. If you have someone working for you that you're calling a volunteer, but he really has an expectation of payment--is really an employee--then you have to pay him wages; at least the minimum wage. The label in and of itself is not that meaningful, except to the extent that it causes confusion in the supposed volunteers' expectations of compensation; under the Supreme Court law applicable to deciding who is an employee under the Fair Labor Standards Act, the test is whether the person has an expectation of remuneration. If that expectation exists, based on the understanding between the parties, then it doesn't matter that the employer considers the individual a volunteer. He is in fact being, in statutory language, suffered or permitted to work, and must be paid.

Unlike Service Contract Act, employees can sue under the Fair Labor Standards Act for minimum wages and overtime wages. They can also sue for liquidated damages, which basically are double wages and double overtime. The Labor Department can sue on the employees' behalf as well.

Because of the uncertainty that was presented by HCFA's regulation, a request was filed with the labor Department by the AHCA for a clarification of whether, notwithstanding the definition in the regulations, for Fair Labor Standards purposes the hospice volunteers are not really employees and do not have to be paid wages. That request was filed almost a year ago now but has not been answered. Last time I checked on it, which was a couple of weeks ago, the request was still at the staff level of the solicitor's office. Having been in government for six years I tend to be cynical about these things. If somebody is working on it that long, they tend to want to come up with reasons for coverage. That's the general bias. Quite frankly, though, I can't fathom how they would find coverage here, and sometimes they do come up with the determination that there is no coverage in a case. The AHCA may wish to follow up on this, as I think a favorable response would be a useful document for you all to have in your hands in case any lawsuits are filed.

There is a pending Supreme Court case, *Alamo*, which comes up in the First Amendment religious facility context, but in a tangential way involves the definition of volunteers. The Supreme Court granted review and expects to have oral argument in about thirty days or so. There is some indication that the Labor Department wants to hold up on the hospice issue to see what the Supreme Court says. It may well have some impact on the hospice issue; it's a different context so it's hard to say. Hopefully it will shed some light on the matter, and if not, at least get the Labor Department to come out with its opinion.

If the Labor Department finds there is a problem, employers will face the possibility of lawsuits, by employees. Also a re-evaluation of the HHS regulations would be required, accompanied by a big debate between the Labor Department and HHS as to how they resolve this regulatory conflict. That would probably have no immediate impact on the industry but ultimately could lead to a change in the hospice regulations. However, you would see a proposal, then final regulation, before any change is actually made effective.

Another labor issue affecting nursing homes is the issue of who are executive, administrative, and professional employees under the Fair Labor Standards. If someone is a professional employee, he does not have to be paid overtime. Who is and who is not a professional, however, is one of the gray areas in health care administration. While the physician is obviously a professional, with the nurses there's a whole range: registered nurses tend to be considered professionals; most practical nurses tend not be be. When you get into these gray areas, what becomes important under the Department of Labor regulations is how much money the employee is paid. Under the regulations, if he earns more than $250 a week, there is a shorter "duty test" (criteria for deciding whether they're professional) that has to be satisfied in order for the employee to be considered a professional. This is true as well for executive and administrative employees.

The Carter administration issued some regulations which would have significantly increased these salary tests. All the various industries were opposed to these regulations. The Reagan administration indefinitely stayed the new regulations.

Having the regulations stayed for four years is highly unconventional, and makes them very vulnerable legally. In fact, it is surprising to a lot of people that the regulations have not been challenged by a union. In any case, there is a recognition on the Labor Department's part that it is going to have to increase the salary tests. The higher test would likely be comparable to that in the Carter regulations ($345 per week), although it may not go that high.

Hopefully, there will be some revision at the same time of the "duties" tests, because a lot of the requirements for these determinations don't mesh with the actual roles of people who are considered professionals or administrative executive employees. Your comments on the regulation both as far as what the various categories of professional employees are paid, and what kind of duties they perform, will be invited, and I would urge you to submit information on this subject. The practical impact for you can be great because professionals do not have to be paid overtime. Most of the people making these decisions in the regulatory section do not have much familiarity with the various industries, and are going to come up with general duty tests which will tend to include as many people as possible in the non-professional category.

SUPPLEMENT TO CHAPTER 16

THE IMPACT OF FEDERAL LABOR AND WAGE LAWS ON LONG TERM CARE PROVIDERS

I. OVERVIEW OF THE UNITED STATES DEPARTMENT OF LABOR AND THE OFFICE OF THE SOLICITOR

   A. The Department of Labor

      1. Enforcement authority

         The Department of Labor (DOL) is charged with administering more than 130 Federal labor laws. Over 60 of these relate to employee benefits and workers compensation (*e.g.*, Black Lung Benefits Act); another 30 to job training, placement services and unemployment compensation (*e.g.*, Job Training Partnership Act); the rest regulate such matters as wage and hour standards (*e.g.*, Fair Labor Standards Act, Service Contract Act, Davis Bacon Act); safety and health (*e.g.*, Occupational Safety and Health Act, the Mine Safety and Health Act); pensions (the Employee Retirement Income Security Act) and civil rights (Executive Order 11246, establishing the Office of Federal Contract Compliance, and sections 503 and 504 of the Rehabilitation Act of 1973).

      2. Overlap with other federal agencies' jurisdiction

         DOL's enforcement responsibility frequently overlaps with other Federal agencies, *e.g.*:

         a. *Civil rights*

            DOL's primary area of responsibility involves Federal contractors. The Equal Employment Opportunity Commission has primary responsibility for enforcing Title VII's nondiscrimination provisions against private employers; the Department of Justice has primary enforcement responsibility for enforcing Title VII against public employers. All agencies enforce nondiscrimination provisions against recipients of Federal financial assistance provided by their own programs. Policy and regulatory positions under these overlapping laws are theoretically coordinated among the various agencies.

b. *Pensions*

DOL is responsible for enforcement of Title I of ERISA (reporting disclosure and fiduciary responsibility provisions). Tax provisions (Title II of ERISA) are enforced by the Internal Revenue Service. Plan termination provisions (Title IV) are enforced by the Pension Benefit Guarantee Corporation. Parallel enforcement issues are supposed to be coordinated among the agencies.

c. *Labor Management Relations*

The National Labor Relations Board (NLRB), which is wholly independent from DOL, is responsible for protecting employees' rights to self-organization and collective bargaining and to refrain from such activities. The NLRB also is responsible for the prevention of unfair labor practices by employers and labor organizations. DOL is primarily responsible for enforcement of the Labor Management Reporting and Disclosure Act, which was passed to remedy abuses in the labor movement by setting standards for demographic principles in union affairs, particularly in the election of union officers, requiring reporting, and establishing provisions to protect the integrity of union finances and union businesses.

B. The Solicitor of Labor's Office

1. Functions

The Solicitor's Office provides legal advice to the Secretary and program agencies with respect to the 130 statutes enforced by the Department; assists in promulgation of legislation and regulations; and represents DOL in administrative enforcement proceedings. Also, unlike most other Federal agencies which are represented by the Department of Justice in judicial proceedings, DOL is responsible for most of its own litigation in the U.S. district courts and courts of appeals.

2. Structure

a. *National office*

Historically, the National Solicitor's Office in Washington, D.C. has been divided into 12 staff divisions. Most of them are organized along program lines to reflect the organization of the client agencies, *e.g.*, Wage and Hour Division, Civil Rights Division, and OSHA Division. The national office handles appellate litigation, some major trial litigation, promulgation of regulations, and other legal services peculiar to the seat of government.

b. *Regional offices*

There are eight Regional Solicitor's Offices and several subordinate Branch Offices throughout the nation. The Regional Offices handle most trial litigation and day-to-day advice to the regional client agencies.

3. Size

The Solicitor's Office has approximately 550 attorneys and 210 clericals and paraprofessionals nationwide.

II. CURRENT DEVELOPMENTS UNDER THE SERVICE CONTRACT ACT

A. Overview of the Act

1. The Service Contract Act (SCA), 41 U.S.C. 351 *et seq.*, applies to every contract of the United States in excess of $2,500, except for enumerated exemptions, "the principal purpose of which is to furnish services in the United States through the use of service employees." *Id.* at 351(a).

2. All service contracts covered by the statute are required to include a wage determination reflecting the wages and fringe benefits DOL has found "prevailing" in the locality.

3. If an existing federal service contractor is covered by a collective bargaining agreement (CBA), a successor contractor is required to pay its employees wages and fringe benefits no less than those to which its predecessor was committed by the CBA (including future increases).

4. The Act was originally passed to cover janitorial and other blue collar workers, but was amended in 1976 to cover white collar workers. However, bona fide executive, administrative, and professional employees are exempted from the Act's coverage. 41 U.S.C. 357(b).

B. Issue: Does the Service Contract Act Apply to Contracts Between the Veterans Administration and Community Nursing Homes?

1. Current DOL position

a. In 1968, Secretary of Labor Wirtz ruled that contracts whereby the Veterans Administration (VA) procures nursing home care for former patients are subject to the SCA. Although the legislative history specifically notes that a contract for medical care is not covered because the use of service employees is only "incidental" to providing medical (*i.e.*, professional) services, DOL found that VA contracts "cannot be deemed contracts for hospital care, *i.e.*, for professional medical services . . . since they do not provide for the type of diagnostic or corrective care . . . normally provided in hospitals." A Solicitor's Office opinion elaborated that the services provided "are mainly custodial and little in the nature of medical services is envisioned."

b. The VA subsequently sought reversal of this position on the grounds that veterans in community nursing homes receive professional medical care similar to that provided in VA hospitals, and that the VA contracts include detailed requirements which require a maximum of professional supervision at both physician and registered nurse levels. The DOL refused to change its position on the basis of the information provided.

2. Impact of DOL position

a. DOL's method of determining prevailing wages and benefits (where no single rate is prevailing in an area, DOL bases rate on "central tendencies, that is, median or mean") has been criticized as having an inflationary impact. Prevailing rates, by their nature, do not recognize the limited skills and experience of newly hired or entry level workers. Once a prevailing rate is established, it quickly becomes a "floor." From a labor relations standpoint, it is difficult to lower the pay rate even if the worker is no longer working on a Federal contract.

b. The requirement that all service employees, including part-time and temporary employees, be paid prevailing wages and benefits is likely to significantly raise the costs of long term care facilities. This is especially so in the case of fringe benefits because most long term care facilities do not pay fringe benefits to any part-time employees. Complying with this requirement would raise facility costs far above current VA contract rates.

c. Because of the impracticability of separating employees working under the VA contract from those who do not or of paying additional benefits to only a few employees, higher benefits would have to be made available to all employees.

d.　The "successorship requirement" imports non-unionized wage rates into unionized work forces.

e.　Substantial paperwork burdens are imposed on service contractors under DOL's regulations.

f.　As a result of these burdens since the typical 100 bed facility has 60 medicaid patients and only 2 VA patients, many facilities may cease to participate in the VA program.

3.　AHCA request for reversal of current position

a.　On December 16, 1983, the American Health Care Association filed a request with DOL seeking reversal of the 1968 position on the ground that the nature of the services provided by the VA nursing home program had changed dramatically since 1968.

b.　That request was subsequently suspended pending implementation of changes in the SCA regulations, discussed below.

C.　The Reagan Administration's Reform of the Relevant SCA Regulations

1.　In the waning days of the Carter Administration, DOL issued new SCA regulations designed to codify enforcement policies developed over the years. *See* 46 Fed. Reg. 4320, 4886 (January 16 and 19, 1981). In accordance with the Reagan Administration's regulatory reform program (Executive Order 12291), these regulatory revisions were never implemented. Instead, a proposal incorporating major regulatory revisions was issued 46 Fed. Reg. 41380 (August 14, 1981). The final rules were promulgated in October, 1983. 48 Fed. Reg. 49 736 (October 27, 1983). These rules were judicially upheld in February, 1984. *AFL-CIO v. Donovan*, 582 F. Supp. 1015 (D.D.C. 1984) (Judge Gasch), *appeal pending*.

2.　One of the most significant changes of the new rules is the elimination of coverage of "bid specifications" where the contract as a whole is not specifically for services.

a.　Based on statutory language stating the Act applies to every "contract (and any bid specification therefor) . . . the principal purpose of which is to furnish services", DOL previously applied the SCA to any separate line item (*i.e.*, bid specification) which was "principally" for services no matter what the "principal purpose" of the whole contract was.

      b.   The new regulations apply the SCA only to contracts which, when viewed as a whole, have the principal purpose of furnishing services. New 29 C.F.R. 4.110, 4.132.

    3.   DOL also modified its regulation addressing the requirement that contracts be performed ''through the use of service employees.''

      a.   The prior regulations apply to any service contract for professional services unless the work performed by non-professional service employees is only a ''minor'' factor. 29 C.F.R. 4.113(a)(2) (1983). In practice, a 10-20% guideline was used to determine if such use was ''minor''. The stayed Carter regulations memorialized this 10-20% measure.

      b.   The new regulations still require coverage of such contracts where the services involve the use of service employees to a ''significant or substantial extent.'' However, the regulations now specify that the question of ''significant use of service employees'' requires consideration of ''the nature of the contract work, the type of work performed by service employees, how necessary the work is for contract performance, the amount of contract work performed by service employees vis-a-vis professional employees, and the total number of service employees on the contract.'' 29 C.F.R. 4.113(a)(4).

      c.   Note, however, that the proposal would have covered only service contracts performed ''principally'' (*i.e.*, in the majority) by non-professional service employees. 46 Fed. Reg. 41381.

D.   Applicability of the New Regulations to VA Contracts

    1.   It can be argued that the ''principal purpose'' of the VA contracts is to provide professional medical care.

    2.   Under new 4.110, it is immaterial that the VA contracts also provide for nonprofessional custodial services.

    3.   The factors set forth in 29 C.F.R. 4.113, taken in tandem with the medicare/medicaid conditions of participation of Skilled Nursing Facilities (SNF) and Intermediate Care Facilities (ICF), can be used to argue that the non-professional support services are only incidental to the provision of professional medical services.

    4.   For SNFs, *see e.g.,*

    a.   42 C.F.R. 405.1121(l)(1) (patient care policies must provide for meeting total medical needs of patients).

    b.   *Id.* at 405.1123(b) ("The facility has a policy that the health care of every patient must be under the supervision of a physician who, based on a medical evaluation of the patient's long term needs, prescribes a planned regimen of total patient care.")

    c.   *Id.* at 405.1124(c), (e) (The facility provides 24-hour nursing services designed to ensure that each patient receives "treatment, medication and diet as prescribed, and rehabilitative nursing care as needed"; the facility has "an active program of rehabilitative nursing care which is an integral part of nursing service").

5.   For ICFs, a closer question exists. However, exclusion from coverage can be argued, *e.g.*, on the basis of

    a.   42 C.F.R. 442.251(a)(1) (Purpose of ICF is to provide "health related care and services to individuals who do not require hospital or SNF care, be whose mental or physical condition require services . . . *[a]bove* the level of room and board.") (Emphasis added.)

    b.   *Id.* at 442.338 (The ICF must provide health services which include "treatment, medications, diet, and any other health service prescribed or planned for the resident" 24 hours a day);

    c.   *Id.* at 442.342 (The ICF "must provide nursing care as needed, including restorative nursing care . . . ")

    d.   VA standards also apply and require, *e.g.*, at least one registered nurse or licensed practical nurse or vocational nurse on duty during each tour of duty.

6.   Additional supporting data would prove useful to obtaining a favorable opinion, *e.g.*, number of professional hours per patient, and the amount of professional observations, assessment, and/or intervention required.

III. CURRENT DEVELOPMENTS UNDER THE FAIR LABOR STANDARDS ACT

    A. Overview of the Act

The Fair Labor Standards Act of 1983 (FLSA), 29 U.S.C. 201 *et seq.*, establishes certain minimum wage and overtime standards for covered employees.

1. The wage standards apply to employees engaged in interstate commerce or in the production of goods for interstate commerce. 29 C.F.R. 776.

2. Generally, all employees of an enterprise whose gross annual sales is at least $250,000 are covered; enterprises comprised exclusively of retail or service establishments require a gross volume of $362,500.

3. Under 13(a)(1) of the Act, bona fide executive, administrative and professional employees are exempted from the wage and hour provisions of the FLSA.

B. Issue: Whether Regulations Issued by the Health Care Financing Administration (HCFA) of HHS are Inconsistent with the FLSA.

Section 122 of the Tax Equity and Fiscal Responsibility Act of 1982, Pub. L. No. 97-248, 96 Stat. 356, 42 U.S.C. 1395(c), provides coverage for hospice care for terminally ill Medicare beneficiaries who elect to receive care from a participating hospice. The statute defines the term hospice program as, among other things, a public agency or private organization which "(1) utilizes volunteers in its provision of care and services . . . and (2) maintains records on the use of these volunteers and the cost savings and expansion of care and services achieved through the use of these volunteers." 96 Stat. 360-361.

1. HCFA regulations

    a. Regulations issued by HCFA to implement the hospice program establish eligiblity requirements and reimbursement standards and procedures, define covered services, and delineate the conditions a hospice must meet to be approved for participation in the Medicare program. Under the regulations, the definition of "employee" includes volunteers. 42 C.F.R. 418.3.

    b. As the preamble to the final regulations indicates, commentators objected to the proposed (now final) definition of a hospice employee. The commentators had primarily two objections to the definition: (1) Several commentators suggested that only paid employees be included in the definition so that volunteer physicians could retain their ability to receive payment under Medicare Part B for the medical care they provide to patients they refer to the hospice program and to prevent hospice liability for volunteers. (2) Several commentators objected to the full time requirement and recommended that part time employment also be accepted.

c.   HCFA was unpersuaded and continues to consider a volunteer as an employee of the hospice. It stated its belief that "characterizing volunteers as employees . . . will [not] in itself alter their legal relationships and responsibilities for other purposes." 48 Fed. Reg. 56009 (December 16, 1983).

d.   Accordingly, the hospice program regulations mandate documentation of cost savings by use of volunteers who are to work in place of regular employees. Under the current regulations, these "volunteers" are considered as employees, despite the fact that they expect no compensation for their work.

2.   AHCA request for clarification

In the absence of the HHS categorization, it would seem clear that the hospice volunteers are indeed volunteers for FLSA purposes. Their categorization by HHS, however, may raise some doubt (on the part of employers and employees) as to whether this is so. Accordingly, on February 21, 1984, the AHCA requested clarification of the volunteers' status from DOL. DOL has yet to issue an opinion. In the absence of such an opinion, the legal criteria discussed below would seem to suggest these volunteers need not be compensated.

3.   FLSA definition of employee

The FLSA defines "employee" as an individual employed by an employer, and defines "employ" as including to "suffer or permit to work." 29 U.S.C. 203(e)(1) and (g).

a.   The Supreme Court, in the case of *Walling v. Portland Terminal Co.*, 330 U.S. 148 (1947), clarified the meaning of the phrase "suffer or permit to work," and in the process set forth the distinction between employees covered by the FLSA and non-covered volunteers:

> The definition "suffer or permit to work" was obviously not intended to stamp all persons as employees . . . [S]uch a construction would sweep under the Act each person who, without promise or expectation of compensation, but solely for his personal purpose or pleasure, worked in activities carried on by other persons either for their pleasure or

profit. But there is no indication from the legislation now before us that Congress intended to outlaw such relationships as these. The Act's purpose as to wages was to insure that every person whose employment contemplated compensation should be compelled to see the services for less than the prescribed minimum wage.

Id. at 152.

b. The HHS/HCFA rules fail to acknowledge the distinction set forth in *Walling v. Portland Terminal Co., supra; i.e.,* an employee "contemplate[s] compensation" for the work he performs, while a volunteer works "without promise or expectation of compensation . . . solely for his personal purpose or pleasure." *Id.* at 152.

c. The Supreme Court has also explained that an individual's legal status as an employee is determined by examining the factual context or "economic reality" of the individual's relationship with the employer (*see Goldberg v. Whitaker House Corp.,* 366 U.S. 28, 33 (1961)), rather than merely accepting the label affixed to that relationship. *See Rutherford Food Corp. v. McComb,* 331 U.S. 722, 729-730 (1947).

d. In the case of HHS' regulation including "volunteers" within the definition of "employee," the HCFA failed to examine the "economic reality" of the relationship between "volunteers" and hospice facilities, as well as ignored its own label which it affixed to those individuals. But it is at least arguable that the very characterization by HHS could alter the individuals' expectation of compensation. As a result, it becomes difficult for a health care provider to be certain that it is in compliance with both Department of Labor and Department of Health and Human Services requirements.

4. The pending supreme court *Alamo* case

The distinction between employees covered by the FLSA and non-covered volunteers is the central issue in a recent case the Supreme Court has agreed to review. In the case of *Tony and Susan Alamo Foundation v. Donovan,* No. 83-1935, the Court has agreed to review the application of the minimum wage and overtime laws to businesses run by the Foundation, an evangelical organization. The Foundation contends that its businesses employ only volunteers, rather than employees covered by FLSA.

a. The United States Court of Appeals for the Eighth Circuit held that the status of some 300 persons, known as associates, who work in the Foundation's 30 commercial businesses and receive lodging, food, transportation, and medical care in return, was that of "employee" under the FLSA because "[b]y entering the economic arena and trafficking in the marketplace, the Foundation has subjected itself to the standards of employees." The Circuit Court rejected the Foundation's contention that the businesses are merely extensions of the Foundation's ministries in that they provide the associates a forum for rehabilitation and a forum for spreading their religious beliefs.

b. On appeal, therefore, the Supreme Court must decide whether people who volunteer their services to religiously affiliated businesses, and in return, receive free lodging, meals, health care and other benefits are "employees" who must be paid the minimum wage and be paid for working overtime.

c. Perhaps the Court's decision will shed some light on the government-created conflict which exists between the regulations issued by HCFA regarding the Medicare program and the FLSA.

C. Issue: Salary Tests for Determining Executive, Administrative, and Professional Employee Status

1. The salary tests

DOL's governing regulation specifies numerous duties which an employee must be performing before he will be considered an executive, administrative, or professional employee (EAP) who need not be paid overtime. *See* 29 C.F.R. Part 541. It also specifies the employee must receive at least $155 per week. If an employee earns more than $250 per week, however, not all the duties need be performed. *See id.* at 541.119, 541.214, 541.315.

2. The Carter administration regulatory revisions

a. On January 13, 1981, the Carter Administration issued final rules increasing the base salary tests to $225 per week, and the higher "upset" salary test to $320 per week beginning

February 1981 and $345 per week beginning February 1983. 46 Fed. Reg. 3010.

b. The Reagan Administration indefinitely postponed the revision, and asked for additional public comments on them. 46 Fed. Reg. 11972 (February 12, 1981); 46 Fed. Reg. 18998 (March 27, 1981).

3. Future action by DOL

a. Susan Meisinger, Deputy Under Secretary for Employment Standards, has informed me that DOL most likely will have to upwardly revise the salary tests from their present level.

b. Upward revision is viewed as necessary by some commentators if the regulations (most notably the shortened duty test applicable to highly paid workers) are to maintain their credibility with the courts.

c. Any revision, of course, would be subject to notice and comment and OMB review.

IV. CURRENT DEVELOPMENTS UNDER THE DAVIS-BACON ACT

A. Overview of the Act

1. The Davis-Bacon Act, 40 U.S.C. 276a, applies to Federally-funded and assisted construction or building contracts in excess of $2,000.

2. The Act requires that the various classes of laborers and mechanics be paid locally "prevailing" wage rates and fringe benefits as determined by the Secretary of Labor.

3. Hill-Burton Act funded projects, among others, are subject to the Davis-Bacon Act.

B. Impact of the Act and Its Implementation by DOL

1. The Act has been severely criticized as having long outlived its purpose of protecting the downtrodden construction workers during the Depression era in which the law was enacted.

2. As with the Service Contract Act, critics assert that the law has a significant inflationary impact. However, because of the larger sums involved in construction as compared to service contracts and because DOL historically has used a method of calculating the prevailing wage which favors union rates, the economic impact of the Davis-Bacon Act is far greater than the SCA, estimated in the billions of dollars each year.

C.   Regulatory Reform of the DOL's Davis-Bacon Rules

As under SCA, new Davis-Bacon regulations were issued during the final days of the Carter Administration. The Reagan Administration delayed implementation of the Carter rules, and ultimately issued revised regulations. 47 Fed. Reg. 23652 (May 28, 1982). The regulations were challenged by representatives of organized labor in *Building and Construction Trades Department, AFL-CIO v. Donovan*, 533 F. Supp. 353 (D.D.C.), *aff'd in part, rev'd in part*, 712 F.2d 611 (D.C. Cir. 1983), *cert. denied*, ___ U.S. ___, 104 S.Ct. 975 (1984). The status of these regulations in light of the decision of the Court of Appeals and subsequent action by the District Court is set forth below.

1.   The 30 percent rule

   a.   DOL's new rule eliminates a prior, secondary method for the computation of the prevailing wage on the basis of the wage paid to 30% of the workers in a given class. Instead, the term prevailing would mean the majority of workers employed in a given class. If there is no majority rule, a weighted average rate would be used.

   b.   The District Court and Court of Appeals both upheld this revision, and it has been implemented. *See* 48 Fed. Reg. 19532 (April 29, 1983).

   c.   The estimated annual cost savings from this change is $120 million.

2.   Exclusion of urban counties from rural wage determinations

   a.   The new rule prohibits the use of metropolitan wage data to set rates in rural counties. Because urban rates tend to be higher, this should result in substantial cost savings.

   b.   The District Court enjoined implementation of this provision, but the Court of Appeals reversed.

   c.   The District Court, however, only lifted its injunction against implementation of this provision on December 21, 1984. Order, *Building and Construction Trades Department v. Donovan*, No. 82-1631 (D.D.C.) (Judge Harold Greene).

3.   Exclusion of federal projects from wage determinations

   a.   The new rule excludes from the prevailing wage calculation existing Federal construction projects subject to the Act. Such wage data, it is believed, inaccurately inflate the new wage determination.

b. The District Court vacated this provision, but the Court of Appeals reversed.

c. Implementation of this provision is now permitted by the District Court's December 21, 1984 order.

4. Expanded use of helpers

a. The prior DOL regulation had been criticized by the non-unionized construction industry as improperly favoring unionized labor because of the rule's strict limitation on the use of helpers. (Helpers, who receive lower wages are frequently used on non-unionized projects, but are viewed by unions as undermining the union apprenticeship system).

b. The new rule modified prior limitations by (1) eliminating the requirement that for use of a helper to be permitted, the scope of duties of the helper must be clearly differentiated from a journeyman, and (2) permitting use of helpers where the helper classification was "identifiable" rather than prevailing as under the prior rule.

c. The District Court rejected both revisions. The Court of Appeals reversed, in part, upholding the first of these.

d. The helper provision has yet to be implemented.

e. It is believed the expanded use of helpers will result in substantial cost savings.

V. DEVELOPMENTS UNDER THE OCCUPATIONAL SAFETY AND HEALTH ACT

A. Overview of the Act

1. The Occupational Safety and Health Act, 29 U.S.C. 651 *et seq.*, is designed to protect employees "so far as possible" (*id.* at 651(b)) from safety and health hazards in the workplace. On the basis of this law, the Occupational Safety and Health Administration (OSHA) regulates virtually every aspect of employees' working environment, from electrical wiring to walking services to hazardous substances used in their job.

2. Perhaps the most stringent aspect of the Act is the provision requiring OSHA, in promulgating regulations addressing toxic substances, to

[S]et the standard which most adequately assures, to the extent feasible, . . . that no employee will suffer material impairment of health or functional capacity even if such employee has regular exposure to the hazard health with by such standard for the period of his working life.

29 U.S.C. 655(b)(5).

3. During the Carter Administration, OSHA had taken the position that this provision precluded the use of cost-benefit analysis in setting toxic substance standards. That issue was pending before the Supreme Court when the Reagan Administration took office. Because the balancing of costs and benefits was central to that Administration's regulatory reform initiative, it asked the Supreme Court to remand the case to the agency to see if a cost-benefit analysis could be performed. The Supreme Court, however, saw no reason to defer its decision. It held that the OSHA Act does not permit the use of cost-benefit analysis as a basis for setting toxic substance standards. *American Textile Manufacturers Institute (ATMI) v. Donovan*, 452 U.S. 490 (1981).

B. The Reagan Administration's Regulatory Reform Program

Notwithstanding the *ATMI* decision, there have been substantial modifications of OSHA standards, and significant new standards issued. To give a few examples:

1. Hazards communication (''labeling'')

A new standard requiring labeling of toxic materials in hazardous industries was issued. The total cost was only 20%, the cost of the previous Administration's proposal. 48 Fed. Reg. 53280 (November 25, 1983).

2. Walkaround pay

A standard requiring that employees who accompany OSHA inspectors be paid for the time thereby spent was revoked. 46 Fed. Reg. 28842 (May 29, 1981).

3. Advisory standards

One hundred and fifty-three general industry standards which were viewed as merely advisory because they used the term ''should'' rather than ''shall'' were revoked. 49 Fed. Reg. 5318 (February 10, 1984).

4. Reduction in recordkeeping

The rule exempts certain groups of employers -- those in standard industrial classifications with injury rates significantly lower than the average lost workday rate -- from OSHA recordkeeping requirements. 47 Fed. Reg. 57699 (December 28, 1982). Medical services, unfortunately, are not among the exempted groups. It should be noted, however, that OSHA is most receptive to paperwork reduction efforts, and might be persuaded to exempt long term health care facilities if their accident rate is significantly lower than other medical services.

C. Regulation of Exposure to Ethylene Oxide, A Medical Sterilant

OSHA has recently issued a new regulation affecting workplaces where ethylene oxide (EtO) is employed.

1. The hazard

OSHA has concluded that EtO presents a carcinogenic, mutagenic, genotoxic, reproductive and sensitization hazard to workers exposed to the substance.

2. Uses of EtO

The primary use of EtO is as an intermediate in the manufacture of other chemical products. In the health industry, however, EtO is sometimes used as a sterilizing agent for the sterilization of medical instruments and heat or moisture sensitive devices.

3. Background of the regulation

When new information came to light as to the health hazards posed by EtO, OSHA published an Advanced Notice of Proposed Rulemaking. 47 Fed. Reg. 3566 (January 26, 1982). The Public Citizen Health Research Group (PCHRG), however, believed an emergency temporary standard (ETS) should be issued, and challenged the agency's failure to issue such a standard in court. The District Court agreed with PCHRG, and ordered OSHA to issue an ETS. *PCHRG v. Auchter*, 554 F. Supp. 242 (D.D.C. 1981). The Court of Appeals reversed on the ETS issue. However, the Court determined that, in light of the medical evidence, the failure of the agency to issue a permanent standard constituted rulemaking action unlawfully delayed. *PCHRG v. Auchter*, 702 F.2d 1150 (D.C. Cir. 1983).

4. The new regulation

a. Pursuant to the Court decision, OSHA issued a proposed rule on April 21, 1983. 48 Fed. Reg. 17284. The final rule was issued on June 22, 1984. 49 Fed. Reg. 25737.

b. The final standard establishes a permissible exposure limit of 1 part EtO per million parts of air determined as an 8-hour time-weighted average concentration. The standard also includes provisions for methods of exposure control (engineering controls and work practices), personal protective equipment, monitoring and medical surveillance, labeling, and recordkeeping.

c. An issue left open by the regulation was whether to include a short-term exposure limit (STEL) (for higher level short term exposure). On January 2, 1985, OSHA issued a supplemental statement of reasons stating that a STEL is not warranted by the health evidence. 50 Fed. Reg. 64. The PCHRG has indicated it intends to appeal this decision.

VI. CURRENT CIVIL RIGHTS DEVELOPMENTS -- FEDERALLY ASSISTED PROGRAM OBLIGATIONS

A. Issue: Whether Receipt of Medicare and Medicaid Subject Health Care Providers to Coverage Under Antidiscrimination Statutes

1. Section 504 of the Rehabilitation Act, 29 U.S.C. 794, provides:

No otherwise qualified handicapped individual in the United States . . . shall, solely by reason of his handicap, be excluded from the participation in, be denied the benefits of, or be subjected to discrimination under any program or activity receiving Federal financial assistance.

2. In a case of first impression in the courts of appeal, the Fifth Circuit has held that Medicare and Medicaid payments subject a hospital to the coverage of section 504 of the Rehabilitation Act of 1973, prohibiting discrimination based on handicap in programs or activities that receive "Federal financial assistance." *United States v. Baylor University Medical Center*, 736 F.2d 1039 (5th Cir.), *petition for cert. filed*, October 16, 1984.[1]

3. The *Baylor* litigation arose out of a complaint received by the Department of Health and Human Services (HHS) that Baylor refused to allow a deaf patient to bring an interpreter into the hospital (at no expense to the hospital) so that she could understand her pre- and post-operative discussions with the

---

1. Because of the interrelated positions taken by the various agencies, both DOL and other agencies' positions (most notably HHS) are discussed herein. HHS (then HEW) was first given the responsibility for establishing guidelines and coordinating enforcement of the Act, but in 1980, responsibility for coordinating agency enforcement of section 504 was transferred to the Attorney General. Each agency providing federal funding to recipients who must comply with the provisions of section 504 including DOL implements those provisions through regulations modeled after the HHS guidelines. 28 C.F.R. 41.1 (1983). Because DOL has primary enforcement responsibility for section 503 of the Rehabilitation Act (requiring non-discrimination on the basis of handicap in employment on federal contracts), DOL has a heightened role in the approach taken with respect to employment discrimination issues in the federally assisted contracts as well.

medical staff. The United States filed suit to enforce section 504 of the Rehabilitation Act and regulations promulgated thereunder by HHS. Specifically, the government filed suit to obtain an order requiring Baylor to comply with the Department's investigatory requests, contending that Baylor's receipt of Medicare and Medicaid funds bring it within the coverage of section 504.2 The district court determined that Medicare and Medicaid do constitute federal financial assistance and that Baylor's inpatient and emergency room services were programs receiving that assistance. 564 F. Supp. 1495 (N.D. Tex. 1983).

4. The United States Court of Appeals for the Fifth Circuit affirmed on the merits, grounding its determination on "three congruent sources: the legislative history of that group of statutes prohibiting discrimination in federally funded programs -- Title VI, Title IX and the Rehabilitation Act, judicial interpretation of these, and regulations adopted pursuant to them." *Baylor, supra,* 736 F.2d at 1042.

5. Other case law regarding the issue

Six other courts have considered the issue and, with a single exception, all have held that Medicare and Medicaid payments invoke the protections of the federal discrimination statutes. *See NAACP v. Wilmington Medical Center, Inc.,* 599 F.2d 1247, 1248 n.4 (3d Cir. 1979), *aff'd in relevant part,* 453 F. Supp. 280, *later proceeding,* 453 F. Supp. 330 (D. Del. 1978) (affirming district court determination that hospital's receipt of Medicare, Medicaid and unspecified "other" assistance triggered section 504 and Title VI); *United States v. University Hospital of SUNY at Stony Brook,* 575 F. Supp. 607 (E.D. N.Y. 1983), *aff'd on other grounds,* 729 F.2d 144 (2d Cir. 1984) (legislative history reveals Medicare and Medicaid are "federal financial assistance for purposes of section 504"); *United States v. Cabrini Medical Center,* 497 F. Supp. 95, 96 n.1 (S.D.N.Y. 1980), *rev'd on other grounds,* 639 F.2d 908 (2d Cir. 1981) (same); *Cook v. Ochsner Foundation Hospital,* Civ. No. 70-1969 (E.D. La. February 12, 1979) (same); *Bob Jones University v. Johnson,* 396 F. Supp. 597, 603 n. 21 (D.S.C. 1974), *aff'd without opinion,* 529 F.2d 514 (4th Cir. 1975) (district court finds Medicare and Medicaid to be federal financial assistance for Title VI purposes); *see also Bernard B. v. Blue Cross and Blue Shield,* 528 F. Supp. 125, 132 (S.D. N.Y. 1981), *aff'd without opinion,* 679 F.2d 7 (2d Cir.

---

2. HHS regulations provide that Medicare and Medicaid constitute federal financial assistance. See 45 C.F.R. Part 80 App. A, para. 121; *id.* Part 84 app. A, Subpt. A.

1982) (district court assumes that Medicare constitutes "federal financial assistance" in holding that if Medicare linked to discriminatory program plaintiffs may state a section 504 case); *Flora v. Moore,* 461 F. Supp. 1104, 1115 (N.D. Miss. 1978) (stating in dicta that Medicare and Medicaid invoke Title VI protection); *but contra Trageser v. Libbie Rehabilitation Center, Inc.,* 462 F. Supp. 424 (E.D. Va. 1977) (Medicare and Medicaid do not constitute Federal financial assistance under section 504) *aff'd on other grounds,* 590 F.2d 87 (4th Cir. 1978), *cert. denied,* 442 U.S. 947 (1979).

6. Administrative interpretation of section 504 concludes that Medicare and Medicaid do constitute federal financial assistance to hospitals and health providers participating in those programs. *See* 45 C.F.R. Part 80, Appendix A, paragraph 121; *id.* Part 84, Appendix A, Subpart A.

7. If the Supreme Court grants *certiorari* in *Baylor,* most civil rights lawyers who have expressed an opinion on the issue believe it will be affirmed.

B. Overview of Baylor's Impact

1. The Fifth Circuit's decision potentially subjects all health care providers to coverage under section 504 of the Rehabilitation Act, and logically, to Title VI as well.

2. The cost of compliance with the statutes will undoubtedly increase the cost of treating Medicare and Medicaid patients. More importantly, if health care providers reject Medicare and Medicaid because of the added costs of coverage under the antidiscrimination statutes, fewer will be able to treat and serve the aged, disabled and needy.

3. As discussed below, the impact of *Baylor* is particularly significant because taken in tandem with other decisions, it can suggest that Medicare and Medicaid recipients are prohibited from discriminating on the basis of handicap in their employment decision as well.

C. The Combined Impact of Baylor and Consolidated Rail Corporation v. Darrone,___U.S.___, 104 S.Ct. 1248 (1984): Recipient Liability for Handicapped-Based Employment Discrimination

1. In a unanimous opinion, the Supreme Court has held that handicapped individuals are empowered to bring suit in federal district court for alleged employment discrimination in violation of section 504, regardless of the designated use of the federal

funds received by the employer in question; *i.e.*, even if the primary objective of those funds is not to provide employment. *Darrone, supra.* This decision is in a sense counterintuitive to the Supreme Court's companion *Grove City* ruling that the prohibition against discrimination in federally assisted programs (there, against sex discrimination in education) only applies to the programs which directly receive Federal money. 104 S.Ct. 1211 (1984).

2. Rather than reach the merits of employment claims under section 504, many lower courts had disposed of such claims on procedural grounds. Those courts held that one of the 1978 amendments to the Rehabilitation Act, Pub. L. No. 95-602, Sec. 120, section 505, 92 Stat. 2955, 2982-83 (1978) (codified at 29 U.S.C. section 794a (Supp. V 1981)), incorporated the limitations on judicial enforcement of private rights of action for employment discrimination claims contained in Title VI of the Civil Rights Act fo 1964, 42 U.S.C. 2000(d)-3 (1976 and Supp. V 1981). Under such an interpretation, section 504 does not provide a right of private action "unless (1) providing employment is a primary objective of the federal aid, or (2) discrimination in employment necessarily causes discrimination against the primary beneficiaries of the federal aid." *Trageser v. Libbie Rehabilitation Center, Inc.*, 590 F.2d 87, 89 (4th Cir. 1978), *cert. denied*, 442 U.S. 947 (1979).

3. The "primary objective" requirement had prevented many handicapped individuals from pursuing any private remedy for discrimination in the workplace. *See United States v. Cabrini Medical Center*, 639 F.2d 908, 910 (2d Cir. 1981); *Carmi v. Metropolitan St. Louis Sewer District*, 620 F.2d 672, 674-75 (8th Cir.), *cert. denied*, 449 U.S. 892 (1980); *Sabol v. Board of Education*, 510 F. Supp. 892 (D. N.J. 1981); *Cain v. Archdiosese of Kansas City*, 508 F. Supp. 1021 (D. Kan. 1981); *Guertin v. Hackerman*, 496 F. Supp. 593 (S.D. Tex. 1980); *see also Brown v. Sibley*, 650 F.2d 760, 767-69 (5th Cir. July 1981) (Unit A) (holding that the receipt of federal financial assistance by a multiprogram entity does not make all programs subject to section 504).

4. In *Darrone*, however, the Supreme Court declined to reach this conclusion and held instead that section 505 of the Rehabilitation Act does not incorporate the primary objective limitation of Title VI. *Darrone, supra*, _____ U.S. at _____, 104 S.Ct. at 1254. *See also Jones v. Metropolitan Atlanta Rapid Transit Authority*,

681 F.2d 1376 (11th Cir. 1982), *cert. denied*, _____ U.S. _____, 105 S.Ct. 1591 (1984).

5.   In reaching its decision in *Darrone*, the Court relied on the legislative history, executive interpretation and purpose of the 1973 enactment.

    a.   The Court found no mention of a "primary objective" limitation in the legislative history, "although the legislators on numerous occasions adverted to section 504's prohibition against discrimination in employment by programs assisted with federal funds." *Id.* (citing S. Rep. No. 93-318, at 4, 18, 50, 70 (1073, U.S. Code Cong. & Ad. News 1973, 2076; 119 Cong. Rec. 5862 (remarks of Sen. Cranston), 24587-24588 (1973) (remarks of Sen. Williams, Chairman of the Committee on Labor and Public Welfare))).

    b.   The Court found that HHS from the outset has interpreted section 504 "to prohibit employment discrimination by all recipients of federal financial aid, regardless of the primary objective of that aid." *Id.* (citing 39 Fed. Reg. 18562, 18582 (1974)) (revising preexisting provisions to implement section 504); 41 Fed. Reg. 29548, 29552, 29563 (1976)(proposed department regulations), *promulgated*, 42 Fed. Reg. 22678 (84.2), 22680 (84.11), 22688 ("Employment Practices") (1977); 43 Fed. Reg. 2132, 2138 (1978)(final coordinating regulations). The Department of Justice, now responsible for coordinating agency implementation of section 504, *see* Executive Order No. 12250, 45 Fed. Reg. 72995 (1980), adopted the HHS (then HEW) guidelines, 46 Fed. Reg. 440686 (1981).

    c.   Finally, the Court found that the "application of section 504 to all programs receiving federal financial assistance fits the remedial purpose of the Rehabilitation Act 'to promote and expand employment opportunities for the handicapped.'" *Id.* at 1255 (quoting 29 U.S.C. 701(8)).

6.   Accordingly, when the *Baylor* and Darrone cases are read in conjunction, recipients of Medicare and Medicaid--which include most long term health care providers--are subject to the substantive duties that section 504 imposes on recipient employers.

D.   The Substantive Duties that Section 504 Imposes on Recipient Employers--Administrative Interpretation

1. HHS regulations prohibit employment discrimination against "qualified handicapped persons." 45 C.F.R. 84.11. The regulations substitute "qualified handicapped person" for the statutory formulation "otherwise qualified handicapped individual" because the Department concluded the change

    > was necessary in order to comport with the intent of the statute because, read literally, "otherwise" qualified handicapped persons include persons who are qualified except for their handicap, rather than in spite of their handicap. Under such a literal reading, a blind person possessing all the qualifications for driving a bus except sight could be said to be "otherwise qualified" for the job of driving.

    > *Id.* at Part 84 Appendix A(A)(5)(analysis of final regulations).

2. A "qualified handicapped person" is "a handicapped person who, with reasonable accommodation, can perform the essential functions of the job in question." 28 C.F.R. 41.32 (1983) (Department of Justice "Standards for Determining Who Are Handicapped Persons").

    a. The term "essential functions" is used to "emphasiz[e] that handicapped persons should not be disqualified simply because they may have difficulty in performing tasks that bear only a marginal relationship to a particular job." 45 C.F.R. Part 84, Appendix A at 299 (1983).

3. Employers must make "reasonable accommodation" to the physical and mental limitations of otherwise qualified handicapped employees and applicants. *Id.* at 84.12.

    a. Under the HHS regulations, reasonable accommodation includes "(1) making facilities used by employees readily accessible to and usable by handicapped persons, and (2) job restructuring, part-time or modified work schedules, acquisitions or modifications of equipment or devices, the provision of readers or interpreters, and other similar actions." *Id.*

4. Employment criteria that tends to screen out handicapped persons must be job related. *Id.* at 84.13.

    a. The Department of Labor regulations provide that job qualifications "which would tend to exclude handicapped individuals because of their handicap . . . shall be related to the specific job or jobs for which the individual is being considered and shall be consistent with business necessity and safe performance." 29 C.F.R. 32.14(b)(1983).

5. Employer need not make reasonable accommodations if they would invoke an "undue hardship." *Id.* at 84.12(a)

   a. The regulations prescribe a detailed set of factors governing the determination of whether forcing an employer to provide accommodations would involve and "undue hardship." *Id.* at 84.12(c). In arriving at this determination, a decisionmaker must consider the cost of accommodations and the size, purpose, structure, and budget of an employers program. *Id.*

6. Future regulations to look out for:

   a. The Department of Justice has developed and circulated to the other agencies a prototype regulation implementing the 1978 Amendments to section 504 of the Rehabilitation Act. The prototype is patterned after existing Federal regulations for the implementation of section 504 in programs or activities receiving Federal financial assistance.

   b. DOL is in the process of preparing new across-the-board regulations applicable to all its federally assisted programs.

E. The Duties Imposed by Section 504 As Construed by The Case Law

Predictably, courts appear to have very different views regarding the extent to which recipients of federal funds are required to accommodate handicapped persons under the Rehabilitation Act. *See e.g.,*

1. *Smith v. Administrator of General Services,* 32 Fair Empl. Prac. Cas. (BNA) 986 (C.D. Cal. 1983)(providing supervision and regular blood tests for an epileptic nursing assistant is a reasonable accommodation);

2. *Nelson v. Thornburgh,* 567 F. Supp. 369, 379-82 (E.D. Pa. 1983)(providing half-time readers for blind social workers is not an undue hardship);

3. *Bey v. Bolger,* 540 F. Supp. 910, 927 (E.D. Pa. 1982) (offering "light duty status" to handicapped employees who had not met five-year minimum service requirement would be an undue hardship to the Postal Service because of losses of efficiency and extraordinary costs);

4. *Upshur v. Lane,* 474 F. Supp. 332, 342 (N.D. Cal. 1979)(section

504 would not require a school district to hire an aide for a blind administrator);

5. *American Public Transit Association v. Lewis*, 655 F.2d 1272, 1277-78 (D.C. Cir. 1981) (Department of Transportation regulations requiring that all public transportation be made accessible to the handicapped would have imposed unduly burdensome costs).

6. In *Southeastern Community College v. Davis*, 442 U.S. 397 (1979), the Supreme Court addressed the issue of how much accommodation section 504 requires. Although the case involved education rather than employment, Justice Powell noted that the issue was important "to the many institutions covered by section 504." *Id.* at 404. A unanimous Court held that section 504 did not require a federally assisted nursing program to admit an applicant with a severe hearing impairment. The Court determined that the language and structure of the Rehabilitation Act "reflect a recognition by Congress of the distinction between the evenhanded treatment of qualified handicapped persons and affirmative efforts to overcome the disabilities caused by handicaps." *Id.* at 410. Nevertheless, the Court noted that it did "not suggest that the line between a lawful refusal to extend affirmative action and illegal discrimination against handicapped persons will always be clear." *Id.* at 412. Moreover, the Court intimated that if, in the future, accommodations no longer proposed "undue financial and administrative burden," it might deem the refusal to provide them discrimination. *Id.* at 412-13.

7. The *Davis* opinion -- containing much of the ambiguity reflected in the lower court decisions -- has perpetuated the inconsistent application of section 504 to employment disputes.

8. Another unresolved issue is whether the duty of "reasonable accommodation": section 504 is the same as that imposed on federal contractors under section 503. If so, DOL's section 503 regulations (41 C.F.R. Part 60-741) and interpretations (which historically have been fairly stringent) would apply.

9. As a result of the *Baylor* and *Darrone* decisions, long term health care providers might find themselves in the middle of this ambiguous area without meaningful guidelines for interaction.

VII. CURRENT CIVIL RIGHTS DEVELOPMENTS -- FEDERAL
      CONTRACT OBLIGATIONS

   A. Overview of Executive Order 11246 and its Implementing
       Regulations

       1. Executive Order 11246 requires that every nonexempt
           government contractor refrain from discriminating against
           employees or applicants on the basis of race, color, religion, sex,
           or national origin, and take affirmative action to ensure that
           applicants and employees are employed without regard to such
           factors. Federally assisted construction contracts are also
           covered.

       2. Executive Order 11246 is enforced by DOL's Office of Federal
           Contract Compliance Programs (OFCCP). Regulations issued
           by OFCCP are published at 41 C.F.R. Chapter 60.

       3. The heart of OFCCP's regulations is the requirements that the
           employer take affirmative action to meet goals and timetables for
           the recruitment, hiring, and promotion of women and minorities
           whenever those groups are "underutilized" in comparison to
           their "availability" based on complicated statistical calculations.

       4. Current regulations require all government contractors with 50 or
           more employees and a contract or subcontract amounting to
           $50,000 or more to institute a formal written affirmative action
           program (AAP), and establish goals if necessary.

   B. Potential Coverage of Long Term Care Providers Under Executive
       Order 11246

       1. Contracts with the veterans administration

           As noted *supra*, arrangements between the VA and long term
           care facilities have been viewed as government contracts for
           Service Contract Act purposes. Absent a compelling reason for
           viewing the VA contract differently for Executive Order 11246
           purposes, these contracts are likely to be viewed by DOL as
           subject to the Executive Order.

       2. Medicare and Medicaid

           a. DOL Solicitor's Office staff is currently examining the
               issue of whether Medicare and Medicaid constitute
               government contracts subjecting recipients to coverage.

           b. The caselaw finding that Medicare and Medicaid constitute
               Federal financial assistance discussed *supra*, while not
               specifically addressing this issue, by their very holdings

suggest the recipients are not government contractors, because for OFCCP purposes financial assistance and direct contracts are two distinct categories.

c. Nonetheless, my discussions with DOL staff suggest that it is possible that they might conclude that some Medicare/Medicaid recipients are government contractors. It should be cautioned that this conclusion is very tentative, and more importantly, has *not* been subject to review within the higher levels of the Solicitor's office or DOL.

C. Future Issues Facing OFCCP

1. Continued existence of the program

Some industry groups and members of the Administration support wholesale revocation or substantial revision of the Executive Order. Such an action would face substantial political opposition.

2. Revision of OFCCP regulations

The Carter Administration issued revisions to the OFCCP regulations which have never been implemented. OFCCP proposed to modify the regulations in 1981. 46 Fed. Reg. 42968 (August 25, 1981). The controversial proposal has never been finalized. Among the issues of greatest interest are:

a. How much to increase the dollar and employee thresholds for the AAP obligation. (The proposal set the thresholds at $1 million and 250 employees; most likely the threshold selected will be lower.)

b. Whether to delete the goals and timetables. *Compare Firefighters Local Union No. 1784 v. Stotts*, _____ U.S. _____, 34 FEP Cases 1702 (1984). This is a major symbolic issue for proponents and opponents.

c. What factors should be taken into account in performing the availability computation.

Chapter 17

Legal and Ethical Issues for Nurses in Long Term Care

Speaker: Kathleen A. Michels

I want to start off by saying that I'm not an ethicist. I'm a lawyer, and although it may seem a bit presumptuous to label my talk "Ethical Issues," these issues do surface again and again in my practice. What I'd like to do today is to discuss them from the point of view of a practicing attorney.

BACKGROUND

Obviously ethical issues arise in health care all through the spectrum, from birth to death. They arise in regard to all types of health care providers, acute care hospitals, the surgicenters, and long term care facilities; but there seem to me to be two places and two ages where the ethical issues crystallize. These are for the newborn--the impaired newborn in particular--in the intensive care unit; and for the elderly, in a long term care facility. Maybe this isn't too surprising. I guess it's conventional wisdom that life is somewhat like a circle; that man starts out being dependent on others for basic care and his basic needs and in many instances ends up in exactly the same fashion. In addition to sharing infirmities and sometimes an inability to speak for themselves, these two age groups also share the characteristic of being in an institution where decisions have been traditionally made out of the sight and mind of the public.

Another thing they share in common is the perception that the cost of taking care of an impaired newborn and the cost of taking care of the elderly is very, very high. We've heard so much about cost today, that I'm not going to talk a whole lot about it and about the need for new beds and the need for long term care. Let's just start off with the assumption that it's true and that it is going to cost some money. That has ethical implications. If you heard the case mix discussion, you could see the ethical issues popping up everywhere. There have been other methods of attempting to analyze and control costs that also raise ethical issues.

Recently there have been a spate of articles on cost benefit and cost effectiveness analyses. These types of analyses apply to health care and have particular implications for the geriatric population for the long term care. Consider for example, that if you are doing a cost benefit analysis of health care, one of the measurements frequently used is the productivity of the individual involved. For example, you might take the amount of money that the individual is going to make over his lifetime; subtract the amount the individual is going to cost society by drawing on Medicare, Medicaid and Social Security, and come up with some kind of net worth benefit from saving the individual. Now if you apply that to an 85-year-old person in a long term care facility, you're going to come up with a minus.

Another problem is measuring the quality of life. It's very difficult to attempt to measure in value the quality of life of an individual who is not able to communicate with you. In fact, what are the pleasures of living when one is senile? I'd like to read you one quote from one of the many articles both pro and con in a variety of journals that have appeared in the last couple of years. One quote particularly struck my fancy from the *New England Journal of Medicine*; this is from a Dr. Alan Stone: "The logic of the human capital argument would thus be perfectly consistent with a concept that youth and age are at least non-treatment. After retirement is the geriatric intervention, with a most favorable benefit-cost ratio. As Woody Allen has noted with equal insight, 'death is a great way to cut down on expenses.' "

Based on the cost and on the real or perceived abuse and neglect of these two populations that I've mentioned, the handicapped newborn of course has received extensive attention over the last few years. In particular, as you're all aware, the last few years saw the extended debate in judicial proceedings involved in the Baby Doe and Baby Jane Doe cases, the promulgation and invalidation of the Baby Doe regulations, and the passage of compromise legislation this year.

The type of issues highlighted in the Baby Doe debate are issues that could well be applied to elderly patients in long term care facilities and it's probably only an accident that we don't have the Granny Doe regulations. For example, when, if ever, is it justified to withhold treatment for handicapped newborns or for the impaired elderly based on the prognosis that they will never have or never again have a functioning cognitive life; based on the quality of their life; based on the cost and burden of caring for these individuals?

Perhaps the primary distinguishing feature between the two populations that I've identified is that at least with the impaired newborns, we have some kind of expectation or hope that if properly treated, they'll have a reasonable life expectancy. Another possible difference is that society has at least traditionally approached infants with a desire to comfort and cuddle them. With the elderly we do not have the expectation that even if properly treated, and aggressively treated, they have the expectation of a long life. Nor have they tended to generate the same type of impulses as have the infants.

INFORMED CONSENT

Now with that as background, I'd like to focus on a few particular ethical/legal issues. As I'm sure you're aware--there are a myriad of them--we have identified in our outlines only some of them and can talk about even fewer today. One that I'd like to start with is informed consent. The issue of informed consent may not seem terribly glamorous or to be the kind of issue that would generate substantial debate, but it is my experience that the concept of obtaining informed consent for long term care residents lies at the heart of a number of ethical issues.

Informed consent is not routinely or properly obtained in some facilities. There appear to be several reasons for this. First, the long term care patient is frequently incompetent or has fluctuating competence due to disease, organic brain syndrome, or what have you. Therefore the ability of the provider to obtain patient consent is questionable. It's also a difficult process and it's time consuming. The second reason is that many types of treatment delivered to patients in long term care facilities may be perceived as being routine--that being the type of decision over which there isn't much choice. Perhaps this stems from a paternalistic attitude towards some long term care residents; a tendency to carry out the wishes of family or physicians without really ever inquiring as to whether or not it is what the patient has consented to. Then the reality is that there are numerous elderly patients who need care and have limited time and resources for obtaining consent from the patient or from others, especially through the judicial process.

Despite these very logical reasons for neglecting consent, failure to obtain informed consent raises serious legal and ethical issues. From an ethical standpoint, the failure to inform a resident and to obtain and follow through on his or her consent, in effect deprives that person of the right to self-determination.

Legally, there are a variety of laws, regulations or policies that require informed consent. In Massachusetts we have a variety of sources which require informed consent. We have case law that says that a physician, at least, has the duty to provide a patient with all the information that's material to the patient to make a decision. We have a patient's bill of rights that extends specifically to nursing home residents and says that they have the right to informed consent as provided by law. Under the Massachusetts Consumer Protection Act, it is an unfair act or practice for a nursing home to fail to provide residents with information concerning the nature of treatments and their effects, and information concerning possible consequences should the patient refuse treatment or drugs. Furthermore, the Medicare conditions of participation contain standards with regard to establishing policies, insuring that patients receive certain information and have a right to participate in planning their own treatment.

While the future Medicare regulations may be more helpful in this regard, at least there's something in the regulations now in regard to informed consent. Now, assuming there is a right to informed consent, is there any possibility that the nursing home is going to be held liable if you fail to obtain it? I think there is. Traditionally, the physician is the party who was found to have the duty and to be liable if the duty was breached.

There are a number of theories under which a nursing home itself could be found liable. One of these is *ostensible agency*. It is certainly a reasonable argument that if a resident comes to your facility, the resident is looking not to the physician for care and treatment, but to the nursing home--its nurses, its aides, and the home itself. There's also a theory of corporate negligence. Maybe it should be the responsibility of a nursing home to insure that patients are giving informed consent, or have someone appointed for them who can do so. Finally there may be a contract theory if your institution has a document that it presents to the patient that indicates that the patient will be allowed the right to participate in planning his or her treatment. Therefore, based on ethical and legal reasons, informed consent *is* important, particularly for major treatment decisions.

Granted all that, what is the process and how do you obtain it? The first step, although it may seem a little bit obvious, is to ask the patient. Sometimes it is overlooked; patients do have fluctuating competence. The President's Commission that came out in 1983 with its decision to forego life-sustaining treatment, stated that a conclusion that a patient is incompetent should be made only when the patient lacks the ability to make a decision that promotes *his* well-being in conformity with *his* values and preferences.

Another question is, who should make this decision? What standards should be used and how should they be incorporated into your policy? In terms of who should make the decision, it's difficult to generalize. The Medicare conditions of participation imply that there may be several ways of determining that a patient is incompetent. One is that the patient is adjudicated incompetent under state law. It's pretty easy and straightforward, but very time consuming. Another is that a physician finds the patient to be medically incapable of understanding his or her rights; this isn't state law but rather suggestions from the federal government as to ways that incompetence may be determined. The last method is to determine if the patient exhibits a communication barrier. I don't know exactly to whom the patient exhibits it or what that means, but for what it's worth, it's in the regulations.

State law varies obviously from state to state. Some will contain requirements that a person be adjudicated incompetent; most do not. In Massachusetts there is no legislative requirement, no statute on the books which says you have to go to court to make a determination that a patient is incompetent. There's also some indication in Massachusetts that the consent of a spouse, for example, who is not judicially appointed, will be sufficient for most treatment decisions, assuming the spouse is acting in good faith.

There's also the indication in Massachusetts law that even more controversial decisions such as Do Not Resuscitate (DNR) orders, may be consented to by the loving family of a patient without prior judicial approval. That's going to be the next case, trying to decide which family is loving. The President's Commission that I referred to before, and which has done some extensive study in this area, points out the fact that there is much uncertainty in state law but that most determinations are in fact not made in court, but are made informally--probably by a physician.

Now, faced with these inconsistencies, one might suggest obtaining a judicially appointed guardian for every resident. But such a guardian is not often available. We have, in Massachusetts, set up various guardian services which are so backed up that we only call them when we have a dire emergency. But in many instances, guardians are simply unavailable. It takes a great deal of time and energy and cost and so forth.

Recognizing and trying to balance both the legal and ethical constraints and practical realities, I might suggest a few guidelines for deciding when it's necessary to seek a judicially appointed guardian. First of all, it's very important to categorize the decisions that are being made: is the decision a routine medical treatment decision about which there is no controversy? Decisions that might fall into this category, depending on the facts, are exploratory surgery to determine whether or not a patient had cancer as was suspected.

To the extent that there is disagreement in the medical community as to the wisdom of the procedure, to the extent that there are serious risks involved in the procedure, and to the extent that the procedure is intrusive and the benefits questionable--the wisdom of accepting surrogate consent with no formal procedures becomes more questionable. Other factors are obviously the involvement of the family, any questions as to the good intentions of the family and any prior involvement of governmental agencies or the court. For example, some of the situations we've encountered have been patients who are being sustained on life-sustaining equipment, whose family has been engaging in essentially a fight over the person's property to be disposed of after death. That type of situation does not engender a great deal of confidence in the surrogate decision-makers. We've had instances where the patient has been referred and has been admitted to a facility after an abuse and neglect petition has been filed against the family. If an agency following the patient is also involved in the aforementioned situation, then utilizing the consent of the family member without looking elsewhere may not be advisable.

Finally, there are some specific decisions in Massachusetts that cannot be made without court authorization. You have to look at your own state law to see if there are any that would be applicable to you, but in Massachusetts, anti-psychotic drugs cannot be administered to patients who are refusing them and who are incompetent without authorization by the court. Similar proceedings are probably required for electroconvulsive therapy.

One of the decisions that's obviously most troublesome and most difficult to make, with or without judicial intervention, is the decision to withhold or to terminate life-sustaining treatment.

Life-Sustaining Treatment

We've been dealing with life-sustaining treatment issues for almost twenty years now. In earlier analyses the brain death issue seemed as controversial as the withholding or withdrawing of respirators does now. We seem to have reached pretty good consensus on the brain death cases with most states having some type of brain death legislation. However, the area that still maintains a certain amount of controversy is the withholding or withdrawing of life-supporting treatment.

Competency and Incompetency

The two general areas that I wanted to talk about in relation to treatment are competent persons and incompetent persons. When you talk about withdrawing or withholding life support treatment, you're doing a balancing act. On one side you're balancing a person's right to privacy or the right to be free from invasion of bodily integrity and on the other side are the states' rights.

In relation to the competent line of cases, a very good example was the 1978 Massachusetts case of *Lane vs. Candura*. In this particular case, Mrs. Candura had suffered from gangrene in her right foot and lower leg. She had refused to consent to an operation that the physicians had been recommending. Her daughter sought to be appointed as her guardian. Ultimately, the court decided that although perhaps the daughter would recommend that the mother have the surgery, the fact that the mother was competent gave credence to whatever her decision was. She didn't want surgery, so she did not have to have the surgery.

In the 1970 *Perlmutter* case out of Florida, we have a gentleman that had Lou Gehrig's disease. He asked to be removed from a respirator, being very cognizant of the fact that being removed from the respirator in his case would mean death within an hour. The court granted his request. One of the factors that they took into account was that there was full approval of the family. The court decided that the state interest in keeping him alive did not outweigh his right to die with dignity. It was his choice and they upheld it.

Thus the competency cases are not as controversial as those dealing with incompetency. The lead decision in the incompetency line of cases is the 1976 *Quinlan* case out of New Jersey. Because Karen Ann Quinlan was in a persistent vegetative state, her parents made the decision that they wanted to have her respirator removed. Although the parents had signed a waiver form, the doctor in the case decided that he did not want to risk the possible criminal or civil liability by withdrawing the respirator and took the issue to court. The final court decision was that as long as the doctor and the family as well as an ethics committee all recommended that the respirator be removed, it would uphold that decision. The court stated that in cases like *Quinlan*, there was no need to get prior judicial approval of a decision to withdraw treatment. The issue of prior judicial approval has been addressed differently by other courts, however.

After the *Quinlan* case we have the 1977 *Saikewicz* case from Massachusetts. The *Saikewicz* case involved a gentleman who had severe leukemia. He had been institutionalized most of his life and due to certain of his maladies, chemotherapy was the treatment of choice. *Saikewicz* is known for its use of the substituted judgment test and determining the four main state interests for purposes of balancing individual and state interests. The substituted judgment test requires the people that are going to make the ultimate treatment decision to do so as if they were the patient himself instead of an interested third party.

The four main state interests that could counterweigh the patient's privacy interests were found to be the preservation of life, protection of interests of innocent third parties, prevention of suicide, and maintenance of the ethical integrity of the medical profession. One major caveat that came out of the *Saikewicz* case was a disagreement with the *Quinlan* decision in the area of prior judicial approval; *Saikewicz* held that these decisions are too important to allow them to be made solely by the family, physicians, and an ethical committee.

Next we have the 1980 *Spring* case from Massachusetts which also dealt with prior judicial approval. The court delineated thirteen different issues to be analyzed in deciding whether you need to go to court first for approval. Those are delineated in the outline and I won't go through them for you now. It gave us some things to look at, but it never really provided detailed guidelines as to how to proceed with them. It is unclear whether, for example, if you have seven of these thirteen criteria you still need prior judicial approval.

The 1981 *Storar* case from New York disagreed with the *Saikewicz* substituted judgment test. Mr. Storar was a terminally ill patient who required two units of blood every eight to fifteen days. Giving him the blood transfusions was something that his mother perceived as being very uncomfortable for him, that he resisted, and her ultimate decision was that she wanted those blood transfusions stopped. That was her substituted judgment of what her son would have wanted. The Court of Appeals of New York, however, disagreed stating that you may typically use a substituted judgment test, except in cases like this where the court didn't like the substituted judgment. The court held that it could not allow an incompetent person to bleed to death because someone felt it was best for a person with an incurable disease. The *Storar* case was a maverick in how it dealt with the substituted judgment test; most courts do use that type of analysis.

What happens when you have some indication of what the person wanted ahead of time? That issue was dealt with in the *Eichner* case. In that 1981 New York case, Brother Joseph Fox had had a cardiac arrest which ultimately left him in a persistent vegetative state and on a respirator. Prior to sustaining his injury, Brother Fox had on several occasions talked with other people about the *Quinlan* case and what he would want if he was put in a similar situation. The court took into account his statements on numerous occasions that he would not want to be kept alive in a Quinlan-type of situation. The court therefore allowed his respirator to be terminated.

That's a bit different than what was done with Karen Ann Quinlan. Evidence in the *Quinlan* case noted that when talking to friends on different occasions, Karen had said that she "would not want to be a vegetable." The *Quinlan* court did not view that as probative evidence to be considered in determining whether they should withdraw the respirator or not. We can only speculate why personal comments were used as evidence in one case and not in another. I think part of the reasoning was that Brother Fox had made his statements very close to the time he actually was injured and that he was an older person. In all honesty, I also think the case law has developed over time and the courts have become more sophisticated since the *Quinlan* case.

Having discussed the impact of prior personal statements on a decision to withhold life-sustaining treatment, let's consider the case of someone who has signed a living will. That issue was dealt with in the 1983 *Bludworth* case. In that Florida case, a man had signed a living will which stated that he did not want to have extraordinary measures used if he was ever in a comatose or persistent vegetative state. The District Court of Appeals held that his signing a living will was probative evidence of what he wanted. The will was not so old that they worried he might have changed his mind either. The court did note that they still wanted these kinds of cases brought to the court for prior judicial approval, however.

The 1983 *Colyer* case in Washington again dealt with the unclear issue of prior judicial approval before terminating life-sustaining treatment. Some states seem to want that determination to be made in advance by the court, while others rule that as long as the physician approves, the family agrees and there is some type of ethics committee involvement in the decision, there is no need to come to court. We may very well need a U.S. Supreme Court decision to finally decide whether or not you need prior judicial approval in these type of cases. In the meantime, although the issues of withholding and withdrawing life-sustaining treatment like respirators seem somewhat resolved, a new area of controversy is arising regarding the withdrawal of nutrition and hydration.

NURTITION AND HYDRATION

The case of *In the matter of Mary Hier* was decided by the Massachusetts Appeals Court in June of 1984. Mrs. Hier was a 92-year-old woman who suffered from severe mental illness and had been hospitalized for at least 58 years with her care being paid for by New York public assistance. She'd been treated off and on with thorazine, which apparently reduced her extreme agitation, but she didn't like the injections. Because of a physical malformation, in 1974 she had undergone a gastrostomy and from that point on, was fed through a tube surgically implanted through her abdominal wall. According to representations by counsel that appeared before the Appeals Court, she repeatedly removed the tube and underwent a series of surgical reinsertions. In April of 1984, after removing the tube several times, she was transferred from the Beverly Nursing Home to Beverly Hospital.

It might have been possible at that time to reinsert the tube without surgery, but Mrs. Hier adamantly refused. She did not have a "communication barrier," so to speak. Because the family was unavailable and very importantly, her care was being paid for by a state agency, the hospital petitioned for appointment of a guardian with the authority to consent to thorazine. In Massachusetts, there is a need to get court authorization in approval of a plan for administration of certain drugs, and the hospital felt it important in this case to get court authorization.

But the hospital didn't ask that the guardian have the authority to consent to the surgery. A guardian ad litem and counsel were appointed for Mrs. Hier and *they* advocated surgery. Applying the substituted judgment test, the probate court decided that if Mrs. Hier were competent, she would decide that she didn't want the surgery. The guardian ad litem appealed, espousing the theory that failure to provide nutrition to a patient who is *not* brain-dead, comatose, vegetative, or facing imminent death cannot be justified by the right to privacy or on any other grounds.

Like the California court in the *Barber* case, the Massachusetts Appeals Court rejected the argument that nutrition should be differentiated from treatment and the right of choice limited to treatment only. The court didn't indicate which, if either, decision it approved, but it did distinguish *Hier* from both *Conroy* and *Barber* both of which are discussed below. The court said that the distinction was not between terminating a procedure and commencing it, but rather between supplying nutritional support by a modestly obtrusive means, that is an IV in the *Barber* case, and an invasive procedure, a surgical reinsertion of the tube in the *Hier* case. The court rejected the distinction between starting something and stopping something, which also seemed to have lost its usefulness in our discussion of these issues, and instead, focused on the obtrusiveness of the procedure, thus in effect performing a benefit-burden analysis for the patient. In weighing the obtrusiveness, the court looked at Mrs. Hier's particular situation, and considered the following facts: the complications presented by virtue of her prior operations, the scar tissue and the burden of the proposed operation on an elderly person in a debilitated state (she was a tiny woman who had not been receiving adequate nutrition, apparently). They were unable to evaluate the possible complications beforehand. There was a 20 percent mortality risk according to the original medical evidence. And then, after the surgery, the evidence was that she would have to be physically restrained to keep from pulling the tube out again, or else the problem would begin again.

The Massachusetts Appeals Court approved the probate court's application of the substituted judgment test and said the court properly took into consideration the fact that Mrs. Hier clearly indicated she wanted no surgical intervention. The court properly took into account that the benefits of a gastrostomy to her were diminished by the fact that she repeatedly dislodged the tube. They also properly took into account the fact that the treating physicians did not recommend surgery and also took into account that her religion, Roman Catholicism, would not impose any ethical constraints on her treatment choice.

The court examined some of the state issues and the other third party interests that have been mentioned and decided that these did not outweigh Mrs. Hier's right. The decision seemed to repeat most things that we have heard in the past, and in fact, to pick up on and reaffirm the decision in the *Barber* case. However, the decision was not the end of the matter in Massachusetts. The guardian ad litem (GAL) persuaded the probate court to authorize transfer of Mrs. Hier to another hospital, St. Elizabeth's in Boston. Ostensibly they were to evaluate Mrs. Hier to determine whether she would be a candidate for hyperalimentation, which would be another method of treatment rather than the gastrostomy, and of course would have much different implications for the court's analysis. A new guardian was also requested by the GAL.

After evaluation at St. Elizabeth's Hospital, the GAL moved the probate court to reopen the evidentiary phase of the hearing, not to present evidence about hyperalimentation, but to present entirely new evidence about Mrs. Hier. Six physicians and the head nurse testified, and their evidence revealed that Mrs. Hier had a voracious appetite. Even though she was unable to keep anything in her stomach, she constantly ate. She wanted to live, and she said she felt she was getting better. She was much less agitated now that she was being treated with thorazine. Medical testimony said that reinserting the gastrostomy tube would be good medical practice, not excessively burdensome, and would offer a reasonable hope of benefit. Medical evidence was to the effect that the procedure was relatively simple, there was little scar tissue, and the risk of mortality was approximately five percent. Finally, without the surgery, Mrs. Hier would die.

The probate court, in a very restrained opinion, said there was a substantial change in the circumstances. Mrs. Hier was now acquiescent to the surgery, so the decision was that her substituted judgment was that she would have the surgery. Additionally, and again in a very restrained fashion, the court said the evidence was "overwhelmingly contradictory" to the previous evidence, specifically in regard to scarring and in regard to the risks of the procedure. A new guardian was appointed with authority to consent to the surgery.

I think the *Hier* case points out some of the difficulties in this area from a practical point of view. These are some things that you can do to reduce the chances that one of your residents or patients would ever be in this type of situation. Practically speaking, it's one thing to talk about the theories and the law which sound good but really do not have anything to do with the person. We have to deal with the fact that there is a lot of dissension within the medical community in regard to withholding nutritional fluids.

In 1983, at the probate court chancery level in New Jersey, the nephew of Claire Conroy petitioned the court to have her nasal gastric (NG) tube removed. Claire Conroy was an 84-year-old nursing home resident, suffering from organic brain syndrome, necrotic decubitus ulcers, urinary tract infection, heart disease, hypertension, and diabetes, among other things. Except for minor movements of her head and neck, and sometimes of her arms and hands, she basically was unable to move, she didn't speak, and she lay in bed in the fetal position. She did apparently sometimes follow people's movement with her eyes, but at other times did not. Medical testimony was inconclusive as to whether or not she was capable of experiencing pain. All the testimony in the case, as well as the judge's own direct observation, led him to believe that she had no cognitive or volitional functioning. There was no reasonable expectation that she would ever improve. The guardian felt that his aunt would not want to continue the nasogastric feeding. Because the physician in the case would not consent to removal of the NG tube, the nephew went to court. I think the word "consent" is very interesting in that instance, because it does show us the symbiotic relationship, or the interrelationships, if you will, among all the parties in these type of cases. Generally we think of a patient consenting, or maybe the surrogate decision-maker, but many more people can become involved. There are nurses, physicians, aides, and friends--all will have something to say about the withholding of treatment.

The court at the probate level rejected the extraordinary-ordinary distinction, once again, and said that the focus should be on whether the life of the patient had become unbearably burdensome to her. He concluded that it had, and he said the NG tube should be removed. In a decision that was perhaps not as restrained as the *Hier* probate decision, he also said that it should be removed even though painful death by starvation and dehydration will follow. This provided the impetus for a lot of concern about this type of situation. The probate judge was not insensitive and attempted to assuage the fears of those who thought that the decision would be applied to all senile patients in nursing homes, and attempted, at least, to carefully distinguish Mrs. Conroy's situation from those senile patients who are still capable of loving and receiving love and having the environment have some effect on them.

The court also said that although it would decline to say whether judicial involvement was always necessary in these types of cases, there would be times when it was appropriate, for example, when there was disagreement, as there had been in this case, as to what was the best course of action. It also mentioned that judicial involvement might be appropriate when nursing homes were involved and there was no ethics committee, as apparently was the case here.

The New Jersey Appellate Court was outraged by the decision, and reversed the lower court decision, saying that it authorized euthanasia. It said that nourishment is not the same as medical treatment referring to the distinction between ordinary and extraordinary care, this being ordinary care. Also mentioned was the fact that the intrusiveness of this particular procedure was minimal.

Very recently the New Jersey Supreme Court decided the case on appeal. I do not yet have that decision in hand, however, I do have the quotations in the *New York Times* and various other reports. It appears to say that if medical evidence established that a patient like Mrs. Conroy is elderly, incompetent, with severe and permanent mental and physical impairments, and with a life expectancy of one year or less--if she would have refused the treatment, then the treatment may be withdrawn. In other words, it reversed the appeals court. It appears to have established a subjective test, in most instances, but required clear proof of what her intent would be.

Alternatively, the New Jersey court has stated that if one cannot meet the subjective test, the limited objective test may be used and if that doesn't work, you can use the pure objective test. So we have now a whole new system of tests to think about. The limited objective and the pure objective move along the spectrum to a best interests analysis.

The New Jersey Supreme Court appears to have said that artificial feeding is not different from treatment, going back to the Probate Court decision and being consistent with Massachusetts and with California. It appears to also have said that withdrawing treatment is no different from not starting it in the first place. One of the things that was different, however, in addition to its tiers of tests, is that it appears to have established special rules regarding nursing homes. The court has said that if a nursing home resident is involved, then we will need the opinion of two other physicians aside from the attending physician, presumably on the issues relating to the standards that the medical evidence has to show, and that the nursing home ombudsman for the state will have to be involved. This may also require some kind of judicial intervention. Once you get one state agency involved, one tends to bring these cases to court. But at any rate, the court did advance a particular concern for nursing home residents like Mrs. Conroy.

If one could summarize it all, the three recent cases--*Barber, Conroy* and *Hier*--all appear to have rejected the distinction between food and fluids and other treatment. I should probably say "artificial feeding" because this is what we're talking about. None of these cases have dealt with providing a patient with a sip of water, hand feeding, holding them and giving them something personally. These have all been artificial means, varying from the NG tubes, IVs, to gastrostomies. They have also rejected the distinction between ordinary and extraordinary treatment as not very useful, and between starting and stopping.

There are some guidelines that will help in making decisions regarding nutrition. The questions to ask are as follows: (1) What treatment is currently being provided to your patient? (2) How intrusive is it? (3) What are the risks?

(4) What are the side effects? (5) If there is pain, how much pain? How often? How long? (6) What is the likelihood of success or benefit from the treatment? (7) What are the risks and side effects of no treatment? (8) What are the alternatives that are available such as hyperalimentation? What are the risks and benefits? (9) What is the certainty with which these issues can be determined, what are the recommendations of the treating professionals? (10) What are the wishes of the patient? (11) Have you asked all of the family members what they think? How involved are they? Do they all agree? Are they acting in good faith? (12) Finally, you might want to ask whether or not there is the involvement of any other kind of state agency.

Assuming that you have a policy for handling all of these issues, have you, the nursing home, complied with all your policies, and are they well documented? This screening process will not give you the answer. A lot of cases will drop by the wayside before you get through it, but at least when you come to make a decision you'll have some facts.

CRIMINAL CASES

The 1983 *Barber* case in California addressed 2 issues: (1) the difference between life-sustaining treatments such as the use of respirators and the provision of nutrition, and (2) whether under the facts of this case, the two physicians involved were guilty of murder and/or conspiracy to commit murder. The two physicians had acceded to Mr. Herbert's family's request to discontinue his life-sustaining machinery and intravenous tubes. Mr. Herbert was in a persistive vegetative state after suffering a cardiorespiratory arrest.

The court of appeals in this case ultimately held that the physicians' actions were not unlawful, even though they did not secure prior judicial approval, and there was no ethics committee involved in the treatment decision. They only had family agreement regarding the decision to discontinue the life-sustaining machinery. The court ultimately looked at whether the physicians had a duty to continue the treatments which meant looking at the medical standard of practice. The court's view was that in this particular case, they were going to look at whether the proposed treatment was proportionate or disproportionate in terms of the benefits to be gained versus the burdens caused to the patient. It was felt that the focal point of the decision should be the prognosis as to the reasonable ability to return to cognitive and sapient life.

Ultimately, even without prior judicial approval, the court felt that because the physicians had adhered to Mrs. Herbert's substituted judgment of the fact that she thought her husband would want the respirator discontinued, the court said that there was not criminal liability in this particular case.

There have been several cases wherein nurses have filed complaints against other nurses' actions. One that deals with a registered nurse reporting another registered nurse was in the 1984 *State of Wisconsin vs. Engel* case. Nurse Engel pled no contest to the crime of practicing medicine without a license, by the fact that he had discontinued a respirator on a patient without a physician's order. The patient had suffered irreversible brain damage due to a stroke and death was imminent.

The particular facts of this case were that the facility had a policy that a respirator would not be discontinued until the patient was dead. The attending physician decided that, even though the family had asked to have the respirator discontinued, he was going to adhere to the policy of the facility and not disconnect. The registered nurse involved, who was dealing with the family on a continuing basis, decided that the family so strongly wanted to have the respirator disconnected that he disconnected the respirator and the patient died.

Action was brought, interestingly enough, under the theory of the unauthorized practice of medicine, and the decision of the court was that the registered nurse would be sentenced to twenty months' probation for his actions. Right now action is pending as to whether Mr. Engel's nursing license will be revoked due to the unauthorized practice of medicine or any other particular violation of the Wisconsin Nurse Practice Act or of the regulations of the Board of Nursing.

REGULATORY AGENCY DECISIONS

In the 1984 *Rafferty* case, out of Pennsylvania, the State Board of Examiners in Pennsylvania revoked a nurse's license because she had disconnected a respirator. The nurse then sued and the court found that although the nurse's actions had deviated from nursing practice, because there was no intent on the part of the nurse to break the law, the required criterion of willfulness was not found to be present. Therefore the court said that the Board of Nursing could not take away that nurse's license, and reinstated the license.

The issue of withholding or withdrawing medical treatment is also being addressed in arenas other than the courts and regulatory agencies. State legislatures are enacting natural death acts or living wills. Statutory requirements vary from state to state especially insofar as how many physicians are required to sign, witness qualifications, expiration dates, and protection from civil and criminal liability.

Essentially, regardless of these differences, states are trying to develop ways in which people can give an indication of what they want before the fact, so that there is documentation of the person's wishes for the family and health care providers to refer to.

Another approach is the use of the durable power of attorney. Some state laws now say that the durable power of attorney can be used to make medical/legal type of decisions. This would affect such activities as withdrawing respirators. An article relating to this procedure is written by Lombard and Emmert and is titled "The Durable Power of Attorney: Underused Tool,"

National Law Journal, vol. 7, number 8, October 29, 1984, pp. 15-19. You should check your particular state laws, however, because the durable power of attorney in some states may be limited to business transactions; a guardian must still be appointed for decisions regarding person. The advantage of the durable power of attorney over the power of attorney is the power of attorney stops when the person becomes incompetent whereas the durable power of attorney allows you to continue to make decisions without going through lengthy judicial proceedings.

Chapter 18

Investigations of Nursing Homes

Speakers: Edwin A. Bladen
Arthur S. Friedman
Gregory J. Naclario
Richard E. Plymale

ARTHUR FRIEDMAN We have a very distinguished panel representing different prosecutorial philosophies and different jurisdictions in terms of size and location. At my extreme right is Richard Plymale, who is an assistant attorney general from Kentucky. He is the director of the Medicaid Fraud Control Unit; he has been so for about 5 years now, and he is the immediate past president of the National Association of Medicaid Fraud Control Units.

To his immediate left is Mr. Ed Bladen, who is an assistant attorney general from the state of Michigan. He is also the director of the Michigan Medicaid Fraud Control Unit, and the present president of the National Association of Medicaid Fraud Control Units. To his immediate left is Gregory Naclario, who is a special assistant attorney general from New York. He is a member of the Office of the Deputy Attorney General for Health and Social Services. He's also in charge of the Long Island Regional Office, which comprises Nassau and Suffolk counties.

Just by way of introduction, my name is Arthur Friedman. I work with the Office of the Inspector General, Department of Health and Human Services. I am the Director of the State Fraud Branch, whose main responsibility is the federal oversight of the state Medicaid Fraud Control Unit grant program, which now includes 36 different jurisdictions and has a total annual budget of about $42 million.

TARGETING

What we'd like to talk about today are nursing homes, nursing home investigations, how they're conducted. Let's start off right and go right for the jugular vein. Many owners, administrators, people of supervisory positions in nursing homes, as well as the lawyers and/or accountants or other professionals who represent nursing homes, feel that nursing homes are being singled out for particular attention when such attention is not warranted, and that their clients or they themselves are being the subjects of witch-hunts, fishing expeditions, gestapo tactics, and the like. Let's throw out something to the panel. How do you choose which nursing home to investigate or to look at? How about Greg, do you want to take that one?

GREGORY NACLARIO   In New York, if we come knocking on your client's door, hopefully it is based upon the fact that our analysis, our targeting, indicates to us that there's a problem there. I'm going to exclude for purposes of our discussion right now any complaints, any allegations, that we have on your client's facility. That aside, you have to look at it from my point of view. I have an office of 43 people consisting of attorneys, auditors, and investigators. I cannot possibly audit, in a given period of time, all the nursing homes in my area. So I have to be selective. I have to try to use my resources to the maximum.

So what we try to do is to do our best to target those homes that have a potential for fraud, and the way we do that is using our accounting techniques. We have an accounting staff who primarily engage in the targeting function for us. They will basically engage in two types of analysis. First, the variation analysis at a given home with respect to its vendors. For example, if you have a food vendor who's there for the last 2 years, and your food costs are running $150,000, and then you change vendors, and the next year your food costs are $250,000, well, to us that indicates there might be something wrong there.

So what we do is compile--and the nursing home industry in New York and on Long Island specifically has been very cooperative--we send out survey letters, ask the homes to give us information concerning their vendors, and they do in fact respond. The vast majority respond. So we put that into an IBM PC and we can play with those figures.

We also have access, through our state's nursing home reporting system, of getting all the costs from all the homes in our region. What we then will do is we'll spread like homes in geographical areas and compare different costs. We'll take the food costs and divide that by the patient days. We'll take repairs and maintenance, divide that by square footage, and do the same thing with housekeeping. What we then try to do is put all the homes in the same category and then we'll see which homes stand out, if any. If everybody else has housekeeping costs of $4 a square foot, and one home is running $6 a square foot, and he's also higher than his norm in a number of other areas, that will be the home we will target for our audit investigation.

FRIEDMAN   Ed?

EDWIN BLADEN   Well, we're not quite as sophisticated as New York in that respect. The first thing, you should understand the state of Michigan has by law the authority of statutory visitorial rights with any Medicaid provider within the state. So we may just simply drop by unannounced and ask to look at the books and records and audit, for example, patient trust funds, as the case may be, absent hours--simply just undertaking at random that effort, or targeting our Upper Peninsula, as an example, and sweeping through there for about a week or two.

Regularly we receive from our single-state agency--which is our Department of Social Services--referrals of what they have determined to be unallowable costs, after either desk audit, or audit of a nursing home's cost reports. From there, we determine whether or not the unallowable costs indeed appear to be false statements in the cost report; if they are, we will execute a search warrant on the nursing home for all of the records relating to those issues. We make copies of what we have taken and take the originals. We ultimately file what would be characterized as similar to a perjury complaint warrant or indictment.

Lastly, the fact is, like any law enforcement agency, we have and do cultivate sources of information "on the street" if you will. These might be workers, they might be disgruntled employees, they might be insiders who give us information for whatever reason that motivates them. I'm sure you all can think of a variety of reasons, some legitimate and some illegitimate--that might motivate people to talk to us. There are some who come to us anonymously, which we have a great deal of concern about. We always somewhat discredit that anonymity but nonetheless do take a quick look and develop those sources and pursue it through our ordinary investigative techniques such as use of grand jury subpoenas or our own office subpoena, or by search warrant.

FRIEDMAN Dick, do you have anything to add?

RICHARD PLYMALE Well, I think they've pretty well covered what Kentucky does. We're not either as sophisticated as New York or as crude as Michigan, just using your terminology. We're somewhere in between, I would say, and our single-state agency, the Cabinet for Human Resources, has a division of audits which conducts the audits for setting of the prospective rates in nursing home reimbursement. As they go through the cost audits, usually at least once every 2-3 years--and in many cases, if you have a problem home, once every year--they refer probably 10-15 cases a year. That's a pretty good percentage in a smaller state like Kentucky.

As Ed has mentioned, one of the primary sources you have to understand in nursing home investigations is a disgruntled former employee, particularly in the larger homes. It's very difficult for an administrator, owner, or proprietor of any kind who handles a great deal of expenses--who is cheating--to hide it from the variety of employees who work and control the books and papers necessary to cover that. The moment that someone gets disgruntled, or leaves the employment, or the love affair breaks up, or whatever, that's a primary source of information and often the documents are well-prepared and it takes months to get into the case. But eventually if you look hard enough we've generally found that--and of course you have to check the reliability out through grand jury process and so forth, just to make sure that the documents say what the employee implies their meaning to be.

BLADEN Let me add, Art, recently in light of what's become unfortunately a large amount of breakups of marriages within this country, we've had a rash of former spouses turn in their spouse with respect to fraudulent cost reports or hiding of kickbacks with respect to nursing homes.

FRIEDMAN Is this during the divorce proceedings, Ed?

BLADEN Sometimes it's during the divorce proceedings, and other times it's just when it's about to happen. It's obviously motivated for a lot of reasons.

PUBLICITY AND INTERFERENCE WITH BUSINESS

FRIEDMAN Well, you know that it seems that now that we've settled on the home to investigate, we're all familiar with reading either the national newspapers or television, or we see so-and-so under investigation or some famous person is smeared that he did something wrong, or somebody makes an allegation against him. It seems that many times, especially a reputable businessman, doctor, or nursing home owner, even if they're under suspicion, there's a great deal of economic loss or loss of prestige in the community or loss of reputation. Many times those charges are unfounded.

When you guys investigate a nursing home, there's a lot of people in the nursing home who are going to find out about it. How do you protect it, or what concerns do you have? Let's make this a two-part question: one, to prevent adverse publicity during the investigation stage, and two, not to interfere by seizing books and records. A grand jury subpoena is looking; auditors are looking; investigators are talking to people. How do we make sure that the nursing home, who is in business to take care of old people, how do we make sure that they continue to do that? Ed's a good defense attorney. Ed, do you want to try? How about you?

BLADEN Well, to begin, in terms of prevention of adverse publicity, we are extremely careful to avoid that as much as possible, and I can assure anyone sitting in this room that we do not initiate any communication with the media with respect to that investigation. To the extent that the media learns of the investigation by whatever means they may have--perhaps an employee within the organization itself who might call them up or whatever--our standard policy is, "No comment." Unfortunately, I suppose, the media tries to make much of "No comment," but I don't know what else to say. It would not be truthful to say there is no investigation, and it would be inappropriate to state that there *is* an investigation, because then, again, they attempt to build upon that. So our comment is, "No comment."

Next, with respect to interference with the ongoing business activities of the organization that we are investigating, let me first deal with the search warrant situation. Obviously, the most severe interference is the seizure of records and their removal from the premises. That has a rather strong interference ratio or potential. We don't take the records and leave the person with none. That is not our policy; that is not how we operate. Quite to the contrary, when we come on scene with the search warrant, we come with a portable microfiche machine, or we may have determined at the outset that there may be a copying facility on the premises. We then make copies of the records we are seizing, leaving the copies with the organization and taking the originals.

In the grand jury context, under Michigan law we have a procedure which affords the subpoena recipient or witness the opportunity to provide to the attorney general directly, in lieu of appearance before the grand jury, the subpoenaed materials pursuant to an affidavit of compliance. The affidavit of compliance provides that the materials that may be provided pursuant to the grand jury subpoena may be copies, but the custodian or the possessor of the records certifies that those copies are indeed copies of the originals and may be used in lieu of originals under the General Rules of Evidence, such as sections 901 and others.

So, from that point of view, there is a minimization of interference, because you should recognize that in most grand jury contexts--this may be true in other states and in the federal system--the grand jury subpoena calls for originals. So it is left to the recipient or witness to make their own copies, and if they fail to do so then, and produce originals, they are out of luck for at least the period of time that the grand jury possesses their records and uses them. These records, of course, you should understand, are *your* records. They are not the grand jury's records once they're turned over to it. They *must* be returned to the possession of the witness at the conclusion of the investigation.

FRIEDMAN Greg, do you have anything to answer that, based on some of the cases that you've had?

NACLARIO Sure. I don't think any responsible prosecutor--at least the prosecutors that I've met with the National Association--would ever engage in any type of smear campaign. I think the prosecutors understand that it is at best unethical, and I know my attorney general and the deputy attorney general that I work for follow the policy that Ed has articulated. We neither confirm nor deny investigations. We don't try our cases in the press. Any investigation we engage in we want to keep confidential for our own reasons. So as far as the investigation per se being thrown onto page two or page three of your local newspaper, I don't think that's too much of a reality.

The reality I think does come in the fact where we're investigating a particular nursing home and we now want to start to interview vendors of that nursing home, or if it's a physician, on his patients to see if they received the goods and services he allegedly provided them. That gets to be a little more of a touchy issue because now we're going out to vendors and we're saying, "We'd like to discuss your relationship with the XYZ Nursing Home, and we'd like to see your bills. We'd like to see your invoices." We try to couch that type of investigation as strictly routine. We are the Medicaid Fraud Control Unit. It's part of our job. We do this to everybody. Now that may or may not be the case. We may be zeroing in on one particular vendor because of our targeting, our interviews, or our audit, but we try to keep that as low-keyed as possible. So the only time I think we'd really start making some waves and really causing some grief for vendors to a nursing home is if we have a pretty strong suggestion that this vendor is in fact in league with the nursing home owner, operator, or whatever, and we're about to consider him some potential target or use him as a witness in the grand jury.

The other thing I think is the matter of interference. That is a charge that is very easily made by the industry. The nursing home industry is a very heavily regulated industry. When other third-party insurers come in to audit books and records, I don't hear too muck flak. I know in our state Blue Cross comes in to do a review for the federal government. They come in as a matter of course without any problems. We knock on the door and right away we're disrupting the entire operation. Every other third party that comes in to do an audit is considered like Inspector Erskine of the FBI. We're considered the B. A. Baracas of the A-Team. You know, we haven't done anything yet. We just knocked on your door and right away we're the guys who are going to cause you the grief.

So, I think the attitude to a certain degree--perhaps justified or unjustified, depending upon that particular circumstance--is meant to keep us out. We also don't audit current records. Right now in New York we're auditing 1981, 1982, and 1983. So if somebody tells me, "I need my '81 records," I have to really look at him and say, "Please. Let's not make fools of each other." Generally, the records are available. Generally they are not being used; as a matter of fact they're in storage--you have to go down to the basement to dig them out for us.

We will do an audit on-site. Most homes want us on-site. Some homes go out and hire very expensive attorneys, and to justify their fees, the attorneys say, "Get them out of the nursing home." So they rent us an office. We've been in a very nice suite of offices. We've been in an 8-by-10-foot room, and right now we are in a trailer. We will audit those books and records any place we have to. So we try our best and we are sensitive, although some people really don't believe that. We are sensitive to the fact that the industry, the nursing home, has to provide a certain level of care to the patients. One of our objectives is to make sure that that level of care is in fact provided and provided well. So we will do everything possible to work with the administration to review those records. We have to review the records and we can work out the details. But we try to minimize as much as possible any interference with the facility.

FRIEDMAN Dick?

PLYMALE Well, I think I agree with Greg. That is, during the investigation it's totally inappropriate for a prosecutor to release or leak information to the press. We have a no-comment policy, but you have to understand that what's considered adverse publicity during the investigative stage--once we've made the determination that a major fraud has occurred, then what was adverse before now becomes deterrence value to a prosecutor's office. Therefore, we do issue press releases and make them public immediately upon indictment. They cover only the facts in the case, not the evidence.

I'm sure all of you have seen those TV coverages where they go out and photograph the administrator's home, and the indictment covers the fact that it was built out of nursing home funds by the general contractor who was building the wing on the home. You've heard those types of stories and it's happened in Kentucky. We don't really feel in that circumstance, after indictment, that the person who has committed the fraud necessarily deserves the type of privacy that the investigative stage entails. The reason is that you filed the public charges in court anyway, and of course we don't aid the press. We don't give them his address and tell him all the facts. The press picks up the indictment and puts the story together basically from the indictment.

BLADEN Let me add one other thing. There is a troublesome area that is one which we feel is quite sensitive; that is, frequently the fraud unit will execute a subpoena upon a financial institution with whom the entity is doing business. That does raise some sensitive issues.

Now, because we're not subject to the federal Financial Right of Privacy Act, the institution's obligation to communicate to the target the fact that the subpoena has been served and all the other implications of the federal Financial Right of Privacy Act do not apply at the state level. Nonetheless, frequently we are contacted by the counsel to the financial institution who wants to know what is going on, what investigation is under way? We learn at that point because they tell us, there is a major loan being worked up. They ask, are we now looking at an individual or an organization that is a substantial credit risk, or can arguably be put out of business, or the resulting liability there would be so substantial that it would undermine the validity of the loan.

Essentially we have to say that this is a routine, regular practice of ours to investigate these institutions and as such we cannot comment any further. We would expect that they would--and we do add this--expect that the financial institution would make their determination in their best judgment in the ordinary course of business and not necessarily determine the worth or non-worth of this particular loan based upon the mere fact that we have executed a subpoena on the institution.

FRIEDMAN Well, I guess it's a pretty touchy situation. If I'm a major vendor for a nursing home, and I extend a lot of credit--maybe $200,000 or $300,000-- they owe me, and I know that they always get a Medicaid billing and it takes them a certain cycle to have cash--to find out that the XYZ Nursing Home has been the subject of a grand jury subpoena. I get to worrying about my money! Next month they may go out of business or they may go into, heaven forbid, chapter 11. I'll get 2 cents on the dollar in 50 years. I think it's a great concern even though you say, Ed, "Well, you know it's a routine investigation but we can't comment any further." That's a tough pill to swallow for somebody who's extending $200,000 or $300,000 in credit.

NACLARIO You have to remember, Arthur, the Medicaid fraud units have been in business for awhile, and we have issued investigations and issued subpoenas conducting investigations over the course of the years where we have in fact, after the investigation has been concluded, not come out with an indictment for any number of reasons. So maybe going back to New York in 1970 or 1975 when we first started, if you wished to subpoena then, in the height of that nursing home scandal, yes, I think you could turn off a lot of vendors and have vendors worried about their stake at the facility. But we've been in business 10 years now and it is routine. It's really the exception to the rule that a nursing home only does get indicted. So I think when you tell a vendor or you tell a lending institution--which is a very good example that Ed brought up--that it is routine, I think that a) it's the truth, and b) they realize that, yes, maybe if you conduct ten investigations, if you come out with two indictments you're doing very well. And I think it's not as much of an impact now as it used to be.

BLADEN It's customary for them to receive a variety of subpoenas, or summons, for financial material. For example, the Internal Revenue Service serves that institution on a regular daily basis, I'm sure, half a dozen or more such subpoenas. Every financial institution of any size that I've ever dealt with, has an officer or a person designated specifically for answering subpoenas or requests from the government.

When talking to the institution's counsel, I always ask--and I didn't--"Why do you want to know? Why does this one subpoena particularly pique your interest? Since you are a regular recipient of these kinds of things anyway, why this particular one? Is there something about it that makes you nervous?" Frequently we discover with that kind of question that the financial institution itself has done some investigating into the background of the applicants, and we discover some very interesting information that *we* might find useful because *they* were a bit nervous, about the persons who had made the application for the loan.

FRIEDMAN I'm intrigued by the fact that you would consent to do the audit off-site away from the nursing home. It would seem to me if I was examining books and records and I was the prosecutor, I would want to be at the nursing home so I could--I don't use the word "interrogate" because that's a little strong--but if I wanted to ask some questions about the books and records, I could have the bookkeeper there or the person who made the entries right there, and I could say, "Hey, Fred, you want to come over here and tell me what all these entries mean?" When you're off-site you're removed from the day-to-day contact, and you may have to work through the attorney for the home who will have to ask the questions for you. Are there any dangers or any traps or problems from working off-site in an area that you guys don't control?

NACLARIO Well, first of all, I would rather do an audit at a nursing home for the very reason that you just stated. After awhile my auditors get to know the chief bookkeeper, and they start talking about "What's this entry?" and "Can you explain that to me?" We're there about 6 or 8 weeks. So you start building up a rapport with certain people at the nursing home. We tell our auditors to keep their ears open and their mouths shut, to keep their eyes open, see what's going on, hear what's going on. So I would definitely prefer to keep auditors on-site. If I ever get out into private practice and defend any nursing homes, the first thing I will do is tell the prosecutor, "You can do the audit off-site." If I was on the other side, I would not want three of the special prosecutor auditors and an investigator hanging out at my nursing home.

FRIEDMAN Are you giving away secrets here?

NACLARIO No.

FRIEDMAN Oh.

NACLARIO Since you let the cat out of the bag, I might as well follow up on it. Now the danger from my point of view is doing an off-site audit. We had a very interesting case. I think Artie is making reference to this, and I'll try to give you in a nutshell. We were going to do a hospital audit and we agreed to do it off-site. And to a certain degree we have to really agree to do it off-site. If I subpoena the books, I can ask you to bring them into the grand jury. You can make a motion to quash--tell the judge, "Judge, I'll have the books available at X location." I think the judge will put a little pressure on me to say, "Listen. Let's not make a big deal over that. He's willing to give you the books someplace else." So I'm in a bit of a tenuous situation.

  In one case, a hospital gave us a very nice room. The attorney for the facility came by and showed us the room and indicated that, if we wanted to use the telephone, this was the telephone we could use. This was an old church that the facility had taken over and had a number of different rooms. We were sort of in the side room to the altar area, if you will, and we were confined to this room. He indicated that there was no overhead lighting, but the home would provide certain lamps for us to put on these long conference tables.

We were going to start the audit on a Monday. That Friday the telephone rings in my office. It's an administrator of another hospital, and he says to me, "Carl's going to bug you guys." I said, "What?" He said, "Carl is going to bug you. You got an audit going down Monday. It's off-site. He's going to bug you." And that's all he told me; he hung up on me. Well, needless to say, we could have gone down and served a forthwith subpoena on the guy to get the information that way, but what we decided to do was we string it along. We went there Monday; we went there Tuesday; we went there Wednesday, being big, fat, dumb, and happy.

Wednesday we also bring in our tech guy, and this guy was a former New York City policeman for 25 years. Never found a bug--never. He said, "That's in movies. It's crazy. I don't want to come." He came, and he's there sweeping the place. Lo and behold, his little handheld meter--whatever they call it-- touches one of these lamps and that needle goes all the way over. He then starts taking apart the lamp and, lo and behold, his eyes look like my daughter's eyes on Christmas. Because inside that lamp was a battery pack, and a transmitter. Well, we put the lamp back together again. My boss decided to call in the FBI, and the FBI disabled one of the mikes and they sat in the place for another 2 days. They ultimately executed a search warrant. The two lamps both had mikes in them. There was a tape recorder on the other side of the altar that was hearing everything we had to say, and my friend the good defense attorney who said, "Anytime, Greg, you want to use this telephone, feel free," may or may not have known that downstairs at the junction box was another tape recorder. So I'm very reluctant to do off-site audits now, but we just swept that trailer about a week ago and we'll do it another couple of times.

Typical Findings

FRIEDMAN Okay. Moving right along. Well, now that we've got our people in there, and we're doing an investigation and we're auditing and we're interviewing vendors, and we're doing all kinds of things, what are the typical kinds of crimes that you would find in a nursing home? Richard?

PLYMALE Well, in Kentucky, and I can't speak for nationally, but in Kentucky the most typical types of crimes in nursing homes are merely expenditures in the cost report which are totally unrelated to the patient care. That's the general standard. What types of expenses? Personal loans. Construction of personal residences, or driveways, or fencing, or heating and cooling equipment if you have a contract going at the home. Kickbacks in terms of the vendors, and particulàrly recently we've had a rash of false employment records, ghost employees basically, family on the payroll--you know, two daughters who are in college during that period of time are being paid full-time and those wages somehow are paid and put in the cost report. The daughters never received the wages, or the wife's on the payroll and she's a schoolteacher. She's working the 8-to-5 shift.

We're having a little problem with ancillary costs right now, and our state is about to issue a warning letter to the nursing home industry because our definition of ancillary cost is a little more restrictive than Medicare's. It involves very strict definitions of what types of supplies and so forth are allowed. We're finding anything from whiskey--anything that can conceivably be prescribed by a doctor or recommended by a doctor even though it's totally unrelated to medical need--is put into ancillary cost, and we're finding substantial inflation of costs in Kentucky.

NACLARIO In New York, the generation of the dollar is the key. Usually we have a progression of kickbacks that usually starts with the typical 10% of your business. The vendor's got to give the home back 10% of the business he transacts, and that's how it starts. Of course, the vendor doesn't take the 10% out of his profit; he just tacks that on to the cost of goods sold, because now he's got a lock on the account. He doesn't care what he charges because he's giving a kickback.

Then it seems that the owners get a bit more greedy and they say, "Well, listen, we're not making enough on the straight kickback. Why don't you inflate a couple of invoices? So, in other words, deliver $5,000 worth of goods but submit a bill for $8,000. We'll pay you the $8,000. You then turn that $8,000 check into cash and you give me back, say, $2,500, you can keep the $500 for your tax liability." So that goes on for awhile.

Then greed gets into it again, and we now get into the area of completely fictitious invoices, such as putting in a new cesspool system when none was done, repaving the same parking lot four times in 3 years. We had one nursing home that was--at least if you go by the books--each nursing home patient received three brand new washcloths every day for 2 years--cleanest patients you'd ever want to see. So those are the ways, in New York at any rate, the schemes are done.

We also had one company--it was a meat company. Meat company A would send an invoice on the first of the month for 10 items. He then printed invoices up for Meat company B, and on the fifth of every month he'd submit another bill on B's invoices for the same items he submitted on the first, only he reversed the order. That went on for about 2 1/2 years. All those invoices on the fifth were phony. So there are ways to generate the income.

We are now seeing a few other new wrinkles where, to get the money back to the owner, a lot of people have thought of a Don King promotion syndrome before Don King. We have Atlantic City not too far away from our office, and you find out from nursing home owners--also from vendors and competitors--that Mr. Johnson takes administrator down to Atlantic City and the administrator doesn't have to worry about buying any chips because the vendor supplies him with the chips. It's a nice way of giving a kickback--buying a couple of thousand dollars worth of chips. Who's going to trace it?

Another method: we have vendors going into partnerships with nursing home administrators in businesses. We have a video store that is now owned by a vendor who put up the majority of the cash for the video store. The nursing home administrator shares equally in the profits of the video store. If you look at the contract between this vendor and the home that the administrator works in, he's a linen vendor and the linen costs at this particular home are higher than any of the other 51 homes we have on the island. So it gives you food for thought.

FRIEDMAN Dick wanted to make one comment.

PLYMALE Let me say that these are typical schemes that I'm sure many of you have heard of in the industry. You know what types of costs have more softness or hardness in terms of audits, whether it's the IRS or the single-state agency. We're not telling you a great deal of new material here, but in the more sophisticated costs, you've got to understand that the fraud units have reached some level of sophistication in their investigation.

What we find is the books and documents normally conform with the audit upon initial review. It takes secondary and tertiary subpoenas, in a very complex and lengthy process, to get to personal bank accounts--not only the business bank accounts of the vendors but the personal bank accounts of the vendors, and then maybe a fourth level of subpoenas after that. Then if you take the personal accounts and filter them back and crossmatch them, they tell a much different story that the documents did.

It's only from complex crossmatching financial information that the more sophisticated frauds are found. Unless you have just boatloads of cash around to hide this type of transaction, there's no way that you're not going to leave a paper trail. You still run the risk of the fact that three or four of your vendors know it, and even if it is in cash, they can still blackmail you. I just wanted to add that.

BLADEN Well, as far as Michigan is concerned, we of course have the run-of-the-mill criminal behavior in the institutional setting like everyone else: kickbacks, continuously lying on a cost report, hoping that someday somebody is going to give up and allow them to have the new swimming pool in the backyard. Even though we are on a prospective payment system and although there may be no actual loss that might otherwise occur, our attitude is that's simply perjury; it's lying and we're going to prosecute those kinds of things.

The more sophisticated types of crimes that occur are things like unrelated party schemes. We have seen where, as I'm sure you know, the regulations provide that if the parties are related--that is, the provider and the supplier or vendor of the goods and services--then it's the actual cost of the vendor or supplier that is to be passed on, not the cost of the institution or the provider. The fact is, we've had extremely complicated multistate related party schemes.

Indeed, not long ago, we recently concluded an extensive investigation and prosecution which resulted in convictions where the Medicaid fraud units from three states cooperated together and conducted simultaneous investigations where each of our people were sworn in as agents of each of the other jurisdictions for the purposes of working together in the course of that investigation.

They're becoming a little bit more sophisticated, but yet there are some providers, particularly in the nursing home area, who simply will not give up. They insist that their country club dues, their girlfriends' expenses at some resort someplace, must get buried in the administrative and general expenses under some heading. They insist on doing that year after year. We said, "Enough is enough." It's a four-year felony to lie or make a false statement and we prosecute those on that basis.

FRIEDMAN This whole thing about prosecuting nursing home owners, is a fairly recent occurrence; within the last 10 years. Medicaid programs started, let's say, in 1966, 1967. A lot of nursing homes established procedures and accounting practices, if we could call it that, where certain kinds of costs were put in the cost report, and if they ever were questioned by the Medicaid agency or the fiscal intermediary, everybody sat down like gentlefolk and they worked it out and they made a settlement. There wasn't any worry about grand juries or indictment. It was treated as an administrative remedy. Things were cleaner then.

BLADEN And a lot cozier.

FRIEDMAN There's no doubt about it. But it seems that from the viewpoint of the nursing home owner--that all of a sudden they're changing the rules on him. What used to be a civil case or administrative case they're now throwing me in jail for. Do we do that? Do we throw people in jail for civil mistakes, or where the issue is question of judgment, or a gray area?

BLADEN Let me begin by saying that really what you're asking, Art, is, how do we distinguish between a civil case and a criminal case? What is characterized by the nursing home administrator owner to be a simple dispute about policy and whether or not a cost is genuinely allowable and related to patient care becomes, all of a sudden, criminal. Well, there's a very simple acid test that we employ. That is, when you put into a cost report for patient care an item that turns out to be a new motorboat engine for your racing machine out on the Great Lakes, that's called lying, cheating, and stealing. No amount of argument, dispute, or good faith, in my view, comes into play to tell me that you took out an 84-year-old lady patient and her husband out on the Great Lakes, and entered her into the Muskegon-to-Mackinaw boat race. Now, if you can tell me how that is a good faith dispute, I'd sure like to hear it. Consequently, we view that as criminal, not civil.

On the other hand, if indeed a full, complete, and good faith disclosure is made, and there is a genuine dispute as to whether or not the new beautification program in the back of the nursing home along with the main road that goes closer to the owner's home is indeed related to patient care, and it's fully disclosed as such, we may have a different story with regard to whether or not that kind of behavior is indeed criminal. But if it's hidden away, secreted away, so that because of the prospective payment systems someone isn't going to get to it until a year or two later--and hope like heaven's name you can get away with it--then we have different feelings.

NACLARIO No prosecutor's going to take a case that shows some expenses were wrongfully included as questionably related to medical care and take them to a grand jury and prosecute you for a felony, in a case where there is any legitimate actuarial accounting theory that would support that being related to patient care. Let's face it, we're looking for false invoices. We're looking for ghost employees. We're looking for completely fabricated expenses--diving equipment or vacations on the Master Charge of the home--or something of that nature. It's really silly for a controller or an accountant to sit down and say, "We need an invoice to cover this expense," and create a false record. That's just a dead case. You have little sympathy in that case no matter what the loss is. The attorney says, "Well, there's no loss to Medicaid. We have a 400-bed home here. This is a $2,500,000 home. What are you talking about? Our budget is so large, that is miniscule."

Well, he should have thought about that before he received the $10,000 and created the false invoice, or got the $500-a-month kickback, or whatever. As Ed says, we have little sympathy for that situation. We have lots of sympathy for the home that has professional accountants and auditors who come in and disclose and cooperate, who let us see the information where the records are rather questionable in terms of putting the categories of cost in the report. There's no question they're related to the business of the home to some degree. That's a tough criminal case. We don't like to lose. We don't like to look bad in the press. Just like you don't like the adverse publicity, most prosecutors are young, aspiring, and have some political goals in mind. You've got to keep in mind the type of mind you're dealing with when you deal with deputy attorney generals, or local or district attorneys, or U.S. attorneys. These guys are real proud of their name. They want to win and they're going to construct the type of case to win.

We're going to make one other comment. Would you lie to the Internal Revenue Service on your tax return the same way you would lie on your cost report to the Medicaid state agency? If you would, I guess you got a problem. But if you're more frightened of IRS than you are of us, maybe we're hoping at least to communicate the notion that we're at least as aggressive.

PLEA BARGAINING

FRIEDMAN Let's move on. Suppose we have made the decision to charge somebody. A fellow has been indicted for a few felonies, possibly substantial money. The defense lawyer comes in representing his client and says, "Alright, nobody wants to have a trial here. It's 6 weeks; it's a loss leader for me. I don't want my defendant to get all this publicity every day. It'll be in the newspaper. Let's settle this out; we'll take a reasonable plea." What are some of the considerations that you would take into mind in considering one, whether to give a plea, and two, what is a plea that you would feel comfortable with? Greg, how about you?

NACLARIO Well, I think if you're talking about a grand larceny where substantial monies--if you're talking about between $50,000 and $100,000--in my view, that individual has to take a felony, he has to pay back the amount that is due the state, plus interest. The only thing that I'm going to be dealing with you on is my recommendation of sentence. You can cry all you want that the guy's got a license, that he's a doctor, that he's God only knows what else, but that's just really too bad. The cases that we go after, the cases that we do indict, and the cases we do make are, in our judgment, cases we could win at trial. The basic rule in our office is, if we can't be 90% sure that we can convict this man after trial, we don't indict him. So we usually go with very strong cases. We will give defense attorneys as much discovery as the federal government does if not more. We will basically stand pat on our case.

If you want to talk about what my recommendation is going to be at the time of sentence, we all have to realize the fact that you probably represent a gentleman who's the pillar of the community, who will have, as I have seen, a defendant presentence memo. The first letter in that report by the defense attorney, of course, is a letter from the local bishop extolling the virtues of this man. I really feel guilty prosecuting some people after I read how good they are, although this one particular gentleman stole in excess of $1,250,000 but the bishop found it in his heart to write a very kind letter for him. He should write a letter for me someday like that.

What we should do is say, "What can you do for me? What can your client do for me on sentence?" Now granted, as I said, your man in all likelihood stands a very good shot of getting probation. He's never been in trouble before-- a pillar of the community. I can get up and yell and scream that I feel this man should get some incarceration. Now it all depends on how much I yell and how loud I scream. Some judges may be inclined to give him 30 days in jail plus probation, or 60 days in jail followed by probation. I was a legal aid attorney before I became a prosecutor, and I was at the local lockup on more occasions than I would like to tell you. Even one day in jail is quite an experience for somebody who's the pillar of the community in New York.

BLADEN   In Michigan it's not so bad.

NACLARIO   So commit a crime in Michigan.   But I would tell your client, "What could you do for me?   What information can you give me to show that you're contrite, that you're willing to clean up this industry?   What can you do for me to make cases?''   I'm not just interested in intelligence.   Check out meat vendors or look at dietary--I'm not interested in that.   If you want me to take no position on sentence, your client is going to have to make a case for me.   If that means making a telephone call where we record the telephone call, or wearing a body recorder and having a conversation with somebody--that's what it takes to get out from under.

FRIEDMAN   Is that a free skate?

NACLARIO   No.   Not guaranteed.   Free skate means straight dismissal, right? One out of 117 got a free walk because of the fact that he cooperated wearing a body recorder, and the only reason he did is he led us down the path to a major political figure.   For that we gave him a dismissal.   That's the name of the game. But, lo and behold, you want a plea?   You want a recommendation of no jail, you're going to have to do something for me.

FRIEDMAN   Ed, what do you think?

BLADEN   Somewhat of the same way.   In terms of plea bargaining, first of all we look at the licensure implications.   In Michigan, under our occupational care, defrauding a third-party payor is loss of licensure under Michigan law--your occupational license, nursing home administrator's license, physician's license, whatever the case may be.   That's the first problem, so a lot of people might want to just simply try the cases in Michigan because they're more worried about loss of license.

You asked why don't we look at the nature of the offense, the size of the theft, and restitutionary ability of the person to determine a plea bargain?   We make no promises with respect to federal liabilities such as civil money penalty liability.   We say you take your chances with the federal authorities.   If you don't like that, we'll try the case because my lawyers haven't had enough time in court anyway, and they're getting stale and too many defendants are asking to plead out.

Now there is one category of case where there is no plea bargain whatsoever: that is patient abuse.   If you beat up an old lady in the home, you can rest assured we will prosecute that case to the fullest.   On the other hand, if it's a plea as charged in those cases then, it's a guilty plea, not a nolo contendere plea--it's a guilty plea as charged.   That's the only plea bargain we'll enter into, in patient abuse cases.

NACLARIO That's tough, Ed.

FRIEDMAN What do we say about Kentucky?

PLYMALE Michigan is tougher than Kentucky, I'm afraid.

NACLARIO But they have better jails.

PLYMALE Let me ask you this, Ed. Is that revocation of license even for a misdemeanor?

BLADEN Yes. Even a misdemeanor.

PLYMALE That is quite, I think, aberrational to most states. Certainly it would put some teeth.

BLADEN It's revocation or suspension so you can get a 2-year suspension, that kind of thing. But it's loss of license for a period of time; you can lose your livelihood.

PLYMALE I see. Well, my training was with the Department of Justice before I came to this job and I generally use those guidelines. I look at the gravity of the crime. I look at the history of this individual. If the home head cost report adjustments were grossly aberrant over a period of 5 years and they refuse to accept the accounting recommendations of the state--I have little sympathy for that home. Do they cooperate during the audit? Sure, it has some human impact, let's face it. There's a lot of human element in these investigations. The interaction of the administrator with the single-state agency, the controller, the accountant, the attorney--it does not hurt to be nice to prosecute--or to the single-state agencies--to know the movers and shakers in those state bureaucracies and to deal with them on a professional and hopefully gentlemanly basis.

Now, it's not going to impact a major felony case. No prosecutor with assault is going to sell out his theory of criminal justice, just because a friend is on the other side. But it's got to have subtle impact. It's got to have some subtle impact, and certainly it might affect the nature of the sentencing recommendation even in New York, for sure. Certainly in Kentucky it might even affect the nature of the level of felony or whatever. Is there a legitimate argument that can be made in defense--and every prosecutor looks, "Am I going to win this case? Could I lose this case, and if I lose it, is there a legitimate defense that can be brought before this jury? If there is, maybe I should consider a plea arrangement where I don't spend $100,000 or $10,000--depending on the length of the trial-- of the state and court's money to try a case that I have a 50-50 shot at."

BLADEN But would you have brought that case in the first place, Dick? If you were doing a very careful analysis and evaluation of the evidence, and you see what purports to be a fairly decent defense, would you have even charged it?

PLYMALE Let me tell you, I'm human, Ed. I have, and I think every prosecutor who's been in the business very long has taken a case based upon a very thorough investigation but not unturned one or two leaves somewhere. Out of the woodwork comes a witness, comes documentary evidence that was never discovered and that is somewhat surprising. Now it doesn't give a total defense in your view, but it seriously jeopardizes the morality and ethics of your case. In other words, it says, "Well, he's real bad here in this part of the indictment but, gee, he has an excuse for about half of these counts."

Well, we had a famous case like that where we thought they were paying for the girlfriend. It turned out to be the daughter. The sex appeal is lost in front of a jury!

You really do and the rollover--of course, you'd always like to have someone come along and give you 1,000 cases as a prosecutor, and if you're going to cooperate, a little over. That's fine.

PATIENT ABUSE

FRIEDMAN We have about 5 minutes left in our official time but we started a little late and I want to leave about 5 minutes of time for questions. I want to hit a very important point that we just skirted around. Nursing home fiscal fraud is important? No question about it. We have to protect the Medicaid funds. We hear about the budget of the U.S. and Medicare, but in the last analysis, we're talking about people; we're talking about patients who are the most vulnerable sector of our society. What does the fraud unit do to protect those people? How about Ed?

BLADEN We're looking at the issue of patient abuse in a real sense. We have a very sophisticated and compulsory reporting system within our state with regard to any harm or related issue associated with what is broadly described as patient abuse. We are on the scene as promptly as possible with an investigative team to determine the actual nature of the activities so that we can determine whether there's a potential for criminal prosecution.

Generally, we have a 24-hour reporting system to our Department of Public Health. We are notified and then should be in there no later than about 48 hours after the occurrence of the event. We do *not*, as a customary practice, rummage or walk through homes to determine whether or not the facilities are clean, whether there's an overwhelming urine stench, or any of those issues. That is not our role. Our role is as a criminal investigative and prosecutive agency. The role of our Department of Public Health performs those inspections. To the extent there is one that they find that is outrageous in terms of those kinds of criteria, then they might refer to us to close the place down.

FRIEDMAN Greg, how about New York?

NACLARIO We basically have a very good reporting system in New York. We have a reporting statute which makes it professional misconduct for any administrative health care professional not to report instances of suspected patient abuse to the Health Department. The Health Department gets those complaints. They send out their own investigator. Simultaneously, we get the complaint and we evaluate it. If it appears that there is a violation of the New York State penal law, which is the only law we can operate under in a patient abuse situation, we will make a decision to send one of our investigators to the home and conduct our own investigation. Based upon that investigation, we'll either send the matter back to the state Health Department or bring the matter to a grand jury. So I think it's something we really are very sensitive to.

PLYMALE In 30 seconds--Kentucky also has a reporting system and does an initial investigation in the single-state agency, the Cabinet for Human Resources. But let me say the worst nursing home cases in Kentucky have come from the coroner's office after the fact. They weren't even discovered or there was no complaint filed before death. Obviously, it would be too imminent to have a report filed, but the worst cases are rarely discovered until it's an outrageously serious situation of amputation or some serious injury in terms of a restraint being improperly administered to a patient: cutting off circulation, turning him into a vegetable, or killing them, or the gross bedsore cases. Yet generally the outrageous cases come from the coroner. The local DAF of the coroner refers it to him, or to the family or friend of the patient.

FRIEDMAN We certainly covered a lot of ground this morning. Do you have any questions?

> *What is the percentage of nursing home facilities under investigation in relation to overall caseload?*

> BLADEN The percentage of a case mix is this: Institutional providers in the state of Michigan account for $.78 on the Medicaid dollar. It is the reverse in terms of case mix in investigations. About one-fourth of the cases that we have in the office, at the most, are institutional, and maybe about half or a third again are nursing homes. I should tell you that we set goals in our office and this quarter goal is five nursing homes

for indictment. So hopefully we'll have five by the end of the quarter.

I'd say 30% of our case mix is nursing homes--the other part being individual providers and hospitals.

PLYMALE I'd say in Kentucky, about 20% maximum of our case load.

FRIEDMAN I think you have to remember there are many more ambulatory providers allowed as transportation, doctors, than there are nursing homes. Nursing home investigations are so much more time consuming, also.

Why are these offices called "Fraud" units? Do you think that people would not be so put off, or a stigma would not attach if the name of the office were different?

BLADEN I think it's a rose by any other name. No, I think whatever you call it, people are going to understand what the purpose of the office is. We could call ourselves the White Cross, and pretty soon after 6 months of us working out there they realize it's just a catchy name for our office.

But ironically the people like Blue Cross and Blue Shield--at least in Michigan, and this may be true in some other Blue Cross plans--have a fraud unit who does indeed conduct these kinds of audits or investigations, though I have to admit--it's relatively new for them. But nonetheless, they're there.

PLYMALE In fact in some of my cases in Kentucky, the losses to Aetna, Blue Cross, and other private insurers far exceed the loss to Medicare or Medicaid.

In Kentucky, you earlier had mentioned that most prosecutors have something basically--got a lot of veto, a lot of positive political innovations. What about turning the tables around in prosecutorial misconduct? I haven't heard that much about that, where occasionally a little extra evidence is to be made particularly, and some ambitious young prosecutor decides he's going to fabricate some evidence. How is that dealt with in the offices? I mean, is that just ripped up?

PLYMALE If we find a prosecutor in our office, and I had one many years ago, who has fabricated evidence or is engaged in a conflict of interest, he is fired.

BLADEN   I'm sure in Michigan, too, he'd be indicted.

PLYMALE   I'm saying, to begin with he is fired and brought to the attention--indeed, we have prosecuted our own.
   Let me say in this regard that, even in Kentucky, I have the same philosophy.   I had an employee, one of my eight investigators, who filed a false travel voucher.   That wasn't much money or whatever.   But she was immediately reprimanded and transferred to another unit, never to testify in a criminal investigation again, probably.

FRIEDMAN   Was she prosecuted?

PLYMALE   Oh, no.   She was not prosecuted because there was no loss.   She paid the money back.   She merely just lied on her--well, what I'm saying is this, it was only thirty or forty bucks; it was only one night.

FRIEDMAN   What's the difference?

PLYMALE   You're right.   The standard is different in some instances.   You have to be realistic about this.   We're not tolerating any major misconduct.

What do you do to make a person . . . when you come up and write an investigation? Do you put ads in the paper that the nursing home is clean?

NACLARIO   I think we answered it.   The first question we asked was, how do we target so that it does not become a witch-hunt?   I think a question that possibly could have been asked is, after you guys investigate somebody, do you give them a letter saying we investigated you and you didn't find anything?   Or, as he says, put an ad in the *New York Times*?

BLADEN   Right!   They deserve it.

NACLARIO   We just go away and that's sort of a sign in the industry that everything is fine.

PART 5

PROVIDERS:
ICFs, CORFs, and Home Care

Chapter 19

Intermediate Care Facilities for the Mentally Retarded

Speaker: Samuel D. Turner

There have been during the past year or two many widely publicized instances of health and safety problems in intermediate care facilities for the mentally retarded, as well as an unusual amount of congressional interest in the subject. The congressional hearings held by Senator Lowell Weicker were part of a continuing inquiry into conditions at many of the large public institutions. The list that Senator Weicker submitted to the department included facilities whose names have cropped up many times in the past, such as the Rosewood facility and the Willowbrook facility. A related issue was the degree to which the civil rights division of the Department of Justice was fulfilling its responsibility under the law to ensure the rights of people residing in these facilities.

During the past year or two, there has also been a winding down of major decade-long law suits which have helped to change the landscape with respect to these facilities--not only in the states where the facilities are located but across the board. The Willowbrook litigation in New York seems to have come to a close; the attorneys have been paid off, which is usually a sign that the activity will cease or at least substantially slow down. The *Pennhurst* case in Pennsylvania is about to be settled and closed out; all that remains is for the judge to sign the settlement agreement. A week or two ago, the Justice Department entered into a Consent Decree with the state of Maryland concerning the Rosewood facility.

The people who live at these facilities are a very vulnerable, sympathetic population--a group that summons forth all sorts of images of despair and chaos and make us want to respond to their needs. They're also involved, through surrogates or representatives, in a struggle to define their rights that in a lot of ways is not unlike other such struggles that we've seen in the past.

Many people are drawn to these issues because of the tremendous amount of money involved. About 13 percent of all Medicaid funds go to take care of people in ICFs/MR, despite the fact that they constitute less than 1 percent of the total Medicaid eligible population. This also is an interesting area for lawyers because the law is in flux, and there is a continuing effort to define specifically the rights of people in ICFs/MR and the rights of the mentally retarded or mentally impaired in general. This area also, inherently, involves conflicts between state and federal governments.

ISSUES INVOLVED IN PATIENTS' RIGHTS

The subject generally can be viewed in terms of four major legal or policy issues: deregulation, deinstitutionalization, individual rights and quality of care, and financing.

DEREGULATION

Deregulation is not usually discussed in relation to care for the mentally retarded, but it has become almost a catchword of the Reagan administration, and it is the absence of deregulation in this area that is significant more than its presence.

Considering the interplay between the 4 issues mentioned, it would seem that deregulation would go hand in hand with deinstitutionalization. And one might expect to find the Administration supporting the concept of deinstitutionalization because there has been a general trend toward the loosening of the kind of rigid guidelines that must accompany the large public institutions. There also has been a trend toward delivery of services in smaller packages. But there are problems in this area that have undermined any sort of effort toward deregulation. There has, in fact, been a tendency to tighten up on regulations rather than to deregulate, a trend that is clearly out of character with current practices in other segments of the Department of Health and Human Services.

Some of the difficulties that arise in terms of deregulating in this context involve establishing methods of policing the quality of care for people in such a vulnerable position, and reassuring the federal and state authorities that their dollars are being well spent. One of the selling points of deinstitutionalization at the outset was the notion that it should cost less to provide care in small community settings. But some studies and data indicate just the opposite--it may cost quite a bit more to provide the sort of care that is necessary in a community setting. Whereas in a hospital setting or many other settings where the administration has deregulated in the hope that market forces will control, in the community setting there simply aren't any market forces at work to ensure that the quality of care is maintained.

DEINSTITUTIONALIZATION

The second issue is deinstitutionalization, an issue which is now beginning to fall into disfavor, at least in its more extreme manifestations. There are a number of reasons for this, one of which is the number of homeless individuals in this country. Most of these are not people who have been released from ICFs/MR, but there is nevertheless a growing concern that if you release people from the large public institutions they might not be able to care for themselves and could contribute to the swelling numbers of homeless.

There are some indications that deinstitutionalization may be more costly, not just per capita but also because some people who would otherwise be living at home with their parents or in some other family setting, may wind up in a community facility even though their parents or family would not be willing to send them to a large public institution. Some studies have also indicated doubts about the clinical benefits of deinstitutionalization, even where it's otherwise appropriate, and finally, once you begin putting people out into the community, each additional person after that becomes more difficult, because there are limited spots in the community. And each person left in the institution is in most cases more severely impaired than those who have been released. It becomes increasingly difficult with each new deinstitutionalized person to ensure that the community setting that you find for the person, if one can indeed be found, is one which will be appropriate.

INDIVIDUAL RIGHTS AND QUALITY OF CARE

The other side of the deinstitutionalization question is a question of individual rights and quality of care. If deinstitutionalization of all or most of the people in these facilities is not carried out then there must be a considerable push to ensure that the quality of care in these institutions will improve or at least be maintained. In that direction, the federal government and public interest groups are attempting to continue to improve the quality of care in large public institutions.

This improvement obviously involves higher levels of financing and is thus obviously somewhat inconsistent with the underlying notion of deinstitutionalization.

FINANCING

The President has proposed a cap on Medicaid contributions to the states, and it seems that the process of tightening up on the amount of federal dollars that will be available to the states in all sectors of the Medicaid program will continue, with an ensuing struggle to ensure that the people in the ICFs/MR get their proper percentage of that money.

At the time that federal funding for ICFs/MR was initiated, many of these formerly state-run institutions were not the sorts of places where the federal government customarily channeled its money. They have been characterized frequently as warehouses for the mentally retarded; they had open wards and generally terrible conditions.

POOR CONDITIONS

One example is the Partlow Facility in Alabama which was in 1980 the subject of the *Wyatt v. Stickney* litigation. As described in documentation related to the 1980 legislation, giving the Justice Department standing to intervene in law suits respecting these facilities, one patient was regularly confined in a straight jacket for nine years, as a result of which she lost the use of both arms. The evidence at trial revealed that four patients died as a result of inadequate supervision, when one patient pushed the wheel chair in which a fellow patient was confined into a shower of scalding water. Another died after ingesting an overdose of drugs which had been left unattended and unsecured.

At the Willowbrook facility in New York, in the absence of adequate supervision, children suffered broken teeth, loss of an eye, and the loss of part of an ear bitten off by another resident. In an eight-month period, the five thousand resident facility reported over thirteen hundred incidents of injury, patient assault, or patient fights. Unsanitary conditions led to one hundred percent of the residents contracting hepatitis within six months of their admission.

These things perhaps only came to the attention of Congress at the time of the passage of the 1980 legislation, but the people at HHS and advocates for the mentally retarded involved in drafting the laws were aware of these problems and sought through the 1974 regulations to take substantial steps toward correcting them.

DIFFICULTIES WITH CURRENT LEGISLATION

A problem that has arisen regarding these regulations has been in their inflexibility. The regulations themselves seem very general, but people from the states complain that in the hands of a federal surveyor, they can become very inflexible and rigid. It is also true that the needs of the residents, the facilities, and the states have changed since the laws were first drafted in 1974. Another problem area in the current regulations is the amount of paperwork required. The association of supervisors of these facilities has suggested that about 20% of their staff time is spent on filling out paperwork that is required by the federal regulations. Another problem for HHS has been that the concept of active treatment, which is very important in the statute, has not been clearly defined in the regulations.

ISSUES UNDER CONSIDERATION FOR FUTURE LEGISLATION

SAFETY

HCFA has indicated that there needs to be better, more clear protection in two general areas of safety for the residents of the facilities. One is the provision of care in case of emergencies and the other is abuse by fellow patients or interlopers in the institutions.

OPEN WARDS

Another area of concern despite the general requirements in the regulations, is that open wards be done away with, and that no more than four people be contained to a room. There is now a provision in the regs for variances, which apparently have been granted so that many institutions still have open wards. The new regulations will seek in some way to tighten up the process of granting these variances. Open wards will exist only when absolutely necessary, such as when a number of patients are in such serious health condition that they must be monitored at all times, and because of staffing requirements, it would be safer and more efficient to have more than four in a room.

Consultation with the states regarding the above problems has resulted in some concrete suggestions which HCFA will probably accept. The process of changing these regulations is one which has been under way off and on throughout this administration. It was identified as a problem early in the Reagan administration, by people in HCFA, and during the first administration there was a lot of consultation with interested groups, with the Association of Retarded Citizens, with the AMA, with the states, with the American Psychological Association, and with the folks who run the ICFs/MR and the states. But if there are any changes in the regulations in response to state suggestions, it will result in more delay.

INTERMEDIATE SANCTION REGULATION

Another regulation which will be forthcoming a bit before any changes in the standards is the so-called intermediate sanction regulation which implements a 1980 statute, the 1980 Budget Reconciliation Act, which provided for the first time for so-called intermediate sanctions. Prior to that time the only sanction that was available for institutions of this sort and also for SNFs and ICFs was termination sanction. Congress felt that it was necessary to provide something other than that blunt instrument for the purpose of sanctioning facilities and insuring that they provide the proper quality of care. What Congress did in the 1980 Reconciliation Act was to provide an intermediate sanction for Medicare, which the Secretary had the opportunity to trigger, and then basically to parrot that same treatment in Medicaid, providing the states with the opportunity for an intermediate sanction as well. Yet in practice that sanction is really only going to work with respect to ICFs/MR in the case of privately run ICFs/MR because, in the case of public institutions, the states will engineer something like a sweetheart arrangement with their own facilities to ensure that they are not unduly jeopardized by the imposition of any sanction on their own facilities, an understandable motive on the part of the states, but a possible flaw in the statute.

HHS is now in the midst of administrative litigation with the state of New York over the application of the intermediate sanction. The state of New York probably has the lion's share of the funding for ICFs/MR, with a number of large public institutions remaining even after they phased out Willowbrook. The attention of HHS is focused specifically on five institutions which, despite all of the numerous extensions, did not make the July 1982 deadline for compliance. Most of the problems did not seriously implicate health and safety; they were, instead, structural problems. The state of New York had anticipated that it would be able to deinstitutionalize many more of its ICFs/MR residents than, in fact, it was able to do. It also encountered community resistance, finding that as facilities were depopulated, it became more and more difficult to find a place suitable for these people because they were more profoundly retarded. There also were limited resources in the community, quite apart from community resistance.

New York had actually done very well, starting with a population of 18,600 and reducing it to about 78% of their goal for deinstitutionalization under the plan of correction that they'd entered into with HHS. In the process they'd spent about $533,000,000 in attempting to update the physical facilities at their institutions. Nevertheless, even by the state's view, the facilities were still not in compliance as of the July 1982 deadline, so the state sought to impose the intermediate sanction on these facilities. The terms of that sanction are that for a period of a year, a facility can be punished for not being in compliance with the regulations simply by not allowing any new admissions.

Now in a context where a state is trying hard to depopulate and trying to move people out of the institutions, it is not likely that that is going to be a very meaningful sanction to simply say we won't admit any new people to the facilities. And there is some opportunity for tinkering by the state to ensure that it will not suffer any hardship as a result of the imposition of this sanction; yet at the same time it seeks to hold the federal government at bay to ensure that the federal government won't impose any sanctions on it.

HCFA was understandably concerned about the possibility of abuse by the state and was also concerned because current surveys showed that there were some lingering health and safety problems at some of these facilities. The matter is now in litigation. Even in the context of facilities that have already come into compliance and subsequently fall out of compliance, it is easy to see from this case there are some possibilities for abuse.

LOOK-BEHIND AUTHORITY

The intermediate sanction regulation, when it goes into effect, will add to the Secretary's arsenal of enforcement techniques such as the look-behind authority, which is the authority to second-guess a determination by the state that a facility should be paid under the program. That was done by regulation and without express statutory authority, but has never been challenged by the state, although it may be now to the extent that HCFA seeks to employ it, because passage of express statutory look-behind authority raises a question as to whether there was ever authority for the regulatory look-behind.

Other enforcement provisions are found in the civil rights laws. There may be some question, however, after the decision in *Alexander v. Choate* as to whether the section 504 remedy is going to be very much help in a context like this. In the latter case the state of Tennessee sought to put a durational limit on the number of inpatient hospital days, and was sued by disabled citizens, who claimed that this was a violation of their rights under section 504 because it had a desperate impact on disabled or handicapped persons. The disabled groups were successful in their litigation through the Sixth Circuit. But the Supreme Court reversed the Sixth Circuit's decision and held that there wasn't any actionable 504 right in a context like that where the change in the program was neutral on its face.

Most of the complaints that are filed on behalf of people institutionalized in ICFs/MR do refer to section 504, but depending on the facts of the particular case, it is doubtful whether this provision will be much help after *Alexander v. Choate*.

CIVIL RIGHTS FOR INSTITUTIONALIZED PERSONS ACT

The Civil Rights for Institutionalized Persons Act is administered by the Civil Rights Division of the Department of Justice. That act was passed in 1980 because of a specific situation arising in connection with the Rosewood facility. For the past decade, the Justice Department had followed the practice of intervening in lawsuits on behalf of the mentally retarded or other institutionalized persons challenging the alleged deprivation of constitutional rights. In the *Rosewood* case, the Fourth Circuit held that the Justice Department lacked standing to intervene in the lawsuit or to file a separate action on behalf of the institutionalized persons there. The 1980 legislation creates no new substantive rights, but makes clear the standing of the Justice Department to intervene in actions like this not only on behalf of the mentally retarded but of people in prisons and other institutions.

The 1980 legislation, although it ultimately passed, was the subject of controversy. People who were in favor of states' rights and against intrusion by the federal government were able to have included in the act provisions requiring consultation with the state government. The Justice Department has initiated contact with state officials and detailed the problems, giving the state a reasonable period of time in which to correct the problems. All of these efforts are beginning to bear fruit; the *Rosewood* case has been settled, and there is a case that was recently settled in Indiana.

The ability of the Justice Department to intervene in litigation of this sort or to bring litigation in its own right, poses, at times, an interesting conflict with HHS. For the most part, the Justice Department is investigating facilities or part of the facilities that are not certified as Medicaid ICFs/MR, because there is something of a logical inconsistency in a situation where HHS is continuing to pay for care provided at a place where allegedly care is not being provided or constitutional rights are being violated.

The new intermediate sanction is not going to be very helpful in most instances, because it basically falls under the control of the state. So to the extent that the federal government has a problem with the quality of care that's being provided in a particular institution, it appears that that's not going to be very much help. And in general, other than for a few well-defined areas like the area of active treatment, the federal government doesn't consider itself to have disallowance remedies, so that it can't take a specific amount of money less than terminating the entire facility to correct a small problem. Frequently, the institutions and the states that run them understand that it is very difficult for the federal government to terminate a facility, to cut off immediately 50% or more of the money that's going to the facility. So in the absence of a more precise kind of instrument of control, the federal government's hands will continue to be somewhat tied.

SOME RECENT CASES

YOUNGBERG V. ROMEO

The Justice Department is no longer advocating deinstitutionalization as a matter of federal law, based on their reading of the *Youngberg v. Romeo* case, which came out of the Pennhurst controversy. As they read that Supreme Court decision, there is no Federal Constitutional right or statutory right to deinstitutionalization, and any right to smaller community settings will have to come from state law if there is any such right under state law.

WILLOWBROOK

There was an interesting article in the past few weeks in *The New Republic* by a Washington lawyer named Joel Klein, who participates in these cases, sometimes on the side of the parents, who may wish to argue against deinstitutionalization. His article is reviewing a new book about Willowbrook entitled "The Willowbrook Wars," and he points out first, the change in the attitude towards deinstitutionalization, the very difficult policy issues that are raised by forcing deinstitutionalization on institutions and on families with mentally retarded children. The conclusion of that article is that the final results in the Willowbrook case sounded the death toll for at least the extreme aspects of deinstitutionalization. In his view, advocates for mentally retarded citizens will no longer be able to go successfully into court and argue that a complete facility should be de-populated or that deinstitutionalization is the appropriate remedy for everyone living in an ICF/MR.

There have been numerous rulings in the Willowbrook case, but perhaps most significant was the one in which the Second Circuit ruled that because of changed circumstances, the state could not be bound by a consent decree which it had entered into years before, and part of the changed circumstances were the changed attitudes of professionals and the courts toward the question of extreme deinstitutionalization.

PENNHURST

The *Pennhurst* case, as I think I mentioned in the outline, raises an important question about the tools available for deinstitutionalization. Studies show that people using the so-called home and community based waiver under section 1915(c) of the Social Security Act are frequently those who otherwise would not have been covered by Medicaid. The Office of Management and Budget has noticed this as well and has suggested to HHS, that the granting of these waivers be considerably tightened up.

ALEXANDER V. CHOATE

It is also important to note the effect that the Supreme Court cases have had on the rights of the mentally retarded. One of them is *Alexander v. Choate*, which as I said, cleared up the applicability of section 504 to gross changes in the Medicaid program. It was shown that unless a public interest group can sue on behalf of residents of institutions, and point to specific ways in which certain categories of persons in that institution have suffered other than because of broad program decisions, then the allegations of a violation of 504 will not be likely to proceed.

CLEBURNE LIVING CENTER V. CITY OF CLEBURNE

Another important case is that of *Cleburne Living Center v. City of Cleburne*, which arose in Texas; in this case the Fifth Circuit basically held that exclusionary zoning practices which discriminated overtly against the mentally retarded were a violation of equal protection.

The specific issue that's before the Supreme Court is the propriety of applying a so-called quasi-strict scrutiny or semi-strict scrutiny to the mentally retarded. That's the issue in which an amicus brief was filed by the Justice Department taking the position that the Fifth Circuit should be overturned. That brief states that the mentally retarded are not the sort of group that should be given advantage of strict scrutiny, which usually applies to discreet insular minorities--discrimination on the basis of race, of national origin, of religion, for example.

The ruling in that case may, depending on its narrowness, have an important impact on the development of the law in this area and the development of the programs. It may, even if the Supreme Court's ruling is the narrow one urged by the Justice Department, cause problems by encouraging local communities to enact zoning provisions similar to that one in Cleburne, Texas.

LETCHWORTH

The *Letchworth* case, which has been filed in New York, will be an interesting one to watch for several reasons. The relief sought there is not for an extreme deinstitutionalization order, but for deinstitutionalization only where it is appropriate. For the most part, the relief seems intended to upgrade the quality of care in the institution, which will eventually bring the lawsuit head on with the problem of funding from the state legislature. That problem, a problem of separation of powers, is really inherent in most of these lawsuits to the extent that they focus not on deinstitutionalization, but on upgrading the quality of the existing institutions. It is also interesting that the federal government is included for the first time in a suit like this. It may have a significant political impact because the federal government is subject to different political influences than the individual states, so the wave of the future may be in this Letchworth suit. All of us that are interested in this area, should keep an eye on it.

LEGISLATION

The other major element that we would hope to hear something from, would be the legislative branch of the federal government, but no major legislation is underway. During the past year or so, there has been little in the way of substantive development from the Hill.

There has been, however, some discussion among some of the states of the idea of block-granting the ICFs/MR, and that might be something that the federal government would be interested in. The states would be interested in it to the extent that it would mean that one would get the money free and clear of a lot of the strings that are attached to the current federal money. The public interest groups generally have been opposed to the concept of block grant because they fear abuses by the states if there are no Federal strings attached. The experience thus far has been a positive one; there have been no serious problems with block grants, but they have never been in as sensitive an area as this.

The lesson of all of this is that the landscape has significantly changed. It's changed in the courts, which have become more flexible. It's changed in the states as well, where a lot of people were unabashedly in favor of deinstitutionalization in the past, and now there are problems of all sorts that stand in the way of at least the extreme manifestations of that. And there are problems for public interest groups who litigate on behalf of the mentally retarded, because of the limitations imposed by new attitudes of the court and of government.

Chapter 20

Relationships Between CORFs and Long Term Care Facilities

Speaker: Calvin P. Johnson

I will discuss CORFs, comprehensive outpatient relay facilities. CORFs came into creation in 1981 as a course of amendments to the Omnibus Budget Reconciliation Act. The legislation was promoted by some rehabilitation groups through Senator Dole, and was opposed strenuously by HEW. They dragged their feet continually after the legislation was passed, and the National Rehabilitation Association wound up suing them in order to get the regulations eventually issued. They were successful in that and the regulations came out.

BACKGROUND

A CORF is an outpatient facility designed to provide occupational therapy, speech therapy, PT, and some social services. I became interested in CORFs when I had a client who said he used a program that was paid for by Part B of Medicare and that seemed like an old-fashioned cost reimbursement program of the type that came into existence when Medicare and Medicaid came along. He was right.

However it was our conclusion that this type of program made little sense because in order to create a free-standing comprehensive outpatient rehab facility, a CORF, you have to buy a building, hire a physician, technicians, then find people to use your service. One of the requirements of the regulations is that people coming into the CORF had to be referred to the CORF by a non-CORF physician.

Thus this seemed to be a wonderful program but one that would stay on the hook since few people would ever really take advantage of it.

That client then fled off to the nursing home business, and looking at the nursing home business, we started thinking about different ways that they could maximize their income from the Medicaid and Medicare programs.

One of the things that nursing homes are required to provide is physical therapy, yet PT generates very little income to the facility. Generally speaking the provider or the operator would farm out his PT to a rehab provider. Or a larger chain would form a rehab agency and contract with themselves to provide that service.

What struck us suddenly was that CORFs may be a solution or a new way of patenting this profit. We know why you had the problem and where the market was becuase we had a whole nursing home full of people who had been receiving physical therapy, occupational therapy, speech therapy; received all the therapies that the CORF could provide. Yet patients in ICF homes are considered by Medicare as if they were inpatients of the ICF facility in order to be outpatients for purposes of receiving services from the CORF.

MANAGEMENT OF CORFs

The law requires that the CORF be a separate facility, which was later interpreted to mean not a separate physical structure but a distinct part of the facility which could be designated as a CORF. There is no requirement or regulations that that CORF be operational 24 hours a day, so an area could be designated to be a CORF for a given set of time. A facility could still use that space outside that period of time, but the CORF could operate within those time bonds during the day. So it was suggested to this client at the time to go into the CORF business.

He proceeded to establish CORFs and began including services to his nursing home patients. However, the income generation wasn't as much as we had anticipated because CORFs are cost reimbursement programs, so that you get what your costs are. What he was able to do was to maximize the rehab potential in his facility by shifting over some of his administrative costs and excess costs to his CORF.

It then became apparent that CORFs were interesting facilities and would provide varieties of services that had not been paid for before. They also had the potential of enhancing the facility's image in the community.

We then began to look at the CORF as a business venture unto itself for which the ready-made clientele would be the nursing home, and we had several discussions with the Health Care Financing Administration to decide a method of payment to the nursing home for use of the services. We hit upon the concept of leasing space from the nursing home and paying for that space. Like any other lease, you are paying directly for the space that you're using. Yet at the same time, however, you are paying for more than just the use of that space, but also for the nursing home's goodwill in the community and for the use of its patient base.

We approached this problem as if the nursing home was a shopping center and we were leasing space and opening a business in that shopping center. In discussing that kind of lease arrangement with the department, they saw no problem.

What we then began to experiment with was a way of reimbursing the nursing home based upon the volumes that the CORF did within the nursing home--the units of service that the CORF provided. What we had now was a way to generate new income to the nursing home facility for a service that they had been required to provide. With any real effort it could be a fairly substantial service in that facility in the amounts of money generated to the facility in non-program income. We then had to begin discussing the reality of placing CORFs in nursing homes on a leased-base arrangement.

CORFs have to remain separate entities, which is a focal point in the entire structure of the arrangement. Medicare imposes regulations if the home and the CORF are jointly owned. This keeps the CORF in an arm's length relationship with the provider.

The regulations also require the specific oversight of the services being provided in the CORF by a physician experienced in rehab services. In many areas, that individual is difficult to find. The Department has been very willing to interpret the regulations liberally regarding the amount of experience required by the provider. The problem is the state regulators' certification and the review of the CORF, which is done in two parts. The first part covers the physical plant and personnel and the second covers the services and the program being provided in the CORF. Depending upon the reviewer in your state, your CORF may either be made to look like a home health agency, or like a hospital, depending upon the type of entity with which the reviewer is more familiar. The Department has been trying to standardize this with some considerable influence from the different regions.

The administrator of the CORF has to be directly responsible to the CORF board. Oftentimes that can create a problem where that administrator of the CORF doesn't work hand-in-hand with the administrator in the facility. It is not unreasonable to require there to be coordination there, but at the same time, because of the regulations and the necessity to maintain the separate entity relationship, it cannot be a situation where the nursing home administrator is giving guidance to the CORF administrator as to what he or she does or does not want to occur in the CORF. That would not be an acceptable relationship.

The CORF will keep separate record keeping. If the CORF were a subsidiary of the nursing home, you've got a double record keeping problem. Where the CORF is a separate entity, it is a dual record keeping, but the CORF records are supplemental to the nursing home records for the services being provided to those nursing home patients. Regarding certificate of need, it is often thought that where a CORF comes in to provide a service, you do not need certificate of need review. Every certificate of need that I have seen ties the need for certificate of need approval to whether or not there is a new service being provided. We have taken the position that the CORF is not providing a new service, but that it is a service that had already been provided in the facility; it's simply a different provider providing that service.

If you were to decide to have a CORF as a subsidiary versus negotiating a leased arrangement with a CORF, and if you are strictly an ICF facility, you may find yourself having to comply with Medicare requirements that you had not heretofore been bothered with, if you are strictly an ICF facility.

On the other side of the equation, if you are an ICF/SNF facility, but the number of SNF patients that you've carried over during the course of the year hasn't gotten you over that threshold for them to come in and review your cost reimbursement, and if you are the CORF provider yourselves as a subsidiary, since CORF services are Part B reimbursable, that is liable to throw you over that threshold, and you will have to deal with Medicare on a cost settlement at the end of the year.

> *You indicated that from these services, a home in a leasing arrangement would get paid a rental from the CORF, and that the rental would then be an income offset in terms of property claim, against the depreciation of property expenditures in the Medicaid cost report. If, in fact the costs of the nursing home who is receiving this rental are going to be reduced by that rental and, therefore, suffer a reimbursement conflict, assuming they're 100 percent better quality, where is the gain?*

Okay, since Medicaid differs from state to state, let me answer in terms of Medicare. This will be an offset based upon the number of Medicare patients and Medicare days you've had over a year's time. So that in that facility if you've 9 percent of your patient base being Medicare, that's the only percentage that you're going to offset again. So you've allocated your cost based upon your Medicare patient days, not against the total number of patient days across the board.

And it's also going to be against your total cost; assuming there are 9 percent Medicare patients, you're going to get a 9 percent impact. There is also the situation of a state program where, in effect, the Medicare and Medicaid program wind up in the identical position and where the total cost is offset by the rental of $100,000, and we can assume that they are all third party patients in the facility and that the reimbursement rates are the same. In New York state you have that problem. If that would be the case, and assuming that 100 percent of the patient load is third party and it's identical to Medicare, therefore, 100 percent of the offset impacts reimbursement. In that type of situation there will be no gain. Yet in Missouri, where there are prospective Medicaids, we're home free because the income generated over the next two years will not be readjusted at the end of each year.

Even if the income is generated when you will have a prospective system, it will be offset in determining your base rate on a prospective basis, but they can't come back and readjust for the preceding term.

To complicate it a little bit more, what if we would put this in a distinct part of our building where we build an accounting wall around it and then it's outside of the view of the program. Could that be possible, just as we do our pharmacy and our other services?

Sure. As I understand what Missouri does to determine your rate, they will look at total non-program income and this will appear as a non-program, as if you had leased some housing space or sold some property to somebody to build a shopping center across the street.

In simple economic terms, what is the advantage to using what you have conveniently referred to as percentage lease?

Not including the state of New York, in simple terms, using a lease arrangement will generate addition of non-program income to the facility, which may or may not be offset. Depending upon how your Medicaid reimbursement works, the effect upon your Medicare reimbursement will generally be minimal because of the amount of Medicare patients that you see in a given year.

For a CORF operator this makes no difference since he is on a cost reimbursement system, and being paid his costs. This is from the nursing home operator's point of view who has leased the space to the CORF.

The CORF operator is also receiving the percentage of profit that's allowable in the program, and in the long run, if he is involved in other businesses and is throwing things into his overhead, that allows him to do varieties of other things.

If we have our own PT now, could we still work with that person?

There's nothing that prohibits the CORF from contracting with your existing provider to continue to provide those services. Instead of the contract being between the nursing home and the rehab provider, the PT provider, the speech pathologist, it becomes the contractors with the CORF. And the CORF handles the Part B billing rather than provider billing directly to Part B.

But I don't want to give up part B billing. Could I let the CORF do some other things I can't do?

The CORF could contract with your PT business and pay your PT business for the provision of the services to CORF. That becomes the CORF's cost, which the CORF bills to Part B.

How much of the time can actually be comingled? For example, if you have a CORF in your facility and you have two full time therapists, do you have to break things out so that the therapists are only doing in-house patients in the morning and co-op patients in the afternoon or can things be just going on simultaneously?

If you have a CORF in your operation it doesn't make any sense for you to have in-house therapists; instead the therapists should become the employees of the CORF. Then all the services that are provided will be on an outpatient basis and will be provided based upon the time frame of CORF's operation. The CORF can be in operation from nine o'clock in the morning to ten o'clock at night.

If you have a dietician, for example, that is your food service supervisor or manager of the diet drink fountain. But she sees CORF patients coming from the community to set some kind of counseling and patient teaching through some physician referral. Now she's still on your staff as a manager and as a clinical person, but she's working within the structure of the CORF to care for patients coming into the CORF area. Can all that be comingled with what she's doing during the day?

I don't know. If she's a salaried person, she could be working anywhere from 30-50 hours a week, depending on what's going on, and from the CORF's point of view that person would have to work for the CORF for a given period of time. It's going to be a matter of blocking out time, but on the other side, when the state comes back in, you will run into an audit problem then, because you're going to have to allocate those times back and forth as to what your respective cost is. If you are truly employing the concept of a CORF, and you're providing patient teaching and counseling with a dietician, a social worker or maybe a nurse practitioner, in addition to physical therapist, speech therapist, and the like, it's very conceivable that you'll have to develop some kind of contractual arrangement whereby the CORF operator is either contracting with you to utilize your in-house staff to work for the CORF, or has to go outside and acquire staff to provide that service. It usually makes more sense for him to contract with you to utilize your staff.

When I first read that legislation it was confusing because I thought that somehow the CORF had to be separated out physically and by staffing, but actually the rooms that you currently use for your therapy are sufficient as long as the CORF has designated hours and the space had been certified by the state agency. In a situation where nursing home A decides it wants to have a CORF so they form a subsidiary corporation, they have now met the separate entity rule. CORF is a separate entity. Nursing home A is owned by you and I. I don't have any interest in the CORF, because it is wholly owned by you. But there is now a related party between the two entities. For cost reimbursement purposes, that's treated as if we're the same. You would be paid based on the depreciated value of your building or the area. But if you were not related then you would get reimbursed from the CORF B based on a cost report, on the full record. That's how you would suffer on a related business.

I'd like to get the built-in patient census, marketing clientele straight. You said that ICF patients are not automatically considered out-patients. Is that also the case with skilled patients within a nursing home?

Skilled patients are considered to be inpatients for Medicare purposes.

In the case of a CORF servicing ICF patients, can you have the same physical therapist treating the SNF patient?

That can be done; it's just a matter of establishing the formalities. When that physical therapist treats the SNF patients, she's not working in the CORF, she's a provider and will bill the nursing home for that service. As long as she is providing the services during the delineated time periods for the CORF, she can have other jobs within the facility.

Regarding the administrator, do you have to have a full time administrator running this CORF?

Generally this depends on state regulations. If you have more than one CORF it is also possible to have one administrator for more than one CORF.

Is it permissible to have subunits like they do at the Golden Home? This is a situation wherein you can have a home health entity and you can have a subunit which gets a different provider number and you can still file a consolidated cost report and just designate those costs to . . . ?

I have discussed that with the Department and they have indicated that they would not have a problem with that. I don't know of anybody who has tried to do that. As of the last time that I checked, there were like 48 CORFs in existence and operation nationwide. What we're talking about right now is fairly theoretical since nobody has tested the waters to see exactly how these things are going to fall into place.

Is the corporate structure of this organization non-related parties?

Yes. The corporation is not related at all to any of the nursing homes where they are currently doing business.

It seems evident that there is not going to be a great deal of profit in this arrangement. Perhaps then a nursing home should just have a contractual agreement with a CORF to provide these services, if you're not losing money doing it that way. Then you don't have to worry about all the detail, conquering all your ancillary costs in house.

I don't agree that there is no potential for the nusing home to make money on this. But at the same time I would agree that it does eliminate a lot of the nursing homes' problems in the provision of these services if they are acquired outside of the nursing homes.

The only way you can make money is if you set up a corporation and you're doing it in somebody else's facilities?

Yes. If you have a lease arrangement with somebody who is a CORF, you have the potential of making money. Nursing homes that create CORFs and rent them in their own facility are not going to make money.

Chapter 21

The Unresolved Dilemma: Institutional vs. Home Care

Speaker: Paul R. Willging

The following are some statistics to ponder: The elderly, those sixty-five years of age and older, will go from being 8.1% of the population in 1950 to 18.3% by the year 2030. This is a group of Americans comprising 55 million individuals. Even more significant is the population 85 years of age and older. This group will grow from 2.2 million today, to 8.8 million by the year 2030. While the American population as a whole will grow by 25 to 30% in the next 45 years, the over-age-85-group will grow by 400%.

What impact will these demographic changes have on long term care? In terms of personal care services, 31.6% of the population 85 or older is receiving some form of personal care. Of those receiving personal care services, 70% receive the services in the community, in their homes, or in alternative settings. Only 20% require nursing homes. And yet, it is obvious from the data, that as one grows older and becomes more debilitated, the chances of residing in a nursing home increase significantly. By the age of 85, the chances are 35.1% of having at least one ADL dependency, that is, the requirement for personal care in terms of some of the very basic functions of living--toileting, transferring, feeding--and that, commensurate with that statistic, the chances of being in a nursing home increase dramatically. So that 22% of American citizens age 85 and older will reside in a nursing home.

As for the statistics regarding nursing home expenditures, both skilled and ICF, these have grown from being less than 1% of health care expenditures in this country in the 1960s to a figure now approaching 10%. This has been propelled by the growth of the nursing home industry itself, from less than 200,000 beds 25-30 years ago to 1.5 million beds today, and a projection of a need for an additional 1.2 million beds by the year 2000. There is some skepticism about the latter statistic. Either based on the idea that the demographic figures are wrong, which is considered unlikely, or that utilization is faulty, that many of those in the nursing home today need not be there, but would be more appropriately cared for in the community.

Depopulation of Nursing

There is a myth that one can, in fact, de-populate the nursing home--move those residents into home care, community-based care, and thereby deal effectively with the financial crisis that is likely to impact on all of long term care. There are three reasons for this belief.

One is simply the question of age and debility. Data suggesting that a large proportion of nursing home residents do not belong in nursing homes is 10-15 years old. Since that time, the nature of the nursing home patient has changed dramatically as evidenced in a GAO report published in 1983. Today, the average patient is 83 years old, and has at least four limitations in the basic activities of daily living. In addition, hospitals are beginning to move critically ill patients out of the acute setting and into the nursing home or home care. This will simply exacerbate the problem of acuity within the nursing home.

Secondly, the infrastructure that needs to be in place to deal effectively with patients within the home care of the community setting is slowly dissolving in this country. To be cared for effectively in the home setting, one obviously needs a caregiver. Traditionally those caregivers have been members of the family, and the family is certainly not what it used to be in this country. More and more women who used to stay home to take care of the infirm elderly parent, are in the work force. Greater geographic dispersion of children is an additional factor. And in terms of increasing life expectancy, it has not been a benefit shared equally by men and women. Men still die earlier than the women, which means that elderly women frequently have no one in the home to act as a caregiver. Among the very old, the chances of moving into a nursing home, once the spouse departs, go from 24 to 54%.

Finally, there is the inevitable question of cost. In terms of the very sick patient, there is no question that, in terms of the patient's preference, and perhaps in terms of therapeutic value, the home is a better place to receive care. Yet, when dealing with patients 83 years of age and older, patients with up to four ADLs, providing the kinds of services in the home that can be provided in the institution is simply not cost-effective. Some preliminary data suggests that it costs as much, and often more, to provide services in the individual's home than to bring the patient into the nursing home to provide those services.

Cost Factors

We have also found with the home and community-based waiver program that the infamous "woodwork effect" does indeed apply. Recent data suggests that of the patients being served in this program, 50% came out of the hospital, 3% came out of nursing homes, and 47% came out of community programs that were informal and non-government supported. In effect, this means that close to half of the patients being served in these programs were patients for whom there had not been previously a federal and state financial responsibility.

Another aspect of the cost factor relates to the Medicaid program, which provides the vast proportion of public funding for nursing home care. There is basic parity in terms of the cost of the health care, or personal care services, but when the patient moves from the institution into the home and community setting, additional costs arise that had previously been included in the skilled care or intermediate care rate. These include the SSI payment, the welfare payment such as food stamps, and a variety of other services that now are provided above and beyond the health care service. Thus the home care setting is not going to deal with the basic problems in this country, or serve as a fiscal panacea in terms of effectively dealing with the vast and inexorable demographic tide.

The problems do not stem from a question of need, but rather from a question of our willingness as a society to satisfy that need. This presents a classic Malthusian dilemma. Malthus, the English economist of some centuries ago, plotted two lines on the graph: the one line being the consumption of resources which was growing geometrically, the other being the production of resources, which was growing arithmetically. At some point, crisis had to come about when those two lines intersected, and we were producing much less than we were consuming.

Malthus did have a fourfold solution involving war, pestilence, plague, and sexual abstinence. None of those four is likely to be our solution when one applies the Malthusian dilemma to the area of long term care, but the dilemma is there. We are in a position of consuming in long term care much more in the way of resources than we are producing.

Assume that by the year 2000 there will be a need for not 1.2 million beds, but only 6 hundred thousand additional beds. That translates into 30-35 thousand additional beds per year. In this country we are currently adding only 10 thousand beds per year and with the current public policy, we will probably build closer to four or five thousand over the next few years.

Regardless of how conservative one chooses to be about the numbers, the Malthusian dilemma exists. Yet there may be solutions. The first solution is not to look to the public sector, or to public funding as a way out.

In terms of the public sector, state and federal, the attitude ranges from denial that a problem exists, through benign neglect, to the point of exacerbating the problem at certain points when the public sector gets involved. States will continue to deny the existence of the need for additional resources. The Certificate of Need Program will continue to be a perversion of the planning process, if this is defined as an analytic method of balancing supply and demand. While organizationally, Certificate of Need health planning will reside in the state's Department of Health, its soul and spirit will continue to call the Treasurer's office its home.

The states for the most part, and for obvious reasons choose to deny the need. The obvious reason is that recognizing the need given the current structure of the industry as a single client, means finding additional resources for that client, namely Medicaid. It is also doubtful that the federal government will offer much relief as far as the dilemma is concerned. Rather, it is more likely to compound the problem; the asset revaluation provision, included in last year's Deficit Reduction Act, was as good an example of that as any.

Say, for example, that an investor is able to work his way through the arcane Certificate of Need process and achieve permission to build a bed. He is now being told by the federal government that the return on his investment 10, 20, or 30 years hence will be zero. This is not a very likely method of inducing new investment in the nursing home industry. And it is highly possible that we will not see a Part C of Medicare in the near future. As evidence of this, even Rep. Claude Pepper is no longer referring to Part C, in terms of a major new federal responsibility for assuring that the long term care needs of America's elderly population are met.

Thus the solution to the dilemma is rather to wean long term care off of its dependence upon public funding. To understand this, it is necessary first to analyze this country's elderly in terms of disposable income. Today 58% of America's elderly have disposable incomes, that is, incomes of less than $10,000 per year. Only 23% have disposable incomes of more than $15,000 per year. In ten years, 47%, 11 percentage points less, will have disposable income below $10,000; 35%, 12 percentage points more, will have disposable income over $15,000 per year.

Projections for the year 2015 are even more dramatic: in 1980 dollars, there will be 25% of America's elderly with disposable income of less than 10,000, and 59% more than 15,000. The causes of this situation include more working women, providing more in the way of savings; pension improvement, both in terms of the value of the pension as well as the coverage; 50% of America's workers having pension coverage today, 80% having pension coverage by the year 2000; Social Security, increased benefits, COLA's indexing, and IRAs. That's disposable income and does not even include the possibility of augmenting disposable income by such new mechanisms as reverse equity mortgages.

Thus the future in terms of disposable income is fairly bright, and from that there will be two results. One is that America's elderly are going to be pricing themselves out of the Medicaid market and into the private pay market, and in doing that, more and more are going to be able to afford chronic care insurance. A study under way by ICF, a Washington-based consulting firm, suggests that by the year 1995, 65% of America's elderly will be able to afford chronic care insurance.

CHRONIC CARE INSURANCE

Several insurance companies have already entered the chronic care insurance market, for example the Fireman's Fund, Massachusetts Indemnity, and United Equitable. Prudential Insurance Company is being dragged into it as well, by the American Association of Retired Persons (AARP). The public sector has become interested in long term care insurance as well. There are at least 25 to 30 states which are at varying stages of discussion in terms of how they can stimulate the growth of that phenomenon. The federal role is being investigated as well, in terms of establishing appropriate standards so as to avoid scandals in the area of long term care insurance that were experienced during the growth of Medicaid.

There is also some discussion about whether the federal government could support concepts ranging from reinsurance proposals and potential allowances for the states to buy in (as they already do) to the Medicare program, to buying into the premium structure for long term care insurance to the commercials of the Blues as well.

The hurdles still to be overcome in this area are not affordability, or the question of need, but primarily the question of market perception. The first thing AARP did in this area was to commission a study of the association's members through the Gallup organization to get a sense of whether or not there was a viable market for such insurance. This survey found that 79% of AARP's membership thought they did not need this kind of insurance because they were already covered. And they were already covered by Medicare. But Medicare provides only one hundred days of coverage by law, thirty days of coverage in reality. And in fact, it falls short of the needs of the Medicare patients who are covered.

Medicare clearly is not the solution, yet most of America's elderly do feel that it is going to take care of their needs. This should not be discouraging; the strength of America's industry has traditionally been in being able to sell the public things it does not necessarily want or need. Thus it will be much easier for the insurance industry to sell America's elderly something that it does indeed need.

CASE INDEX